Finding
a Way to
the Heart

Finding a Way to the Heart

FEMINIST WRITINGS ON ABORIGINAL AND WOMEN'S HISTORY IN CANADA

Edited by ROBIN JARVIS BROWNLIE *and* VALERIE J. KORINEK

UNIVERSITY OF MANITOBA PRESS

University of Manitoba Press
Winnipeg, Manitoba
Canada R3T 2M5
uofmpress.ca

16 15 14 13 12   1 2 3 4 5

Printed in Canada
Text printed on chlorine-free, 100% post-consumer recycled paper

Cover design: Mike Carroll
Cover image: Lita Fontaine
Interior design: Jessica Koroscil

Library and Archives Canada Cataloguing in Publication

Finding a way to the heart : feminist writings on
aboriginal and women's history in Canada / Robin Jarvis Brownlie and
Valerie J. Korinek, editors.

Includes bibliographical references.
ISBN 978-0-88755-732-3 (pbk.)
ISBN 978-0-88755-421-6 (PDF e-book)
ISBN 978-0-88755-423-0 (epub e-book)

1. Van Kirk, Sylvia. 2. Native peoples—Canada—Historiography. 3. Native
women—Canada—Historiography. 4. Feminism and higher education—Canada.
I. Brownlie, Robin, 1963– II. Korinek, Valerie Joyce, 1965–

E76.8.F56 2012   971'.0049700722   C2011-908247-0

The University of Manitoba Press gratefully acknowledges the financial
support for its publication program provided by the Government of Canada
through the Canada Book Fund, the Canada Council for the Arts, the Manitoba
Department of Culture, Heritage, Tourism, the Manitoba Arts Council,
and the Manitoba Book Publishing Tax Credit.

Contents

Acknowledgements

IF, AS HILLARY CLINTON HAS ASSERTED, "it takes a village" to raise a child, it takes a small town to complete an academic anthology. We wish to thank a number of key individuals without whom *Finding a Way to the Heart* would never have seen the light of day. First, we thank Franca Iacovetta and Heidi Bohaker for initiating this project in 2007 when they organized the Canadian Historical Association Roundtable "Many Tender Ties: A Forum in Honour of Sylvia Van Kirk." This panel brought together scholars, students, and colleagues to provide a retrospective assessment of Sylvia's academic accomplishments. The enthusiasm generated by that panel convinced us that something more permanent would be beneficial for scholars and students, and clearly indicated that there was a receptive audience. Having provided us with an excellent start, Franca and Heidi passed the baton to Jarvis and myself, who agreed to take over the next stage of producing a scholarly anthology.

When we mapped out our editorial strategy, we envisaged that the luxury of space and time provided by a book allowed us a more sustained focus on the two major analytical arcs of Sylvia's career—First Nations and women's history. A call for papers was circulated, our original panel participants were invited to contribute and, additionally, we sought out other academics that we believed had important contributions to make. In the end, we wish to thank the amazing group of scholars who contributed to this volume: Jennifer Brown, Victoria Freeman, Franca Iacovetta, Rob Innes, Betsy Jameson, Pat McCormack, Kathryn McPherson, Adele Perry, Katrina Srigley, and Angela Wanhalla. They have been a great crew to work with, consummate professionals, and excellent scholars. The essays they produced for this volume offer important contributions to Canadian history and historiography, perspectives on the hidden aspects of the academy, and represent scholars at all career stages, from emerging and established scholars to those at the pinnacle of their careers. We appreciate their patience and their confidence in us.

Moving from our contributors to our "producers," we cannot praise the editors and staff at the University of Manitoba Press too highly. They have been simply fantastic to work with at every stage of this project. Our editor David Carr was enthusiastic about *Finding a Way to the Heart* from our first informal discussions. He expertly shepherded us through the submission and review process, providing sage, timely, and encouraging advice. Glenn Bergen, who has led the editorial team since the manuscript arrived at the UMP offices, displayed great calm under pressure and has been responsive to all of our requests and questions. We are fortunate that the editorial staff, the copy-editors, designers, and all others involved in the production of this book have brought such creative energy and excellence to our volume. We've been privileged to work with them and wish to thank them for making this handsome publication possible.

Finally, on our respective home fronts, we wish to thank our partners Roewan Crowe and Penny Skilnik for their encouragement and support. Both of them gave us the gift of time, much of which was "stolen" from weekends and evenings, to finalize this project. They shared our understanding of the political and academic importance of this feminist academic project. In many conversations over the years, they have helped us deepen our grasp of feminist questioning and analysis, and we are very grateful.

Robin Jarvis Brownlie
Valerie J. Korinek

Finding
a Way to
the Heart

SYLVIA VAN KIRK (LEFT) and JENNIFER S.H. BROWN at the
Rupert's Land Colloquium, Stromness, Orkney Islands, June 1990.
PHOTO BY WILSON B. BROWN.

Introduction

WHEN SYLVIA VAN KIRK SET OUT IN THE EARLY 1970s to write her dissertation on the history of women in the fur trade, she encountered considerable resistance in the academy. "What history?" was a common theme, ridiculing the idea that women were involved in the trade at all. Until then, the fur trade had been narrated largely as a story of European men exploring the continent, mastering the wilderness, and building a commercial empire that paved the way for European resettlement.[1] Aboriginal men were bit players at best in most of these works, and women were completely absent. But Sylvia persevered, reading the male traders' records "against the grain" and demonstrating that, in fact, the fur trade could not have proceeded at all without the active participation of women. As Sylvia's former student Christine Welsh pointed out in her 1992 film *Women in the Shadows*,[2] Sylvia's work "turned the conventional view of history upside down." Her feminist questions and insights helped pry open the narrow parameters of historical inquiry to expand the areas of life considered worthy of investigation, and to admit new kinds of questions. Sylvia showed that the fur trade was more than simply commercial exchange—it became a full-fledged multicultural society whose social, sexual, and familial arrangements were central to trade, governance, and intercultural relations. By doing so, she played an important role in revealing how new questions about women's lives could radically transform our understanding of the past. Instead of mere exchanges of goods between two discrete, virtually unconnected groups of men, the fur trade now became visible as an integrated, multicultural social world, where intimate relationships between European men and Aboriginal women forged kin networks linking traders and hunters. The families, kinship obligations, and mixed-descent, culturally versatile children that resulted shaped the lives and actions of all participants in the trade.

The genesis for the present volume came from a call to participate in a 2007 Canadian Historical Association roundtable organized to commemorate Sylvia Van Kirk's scholarship. A few years prior, Sylvia had quietly taken early retirement to Victoria, BC, after a distinguished career in the Department of History at the University of Toronto. In the roundtable, a group of former colleagues, students, and research collaborators convened to reflect on the role that Sylvia's work had played in their careers, including her groundbreaking scholarship on Native-Newcomer relations as well as her teaching and mentorship.[3] The response to that panel was heartening, and in the days afterwards many people inquired about future intentions for the papers. Ultimately, we decided to forge ahead with an edited collection that would strive to preserve some of the spirit of the panel but also function more broadly to showcase the ways that the ideas advanced by Sylvia and her generation of feminist scholars have been taken up and developed in the succeeding three decades. The book's contributors are former students, fellow researchers, and scholars in Native-Newcomer relations, western Canada, and women's history whose work has been inspired by Van Kirk's.

In offering this volume of essays in honour of Sylvia Van Kirk's scholarship, we also seek to mark the substantial changes in the historical discipline that have occurred since the battles of the 1970s over the meaningfulness and even the possibility of women's history. One of the contributors to this volume, Adele Perry, holds a Canada Research Chair in Western Canadian Social History. As she acknowledges, her current work bears clear connections to Sylvia's, taking as its point of departure the intimate fur trade relations that Sylvia has explored throughout her career. Perry's research is situated within a transnational/ transcolonial/ transborder field of inquiry that did not exist when Sylvia's widely circulated monograph "*Many Tender Ties*" was published, but whose methods, questions, and analytical frameworks were prefigured in Sylvia's writings. Thus, the kinds of inquiry that were marginalized in the early years of Sylvia's career have become cutting-edge research worthy of one of the academy's highest rewards—an enormous change in some three decades.

In her contribution to this volume, "Ties Across the Border," Elizabeth Jameson provides an important explanation of the international impact of Sylvia's work—especially in the United States—outlining the structural, temporal, and conceptual factors that combined to make "*Many Tender Ties*" well-known south of the border. Jameson is herself a distinguished historian of western women's history and the Imperial Oil-Lincoln McKay Chair in American Studies at the University of Calgary, another indication of the recognition women's historians have won in the past several decades. She shows how Sylvia's scholarship emerged in a historical moment that witnessed new challenges to older historical frameworks focused on settler men, imperial expansion, and the development of the nation state. By placing Aboriginal women at the centre of her narrative and demonstrating the vital importance of women's labour, marital choices, reproduction, and cultural mediation, Sylvia's research helped generate new studies in several major fields, including not only fur trade history but also the history of women (especially Aboriginal women), the west (U.S., Canadian, and trans-border), Native-Newcomer relations, and multicultural history.

As Jameson shows, Sylvia's work, especially *Many Tender Ties,* is cited in studies whose historical interests span three centuries and much of the western third of the northern Americas. One of the most overt nods to her influence occurred in the title of Ann Laura Stoler's well-known review article, "Tense and Tender Ties: The Politics of Comparison in North American History and (Post) Colonial Studies."[4] Stoler was interested in the ways that writings within both North American history and postcolonial studies "address how intimate domains—sex, sentiment, domestic arrangement, and child rearing—figure in the making of racial categories and in the management of imperial rule."[5] Citing Sylvia's call two decades earlier for attention to "tender ties," Stoler noted how effectively her study had demonstrated the ways that these ties were also "tense," thanks to the colonial inequities they revealed. She added a tribute to the lasting resonance of these insights, commenting: "Among students of colonialisms in the last decade, the intimacies of empire have been a rich and well-articulated research domain."[6] Scholars outside the Americas have also participated in the conversation about Indigenous women's contributions and experiences in colonial contexts. Angela Wanhalla's work in this volume examines questions about Maori women, intermarriage, and mixed-descent offspring with respect to New Zealand, exemplifying the scholars in other former British colonies who have pursued this kind of analysis.

Sylvia's research was also path-breaking in its attention to race, class, and gender. Though her research career began before gender history developed as a field—in fact, before feminist thinkers coined the term as an analytical construct—Sylvia's attention to the difference gender made helped reveal the tremendous potential this analytical framework offered for new insights into human experience and the workings of society. She showed how the introduction of Victorian ideas about gender and race made intercultural conjugal relations increasingly difficult and diminished the economic and social options open to the children of marriages contracted "*à la façon du pays.*" In her later work she explored the ways that gender as well as race shaped the fortunes of mixed-race children of the fur trade, as their parents' integrated, multicultural fur trade world was pushed aside in favour of new agrarian, commercial, and industrial interests.[7]

Sylvia's insights about the centrality of Indigenous peoples to trade—and about the long-lasting reality of intimate, committed relationships between European men and Indigenous women—provided important paths for other scholars to follow. As Elizabeth Jameson notes, the popularity of Sylvia's work in the U.S. "had to do at least partly with the power of her interpretive framework to inform western, women's, and ethnic histories in the 1980s."[8] In its challenge to the classic metanarratives of both U.S. and Canadian nation-building, her research "disrupted a mythic West that had marginalized women and people of color."[9] Sylvia's work fell on particularly fertile ground in the U.S. because that country has emphasized the west so much in its national mythology. Indeed, one of the key differences between the U.S. and Canadian literatures, which has effectively diminished Van Kirk's accomplishments in her own country, is that the Canadian west is not as prominent in our "national" history as the American west is in the U.S., where it serves a foundational, central function in defining the glory of a nation. Though a myth, it is one that resonates in New England and California, as well as in the "west" itself. By contrast, the dominance of central Canada as the pre-eminent focus of "Canadian history" has led to the distortion of the west's historical role and to a relative neglect of its people and significance—hence the purchase of the "new western history" in the U.S. and the lesser attention granted to its Canadian counterpart. Bill Waiser, himself a prominent prairie historian, recently lamented that the vitality of the field "appears to have waned," despite the fact that it "has explored promising new avenues of inquiry, especially in the area of Native-Newcomer relations."[10] In a bid to reverse the field's fortunes and to re-explore the Canadian west from an interdisciplinary perspective, in 2008 organizers at the University of Alberta hosted the first western Canadian studies conference since the 1980s. This conference, and the edited volume *The West and Beyond* subsequently published by Athabasca University Press, may portend a renewed interest in the field both from established and emerging scholars.[11] In 2012, the University of Calgary will host the third iteration of this event.[12]

Indeed, innovative work relating to Native-Newcomer relations has been a particularly vital aspect of western Canadian history, and Sylvia has been an important contributor to it. One might almost say that Sylvia added "people" to the fur trade, such was the earlier emphasis on the commercial nature of this world. Moreover, she depicted the west itself as a place where history happens, not just as an iconic terrain to be traded and schemed over by commercial, national, and imperial interests. Her work bridged the old notion of the "prehistoric" world of Indigenous people and the beloved "pioneer" history of the Euro-Canadian settlers moving west to establish their new life. It moved beyond political and economic analyses to examine social questions and consider individual experiences, adding to historical investigation several groups who were traditionally excluded: women, Aboriginal peoples, and the non-elite, including the working class. It was in the field of fur trade history that the questions and insights of social history, particularly its emphasis on the experience and agency of ordinary people, were first translated into the study of Aboriginal peoples. Sylvia played an important role in this shift.

Of course, *"Many Tender Ties"* has also had its critics. Adele Perry is not the only scholar to have found the book "a simultaneously ambivalent and inspiring intervention."[13] While the book's interest in labour suggested a Marxist influence, its attention to Aboriginal women's actions and choices, without the requisite consideration of colonial power relations, signalled an apparently liberal conception of agency. Its romanticist perspective on sexual relations in the fur trade did not always sit well with readers either. In a critical article focusing on *"Many Tender Ties"* and an article by Marxist historian Ron Bourgeault, literary scholar Julia Emberley accused Van Kirk of producing "an impressionistic and sentimental historical narrative" and using a "naive realist" approach, especially in her account of the eighteenth-century Chipewyan woman known to posterity as Thanadelthur.[14] Though Sylvia's book did not deny the existence of more exploitative forms of sexuality in the trade, such as short-term opportunistic liaisons and outright prostitution, it chose to concentrate on the long-term unions that were most similar to Western monogamous marriage. The title itself betrays a certain romantic bent that is evident in the text. Moreover, some scholars criticized *"Many Tender Ties"* for speaking on behalf of Aboriginal women, and others for disregarding the importance of place and ethnicity in examining the women's experiences.[15]

Yet it is also true that this work has never been superseded. With her feminist rereading of classic fur trade sources, Sylvia revolutionized the historical understanding of how the trade functioned and what it meant. The book's explanatory reach, its temporal and conceptual scope, and its compelling narrative and analysis have ensured that it remains an important contribution to both scholarship and pedagogy in universities throughout North America. Its writing style is lively and accessible, a quality Sylvia has prized in historical writing as part of her emphasis on educating the general public—not just university audiences. Students respond well to her work for a variety of reasons: its clarity, its attention to individual lives, and its appeal to the heart as well as the head. Christine Welsh, whose powerful filmmaking began with personal inspiration she experienced from Sylvia's teaching and writing, is not the only former student to have become "hooked" on history from works such as these.

Though Sylvia's scholarly articles have not become as well-known in the U.S. as her monograph, in Canada they have continued to enjoy extended lifespans, and have been widely anthologized in edited collections. It is probably impossible to acquire an undergraduate history degree in this country without encountering some of her writings. Her early articles on women in the fur trade, derived from her dissertation work, enjoyed particular prominence for many years. They were important historical contributions, and their popularity no doubt *was* enhanced by the factor Jennifer Brown has noted about her own work and Sylvia's—that in studying both women and Aboriginal people, they cover "two constituencies at once, killing two birds with one stone, as it were."[16] Sylvia's later work has also been well-received and has graced many historical anthologies. After her dissertation, she became interested in the fortunes of fur trade families in the period following the decline of the main trade era.[17] Turning her attention to families like those of Alexander Ross, James Douglas, Charles Ross, and several others, she investigated "what happened to elite HBC-native families as they moved from fur-trade post to colonial settlement."[18] This research confirmed the importance of a gendered analysis, as Van Kirk found significant differences between the experiences of sons and daughters in the second generation—those who were raised mainly in colonial settlements, not fur trade posts. The daughters were generally more successful in colonial society, acculturating themselves to their new surroundings, shedding the signs of their bicultural heritage, and attracting suitably elite husbands. The sons, on the other hand, had difficulty integrating themselves into the newcomer economy and finding elite wives. In this work Sylvia once again demonstrated her ability to bridge literatures, situating her questions about gender, race, and class at the nexus of several fields that do not communicate as well as they might, particularly the histories of the fur trade and of (re)settlement.

The Historiographical Context

The first academic histories of "the west," both in Canada and the U.S., were produced by easterners who tended to view this vaguely defined region as a vast hinterland serving the needs of the metropolis in Europe and subsequently eastern North America. It was thus initially valued for economic and symbolic reasons. In the U.S., it was the locus of Frederick Jackson Turner's shifting frontier, the crucible of American democracy and exceptionalism, whose importance centred on cheap land.[19] In Canada, it was the source of Harold Innis's first "staple," fur, a primary commodity that decisively shaped Canadian history, politics, and economics.[20] For these reasons, the history of the fur trade was long treated as "largely synonymous with the history of northern and western Canada" before 1870, a story that was at least as much about imperial and corporate exploration and expansion as about furs or trade.[21] In keeping with these subjects, early histories of the west often engaged in considerable valorization of the Europeans who pushed the fur trade frontier steadily west and north, fighting each other as they went—the French and English, the Scots and Orkneymen, the Nor'Westers and Bay men. The emphasis was on male exploits, commercial and military competition, and imperial expansion. To the extent that there were "people"—that is, individuals—in this story, they were white men, usually of the elite echelons of the fur trade hierarchy. To a large extent, however, the protagonists were nations, empires, and corporate commercial entities. Only gradually did "the west" become worthy of history in a broader sense—as something more than a far-off land of opportunity where staples could be exploited or vast tracts of land changed hands with little regard to the original inhabitants.

"The west" was also the place, according to Canadian nationalist narratives, where agricultural settlers conquered a harsh environment to extend "civilization" and secure the transcontinental Canadian nation. In this discourse, the presumptively "white" pioneers (who were actually ethnically and racially diverse) underwent personal hardship and sacrifice, ultimately triumphing over both nature and the U.S. annexationist threat. This story almost entirely elided Aboriginal peoples, in contrast to the U.S. historiography, which featured hostile Indians as an important part of the settlers' challenges and ultimate triumph. But both countries' pioneer histories implicitly or explicitly presented Aboriginal peoples as opponents of progress and civilization. As Elizabeth Jameson and Susan Armitage noted in the introduction to their edited collection on the U.S. west, *Writing the Range*, "The story of intrepid pioneers coming west, persevering, and overcoming hardship and obstacles to tame a difficult land and win a better future is highly seductive—unless, of course, you are one of the 'obstacles' the pioneers 'overcame.'"[22] The pioneer narrative has always been particularly prominent in popular histories and heritage politics, but early academic history writing contained these tropes as well. Most famously, G.F.G. Stanley presented the resettlement of the west as a contest between civilization and savagery, in which the Métis struggle against Canada's attempted assumption of authority over their land was depicted as the last gasp of resistance by a people unfit to enjoy the benefits of civilization.[23] University of Toronto professor Edgar McInnis's well-known Canadian history textbook, published in 1947 but assigned to students well into the 1970s, had only a few words to say about Aboriginal peoples. Noting the European view of North America as a "vacant continent, which lay completely open to settlement," McInnis stated that "this assumption was justified," since the "aborigines made no major contribution to the culture that developed in the settled communities of Canada" and "remained a primitive remnant clinging to their tribal organization long after it had become obsolete."[24] These kinds of attitudes were widely held at the time and, indeed, still have their adherents today.[25]

Early versions of western history were written by historians trained in Britain and central Canada who saw western Canada from the vantage points of Oxford, London, Edinburgh, and Toronto.[26] These histories were initially embedded within the national literature and largely subservient to a nation-building agenda, rather than presenting a history worth telling on its own. The literature began to change when western historians emerged who lived in the west, like A.S. Morton, or who were actually born and raised there, like L.G. Thomas. These men's experiences of the west as a home and lived reality—complete with Aboriginal people, racial tensions, and divisions, with land that meant more than just the harvesting or mining of staples—allowed them to produce more nuanced work about the place. Moreover, they wrote the first histories devoted entirely to the region. A.S. Morton was the first western-based academic historian to write extensively about the region, publishing his monumental work, *A History of the Canadian West to 1870–71*, in 1939.[27] This was a more inclusive treatment, advancing a nuanced view of the region and its peoples. Morton's work bore the markers of its era, particularly in its privileging of the European perspective, and often was reflexively insensitive to First Nations and Métis perspectives. Nevertheless, it also offered important contextual information about the west and often treated Aboriginal people as actors and participants in the region's history. The shifts introduced by scholars like Morton and Thomas illustrate the importance of regionally based historians, whose deep knowledge of the west would begin to forge a different regional history.

It was the explosion of social history in the 1960s that finally brought to fruition a broader view of the west's past. Western peoples were deemed full subjects of history, people who pursued their own agendas and who came from a range of backgrounds, including Aboriginal peoples. Sylvia was part of a new generation of scholars who began to ask questions about Aboriginal participation in historical events and processes. In 1973, L.G. Thomas's survey of fur trade history could still note accurately that historians had written "pitifully little" about Aboriginal peoples.[28] Only gradually, from the 1970s on, did a relevant scholarship appear that made it possible to offer university courses on Aboriginal history. The shift in Euro-Canadian consciousness that fostered a new interest in the Aboriginal past has often been attributed to the broad paradigm shift that followed the Second World War, when international decolonization movements prompted analysis of the wrongs of the colonial enterprise. While this context was clearly important, it is also no accident that academic research into Aboriginal history vastly increased in the early 1970s, just after Aboriginal people in Canada had gained the country's attention by vocally attacking proposed Indian policy changes in 1969—71 and beginning to publish their own thoughts on the events and meanings of the past.[29] Aboriginal perspectives and thoughtful academic scholarship helped to reveal the much-celebrated "opening of the West" as a process that also involved "the closing of the North West for its fur trade, Métis and Indian residents."[30] This understanding, enriched with stories of individual human experiences, was one of the great contributions of Sylvia's generation of scholars.

Sylvia Van Kirk and the Feminist Project

Sylvia is best known for her book *"Many Tender Ties": Women in Fur-Trade Society in Western Canada, 1670–1870*, published in 1980. In this book, a revised version of her dissertation, she made her most influential intervention into historical analyses of the fur trade and the history of Aboriginal women. In the same year, her colleague and friend Jennifer Brown published her own revised dissertation, *Strangers in Blood: Fur Trade Company Families in Indian Country*.[31] Both books took fur trade marriages as their point of departure, examining the marital "custom of the country" that created a long-lasting fur trade society throughout the territory from the Great Lakes to the Pacific coast. Beginning with the feminist premise that women's lives and actions mattered, they demonstrated conclusively that Aboriginal women were crucial to the success of the Aboriginal-European trade system and that many of them worked actively to promote trade relations and secure trader husbands. For their part, male European and Euro-Canadian traders relied on Aboriginal women for an array of vital activities including the processing of furs, the production of clothing and footwear, the snaring of game for food, cleaning and cooking in the forts, and cultural mediation in moments of conflict. Just as importantly, these conjugal relationships created kin ties that helped ensure the women's families and clans brought their game and furs to the post.

In thus inserting women into the story of the trade, the two scholars did more than just demonstrate their presence. They showed how the whole enterprise was founded on women's economic and social labour and, in so doing, revealed the limitations of previous accounts that had incorrectly depicted an all-male world. The implications were far-reaching. In Sylvia's telling, particularly, the economic importance of women's labour was highlighted. Both books foregrounded the domestic sphere as one that intersected closely with commerce, economics, and governance. Both explored the ways that intimate and sexual relationships helped shape trade, empire, and nation. They also examined child-rearing, family life, and the impact of gender, racial, and sexual norms in fur trade country. As Valerie Korinek observes in her contribution to this volume, they "researched and wrote about matters marital long before it was fashionable." Finally, they put old, well-worn sources to brand new uses, suggesting the richness of even the most conventional sources for the investigation of women's pasts.

Van Kirk, Brown, and other contemporary feminist scholars asked new questions. They started with a deceptively simple one: where were the women? They proceeded to further questions such as whether traditional periodizations corresponded to women's experience (a query most famously posed by Joan Kelly-Gadol in her 1977 article "Did Women Have a Renaissance?"[32]). They asked how ideas about women's roles, characteristics, and "nature" shaped their historical experience, and how men's experiences differed from those of women. These approaches opened up whole new fields of inquiry that made women's activities and experiences more visible and changed prevailing ideas about what mattered, what counted as history, and what helped to shape historical development. These questions and methodologies have come to be taken for granted in many circles, obscuring the audacity and freshness of Sylvia's work (and that of her feminist colleagues) in their own time. They were innovators who set out to introduce formerly invisible historical actors and to reinterpret the meanings of the past at a fundamental level.

Overview of the Chapters

This volume brings together work from researchers whose careers have intersected with Sylvia's as students and colleagues. Their contributions build on Sylvia's questions, insights, and methods, and move into new areas of inquiry. Gender, race, and material realities remain important, while our era's characteristic interest in identity takes a more prominent place. These works are interested in Aboriginal people's experiences, the multicultural worlds they inhabited (with and without Europeans), and the social and material realities that shaped their lives. The chapters also examine the ways that Euro-Canadians have told stories about Aboriginal peoples and the meanings we can extract from these discourses about the colonial encounter.

There are effectively two sections to the book. The first three contributions are about Sylvia herself and aspects of her academic career, while those that follow examine a range of historical themes related to the ones Sylvia has investigated in her work. Opening the volume, the three reflections on working with Sylvia explore academic collaborations from different perspectives: Jennifer Brown discusses the intellectual support and cross-fertilization of two friends working in the same field, Franca Iacovetta reflects on the interaction of colleagues in the same department, and Valerie Korinek writes of the student-professor relationship in graduate school. These three chapters offer an expanded definition of scholarship, discussing both personal experiences with Sylvia and the academic and political context in which her career unfolded. In different ways, each addresses the significance of feminism in these years, women's experiences in the academy over several decades, and the resistance they encountered to feminist ideas. These chapters bring an additional dimension that is not often found in historical collections: a recognition of the power of feminist pedagogy, mentoring, collaboration, and committee work. They also do some crucial work in evaluating social and political change within the academy since the 1970s and the many remaining challenges in trying to create inclusive, collaborative, intellectually rich university settings that can help foster fresh feminist insights.

In her contribution, Jennifer Brown looks back on her long collegial and personal relationship with Sylvia and evaluates her friend's academic experiences, development, and impact. Brown reveals the underlying humanity and empathy that animate Van Kirk's work, her rejection of "the dehumanized way in which our history has been written," and her determination to illuminate the lived experience of real people. The friendship also models an intellectual relationship based on collaboration and mutual support rather than competition. Although Van Kirk had been working with the Hudson's Bay Company records for two years when Brown began to examine the same archive, she welcomed her new colleague, suggested interdisciplinary cooperation, and observed that there was "room for both our studies and more."[33] At the same time, the chapter considers how sexism shaped the experience of women entering the academy in the

1970s. With few women in the professoriat, Brown describes feeling marginalized and disadvantaged as a woman, an experience she shared with other female graduate students. She discusses the cool reception Sylvia's work received from certain senior male professors, and the impact this attitude had on her early career. Looking back over a friendship and career lasting more than thirty years, Brown provides a valuable retrospective that highlights tremendous change in academic research, pedagogy, and climate.

Next, Franca Iacovetta discusses her lengthy collegial association with Sylvia in the Department of History at the University of Toronto. She focuses on one of the least-mentioned elements of a scholarly career—committee and administrative service—describing the "front-line" feminist work that she witnessed Sylvia accomplishing within the History Department, on search committees, and in administrative roles. While academics are sometimes reluctant to devote their time to service work—Iacovetta initially viewed it as a "monumental inconvenience"—the article considers the significant results Sylvia obtained by willingly taking on this kind of invisible, behind-the-scenes work in order to promote change in the academy. She reveals just how extensive Sylvia's service and administrative commitments were (nearly 100 committees during her career, and over a decade of serving in administrative positions), and how she promoted change through her "polite but persistent" practice of offering reasoned argument to overturn conventional, dismissive views of women's academic work. In these ways Sylvia was a significant part of that path-breaking generation of feminist scholars who "carved out an intellectual and political space for women's history and feminist studies."[34]

Finally, Valerie Korinek reflects on the experience of working with Sylvia as a graduate student, in and outside the classroom. She reveals a number of important ways Sylvia found to support and advance women graduate students in a period when male dominance in the profession was still entrenched. Indeed, this chapter also serves as a larger discussion of the role of mentoring in academic life, with a kind of case study of the ways that Sylvia's feminist mentoring helped ease early career paths for her students, particularly those working in women's history: "When I think back to my experiences in Van Kirk's over-subscribed classes in women's history and Native-Newcomer histories, there was an incalculable value in participating in classes where female voices predominated; where competition and collaboration were in evidence; and where we learned much more than the subject matter in question."[35] Korinek's reflections are a reminder of the necessity of feminist mentoring, given the continued gender imbalance in the historical profession and the woeful over-representation of middle-class Euro-Canadians among faculty. While some progress has been made in broadening the demographic base of the profession, there is an ongoing need to support diversity, and in particular to encourage scholars outside of the traditional white, middle-class groups who predominate within the profession. The chapter also highlights the additional ways that Sylvia helped pave the way for others to follow through her own audacious research questions, her service in administrative roles where she could advocate for external funding for women students, and her presence, which helped raise the profile of women's history scholarship at a time when it was still largely marginalized at the University of Toronto.

Section two of the volume begins with historiographical chapters that evaluate Sylvia's work, positioning it within the Canadian and American scholarly context. First, Elizabeth Jameson assesses the reach and influence of Sylvia's academic work in the U.S. context, showing how she demonstrated the value of new historical questions and methods at a critical moment in the historiography of the west. Second, Adele Perry offers a historiographical and methodological reflection on "historiography that breaks your heart"—that is, the notion of scholars as vulnerable observers whose scholarly analyses take into account their emotional responses to their sources. Beginning with this idea, Perry analyzes *"Many Tender Ties"*, its continuing resonance, its problematic features, and the implications of all this for her own research on the transcolonial careers of the Douglas-Connolly family. Returning to the same Douglas archive that Sylvia found so rich, and with a perspective similarly attuned to the artificiality of public-private distinctions, Perry sets out to track new questions and connections in the translocal, transcolonial world of peripatetic imperial subjects.

After the historiographical contributions, the chapters are organized in a roughly chronological fashion, though many of them cover a considerable temporal range. We begin with Angela Wanhalla's translation of some of Sylvia's questions, ideas, and insights into the context of nineteenth-century New Zealand, investigating the experiences of mixed-descent people in New Zealand, and relations between Maori and newcomers more broadly in the early period of colonization. She conveys a fascinating picture of interracial conjugal relations fostered by the whaling industry, in which the Indigenous Ngāi Tahu formed conjugal and kin ties with whaling men from many countries. She also considers the broader question of why the large population of mixed-descent children did not develop a separate identity in the way that some Métis in Canada did, finding her answer in the experience of colonization and economic marginalization that mixed-descent people shared with their Ngāi Tahu kin.

Robert Innes's chapter continues the theme of family and kinship in an important conceptual intervention that demonstrates how scholars' focus on "tribes" obscures the greater importance of band-level organization and the central role of kinship in the formation and maintenance of bands. Innes points out that most groups living on the plains were (and are) tribally mixed, containing individuals of varying cultural descent: Cree, Saulteaux, Assiniboine, Métis, English half-breed. What counted most in terms of identity and relations with others was not language or tribal affiliation, but kinship connections. This insight can lead to a more nuanced understanding of the history of the plains, where band-level relations were often paramount and where kin relations and obligations frequently determined the choices and actions of individual members.

Patricia McCormack's chapter further pursues an understanding of multiculturalism in her analysis of the integrated, pluralistic fur trade world that Sylvia examined in *"Many Tender Ties."* Outlining the social and economic structure of Fort Chipewyan during the fur trade, McCormack gives substance to the recognition that fur trade society in the north long outlasted the demise of the fur trade world further south. Like Innes, she underlines the importance of kinship and the fluid and situational identities of the region, which were complicated and extended by the actions of the Cree and Chipewyan in intermarrying to form a "new multi-ethnic regional band" out of "ethnically distinctive local bands."[36]

Jarvis Brownlie's chapter begins a set of papers investigating colonial discourses about Indigenous peoples. Exploring the images and notions of First Nations that were promoted in Upper Canadian newspapers, she considers the ways that these messages legitimized both the dispossession of Aboriginal people and the unification of disparate settlers under the notion of a white race. At the same time, Brownlie considers Aboriginal texts from the time, finding that Aboriginal counter-discourses sought to use shared notions of masculinity to build connections with the newcomer society and to project a shared future. The chapter pairs well with Victoria Freeman's paper analyzing attitudes toward miscegenation in Anglo colonies in the nineteenth century. Extending her analysis over a large geographic area, Freeman also considers the other side of the coin examined in *"Many Tender Ties,"* taking into account intermarriage, but also coerced, temporary, and casual sexual relations. Overall, she discovers some broad patterns of intermarriage, finding it most common where colonies were based on mercantile relations with Indigenous peoples, least common where white settlement was the rule.

The last two contributions investigate inter-relationships, competition, and co-operation between different groups of racialized and classed women, and considers how these classifications have affected their experiences and relations. Kathryn Mc-Pherson extends Van Kirk's insights about race and gender relations in the fur trade to a later period in the prairie west—the last decades of the nineteenth century. She takes up the narrative, so common in pioneer accounts, of settler women surprised and trapped in their homes by the unwelcome visits of their Aboriginal neighbours. Often written years after the fact, these stories are surprisingly consistent in their plots and themes, particularly in their portrayals of gender, sexuality, and domesticity. Ultimately, McPherson sees these narratives as devices that displayed the fortitude of pioneer women, underlined their class and racial gendered respectability, and helped produce a collective identity that located white settler women at the heart of the Canadian narrative of colonization and nation-building.

The themes of family, ethnicity, and race that are woven through the other chapters remain important in Katrina Srigley's work, which completes the volume. This work of contemporary history utilizes oral history methods to shed light on the ways that a group of ten Anishinaabe, Cree, and Métis women from the North Bay area in northern Ontario define their Aboriginality, looking particularly at the impact of Bill C-31 on women's identity and experiences. The chapter explores how the women have dealt with "the ongoing destructiveness of colonialism" in their lives, as well as "the intimate connection between identity and status, and the essential role of cultural reclamation to healing."[37] Federal classifications of Aboriginal identity, including those codified in Bill C-31, An Act to Amend the Indian Act (1985), have created deep, lasting rifts in communities and families, with significant human costs. Yet Srigley finds that the women she interviewed, despite these challenges, have also worked hard to assert their own identities, reconnect with their cultures, and resist the status categories imposed by the colonizing nation state.

Conclusion

Taken as a whole, these contributions offer an array of new historical questions and interpretations. Inspired by the methodological, interpretive, and analytical innovations of Sylvia Van Kirk and her generation of scholars, they also seek to push scholarly inquiry further and to question received wisdom such as the tribal organization of plains groups or the personal distancing required by academic analysis. Examining a range of questions over a time period extending from the early nineteenth to the late twentieth century, and a geographic area reaching from the western plains to southern Ontario to New Zealand, they nevertheless share concerns about race, gender, identity, colonization, and the meanings conveyed by the many different ways to tell a story.

This volume reflects the enduring legacy of Sylvia Van Kirk's research, the ongoing resonance of her feminist questions, and the wide-ranging influence she has exercised among scholars studying Native-Newcomer relations in settler societies. She helped counter the absence of women and Aboriginal people in early histories, which had focused almost entirely on elite white men. Sylvia played an important part in dislodging this kind of exclusive, partial history writing and showed how vital women's contributions were, revealing a whole social world that had been made invisible. By discarding the old "hinterland" approach and placing the west at the centre of her narrative, she contributed to the dynamic process in which westerners reclaimed their own history and brought to bear a greater range of lived experiences and local perspectives. At the same time, she worked to disrupt national myths about the west and its place in national histories. In rejecting the "dehumanized" narrative about the fur trade that focused on commerce and empire, she was able to reveal the lives and agency of ordinary people. Thanks to the breadth of her research contributions, Sylvia's work helped generate new studies in several major fields: fur trade history, gender history and the history of women, Aboriginal women, the North American west, Native-Newcomer relations, multicultural history and more. Her writings continue to inform scholarship in all these fields and across a considerable geographic and temporal range.

The chapters in this volume also demonstrate the agency individual historians have to ask audacious questions that challenge historical norms and assumptions, both in our own research areas and within the academy, our departments, and amongst students of Canadian history. Van Kirk's innovations are a prime example of the importance of greater diversity within the scholarly profession—in her case as a western-Canadian feminist scholar—in making space for different questions, perspectives and, ultimately, research contributions. So many years later, while the profession has made gains in attracting more women historians, we have considerable room for improvement in making history departments reflect a truly representative cohort of Canadians. The more we do so, the more we shall further the goal of producing histories more attuned to racial, gender, regional, class, and sexual differences.

Notes

1   Michael Payne, "Fur Trade Historiography: Past Conditions, Present Circumstances and a Hint of Future Prospects," in *From Rupert's Land to Canada*, eds. T. Binnema, G. Ens, and R.C. Macleod (Edmonton: University of Alberta Press, 2001), 4.

2   *Women in the Shadows*, directed by Norma Bailey, produced by Christine Welsh and Signe Johansson (Direction Films/National Film Board, 1992).

3   Franca Iacovetta and Heidi Bohaker organized the celebratory panel, entitled "Many Tender Ties: A Forum in Honour of Sylvia Van Kirk" at the Canadian Historical Association Annual Meeting, 29 May 2007. Panel participants included: Patricia McCormack, Valerie J. Korinek, Mary-Ellen Kelm, Tony Hall and Jennifer Brown.

4   Ann Laura Stoler, "Tense and Tender Ties: The Politics of Comparison in North American History and (Post) Colonial Studies," *American Historical Review* 88, 3 (December 2001): 829–65.

5   Ibid., 829.

6   Ibid., 830.

7   Sylvia Van Kirk, "A Transborder Family in the Pacific North West: Reflecting on Race and Gender in Women's History," in *One Step Over the Line: Toward a History of Women in the North American Wests*, eds. E. Jameson and Sheila McManus (Edmonton: Athabasca University Press, 2008), 81–98; "Tracing the Fortunes of Five Founding Families of Victoria," *BC Studies* 115/116 (Autumn/ Winter 1997/98), 149–179; "'What If Mama Is an Indian?': The Cultural Ambivalence of the Alexander Ross Family,"in *The New Peoples: Being and Becoming Metis in North America*, eds. Jacqueline Peterson and Jennifer S.H. Brown (Winnipeg: University of Manitoba Press, 1985), 207–217.

8   Elizabeth Jameson, "Ties across the Border," this volume, 65.

9   Ibid.

10 Bill Waiser, "Introduction: place, process, and the new prairie realities," *Canadian Historical Review* 84, 4 (Dec 2003): 2–3.

11 *The West and Beyond: new perspectives on an imagined region*, eds. Alvin Finkel, Sarah Carter, and Peter Fortna (Edmonton: Athasbasca University Press, 2010).

12 In 2010, St. John's College at the University of Manitoba hosted a second meeting of the renewed Western Canadian Studies conference.

13 Adele Perry, "Historiography that Breaks Your Heart: Van Kirk and the Writing of Feminist History," this volume, 81.

14 Julia V. Emberley, "'A Gift for Languages': Native Women and the Textual Economy of the Colonial Archives," *Cultural Critique*, 17 (1990–1): 29–30.

15 Jacqueline Peterson with John Anfinson, "The Indian and the Fur Trade: A Review of Literature," in *The Prairie West: Historical Readings*, eds. R. Douglas Francis and Howard Palmer (Edmonton: Pica Pica Press, 1992), 88; Ruth Roach Pierson, "Experience, Difference, Dominance and Voice in the Writing of Canadian Women's History," in *Writing Women's History: International Perspectives*, eds. Karen Offen, Ruth Roach Pierson, and Jane Rendall (London: Macmillan; Bloomington and Indianapolis: Indiana University Press, 1991), 79–10.

16 Jennifer Brown, "The Blind Men and the Elephant: Fur Trade History Revisited," in *The Uncovered Past: Roots of Northern Alberta Societies*, eds. Patricia A. McCormack and R. Geoffrey Ironsides (Edmonton: Canadian Circumpolar Institute, University of Alberta, 1993), 15.

17   Sylvia Van Kirk, "Tracing the Fortunes of Five Founding Families of Victoria," *BC Studies* 115/116 (Autumn/Winter 1997/98), 149–179; "A Transborder Family in the Pacific North West: Reflecting on Race and Gender in Women's History," in *One Step Over the Line: Toward a History of Women in the North American Wests*, eds. E. Jameson and Sheila McManus (Edmonton: Athabasca University Press, 2008), 81–98; "Colonised Lives: The Native Wives and Daughters of Five Founding Families of Victoria," *Pacific Empires: Essays in Honour of Glyndwr Williams*, eds. Alan Frost and Jane Samson (Vancouver: University of British Columbia Press; Melbourne: Melbourne University Press, 1999), 215–236.

18   Van Kirk, "A Transborder Family in the Pacific North West," 81.

19   Frederick Jackson Turner, "The Significance of the Frontier in American History," in *History, Frontier, and Section: Three Essays by Frederick Jackson Turner*, ed. Martin Ridge (Albuquerque: University of New Mexico Press, 1993), 62–71. Turner first delivered "The Significance of the Frontier" as a paper at the American Historical Association meeting in Chicago, 12 July 1893.

20   Harold Innis, *The Fur Trade in Canada* (London: Oxford University Press, 1930).

21   Payne, "Fur Trade Historiography," 3.

22   *Writing the Range. Race, Class, and Culture in the Women's West*, eds. Elizabeth Jameson and Susan Armitage (Norman: University of Oklahoma Press, 1997), 12.

23   G.F.G. Stanley, *The Birth of Western Canada* (1936).

24   Quoted in Sarah Carter, *Aboriginal People and Colonizers of Western Canada to 1900* (Toronto: University of Toronto Press, 1999), 5.

25   See, most prominently, Tom Flanagan, *First Nations? Second Thoughts* (Montreal/Kingston: McGill-Queen's University Press, 2000), and Frances Widdowson and Albert Howard, *Disrobing the Aboriginal Industry: the Deception behind Indigenous Cultural Preservation* (Montreal/Kingston: McGill-Queen's University Press, 2008).

26   For an insightful account of prairie historiography organized by generation, see Gerald Friesen, "Critical History in Western Canada," in *The West and Beyond: New Perspectives on an Imagined Region*, eds. Alvin Finkel, Sarah Carter, and Peter Fortna (Edmonton: Athabasca University Press, 2010), 6.

27   Arthur Silver Morton, *A History of the Canadian West to 1870–71: Being a History of Rupert's Land (the Hudson's Bay Company's Territory) and of the North-West Territory (including the Pacific Slope)* (London/ New York: T. Nelson and Sons, 1939).

28   L.G. Thomas, "Historiography of the Fur Trade Era," in *A Region of the Mind*, ed. Richard Allen (Regina: Canadian Plains Research Center, 1973), 83, cited in Payne, "Fur Trade Historiography," 3.

29   See, for instance, Harold Cardinal, *The Unjust Society: The Tragedy of Canada's Indians* (Edmonton: M.G. Hurtig, 1969); *The Only Good Indian: Essays by Canadian Indians*, ed. Waubegeshig (Toronto: New Press, 1970); Maria Campbell, *Halfbreed* (Toronto: McClelland and Stewart, 1973); Howard Adams, *Prison of Grass: Canada from a Native Point of View* (Toronto: New Press, 1975).

30   Payne, "Fur Trade Historiography," 5.

31   Jennifer S.H. Brown, *Strangers in Blood: Fur Trade Company Families in Indian Country* (Vancouver: University of British Columbia Press, 1980).

32   Joan Kelly-Gadol, "Did Women Have a Renaissance?" in *Becoming Visible: Women in European History*, eds. Renate Bridenthal and Claudia Koonz (Boston: Houghton Mifflin, 1977), 137–163.

33 Sylvia Van Kirk to Jennifer S.H. Brown, 26 April 1972, quoted in Brown, this volume.

34 Franca Iacovetta, "Sylvia Van Kirk: A Feminist Appreciation of Front-line Work in the Academy," this volume.

35 Valerie J. Korinek, "Daring to Write a History of Western Canadian Women's Experiences: Assessing Van Kirk's Feminist Scholarship," this volume, 37-48.

36 Patricia A. McCormack, "'A World We Have Lost': The Plural Society of Fort Chipewyan," this volume, 146-169.

37 Katrina Srigley, "'I am a proud Anishinaabekwe:'" Issues of Identity and Status in Northern Ontario after Bill C-31," this volume, 241-259.

Works by Sylvia Van Kirk

"The Impact of White Women on Fur Trade Society," *The Beaver* (Winter 1972): 4–21. Reprinted in *The Neglected Majority: Essays in Canadian Women's History*, eds. Susan Mann Trofimenkoff and Alison Prentice (Toronto: McClelland and Stewart, 1977), 27–48; and in *Sweet Promises. A Reader on Indian-White Relations in Canada*, ed. J.R. Miller (Toronto: University of Toronto Press, 1991), 180–204.

"Thanadelthur," *The Beaver* (Spring 1974): 40–45.

"'Destined to Raise Her Caste': Sarah Ballenden and the Foss-Pelly Scandal," *Historical and Scientific Study of Manitoba*. Series III, 31 (1974–75), 41–52.

"The Role of Women in the Fur Trade Society of the Canadian West, 1700–1850." PhD dissertation, University of London, 1975.

"'The Custom of the Country': An Examination of Fur Trade Marriage Practices," in *Essays in Western History*, ed. L.H. Thomas (Edmonton: University of Alberta Press,1976): 49–68. Reprinted in *Canadian Family History: Selected Readings*, ed. Bettina Bradbury (Toronto: Copp Clark Pittman, 1992), 67–92.

"Women in Between: Indian Women in Fur Trade Society in Western Canada," Canadian Historical Association, *Historical Papers* (1977), 30–47. Reprinted in *Pre-Industrial Canada, 1760–1849*, eds. Michael S. Cross and Gregory S. Kealey (Toronto: McClelland and Stewart, 1982), 191–211; *Interpreting Canada's Past: Volume 1, Before Confederation*, ed. J.M. Bumsted (Toronto: Oxford University Press, 1986), 168–83; *An Introduction to Canadian History*, ed. A.I. Silver (Toronto: Canadian Scholars' Press, 1991); *A Passion for Identity: An Introduction to Canadian Studies*, 2nd ed., eds. David Taras, Beverly Rasporich and Eli Mandel

(Scarborough: Nelson Canada, 1993), 53–68; *Out of the Background: Readings on Canadian Native History*, 2nd ed-., eds. Ken Coates and Robin Fisher (Toronto: Irwin Publishing, 1998), 102-117.

"Many Tender Ties": Women in Fur-Trade Society in Western Canada, 1670–1870 (Winnipeg: Watson and Dwyer, 1980).

"Fur Trade Social History: Some Recent Trends," in *Old Trails and New Directions*, eds. Carol Judd and Arthur J. Ray (Toronto: University of Toronto Press, 1980), 160–173.

"'What If Mama Is an Indian?': The Cultural Ambivalence of the Alexander Ross Family," in *The Developing West*, ed. John Foster (Edmonton: University of Alberta Press, 1983), 123–36. Revised version in *The New Peoples: Being and Becoming Métis in North America*, eds. Jacqueline Peterson and Jennifer S.H. Brown (Winnipeg: University of Manitoba Press, 1985), 207–217; and in *The Invention of Canada: Readings in Pre-Confederation History*, ed. Chad Gaffield (Toronto: Copp Clark Longman Ltd., 1994), 402–12.

"The Role of Native Women in the Fur Trade Society of Western Canada, 1670–1830," *Frontiers* 7, 3 (1984): 9–13. Reprinted in *Rethinking Canada: The Promise of Women's History*, 2nd ed., eds. Veronica Strong-Boag and Anita Clair Fellman (Toronto: Copp Clark Longman Ltd., 1986), 73–80; *The Women's West*, eds. Armitage and Jameson (Norman, OK: University of Oklahoma Press, 1987), 53–62; *Perspectives on Canadian Economic Development: Class, Staples, Gender, and Elites*, ed. Gordon Laxer (Toronto: Oxford University Press, 1991), 353–361; *Women in Pacific Northwest History*, Vol. 1, ed. Karen Blair (Seattle: University of Washington Press, 2001).

"George Nelson's 'Wretched' Career, 1802–1823," in *Rendezvous: Selected Papers of the Fourth North American Fur Trade Conference, 1981*, ed. Thomas Buckley (St. Paul: North American Fur Trade Conference, 1984), 207–13.

"What Has the Feminist Perspective Done for Canadian History?" *Knowledge Reconsidered: A Feminist Overview*, ed. Ursula Martius Franklin (Ottawa: Canadian Research Institute for the Advancement of Women, 1984), 46–58.

"'The Reputation of a Lady': Sarah Ballenden and the Foss-Pelly Scandal,'" *Manitoba History* 11 (Spring 1986): 4–11. Reprinted in *Unequal Sisters: A*

Multicultural Reader in U.S. Women's History, 2nd ed., eds. Ellen Carol DuBois and Vicki L. Ruiz (New York: Routledge, 1994), 128–138.

"Toward a Feminist Perspective in Native History" (Toronto: Ontario Institute for Studies in Education, Occasional papers 14, 1987).

"Commentary," in *Western Women, Their Land, Their Lives*, eds. Schlissel, Ruiz, and Monk (Albuquerque, NM: University of New Mexico Press, 1988).

"'This Rascally and Ungrateful Country': George Nelson's Response to Rupert's Land," in *Rupert's Land: A Cultural Tapestry*, ed. R.C. Davis (Waterloo: Wilfrid Laurier University Press, 1988), 113–30.

"A Vital Presence: Women in the Cariboo Gold Rush, 1862–1875," in *British Columbia Reconsidered: Essays on Women*, eds. Veronica Strong-Boag and Gillian Creese (Vancouver: University of British Columbia Press, 1992), 21–37.

"Tracing the Fortunes of Five Founding Families of Victoria," *BC Studies* 115/116 (Autumn/Winter 1997/98): 149–179.

"From 'Marrying-In' to 'Marrying-Out': Changing Patterns of Aboriginal/Non-Aboriginal Marriage in Colonial Canada," *Frontiers* 23, 3 (2002): 1–11. Reprinted in *Rethinking Canada: The Promise of Women's History*, 5th ed., eds. Mona Gleason and Adele Perry (Don Mills: Oxford University Press, 2006), 115–123.

"A Transborder Family in the Pacific North West: Reflecting on Race and Gender in Women's History," in *One Step Over the Line: Toward a History of Women in the North American Wests*, eds. E. Jameson and Sheila McManus (Edmonton: Athabasca University Press, 2008), 81–98.

"Colonised Lives: The Native Wives and Daughters of Five Founding Families of Victoria," in *Pacific Empires: Essays in Honour of Glyndwr Williams*, eds. Alan Frost and Jane Samson (Vancouver: University of British Columbia Press; Melbourne: Melbourne University Press, 1999), 215–236.

"All These Stories about Women": "Many Tender Ties" and a New Fur Trade History

Jennifer S.H. Brown

ON 29 MAY 2007, I WAS PRIVILEGED to be the commentator for a Canadian Historical Association (CHA) Forum in honour of Sylvia Van Kirk, at the annual CHA meeting in Saskatoon. The occasion led me to look back over Sylvia's and my considerable correspondence over the years and to reflect on our work, our mutual interests, and our long friendship. I am happy to have the opportunity to express these thoughts more fully for this book.

Sylvia and I have known each other since 1972. Our association over almost four decades has encompassed a period in which women's and Aboriginal history have secured a permanent place in Canadian history. Much has changed in those years—when we began to walk the historical trails we had chosen, they were narrow and we did not have much company. Now they are broad and well-trodden by scholars of many backgrounds who are shedding light on subjects and areas scarcely thought of in the 1970s, as exemplified by several of the studies in this volume.

This essay makes no attempt to review the history of these fields over the last decades. I shall try, however, to tell a small piece of their story through some of Sylvia's and my own experiences, beginning with our mutual starting point in the early 1970s. Our scholarly correspondence, begun in 1972, fuelled a friendship as we discovered and shared our research and our common interests and enthusiasms. In following years, our studies were intertwined in continuing conversations, even as our careers followed rather distinct paths. This is personal history on a microcosmic scale, but any history must build on concrete particulars, well-documented and well-remembered. And since this is Sylvia's book, this essay may help to tell parts of her story that reach beyond her students' memories, and may even help her students' students to know her and her work better. I take the liberty of referring to her by her first name because we are friends and she would do the same for me.

I first heard of Sylvia when I was a graduate student in anthropology at the University of Chicago. After various peregrinations through other fields and to other parts of the world, my Canadian familial roots finally exerted a pull on my academic studies, leading me to focus on the ethnohistory of northern North America with special attention to fur trade and mission sources. My dissertation became a study of fur traders and their Native families. Both fur trade historians and anthropologists looking at the Aboriginal groups involved in the fur trade had largely ignored this topic, even though trade relations "on the ground" relied greatly on these familial and kinship bonds, which themselves had great social and demographic consequences.

In March 1972, as I was beginning my dissertation research, I wrote to the Hudson's Bay Company Archives at Beaver House, Great Trinity Lane, London, England (the HBCA did not move to Winnipeg until 1974). I asked to use the pre-1870 microfilm copies of their records, which they had deposited in the Public Archives of Canada in Ottawa; at that time, formal advance permission was still required. Mrs. J. Craig, Archivist, approved my request, but added, "We should mention that for the past two years Miss Sylvia Van Kirk has been undertaking research in the Company's archives for her Ph.D. thesis on the role of women in the fur trade of the Canadian Northwest, c. 1670–1850. Miss Van Kirk, registered at the University of London, is working under the supervision of Dr G[lyndwr] Williams, General Editor of the Hudson's Bay Record Society. As this study will clearly overlap with your proposed subject, you may care to contact Miss Van Kirk." She suggested I write to her c/o Dr. Williams at Queen Mary College, and I did so. On 26 April 1972, Sylvia sent me a reply addressed, "Dear Mrs. Brown"; thereafter we went to first names. (This was all before the use of "Ms." became standard; one could not address women formally without implying their marital status.) I will quote from it at some length, as it is vintage Sylvia, and set the tone for a long friendship. She was "very interested" to hear of my topic, and said she "would welcome a correspondence." She went on to outline her own topic and then added,

Of course, the bulk of my thesis does concentrate on the relationships which developed between the traders and their Indian or mixed-blood wives. Evidence confirms that marriages "a la façon du pays" certainly were customary and formed an important element in fur trade society which was indeed an indigenous society combining aspects of the Indian, British and French-Canadian way of life.

As an anthropologist you will likely be applying a different set of criteria to the primary source material. Although concerned with underlying trends and themes, I am more interested in the individual experiences per se than in using them to illustrate certain patterns or trends. As a Western Canadian myself, I feel quite strongly about the dehumanized way in which our history has been written. My thesis will also say little about the mixed-bloods as a group. I am primarily concerned with the initial relationship between the White trader and his Indian wife, and will be dealing with mixed-blood women only in terms of their relationships with White men.

In closing, she wrote, "I am very pleased that you contacted me and hope that this will help you to determine the limits of your thesis. There has been so little work done in this fascinating field that I am sure there is room for both our studies and more. It seems to me that there has not been enough co-operation between scholars particularly at the inter-disciplinary level. I hope we will be able to co-operate to our mutual benefit and I look forward to hearing from you."[1]

The letter expressed not only her intellectual focus and passion (in her usual understated way), but also her already strong stance about cooperation and mutuality. I was much relieved when she replied in this vein. To explain this relief, it may be useful to step back for a moment and talk about being a female graduate student in the 1960s and 1970s. I cannot speak for Sylvia's experiences then, but she, like other women of our generation, probably has numerous recollections along similar lines.

While growing numbers of women were pursuing advanced studies in those years, we were still a minority. Many of us were also not very sure of our positions or our futures in academe.[2] One striking feature of our universities, which we certainly noticed, was the shortage of women professors at any level. In my entire academic career, I never had a class with a woman professor (I believe Sylvia did have one as an undergraduate at the University of Alberta). At Harvard University, where I began graduate studies (first in classical archaeology and then in anthropology), the admittedly small sample of women I knew felt at a disadvantage among the men, and sensed that we were not being taken very seriously. We joked about certain "fair-haired boys," as we called them, male graduate students who were the most likely candidates to go on our professors' major archaeological digs and received other encouragement. A certain professor we knew appeared to reserve his B-plus grades for the women in his seminars. The atmosphere in seminars often tended to reward one-up-man-ship and to encourage territoriality rather than collaboration. In fairness, I was spared such experiences once I moved to the University of Chicago in 1970, but the Harvard legacy meant that a warm and open reception from a fellow graduate student in an overlapping field was a welcome event.

Over the next three years, Sylvia and I exchanged a number of letters, some of which delved deeply into the intricacies of the fur trade families we were both trying to trace. We came to feel sometimes like a pair of old gossips as we tried to sort out the various fur trade marriages and wives, and to trace the children of the traders' sometimes multiple unions. Of course, we were sorting through the fur traders' own gossip; women have no monopoly on that genre despite the stereotypes. We traded thoughts on the problems of organizing our materials, and on issues of terminology: when and whether to use Métis/métis, halfbreed, mixed-blood, and the like. Meanwhile, Sylvia's then-husband was finishing his dissertation, which she took time to help type. In the fall of 1973, she wrote me that, "after months of uncertainty," they both "landed up at Dalhousie University. It's a difficult job to secure one position let alone two—and our situation this year is that we each have what amounts to half a position."[3]

Sylvia and I finally got to meet at the Canadian Historical Association meetings in Toronto in early June 1974, where she presented a paper on marriage according to the custom of the country. As I recall, a senior professor introduced her as "Mrs. Dowler," and we quietly raised our eyebrows.[4] But a highlight was the presence of Irene Spry as commentator—a warm and wonderful senior female scholar who greatly encouraged and inspired us both through those years and until her death in 1998.

In 1974–75, Sylvia stayed on at Dalhousie, while her husband took an improved position at the University of Toronto, Scarborough. Sylvia defended her thesis on 22 May 1975, beating me by a year. "It was a real grilling," she wrote, "but nevertheless went well. The internal examiner was E.E. Rich, who seemed not entirely convinced that all these stories about women constituted 'real' history."[5]

The following year, Sylvia took up a one-year position in history at the University of Toronto, and became a candidate for a tenure-track position, for which she had considerable support. But it emerged that "since a small minority was critical of the thesis, they decided to give me a 2-year contract instead of a tenure-stream appointment." A certain non-Canadianist held that her thesis was only a regional study that lacked comparative material and broader generalization, and needed much work before publication.[6] The situation was not very comfortable for a while. Sylvia's tenure-track position eventually came through, however, and she achieved tenure in 1980.

Our revised dissertations came out as books in the same year (1980), and we shared the Honourable Mention award for the Sir John A. Macdonald Prize in Canadian history from the Canadian Historical Association.[7] We became, it seemed, the Bobbsey Twins of fur trade social history, often cited in the same breath or footnote by writers who might or might not have read the books, as well as by a generation or more of graduate students who were obliged to include us on their comprehensive reading lists. It seemed that fur trade history began to be seen in a new light, and that people began to think and write about it differently. The appearance of Sylvia's work also coincided with the rise of women's history courses and programs in many universities across North America. Her becoming established at the University of Toronto was a most fortunate development for women's studies at that university, as well as for her students and herself.

In following years, Sylvia was increasingly occupied not only with new courses and growing numbers of graduate students, but with administrative duties, especially in women's studies. But we kept in touch—summertime often brought chances for visits at my old family cottage on an island near Parry Sound, Ontario. We canoed and picked blueberries, and Sylvia was a devoted gatherer of pinecones for the wood stove and trimmer of island trails.

The visits also allowed time for lots of talk. In the 1980s we became absorbed in working on the writings of fur trader George Nelson, who became our favourite among the many traders we had met in our archival researches. Sylvia had found him first, discovering his remarkable journals and reminiscences (perhaps around 1200 pages) which had been sitting in the Metropolitan Toronto Public Library, virtually untouched, since the 1930s. We arranged to get photocopies made, and Sylvia secured grant money for an assistant to transcribe the Nelson texts onto an early computer mainframe at her university. In 1983, I moved from Illinois to a teaching position in history at the University of Winnipeg, and was able to make some contribution to the work from that new base, aided by the proximity of the Hudson's Bay Company Archives, now only three blocks away.

George Nelson was an obscure North West Company clerk who ended his fur trade days working for the Hudson's Bay Company after the two firms merged in 1821. He appealed to us as a fresh voice, scarcely known, who was remarkably perceptive and observant both about his peers and about the Aboriginal people with whom he traded; some of his accounts of Ojibwe and Cree people from northern Wisconsin to northern Manitoba and Saskatchewan between 1802 and 1823 are among the most detailed we have. He was never a great explorer; nor did he assume the heroic rhetoric of an Alexander Mackenzie or a George Simpson. He listened, learned the language (Ojibwe in particular), admitted making mistakes in his actions and writings, and was open about failing to understand what he saw, as when he took part in a Cree shaking tent ceremony in 1823.[8]

Of particular interest for us were his relatively frank and reflective writings about his series of Ojibwe marital ties—one early and temporary, the other longer and ultimately tragic, as his second Ojibwe wife and children all died relatively young (he had no surviving heirs). Perhaps more than any other trader, Nelson opened a window into those relationships and their challenges, and into the rather fraught fur trade contexts around them. Sylvia and I collaborated on his biography for the *Dictionary of Canadian Biography*, and she achieved the feat of deciphering an extensive coded journal that Nelson kept as a Nor-Wester in 1816 when he felt at serious risk of losing his post and records to the rival Hudson's Bay Company (HBC) nearby. She published two papers on him, and both we and other colleagues have continued to build on her work, finding other means to explore and bring forward his writings.[9]

Sylvia and I also remember the 1980s as a time of dealing with issues around Peter C. Newman and his books on Hudson's Bay Company history. The controversy that his books on that topic provoked is readily visible if one compares and contrasts the varied reviews of *Company of Adventurers* and *Caesars of the Wilderness*. A review essay on *Company of Adventurers* that I published in the *Canadian Historical Review* in 1986 covered the debate by looking at the varied responses to his work.[10]

In retrospect, we were both naïve in dealing with Newman, a well-known popular author of trade books who had received a very large advance for writing his HBC history. While preparing his books, he had approached each of us, and a number of others, for interviews that we gladly gave him. We had hopes of seeing a high-quality popular history emerge from his project—we wanted to see good results. Unlike some of our more experienced colleagues, we asked for (and received) no compensation for our time or expertise.

The reviews and other responses (including comments to Newman himself) that we and other scholars felt compelled to write when *Company of Adventurers* was published reflected our disappointment with his work. In short, both this book and its sequel were characterized by purple prose, simplistic stereotypes, and errors, along with inflated claims about the author's research in the HBC Archives. Further, we found ourselves cited and credited as if we had endorsed Newman's work, even though we'd had no chance for any advance review or comment. On a larger scale, it was troubling to see him dismiss his numerous historian critics as narrow, territorial, envious malcontents who couldn't write. As historians who set great store by writing well and communicating effectively, we were unhappy to see an artificial gulf opened between academic and popular history, as if ne'er the twain could meet, when in fact, we have had a strong interest in bridging that gap all along.[11] Looking back, we probably allowed the issue to consume more time and energy than it should have, but it was in many respects an instructive experience.

Once I had settled at the University of Winnipeg, our involvement with the Centre for Rupert's Land Studies engaged us both. I helped the centre begin in 1984 as an organization to promote the use of the Hudson's Bay Company Archives, so central to our work. A feature of the Centre's activities soon became its biennial colloquiums, which continue to bring together scholars, students, and many other people interested in the fur trade and Aboriginal history of Rupert's Land—the huge Hudson Bay watershed that the Hudson's Bay Company held by royal charter from 1670 to 1870. From the beginning of the Centre, Sylvia has been an active supporter and participant, and has helped bring together academics and others who share a consuming interest in fur trade and Aboriginal history.

A good many people who have become connected with the Centre have strong family roots of their own in the history of old Rupert's Land. When Sylvia and I were graduate students in the 1970s, the older generations of these families still denied or set aside their Native roots and connections because of harsh experience with racism and prejudice. As a result, our own research was largely confined to working with documents; back then, we could not have begun to do the family and oral histories that newer generations are now pursuing with pride and fascination. Among the people we know who have been immersed in tracing their roots and putting them in a new and broader context are Shirley

Wishart and Vernon Wishart, Heather Devine, Virginia Barter, Sherry Farrell Racette, and many others. Their research is making a difference on the larger stage of Canadian history.[12]

The present generation of students takes it almost for granted that women's history, the roles of Aboriginal women in the fur trade, and gender history are part of their graduate and undergraduate texts and courses. But Sylvia (and I) can tell you this has all happened in the last twenty to thirty years. It was not easy; there was indeed an element of risk and daring involved (as when Olive Dickason in the 1970s challenged convention with her doctoral work in Aboriginal history). Now, the tide has turned remarkably for both women and "Indians." I regularly have had more women than men in my history courses at all levels. Sixty-five per cent of students at the University of Winnipeg are women (a proportion replicated at many other universities), and the university also has close to 900 Aboriginal students. "Women" now make it into the indexes of books as a marked category. (It's interesting that "men" are still not indexed, being the unmarked category that is always present. Maybe that will have to change sometime, if [or as] males begin to suffer the neglect that women endured for so long in history.)

Sylvia's and my paths have diverged in some respects. Sylvia has focused especially (and most productively) on the situations of Native wives in fur trade settings where they were increasingly subjected to the Victorian values of Euro-Canadian men and women. While I was teaching in Winnipeg for twenty-eight years, the centre of her world increasingly shifted from Toronto to Victoria where she now lives. There, she continues to research the old Fort Victoria fur trade families whose mixed descent confronted them with challenges in that rapidly changing community in the mid- to late-1800s. More broadly, her sphere of work and teaching increasingly became women's history, while mine became Aboriginal history.

Yet we still have much in common. We have both reacted against, as Sylvia put it in 1972, "the dehumanized way in which our history has been written." From the 1970s onward, Sylvia brought the women of the fur trade into history as real persons whose voices could be heard (or at least imagined) even if they never wrote their stories for themselves. She has always had a concern to read through and beyond the limited sources to find or envisage those hidden lives, the "Women in the Shadows," to cite Christine Welsh's film on which she advised. She has done those things wonderfully.

At the CHA forum in Sylvia's honour, some presenters made occasional reference to theoretical concepts of recent generations that Sylvia has not used, although they did find that some of those concepts are implicit in her writing. Should she indeed have turned a page at some point, to invoke Homi Bhabha, Clifford Geertz or other theorists of our times? Certainly, concepts such as hybridity and intersectionality have their place in analysis and have heuristic value. But taking a longer view of our historiography, I am struck by how almost all such concepts have a "shelf life"; after a while they become dated, and almost everyone moves on to something new.[13] Theory has its uses but needs to be kept in its place.

At the same time, I am grateful that I had an early immersion in anthropological theory and models—they challenged me to question our concepts and categories. Sylvia's first letter to me compared her historical focus to my anthropological orientation, and indeed, my courses and professors directed me towards broader issues of method and theory that she did not have to face. I benefited from confronting the multiple problems around defining such categories as "marriage," "custom," and "society," which she tended to accept more as given. Many people used the phrase, "marriage according to the custom of the country" in the nineteenth century, but the same words meant quite different things to different fur traders, to Aboriginal people, and to judges and courts of law when they got hold of the phrase.[14]

It is also useful to remember that Sylvia was given a solid training in historical research and documentation by Glyndwr Williams at the University of London, and she was allowed to specialize early in that research; I recall her telling me of the challenges she later faced in teaching broad survey courses because she had plunged into her doctoral specialty so early. Pursuing that specialty, Sylvia religiously attended to the voices that spoke to her through the archives. Too much reliance on the theories of modern outsiders risks silencing those voices, a serious problem seen also by Aboriginal writers. Theory can be dehumanizing; some postcolonial writings tend to foster a new crypto-colonialism in themselves, sometimes drowning out with their superstructures the very voices we should hear and to which we should be listening more attentively.

Sylvia's work has many enduring strengths. She has asked new questions. She has listened hard and carefully to the sources for voices that others had not heard, which she continues to do through her collaborations with their descendants. Her work will survive the theoretical re-fashionings of our fields. *"Many Tender Ties"* is still in print after almost three decades, and that in itself tells us that her work lives and continues to resonate.

Some final thoughts arise from contemplating the title of Sylvia's book. As her readers know, the book opens with a quotation from Chief Factor James Douglas in 1842. Referring to life in the fur trade country, Douglas wrote in reference to traders' family bonds that "habit makes [this life] familiar to us, softened as it is by *the many tender ties*, which find a way to the heart."

The title choice is classic Sylvia. Both she and I found that fur trade unions ran the gamut from tender enduring affection to abuse and neglect, and we recognized that in our work. But she had a devotion to the ones that worked, the relationships that proved the validity and viability of "fur trade society." I have shared that bias to a fair extent; we have both felt special affinity to George Nelson, David Thompson, James Douglas, and several others whose marriages did work. But my book title, *Strangers in Blood*, picked up a different angle: the challenges these unions faced when British and Canadian courts tried to assess their legitimacy and that of their children. "Strangers in blood" was an English legal category. If Native fur trade wives and children could not be shown to be legitimate, their legacies were subject to a higher duty, a kind of tax assessed on non-relatives who as heirs were declared to be strangers in blood (a cruel irony for children who certainly shared their fathers' "blood"). The term highlights the enduring problematics of these relationships both within and outside the world of the fur trade.

Sylvia has strong ideals and values, and tremendous empathy for her subjects of study. She is also a romantic, in the best sense. It is entirely fitting that in retirement in Victoria, BC, she celebrated her marriage to Geoffrey Hart in April 2006 with a fine enactment of a full-scale Victorian wedding, in the Church of Our Lord, spiritual home to many old fur trade families. After almost two decades of being on her own, she finally regained for herself "the many tender ties, which find a way to the heart." Of course, in non-Victorian fashion, she is still Sylvia Van Kirk!

Notes

1   The personal letters drawn upon for this paper are in my files, and are quoted with the kind permission of Sylvia Van Kirk.

2   I and many other women were encouraged at the time into graduate studies by the opportunity offered by the Woodrow Wilson Fellowship program. Aspiring graduate students who had an excellent academic record, good references, and a successful interview could gain financial support to enter graduate school and continue the pleasures of studies at higher levels without having to face real-world issues of where they might lead.

3   Sylvia Van Kirk to Jennifer Brown, 20 November 1973.

4   In the 1970s it was still unusual for women to keep their own names upon marriage. This was an issue that I was spared in the 1960s, as I was a Brown who married a Brown. Sylvia commented on the issue to a *Globe and Mail* interviewer, Constance Mungall, in 1976, admitting, "I've kept my own name professionally, but I've been schizophrenic about it. When we travel together [she and her husband], I use a passport with my married name. I just can't face the explanations at each hotel" ("Course on History of Women in Canada Seen as Part of Way to Discover Identity," 3 May 1976). Times have changed.

5   Van Kirk to Brown, 17 July 1975. Rich's comment evokes a parallel with the experience of distinguished Métis historian Olive P. Dickason when she applied to do a PhD in Native History at the University of Ottawa in the early 1970s. The university "did not acknowledge that Indians had any history, and suggested that she take anthropology instead." However, she later recalled, "A Belgian fellow [Cornelius Jaenen], who didn't know very much about Native people, but knew a lot about discrimination, took up my cause, and the university eventually admitted me." R. John Hayes, "Historian Awarded Order of Canada," *Windspeaker* Feb. 1996, 8.

6   Van Kirk to Brown, 19 June 1976.

7   *"Many Tender Ties": Women in Fur-Trade Society in Western Canada, 1670–1870* (Winnipeg: Watson and Dwyer, 1980) and *Strangers in Blood: Fur Trade Company Families in Indian Country* (Vancouver: University of British Columbia Press, 1980).

8   See Jennifer S.H. Brown and Robert Brightman, *The Orders of the Dreamed: George Nelson on Cree and Northern Ojibwa Religion and Myth, 1823* (Winnipeg: University of Manitoba Press, 1988).

9   Sylvia Van Kirk, "George Nelson's 'Wretched' Career, 1802–1823," in *Rendezvous: Selected Papers of the Fourth North American Fur Trade Conference, 1981*, ed. Thomas Buckley (St. Paul: 1984), 207–13; and "'This Rascally & Ungrateful Country': George Nelson's Response to Rupert's Land," in *Rupert's Land: A Cultural Tapestry*, ed. R.C. Davis (Waterloo: Wilfrid Laurier University Press, 1988), 113–30. See also Brown and Brightman, *The Orders of the Dreamed*; and George Nelson, *My First Years in the Fur Trade: The Journals of 1802–1804*, eds. Laura Peers and Theresa Schenck (St. Paul: Minnesota Historical Society Press, 2002).

10 Newman's *Company of Adventures* in "Two Solitudes: A Look at Reviews and Responses." *Canadian Historical Review* 67, 4 (1986): 562–571. Newman's two books were published in 1984 and 1987, respectively, by Penguin Books, Markham, ON.

11 In fact, Sylvia Van Kirk's and other works in our circles have generally been viewed as well-written (the fur trade historian most notorious for bad writing was Harold A. Innis of two generations ago). Our books have been reprinted several times, sometimes in the USA (University of Oklahoma Press), and have stayed in print for thirty years. Sylvia has been active in popular and public history through much of her career; witness, for example, her *Life in the Western Canadian Fur Trade 1770–1870*, vol. 32 in the *Canada's Visual History* series published by the National Museum of Man and the National Film

Board (Ottawa: 1979–80); her vital role as consultant on Christine Welsh's 1989 film *Women in the Shadows* (Direction Films); and numerous other contributions. Currently she continues her public history work in connection with the old fur trade families' church, the Church of Our Lord (Reformed Episcopal), in Victoria, BC.

12 For recent essays by Devine, Barter, and several others on these themes, see *The Long Journey of a Forgotten People: Métis Identities and Family Histories*, eds. Ute Lischke and David T. McNab (Waterloo, ON: Wilfrid Laurier University Press, 2007). Vernon Wishart's *What Lies behind the Picture? A Personal Journey into Cree Ancestry* (Red Deer: Central Alberta Historical Society, 2006) is an evocative book on his sister's and his searches for their hidden Cree roots and forebears.

13 As an older example, in the 1930s and 1940s, acculturation theory and Rorschach tests had their days, and one of my favourite anthropologists, A. Irving Hallowell, bought heavily into them in that period. His work endured, however, mainly because of the solidity of his research and the quality of his ethnography. His later writings virtually dropped the use of those tools; they served him for a while, but he then set them aside.

14 Jennifer S.H. Brown, "Partial Truths: A Closer Look at Fur Trade Marriage" in *From Rupert's Land to Canada*, eds. Theodore Binnema, Gerhard J. Ens, and R.C. Macleod (Edmonton: University of Alberta Press, 2001), 59–80.

Sylvia Van Kirk:
A Feminist Appreciation of
Front-line Work in the Academy

FRANCA IACOVETTA

"THE 18 WOMEN AND TWO MEN ATTENDING a course called History of Women in Canada" at the University of Toronto, wrote a *Globe and Mail* reporter in spring 1976, "could hardly wait to comment on their own experiences when instructor Sylvia Van Kirk introduced the subject of women's rights in Canada." The journalist, Constance Mungall, went on to describe the course—a new third-year seminar being offered by the (now defunct) interdisciplinary studies department at the University of Toronto—and the class ("After the vote: Did it make any difference?") she had just observed. Sylvia had promoted discussion in the seminar by noting that "in the 1930s suffragette Nellie McClung had said the place of women in dating is 'to wait…wait…wait'" and then asking if they thought it was still true today. Various students jumped in with their opinion and "the consensus was that it's still the same and it's hypocritical."

Mungall had attended the class as the course was nearing its end. By then, the seminar had covered a series of topics that would become standard fare for survey courses in Canadian women's history, including Native women in the fur trade (a topic that, of course, Sylvia's own research had helped make possible), white settler pioneers, and women in education, medicine, waged work, and moral and political reform movements. But these were also early days for women's history and Sylvia was drawing on limited resources—still convincing people of the value of the field—and introducing little known historical female subjects. Clearly, the reporter had thought the idea of teaching women's history novel enough to write an article about Sylvia, then a newly minted PhD who had just joined the faculty at the University of Toronto as an instructor (a tenure-stream job would come later). The photo accompanying the article featured a young Sylvia wearing glasses and sporting a classic seventies hair style—straight shoulder-length hair with long bangs split in the middle. Noting that "there are whole areas in Canadian history where the role of women has not been inves-tigated at all," Sylvia added that even while she could rely on her own work to teach about Native women in western Canada, "we need more work on women in Indian society in Eastern Canada, in New France, in the Maritimes, in ethnic groups." Several students told Mungall they had never heard of McClung or ever read the works of critically acclaimed nineteenth-century Canadian women novelists and poets before taking this course. "That reflects the social situation in Canada," Sylvia explained, adding that "integrating women into our social and economic history has to be part of our attempt to find out who and what we are in Canada." The journalist cavalierly called this modest "women's lib" talk. But she also went on to emphasize the favourable response of the students, including one of the men who had taken the course purely as an elective and expected to be constantly "put on the spot" by his female "prof" and classmates. Instead, he enjoyed Sylvia's teaching style, including her willingness to share with students her personal stories of being a feminist in the academy (and wider society of 1970s Canada) as a way of encouraging them to reflect on their own circumstances and values. Of his female classmates, he said they were "radical" (by which he appeared to mean they were in favour of women's rights) yet he often found himself agreeing with them. When he didn't, he added, they usually respected his divergent opinion.

Given the opportunity to articulate her teaching objectives and methods, Sylvia stressed in the *Globe and Mail* interview that while she did not want to turn her women's history class into "a consciousness raising group" shaped by a particular feminist agenda, she did wish to encourage students to ponder the ways in which an understanding of women's different priorities and experiences might lead to a new way of thinking about the Canadian past. Of her students, she observed that "I haven't sensed any currents of revolution. Both [seminar] groups seem aware [of women's issues], but [are] a little conservative." She ex-plained that for her, teaching women's history was not propaganda but rather a process of informing students about the little-explored lives of women. She was satisfied that she had made a difference. "I think a lot of minds were opened to issues they never thought about before," she told Mungall. "There's room for challenge and questioning not only in the contemporary sphere, but about why things were the way they were back when."[1]

This type of feminist position in favour of reasonableness—that is, the view that one can find effective ways of challenging and questioning people's understandings of the past or a contemporary situation—nicely sums up, I think, the way in which Sylvia led a long and successful, and also very demanding, career at the University of Toronto. The newspaper piece cited above dealt primarily with her teaching and, to a lesser degree, research, but I would suggest that, as I observed it, a desire to challenge and question people's conventional understandings by reasoned argument also characterized the way in which Sylvia conducted herself as a feminist colleague on the front lines of the academy— how she approached her responsibilities on numerous search committees and carried out her many administrative duties in the university.

It is this aspect of Sylvia's academic career that I wish to highlight in my contribution to this volume. In contrast to many of the other contributors who knew Sylvia as a contemporary, friend, or student, I came to know her best as a colleague at the University of Toronto, whose history department I joined almost fifteen years after she introduced the History of Women in Canada course described above. While we continue to be very different kinds of personalities with both similar and distinct politics, I came to appreciate and respect Sylvia's polite but persistent approach to bringing feminist perspectives into the academy—one step at a time, one committee at a time—working with the assumption that most colleagues (like students) are reasonable if not revolutionary minded people who will listen and ponder alternative views if presented in clear and compelling ways. I also chose to highlight this topic because we do not talk enough about all of the time and energy that goes into committee and administrative work or fully appreciate its significance as a mechanism for social change. For feminist scholars in the 1970s and 1980s, this workload was compounded by the challenge of trying to convince colleagues hostile to (or ignorant of) feminist theories and methodologies to expand their horizons and recognize feminist scholarship as a legitimate endeavour (as opposed to "a merely ideological enterprise," as some critics dismissively declared), and even to entertain the notion that a female candidate could be as "excellent" as a male. I offer a personal and professional appreciation of a senior colleague belonging to that group of feminist scholars who, beginning in the 1970s, took on faculty positions in Canadian universities and carved out an intellectual and political space for women's history and feminist studies. These are my opinions. When I recently tried to interview Sylvia, she made it clear that she thought it best that I write the piece my way—without her intervention—and without treating her as some kind of feminist authority on university affairs. I have taken that advice to heart.

When I was first hired at the University of Toronto in 1990, I never expected to become a friendly colleague or friend of Sylvia Van Kirk. For one thing, she was a feminist historian icon—the author of one of the foundational books in Canadian women's history, *"Many Tender Ties"*.[2] By my time, anyone who had ever taken a Canadian history course—be it an introductory survey, a social history, or women's history course—had been exposed to Sylvia's work, especially on Native women in fur trade society in lectures and in tutorial or seminar readings. For many of us across the country, our first introduction to women in Canadian history was through Sylvia's scholarship. In international circles, feminist historians often cite the U.S.-based European historian Joan Kelly and her pioneering piece, "Did Women Have a Renaissance?" as a critical starting point in the field of women's history—and rightly so.[3] Feminists in labour and left history also cite Alice Kessler-Harris' now "seminal" article "Where Are the Organized Women Workers?" for similarly compelling reasons.[4] In seeking to research such deceptively simple questions, these and other pioneering feminist historians not only discovered women in history but gained a better understanding of how women's lives differed from men's as well as how gendered power dynamics had often imposed limitations on women. It is equally important that, as Canadianists, we recognize (or remember) that at roughly the same time, Sylvia was asking her own deceptively simple question: where were the women in the fur trade society of the early Canadian west? As a PhD student, she went off to England and the Hudson's Bay Company (HBC) Archives armed with little more than this research question—to see whether one could find women in the fur trade—and, as she later explained, she more or less stumbled along, reading the archival records, poring over fur traders' diaries and HBC records looking for women. She had not committed to any particular theoretical paradigm other than a feminist understanding that women had to be there, somewhere. And the rest, as they say, is history. Along with Jennifer Brown, she brought Native women from the margins to the centre of Canadian history, even though they came to us largely through white male records. If undergraduate students of Canadian history could not remember anything else about women in the Canadian past, they could remember that Aboriginal women mattered to fur trade economics, politics, and society because Sylvia Van Kirk had demonstrated this to be so. For all of my chutzpah—and I had plenty in those days—I was shy about meeting such a major name in Canadian history.

I also assumed that there would be a personality divide—both generational and political—between Sylvia and me, an assumption that had much to do with my own self-perception, biases, and positioning. I belonged to a later group of feminist historians trained in the 1980s whose careers had been made easier because of senior colleagues like Sylvia. If this sometimes made us appear more brash than those colleagues, it was largely because the presence of these feminists in the academy—and their success as scholars whose work had helped define an entire field of history—gave us a sense of entitlement to be in the university and to carve out our own careers while also continuing to challenge the academy's traditionally elitist conventions. I was also working class, the daughter of immigrant parents of peasant background who had culled together a third-grade education in one of southern Italy's deeply impoverished rural regions. I belonged to the first generation in my family to go to university. Earning a PhD and landing a job as a professor was unheard of in my very large extended family. Although proud of my accomplishments, I was also a socialist and feminist with a political critique of the academy and what I saw as Anglo-elitism at work. I was a scrappy feminist, quick to loudly voice opinions and to dismiss—and on occasion even denounce—male colleagues as hopelessly conservative or anti-feminist. Having gotten a position in the job-starved early 1990s, I had joined a department dominated by senior men with degrees from Ivy League and other prestigious universities. The departmental meetings held to make decisions of any sort invariably involved debates among colleagues who reported on how "we did things" at Harvard, Princeton, Yale—and, on occasion, Oxford, Cambridge, and Chicago. At times, I couldn't resist invoking my alma mater, York University, which prompted strange stares or bemused smiles. My naive assumption, based on my class, ethnicity, and training outside elite schools (apart from one disastrous year at Queen's University), was that Sylvia easily "fit" into the department. After all, to me she was "WASP" (an assumption that denied Sylvia her Dutch immigrant background), middle-class, and seemed to possess the same professional confidences and cultural polish as did the senior men. I also knew she was married to a colleague whose primary appointment was at the Scarborough campus, where I had also been hired. It was only later that I learned from others (never from Sylvia) about the difficulties she had faced as one of the few women and feminists in the department. Having given up a tenure-stream job at Dalhousie University to join her then-husband in Toronto, she had struggled for a number of years on insecure contracts as a sessional instructor before landing a tenure-stream job at the University of Toronto. And in those years, her research had been ridiculed, I learned from others, sometimes in especially nasty terms. "She studies beavers" was one particularly crude double entendre I was told about, suggesting how even well-educated men can behave like immature louts. Little did I know that men in my department felt similarly about the shameful behaviour of other male colleagues. In his recently published autobiography, Michael Bliss offered the following blistering comments:

> With the heady days of expansion long passed, we had few appointments to make in the department. The positions that did come open were hotly contested. Edward "Ned" Shorter, a prolific Europeanist, and Bill Eccles, probably a misogynist, did not think much of the scholarship of Sylvia Van Kirk, whose thesis on the role of women in the fur trade would soon be published to great acclaim. At the crucial meeting of our search committee to consider Sylvia's candidacy for a job, Ned, a free spirit, sauntered in dressed in his working professor's garb—jeans and a denim shirt opened to the middle of his chest. "Hiya, Motherfuckers," he announced, and then launched into his objections to Sylvia, mostly to the effect that her approach to history was antiquarian. We eventually hired Sylvia, and she served the department long and well despite being shabbily treated by the remnants of patriarchy.[5]

The other thing I had not really realized, though I should have done so, was that by the time I met Sylvia, she was not only a veteran teacher whose history and women's studies courses attracted a steady stream of students, but a veteran administrator and committee member. I might have presented myself as the serious socialist feminist with working-class credentials, but Sylvia knew a thing or two about strategy and how to effectively challenge and educate a university committee on gender and equity issues. For almost half of her nearly twenty-five-year career at Toronto, Sylvia held some sort of administrative position. From 1977 to 2000, she was cross-appointed to history and women's studies—and, as we know, cross-listed appointments can be especially burdensome to the person trying to meet the demands and expectations of both departments. Although history was her home base, she was teaching courses, supervising students and serving on committees in both constituencies. Between 1981 and 1984, she directed the women's studies program, a chronically under-funded program staffed with cross-appointments and contract faculty. For most of the

1990s, she served as one of the senior administrators in the history department, completing a five-year term as graduate co-ordinator and a four-year term as associate chair (in charge of the undergraduate program). In addition, she served on innumerable committees—a point to which I return below.

She also served her profession outside the university. An interest in documentary publishing led to her serving as general editor of the Champlain Society for five years in the mid-1980s. This was a time-consuming task involving the supervision and editing of five major volumes of documents in Canadian history. She continued to be active in the society as a council member and vice-president, and served professional societies in history and women's studies. In the mid-1980s, she held a three-year term as an elected council member of the Canadian Historical Association. She helped to found the Canadian Women's Studies Association in 1982 and was a board member of the Canadian Research Institute for the Advancement of Women (CRIAW) for several years. In the 1990s, she sat on the international editorial board of the *Journal of Women's History* and on the executive of the International Federation for Research in Women's History. In Canada, she served on doctoral scholarship committees for the Ontario Graduate Fellowship Program, the Queen Elizabeth Scholarship Program, and the Imperial Order Daughters of the Empire Scholarship, and was on the advisory council for the Centre of Rupert's Land Studies at the University of Winnipeg.

But I want to return to all of those committees on which Sylvia served at the University of Toronto because I have come to understand their significance for effecting important—if not revolutionary—change within the university. Always time-consuming and often under-appreciated, committee service can be politically and intellectually important work if what you want to do is challenge the university and your colleagues to recognize women's talents and credentials and their legitimate—indeed critical—contributions to scholarship and the academy. As far as I can tell, over the course of her career at Toronto, Sylvia sat on close to 100 committees at the departmental (history and women's studies), college (especially New College, which became the administrative home of women's studies), and university-wide level, in some cases serving several terms. She served on dozens of merit and promotion committees, departmental policy committees, undergraduate and graduate program committees, hiring and tenure committees, search committees for chairs and deans, gender equity committees, and committees running endowed guest lecture series and special events.

Of course, a list of committees cannot capture the amount of time and energy that goes into this kind of work. Perhaps it is particularly appropriate that

I acknowledge this fact since I was once a brash young feminist too caught up in her publishing commitments to understand the importance of committee work. I found every reason not to serve on a committee—when I did serve on a committee I treated it as a monumental inconvenience. This was hypocritical. It is one thing to demand changes in the university, and quite another to work persistently at the committee level, changing people's minds and opening up opportunities for bright and educated women who deserve it. While I ranted about political change but stuck to my teaching and publishing, Sylvia was doing a great deal of this critical front-line work, with some significant results.

I want to share a few examples of how I learned about the importance of committees for effecting specific but important change through observing Sylvia at this work. The first example concerns the graduate history program. Not long after I had been appointed to the graduate history faculty in the early 1990s, a group of female faculty members with specialties in women's and gender history (including myself) became interested in creating a new graduate field area in comparative gender history. A comparative field in women's history already existed thanks in large part to Sylvia's work several years before. This was also the time when feminists of various types and working in different national contexts had become involved in the controversy surrounding gender history and the debate, whether it represented the logical conclusion of women's history (as Gisela Bock put it) or its demise—or at least its less politically edgy sibling. Our group of feminist historians felt that the growing field of gender history and its attendant debates ought to become a recognizable field within the graduate program, especially as more and more of our graduate students, male and female, wished to pursue gender questions in their research. In our department, creating a new graduate comprehensive area required presenting a proposal to the department, which then voted on it. All we needed was a simple majority. Immediately, however, we assumed we would encounter hostility to the proposal. Thus, our preparatory meetings, set up to decide on a common international literature that would be central to the field, were characterized by much tension and anxiety. Having assumed a hostile department, we became preoccupied with the need to strategize. Should we start lobbying the male colleagues one by one, beginning with the ones we knew were friendly to us and/or women's history? Should we do the work of putting together a massive bibliography in women and gender history to wave before our opponents when they declared that the field lacked a legitimate body of scholarship? We even considered a contingency plan for after the department had rejected our proposal.

Although a member of our group, Sylvia was too busy with administrative duties and committee work to attend our meetings, though she had given us her support. Feeling increasingly frustrated by all the time spent at these preparatory meetings, I decided to approach Sylvia for advice. I had never done this before. I had hesitated doing so earlier because my understanding was that although generally supportive of our plans, Sylvia herself had not yet reached a decision on the value of gender history. But she was polite and firm in her advice, telling me that all this hand-wringing was entirely misplaced because we did not understand the department. Sylvia, with her years of experience in the department, said this was not the way the history faculty worked; rather, whatever individuals might think of gender history, women's history, or any other comparative or thematic history, there was a basic shared understanding that colleagues had the right to pursue their different interests provided they offered a reasonable rationale and program. She told me to tell the others to stop wasting valuable energy obsessing over the issue and simply complete the terms of the proposal—which involved producing a statement of our objectives and presenting a core list of books and articles. She offered to present the proposal and told us not to assume there would be a major backlash. She was confident the department would approve it regardless of whether certain individual faculty members disapproved of the field. She also noted a certain irony: we were largely creating more work for ourselves by introducing a new field that would need to be taught and supervised, and even the odd cynic would respect our right to increase our workload. The proposal was passed, without any negative comment, within minutes.

In retrospect, I wonder whether we had not first approached Sylvia because, despite her expressed support, we weren't sure that a colleague so closely associated with women's history would support our gender history proposal. In fact, Sylvia's position on the women-versus-gender history question (to use a shorthand) had changed from an initial suspicion of gender history (and specifically, the history of masculinity) to a support for feminist-informed gender history. As she explained to me, she had reflected on how a gender history approach might challenge her research on women in fur trade society and had decided it would complicate matters in interesting ways. At the time, she was working on her Five Founding Families project, which involved tracing the Native and Métis wives of Victoria's colonial elite and their daughters. As she was completing the article on the two generations of women that would later appear in *BC Studies*,[6] she began to reflect on how a gender perspective that, for instance, would require her to pay closer attention to the differing fortunes of the sons and daughters of these elite families would raise new and challenging questions sure to complicate the story. For example, it raised a question that still needs answering: why did the daughters of these mixed-race families go on to lead far more comfortable or successful (albeit conventional) lives than their brothers? She chose not to enter the debate in any public way despite the fact that Canadian feminist scholars of different persuasions invoked *"Many Tender Ties"*, and despite the fact that she was somewhat troubled by the way in which scholars attributed motives to her that she did not hold at the time she was researching the thesis and writing the book. Equally worrying was a tendency to treat the presence of a few early texts on Native women's history as tantamount to a historiography. When we submitted our formal proposal for a comparative gender field in our department, Sylvia was our spokesperson. As someone with plenty of committee and administrative experience in the department, she mentioned our group's wishes, briefly noted how we as a department tended to handle such matters, and presented our case. The proposal was passed without comment— we were all relieved. But I also learned the value of that old but valuable adage: save your energy for the real battles.

Sylvia's work on committees also opened my eyes to how this front-line work can make a difference, if a modest one, for a larger feminist presence in the university, while at the same time dramatically affecting individual women's professional lives. In my view, one of Sylvia's triumphs for feminist scholarship and equity hiring in the university—though she never boasted about it—concerns the impact she made as a member of the search committee for the School of Theology. By the time she served on this committee, we had become friendly colleagues and occasionally had dinner together at the end of a work day, usually at one of the restaurants in the vicinity of the St. George campus. As women without children, we were free to make on-the-spot decisions to go for dinner. Without betraying any confidences, she noted during these meals that she was trying to sort out how best to challenge the committee to take the application of women candidates who studied female spirituality and female healing as seriously as that of the male candidates studying more traditional religious subjects. In telling me this, she was entirely discreet; at no time did she name any names, nor did she disparage any committee member. She understood the situation in the same way she understood how best to get students to appreciate women's roles and lives in the past. She would have to make a case to the committee and it could not simply amount to lecturing them on the need to hire women. She had to demonstrate the value of her argument. As I saw it, she was working from the perspective that her colleagues were bright and reasonable people who could be persuaded by sound argument; she wanted to be both respectful and compelling. In the end, the committee was persuaded enough to include a young feminist who studied birthing rituals among a particular ethno-religious group on the short list. She performed extremely well, impressed them all, and got the nod. Sylvia was delighted with both the outcome and the process. To this day, I do not know if the woman who was hired is even aware of the intellectual and political feminist work Sylvia carried out on that committee. I'm not sure that she needs to be, and Sylvia would probably be embarrassed by the prospect of anyone thinking they were somehow beholden to her. But I hope she does know.

A few years later, I saw Sylvia carry out a similar campaign in my own department; once again, it was clear that she had worked diligently to convince our mostly male department to hire a female candidate not for any personal or ideological gain, but because she believed this candidate brought new strengths to the department. It was one of those difficult hiring situations which had come down to two candidates—one a woman, the other a man. In this case, Sylvia was a member of the hiring committee who in the end decided to produce a minority report that disagreed with the decision of the majority, who supported the male candidate. To be fair, the majority (which included several progressive men who had consistently supported gender equity initiatives in the department) concluded that they would be pleased to accept either excellent candidate but considered the male candidate to have superior credentials. It was impressive to watch Sylvia in action. True to form, she had produced a carefully written report in which she laid out all of her reasons for recommending the female candidate. Throughout, she took pains to not insult anyone, and her report included no disparaging comments about the male candidate. Instead, she focused on the talents and credentials of the female candidate and on the new possibilities which this candidate's field—material history—would open up for the department at the graduate and undergraduate level. Sylvia's report prompted a fascinating discussion—perhaps the most interesting departmental meeting I have ever witnessed in my twenty years at the University of Toronto—and, in the end, the majority of the department agreed with her. It was a modest triumph in the sense that it was only one candidate and one job, but it did open us up to a field never before taught in the department. Again, I stress here less the actual outcome than the process—that is, Sylvia's premise that we can challenge reasonable people to think outside traditional categories.

When former colleagues and students produce festschrifts, much is said about them as a scholar or PhD supervisor and mentor. I wanted to highlight the less glamorous but equally important legacy—the committee work—because sometimes, real change happens behind the scenes, one candidate or one program at a time. It might not be revolutionary, but it is feminist and equity sensitive. As I become a senior member of my history and humanities departments on the St. George and Scarborough campuses respectively, I still rant about political change but also do a lot more front-line committee work. I have come to understand its importance; Sylvia Van Kirk helped me to appreciate the value of this work.

Notes

1   Constance Mungall, *Globe and Mail*, March 1976, clipping, Promotion File, Sylvia Van Kirk, Department of History, University of Toronto. I thank Sylvia for sharing this item with me.

2   Sylvia Van Kirk, *"Many Tender Ties": Women in Fur Trade Society in Western Canada, 1670–1870* (Winnipeg: Watson and Dwyer, 1980).

3   Joan Kelly, "Did Women Have a Renaissance?" in *Becoming Visible: Women in European History*, eds. Renate Bridenthal and Claudia Koonz (London: Houghton Mifflin, 1977).

4   Alice Kessler-Harris, "Where are the Organized Women Workers?" *Feminist Studies* 3, 1 (Autumn 1975): 92–110.

5   Michael Bliss, *Writing History: A Professor's Life* (Toronto: Dundurn Press, 2011), 172.

6   Sylvia Van Kirk, "Tracing the Fortunes of Five Founding Families of Victoria," *BC Studies* 115/116 (Autumn/Winter 1997): 148–79.

Daring to Write a History of Western Canadian Women's Experiences: Assessing Sylvia Van Kirk's Feminist Scholarship[1]

VALERIE J. KORINEK

IT IS ONE OF THE SUPREME IRONIES OF ACADEMIC LIFE that the careers we trained for and imagined in our graduate school years, once attained, race by in a blur of undergraduate and graduate teaching, research and writing, and administrative tasks. One seldom has the opportunity to reflect upon them until one hits the ubiquitous "mid-career" stage, when life events and the retirement of supervisors, colleagues, and former professors occasion such thoughts. Such was the case with the early retirement of Sylvia Van Kirk, who moved "to the coast" (Victoria, BC) after a distinguished career at the University of Toronto. It occasioned reflections (and naturally, some good-natured envy) amongst a cohort of current and former students, colleagues, and researchers. As one of Sylvia's former graduate students (MA, University of Toronto, 1990), I am honored to have an opportunity to contribute some reflections and commentary that would highlight her significant accomplishments in the field of Canadian women's history, feminist scholarship and mentoring, and histories of gender and sexuality in the prairie region. My paper is one of a trio of papers, including those by Jennifer Brown and Franca Iacovetta, which offer personal and scholarly reflections based upon our different relationships with Sylvia—research collaborator, colleague, and student. These essays add up to an intriguing three-dimensional perspective of Van Kirk's scholarly career.

My primary point of reference is the late eighties through mid-nineties, when I completed an MA and a PhD at Toronto. While the pioneering days of women's history research in the sixties and seventies were long past—female historians had by that time made their successful forays into the profession—the legacies of that earlier time and the post-traumatic stress of those battles lingered. A number of new hires, many of them female and working in gender or women's history, were appointed in that era, and thus there was reason for optimism. However, it was instructive to have the opportunity to take classes from scholars like Sylvia, whose career had been forged in the earlier era when asking daring research questions about women's history in western Canada was a risky enterprise. Her personal experiences with such risks and rewards, and the fact that she had prevailed during those tumultuous political years, affected the nature of her classes. Others taught courses, seldom offering additional commentary about the role of the historian in the classroom, the institution and/or within Canadian society—Sylvia's continued engagements and experiences with such matters left her with an astute assessment of the role of the university, its faculty, and of the particular burdens and expectations faced by 'non-traditional' faculty. Not one to belabour the hardships of the past, she preferred to stress strategies for success. Still, it was clear that she regarded the university as an institution where one had to be continually vigilant about systemic discrimination and the myriad ways one could find oneself marginalized.

Naturally, one is always hopeful that such topics and discussions will one day become anachronistic, and that female scholars might just concentrate on their scholarship and teaching. But the misguided and misogynistic notions of women's academic abilities maintain traction, and often in very influential corridors of power. The latest, most jarring example was the announcement of the Canada Excellence Research Chairs (CERC) by the Government of Canada. Intended to be a flagship for the federal government's Science and Technology Strategies, the announcement that these prestigious, international appointments would all be bestowed upon senior male scientists was criticized in the press. Even the minister responsible, Industry Minister Tony Clement, recognized the poor optics of appointing an all-male team, and worse still, from an all-male shortlist of thirty-six candidates. Clement called for an ad hoc committee to investigate how this inequitable situation occurred. The final report, entitled *Ad Hoc Panel on CERC Gender Issues* (written by Elizabeth Dowdeswell, President of the Council of Canadian Academics, Dr. Suzanne Fortier, President of the Natural Sciences and Engineering Research Council and Dr. Indira Samarasekera, President of the University of Alberta), succinctly analyzed the process and outcomes for gender bias. In their findings, the authors noted that the narrowly defined science and technology fields, the short timelines for both phases of the application process, the informal research networks from which the shortlist of candidates was assembled, and the demographic under-representation of women in senior scientific positions all combined to produce this inequitable outcome.[2] In the future, they recommended a number of different measures to increase women's participation in this program. Equally, they requested a "more thorough assessment by a third-party body, such as the Council of Canadian Academies, of the data and issues around the advancement of women in Canadian university research."[3] Importantly, the report ends by reminding Canadians why this issue of gender equity in such exclusive research programs matters, as the report's authors state: "Given the demographic challenges of our projected aging workforce, the need to ensure the full contribution of everyone is not only an equity imperative, but also a pragmatic reality."[4]

This Canadian situation follows upon an earlier, equally explosive, American controversy. In 2005, the controversial comments by Dr. Lawrence H. Summers, then president of Harvard University (and formerly the director of the National Economic Council), vividly illustrated that women in the academy (particularly in science) are still a matter of contention, debate, and gendered notions about the qualifications for scholarship.[5] Summers' speech (ironically, delivered in a workshop intended to address the issue of the under-representation of women in the science and engineering faculty), advanced his "provocative" opinions that female faculty chose not to work the requisite eighty-hour work weeks, particularly if they were married and had children. Additionally, he opined that far fewer teenage girls had the top math and science scores of their male peers, and that those two factors were far more likely to be the cause of women's under-representation than the oft-cited discrimination. In the ensuing uproar, what was most fascinating was not the length of time that elapsed before the requisite apology (in this case multiple *mea culpa*s were offered the week after press coverage of the workshop) nor the anticipated announcement that Summers would not seek another term as Harvard's president, but the significant support (much of it off the record) that was recorded for Summers' statements. While Harvard was ultimately able to smooth over this public relations storm by appointing a female president, Dr. Drew Faust, one cannot help but appreciate the irony that her scholarly expertise is in the history of American women.

Summers' critique was a catalyst for scholars, including many women's history scholars who published articles and roundtable discussions about the fate of women in the historical profession and academy at large.[6] Space prevents an expanded discussion of such matters, but it is important to note that in evaluating Sylvia's career contributions, it made for an oddly circular frame of reference to once again be engaged with professional debates about the fate of women academics, and in particular of the fate of women's history and women faculty in the historical profession. While I wish to highlight Sylvia's scholarly accomplishments, I want to shift the discussion somewhat to also reflect upon her contributions as a feminist teacher, mentor, and administrator, which were equally significant.

Jennifer Brown's excellent essay in this volume offers a detailed overview of Sylvia's graduate student experience at the University of London. What it doesn't mention, except briefly, is Sylvia's undergraduate experience at the University of Alberta, where she first began to ask those audacious questions about women's experiences in the west. Sylvia was originally from Edmonton, and her interest in Canadian history was always primarily oriented to her home region. Memorably, in her Native-Newcomer history classes, she spoke about how her interest in First Nations people had begun in elementary school. Perhaps not surprisingly, early First Nations culture, history, and society had seemed more fascinating (perhaps mysterious) than the predominant Euro-Canadian narrative of immigration and settlement that followed. Given the paucity of western-Canadian work that addressed the historical experiences of women and Sylvia's curiosity about the Aboriginal people's experiences, it was not surprising that an engaged, inquisitive, western-Canadian woman like Sylvia would begin to ask those questions. Returning to Canada after her time in London, Sylvia accepted a Killam Fellowship at Dalhousie University in Halifax. Once her degree was defended she was hired at Dalhousie as an assistant professor, a position she held for one year before accepting a term position in the Department of History at the University of Toronto in 1976. She was hired into a tenure-track position in 1977–78.

As a member of the history department on the St. George Campus, she was affiliated with New College and one of a small group of female faculty members cross-appointed in the Women's Studies Program. Toronto's Women's Studies Program was the first in the country, initiated in 1971–72 with a co-taught class in women's history offered by Jill Kerr Conway and Natalie Zemon Davis.[7]

Very shortly thereafter, New College and its interdisciplinary faculty became the home college for the program. A minor in Women's Studies was approved in 1974–75. By 1980, the Women's Studies program was solidly established, offering undergraduate minor, major, and specialist programs of study, with a core group of courses and a wider selection of cross-listed classes. Sylvia was an active participant in the Women's Studies faculty and in their programs, and thus played a formative role in instructing undergrads in this popular and influential program. She also paid the price of a cross-appointed faculty member—her administrative work was doubled. Furthermore, though it was successful, there were always concerns about Toronto's commitment to the program, and that continual uncertainty was a worrisome distraction from teaching and research.

Within the Department of History, Sylvia taught courses in western Canadian history, women's history, and Native-Newcomer classes at the undergraduate level, as well as Native-Newcomer relations and comparative women's history classes at the graduate level. Despite completing all my degrees at Toronto, I did not encounter Sylvia until I was a graduate student—my undergrad years were spent at Erindale College (now the University of Toronto at Mississauga), where my first introduction to Canadian and European women's history came via wonderfully privileged, small seminar classes with Professors Laurel McDowell and Claire LaVigna. While Erindale students could take classes downtown, it meant taking the dreaded campus shuttle bus, and so I was quite content to enjoy the rather bucolic natural setting that then existed out there in the suburbs (albeit in concrete bunkers that were completely at odds with the Credit Valley "pastoral"). The bustle of main campus was reserved for graduate work, and it is there in the first year of my MA degree that I met Sylvia, who became my master's supervisor, course instructor, and later supervised one of my doctoral fields and served as a member of my PhD thesis committee. In the early nineties, her position in the graduate history program was significant, as she offered an extremely popular graduate class in comparative women's history with a companion doctoral reading field in Canadian, British, and American women's history. This she did in addition to offering a graduate course and field in Native-Newcomer history. While most Canadian doctoral programs offered women's history classes and doctoral reading fields at that time, Toronto's more conservative academic climate gave these classes a frisson of radicalism. It was clear that this minor field was different from other thematic fields that students might elect to prepare, and one often heard dismissive comments from senior faculty, and less frequently from fellow students, about working on such a suspect field of historical inquiry.

While preparing this essay, I had occasion to look through my copy of Van Kirk's women's history field list. As I perused the reading list, what struck me most was how that document is now a historical artifact from a time when women's history still had to make a case for the legitimacy of doctoral field specialization. Indeed, in rather Swiftian language it is entitled "Proposal for a Minor Field in Women's History." One has only to look at this immodest list to be struck by the fact that it contains over a hundred books and articles, double the recommended minor field maximum of fifty works. It was a major field in all but name. There was a very definite sense that we were proving ourselves and making a case for this field. Academic studies of women's advancement into male-defined professions enumerate a variety of strategies that women employ to gain entry. Not surprisingly, Sylvia utilized one of the tried and true means by which women gained access to many unconventional careers: she worked her students twice as hard as required to make her point to us about what it took to succeed in the profession, and to her colleagues about the inherent rigour and intensity of what some might derisively have labelled a "boutique" field. Naturally some weeks my colleagues and I cursed our good fortune to be preparing two major fields, but her demanding courses and reading list served me well when I had the opportunity to offer women's history classes at the University of Saskatchewan. Given her wide-ranging interests in Canadian women's history, she supervised a number of people through MA research papers, including my own work analyzing religious gendered discourses about the contentious notion of women's ordination in the United Church of Canada. According to University of Toronto records, she also successfully supervised seven doctoral candidates to completion—many of whom are employed in the profession today.[8]

Thus, her role as a supervisor and mentor for female graduate students has made a significant contribution to the historical profession. Supervising graduate students is, as we all know, a time-consuming commitment for humanists that seldom results in the research productivity gains conferred upon our colleagues in the sciences. Still, it is an important component of our careers, because despite the ever-increasing numbers of female undergraduates taking history degrees, statistics indicate that there is an attrition rate of female students through the two levels of graduate programs. At the faculty level, female historians' progress through the professional ranks continues to give us cause to wonder not, *pace* Summers, if women have the innate capabilities or drive to be professional historians, but how inclusive and attractive history appears to students and younger faculty alike? According to the 2007 version of the *Canadian*

Association of University Teachers (CAUT) Almanac, women account for 51.5 percent of undergraduates yet women represent only 48.6 percent of MA candidates and 44.9 percent of PhD students.[9] While there is significant variance in gender ratios across the professorial levels, male historians outnumber their female counterparts at all levels (female assistant professors are 43.9 percent; female associates are 37.5 percent, and female full professors are 20 percent of full-time tenured or tenure-track faculty).[10] The CAUT average across all ranks, for tenured or tenure-track history faculty, indicates that 33 percent of the history professors in Canadian universities are women.[11] At the recent Canadian Historical Association (CHA) Annual Meeting, held at Concordia University (2010), council member Dr. Tina Chen indicated that the CHA plans to undertake an equity audit to compile a demographic profile of Canadian history faculty.[12] Regardless of how the professoriate is enumerated, the numbers reflect the ongoing requirement to be conscious of and to speak out about the challenges women continue to face in the academy.

Obviously, one of the crucial means to work towards systemic change is to have prominent female professors, supervisors, and mentors willing to encourage their bright female students to consider professional history careers. At the opposite end of the spectrum, we must maintain our efforts and advocacy on hiring committees and, most importantly, mentor junior faculty so they do make upward progress through the ranks. When I think back to my experiences in Van Kirk's over-subscribed classes in women's history and Native-Newcomer histories, there was an incalculable value in participating in classes where female voices dominated, where competition and collaboration were in evidence, and where we learned much more than the subject matter in question. We were mentored in how to succeed in the profession, the pitfalls of which to beware (not that we always heeded these warnings), and the more obvious steps to take in forging academic careers. In particular, Sylvia was excellent at demystifying the processes of graduate work and career planning, which was particularly useful to those of us who were new to the universities and from families where academic careers were not fodder for dinner-table conversations. And so, she made many of the processes far more transparent, relieving at least some of the worries about how to navigate the system. Many of us were mentored through the process of applying for conferences; indeed, some people attended their first academic conference with Sylvia (in my case, I gave my first academic paper at her behest). As graduate director, she organized a panel of graduate students to talk about their research, and their so-called "new approaches" to women's history research at Toronto. Despite my intense trepidation at the thought of addressing an audience of advanced students and a veritable who's who of gender and women's history scholars from across southern Ontario, Sylvia was very matter-of-fact about my participation; she offered the usual encouragements one does to anxious students, then politely waited until I realized that her request did not actually involve any choice on my part! Others were routinely encouraged to give papers in both the history department and Women's History Discussion group seminar series, to publish articles early and often, to attend national conferences, to join the CHA, and later (when all of the graduate student hurdles had been cleared), we got some useful instructions and practical tips about how to handle job interviews (wear comfortable shoes).

Beyond giving advice, Sylvia took a genuine interest in her students and graciously gave of her time. It was not uncommon for her to join us for post-class drinks after our evening seminar classes, and term's end, when the seminar classes concluded, were occasions for memorable potluck dinners held at her house. Those students who were fortunate to be involved in these scholarly communities forged formative friendships that would serve as the basis of future professional networks. Above all, Sylvia was very persuasive in her belief that we could and should succeed, and her confidence in us was vital. As part of her work to "change the system from within," Sylvia accepted an administrative stint as departmental grad director which enabled her to advocate for external funding for many of us, and gave women's history scholarship a profile that was much needed at Toronto. The encouragement of Sylvia Van Kirk and Paul Rutherford, my doctoral supervisor, was formative, and I question how well I would have navigated the system without their strategic and sage advice. Now, as a supervisor myself, I have thought often about how those courses, fields, and sustained mentoring affected my career, and I realize that I was fortunate to be taught by scholars who were very generous with their time. The books and articles on the comprehensive examinations lists change over time, but the fundamental techniques of teaching and mentoring don't change. Thus the legacy of my experiences at Toronto is now offered, with some translation, to my students at Saskatchewan.

Moving from feminist mentoring and pedagogy, it is important to highlight that Sylvia was also committed to engaging with the public and disseminating her scholarship to the wider community of Canadians. In recent years, because the Social Sciences and Humanities Research Council has prioritized this facet of our research agendas, there has been a renewed emphasis on the importance of such work. But this is something that feminist historians have always understood as both a motivation and a goal of scholarship—it was not merely an individual research pursuit, but instead a precursor to political, social, and economic changes. In the late seventies, Van Kirk was part of an impressive collection of Canadian historians who participated in a venture aimed at elementary and high school students called Canada's Visual History Series. A joint production of the National Film Board and what was then known as the National Museum of Man, the series featured a collection of slides and accompanying textual information that teachers could utilize for their lesson plans. Van Kirk's contribution, entitled "Life in the Western Canadian Fur Trade," allowed students access to her findings and, one hopes, encouraged other nascent historians to think about careers in history.

For example, Van Kirk's work inspired Christine Welsh, a former student, to write and produce a documentary film entitled *Women in the Shadows*.[13] This National Film Board of Canada production, which originated as a term paper in Sylvia's class, depicts Welsh's moving, autobiographical search for her hidden Métis roots. Subsequently, Welsh produced a succession of critically acclaimed documentary films, and currently holds a faculty position in the Department of Women's Studies at the University of Victoria. Having screened excerpts from Welsh's original film in my classes, I am always impressed by Van Kirk's role both as a historical consultant and as a willing participant in this venture, as well as the way the film affects my media-savvy students in a way that written publications do not. Such media and public history work is time-consuming and often not valued too highly in the stakes for peer-reviewed publications, yet it is precisely contributions like those that further engage and politicize people about the importance of historical research, and of women's histories in particular. In retirement, Sylvia has been able to devote more time to her passion for public and local church histories in Victoria.

This brings me full circle to Van Kirk's research accomplishments and their impact on the teaching and writing of women's history in the west, and my own work in particular. Because of the longevity of Van Kirk's monograph and articles, and the way in which her work has been anthologized in readers in a triumvirate of fields—women's history, Native-Newcomer history, and Canadian history—our familiarity with her work has made us lose sight of how daring her original methodology was. Elizabeth Jameson and Adele Perry's essays in this volume eloquently remind us of Van Kirk's contributions and her long scholarly reach. In classes and conversations, Sylvia always modestly offered her perception that she just thought someone ought to ask different questions of those well-scrutinized fur trade records. She was interested in women's experiences and so she sought answers to the questions: Where were the women? What roles did they play? What might the Hudson's Bay Company (HBC) records reveal about women and men's social relations? Van Kirk's decision to audaciously ask those simple, logical questions about Aboriginal women's involvement in the fur trade proved to be a watershed moment in gendered histories of the west. In focusing on the Aboriginal women in the region—their marital, sexual, and economic linkages with fur trading men—Van Kirk's work presciently highlighted a number of issues with which historians still grapple today: the construction of racial, gender, and sexual norms in the west, the diversity of women's history, and the way in which white female settlers (those individuals so often romanticized by the settlement histories) were, themselves, agents of colonialism.

For historians interested in histories of sexuality and marriage, Van Kirk's work is significant because of her recognition that marriage and heterosexual couplings in the west were central, not peripheral, to that world. Rather boldly, she researched and wrote about matters marital long before it was fashionable.[14] The detailed analysis offers us much valuable information about the agency of women and men and how heterosexuality operated in the northwest. Other fur trade historians had, at best, dismissed sexuality as mere biological urges, issues of little consequence to the real story—the economic quest for furs and the resultant issues of commerce, empire, colonization, and nation building. Naturally, post-Van Kirk, we now know very differently. In writing the history of heterosexual relations in the northwest, Van Kirk's work illustrates how contested and complicated such histories were, and how intrinsic they were to the social and economic world created in the region. Subsequently, she has turned her attention to analysis of mixed-race families and of the ways in which marriage, child rearing, politics, and constructions of Euro-Canadian norms of "respectability" have played out at a micro level in mixed-race families in the west.

In seeking to answer similarly simple but no less disruptive questions in my current research, I have drawn upon her insights and early work on histories of sexuality in the West. How did people fashion a queer existence in western Canadian prairie cities? How did those queer subcultures, and later openly gay and lesbian communities, change throughout the post–World War II era? This project, what I have previously referred to as employing a "queer eye view of the prairies," attempts to revise our understanding of prairie history and society.[15] And, naturally, once one starts to ask those questions, to look at the conventional and unconventional archival and oral histories of the region from a different perspective, one starts to find some interesting and destabilizing answers.

Appropriately, to use the city of Winnipeg as but one example, one may reconstruct a small, but well documented, queer male subculture in the city from the 1930s to the 1970s.[16] Uncovering oral interviews and published recollections of George M. Smith, Bert Sigurdson, Jerry Walsh, and other men and women provides us with a very different historical portrait of Winnipeg during the Depression, World War II, and post-war years.[17] While space doesn't permit a lengthy discussion of these materials, two recollections, one from the thirties and the other from the immediate post-war era, illustrate the vibrant subcultural world that existed in Winnipeg and the ways that queer men utilized the city's urban core, commercial landmarks, and transportation hubs to create a queer geography of Winnipeg's oft-historicized streets. Asked to recall Depression-era queer activities in Winnipeg, George Smith noted to interviewer David Theodore that "one time these friends of ours, and this other queen, Bobby Turner, well we used to go every week to this place in St. Boniface to play cards—a straight place. We went by streetcar in our drag and we walked in there and they just about fell over. But they enjoyed it. I don't know how wise they were to us, but they thought it was terrific, and many of the men asked me to dance. We did some silly things."[18] Smith offered largely positive memories of his queer experiences in Winnipeg, and helpfully contrasted them with his observations of New York, Toronto, and London, all cities he visited while in the Canadian army. Other oral informants, however, provided more nuance to the urban queer culture. In particular, Bert Sigurdson noted that while most Winnipeggers where largely unaware of this male subculture located within walking distance of the downtown train station (including hotel beer parlours, Chinese cafés, the Red River trails, and the docklands area), these spaces were not without risk. Verbal and violent assaults were not unknown in Winnipeg. "Dirt was what we called the gay bashers," Sigurdson recalled. "They would be looking out to bash you, trying to take your money. We also called dirt anybody who chased us. When we walked home after our night on the beach…they would call out 'tutti-fruitti' and we'd have to take off."[19]

In the immediate aftermath of World War II, Winnipeg's queer male world was in a period of expansion created by a confluence of factors: better employment opportunities, a more expansive economy, improved access to rental housing and better housing opportunities, and less restrictive liquor licensing laws (which extended hours, in addition to establishing cocktail lounges where both women and men were legally allowed to drink). It was also, for those who experienced this era, a "safer time" in contrast to the violence forthcoming in the seventies and eighties when an increase in gay bashing and homophobic violence (including a handful of sensationalistic murder/criminal cases and a police raid on the city's gay bath house) put the gay male community on heightened alert. Jerry Walsh, a participant in and chronicler of this late forties/early fifties world, offered his nostalgic view of the possibilities available in the city of Winnipeg: "unlike today, back then Main St. was a safe place to cruise day or night. The street's crowning jewel was the Royal Alexandra Hotel at the corner of Higgins and Main. It was elegance at its greatest.... East of the hotel was the CP Station... it was a bustling place both day and night as train travel was at its peak."[20]

In the house parties that were increasingly popular, lesbian women began to make their appearance in the recollections of those interviewed; equally, working-class lesbians were participants at some of the commercial venues. As Walsh continued to sketch his detailed geography, he observed "across Higgins was and still is the Mount Royal Hotel, which was where the gay girls hung out, but it also had its share of sleazy drag queens. It was a lively and noisy place with frequent bouts of dykes duking it out.... It was the first place that I ever saw two guys dancing together; no one seemed to mind." Post-war Winnipeg lesbian and queer male opportunities were expanded, but class, gender, and racial divisions were marked. The few working-class lesbians interviewed about this era confirmed that the Mount Royal was a popular site, and that it also often attracted Aboriginal lesbians.[21]

Mapping and historicizing the desires and activities of Winnipeg's queer men and lesbians revises our knowledge of the city's composition and the multiple ways that city residents tailored public spaces, city landmarks, and commercial venues for their own purposes. The men who cruised the area known as the "hill" behind the Winnipeg legislature in the evening (under the beguiling light of the Golden Boy, Winnipeg's most famous icon), and those who found liaisons at bars and cafés or in commercial landmarks like the flagship Hudson's Bay Company department store on Portage Avenue, were part of the fabric of urban life. Such experiences in the downtown core, as well as the popular lesbian and gay house parties, paved the way for the gay and lesbian activism that would emerge on the University of Manitoba campus and in the city in the seventies and eighties.

My work has been influenced by an interdisciplinary collection of scholars in the fields of sexuality studies (history, geography, theory), western Canadian history, and urban history. While much urban history has been written about Winnipeg, including of the red-light districts and boomtown atmosphere of the early city, there has been no mention of queer residents. This is commonplace, according to scholar Mark Turner, and he has been critical of urban histories in general for marginalizing queer encounters to the "footnotes at the bottom of the page, notes and queries in the margins or unarticulated suggestions."[22] Far more commonly, urban histories have omitted any reference to queer citizens entirely. Prairie urban histories, many of which are commemorative in nature, have routinely fallen into this second category, offering us celebratory, sanitized images of these cities. Revising this literature to include the histories of queer people's struggles to discover others, to take lovers, carve out lives and social spaces, and create cultural (and later political) organizations offers important insights into prairie societies and cultures. Same-sex liaisons, the formation of a homosexual subculture, and an explicitly gay and lesbian political and social community in Winnipeg have done as much to transform and remake cities like Winnipeg as have the heterosexual families, farmers, and the faithful—the far more conventional Prairie historical protagonists.

Such research is confirmation of Van Kirk's original, rich insights into the variety and value of studying regional sexual histories. Whether one studies the fur trade era or the modern western experience, sexual relationships and societal perception of those experiences are significant to understanding those societies. Historicizing sexual relations provides us with very valuable insight into the multiplicity of ways in which people adapted, negotiated, and resisted the legislators' and moralists' calls for "respectability." Equally, queering our view of the prairies illuminates some important characteristics about the modern prairies. First, like the rest of Canada, the majority of prairie residents now reside in urban centres despite the continued economic importance of agriculture (now largely the purview of agribusinesses, not farm families). Second, despite statistics that illustrate that prairie provinces' acceptance of sexual minorities lags behind that of other Canadian provinces (Quebec always leads these polls as the most tolerant and progressive province), acceptance rates amongst younger prairie residents are far closer to Canadian averages. Third, focusing on the prairies offers some unique perspectives on queer history and activism, including models of cooperative and cross-gender alliances that were not employed elsewhere. Those were, in some respects, prairie models of organizing that were familiar to the queer community, and offered linkages with other activist communities.[23] Regional sexual histories are important in their own right, but they also form important elements in the social and political histories of a nation; they complicate and challenge our preconceived notions of the modern nation, just as Sylvia's previous work challenged the myths of the fur trade empire, and later, the settler nation.

In conclusion, Sylvia Van Kirk's accomplishments as a feminist scholar, teacher, mentor, and popular historian have paid significant dividends for the historical profession and for the study of women's, sexual and Native-Newcomer histories of the West. As a teacher and supervisor, she inspired students to embark on feminist research topics and to imagine themselves taking their place in a male-defined academic profession. Her willingness to take time from her research and teaching to undertake media and public history work allowed her to enlarge the audience for her feminist, multi-racial version of western history, and provided many people who would not have the opportunity to take her classes with the benefit of her research findings. Finally, in daring to write about Aboriginal and Euro-Canadian women's history in the west, she has brought a much-needed feminist scholarly analysis to a region still overwhelmingly dedicated to masculinist narratives of exploration, resource economies, colonization and settlement. On a more personal level, asking those audacious "emperor has no clothes" questions paved the way for others—in particular her graduate students—to follow with audacious questions of their own.

Notes

1   The genesis for this paper came from a call to participate in a roundtable organized to commemorate Dr. Sylvia Van Kirk's scholarship. My thanks to Franca Iacovetta and Heidi Bohaker for inviting me to participate in the panel, entitled "Many Tender Ties: A Forum in Honour of Sylvia Van Kirk" at the Canadian Historical Association Annual Meeting, 29 May 2007 in Saskatoon. Panel participants included: Patricia McCormack, Valerie J. Korinek, Mary-Ellen Kelm, Tony Hall, and Jennifer Brown.

2   Elizabeth Dowdeswell, President, Council of Canadian Academies, Dr. Suzanne Fortier, President, Natural Sciences and Engineering Research Council, and Dr. Indira Samarasekera, President, University of Alberta, *Report to the Minister of Industry of the Ad Hoc Panel on CERC Gender Issues*, 23 April 2010, 17 pages. http://www.ic.gc.ca/eic/site/icl.nsf/eng/h_05589.html (accessed 7 July 2010).

3   Ibid., 17.

4   Ibid.

5   Lawrence H. Summers, "Remarks at NBER Conference on Diversifying the Science and Engineering Workforce," 14 January 2005. The Office of the President, Harvard University website. http://president.harvard.edu/speeches/summers_2005/nber.php (accessed 30 April 2008).

6   See Linda K. Kerber, "Risking Our Dreams," *Journal of Women's History* 18, 1 (2006): 121–32. Kerber's paper was part of an important roundtable entitled "History Practice: Conditions of Work for Women Historians in the 21st Century." Other participating scholars included Terri Barnes, Janaki Nair, Franca Iacovetta, Dora Barrancos, Leisa D. Meyer, Maria Montoya, Deena Gonzalez, Catherine Jean Kudlick, Erika Lee, Berteke Waaldijk, and Fumiko Fugita.

7   Women's and Gender Studies Institute website, University of Toronto. http://www.wgsi.utoronto.ca/about/history (accessed 29 April 2008).

8   The University of Toronto Graduate History program confirmed that Van Kirk supervised seven doctoral students to completion, including Dr. M.E. Kelm, Dr. R.J Brownlie, and Dr. H. Bohaker, all of whom hold tenured appointments in history.

9   Table 3.11: FTE Bachelor's and Other Undergraduate Degree, Master's, and PhD Enrollment by Major Discipline, Field of Study and Sex, Canada 2004–2005, *Canadian Association of University Teachers Almanac of Post-Secondary Education in Canada, 2007* (2007): 29.

10 Table 2.11: Full Time Canadian University Teachers by Subject, Rank and Sex, 2004–2005, *Canadian Association of University Teachers Almanac of Post-Secondary Education in Canada, 2007* (2007): 13.

11 Ibid.

12 CHA Annual Heads of Canadian History Departments Meeting, May 2010.

13 Christine Welsh, producer and writer, *Women in the Shadows*, National Film Board of Canada, 1991.

14 There is a fairly extensive historiography that explores the "history" of marriage, See Nancy F. Cott, *Public Vows: A History of Marriage and the Nation* (Boston: Harvard University Press, 2000). More recently, Sarah Carter has picked up this thread, and produced a history of marriage in western Canada, accentuating the role accorded race in legal and social constructions. See Sarah Carter, *The Importance of Being Monogamous: Marriage and Nation Building in Western Canada to 1915* (Edmonton: University of Alberta and Athabasca Press, 2008).

15 See Valerie J. Korinek, "A Queer-Eye View of the Prairies: Reorienting Western Canadian Histories" in *The West and Beyond*, eds. A. Finkel, S. Carter and P. Fortna (Edmonton: Athabasca University Press, 2010), 278–96.

16   See Valerie J. Korinek, "'We're the girls of the pansy parade:' Historicizing Winnipeg's Queer Subcultures Prior to 1970," *Histoire Sociale/Social History* (forthcoming).

17   In 1990, community activists in Manitoba undertook an oral history project to collect histories of the experiences of gays and lesbians in Manitoba. Ultimately, the Manitoba Gay and Lesbian Oral History Project produced a collection of 22 oral interviews with Winnipeg and Selkirk residents. This archive, known as *Lesbians and Gays in Manitoba: The Development of a Minority*, contains recollections from the early 1930s through to the 1970s. Copies of these materials are available in the Provincial Archives of Manitoba, Manitoba Gay Lesbian Archives Committee, C1861-1903, 1990. The original interviews are now part of the University of Manitoba Archives and Special Collections, Winnipeg Gay and Lesbian Archives Collection (A.08-67, A.09-28), collection in processing.

18   PAM, Manitoba Gay and Lesbian Archives Committee, C1869-70, Tapes 9 and 10. George M. Smith interviewed by David Theodore, 25 June 1990.

19   Rainbow Resource Centre (RCC), Manitoba Gay/Lesbian Oral History Project Bert Sigurdson interview, 29 June 1990 with David Theodore. Rainbow Resource Centre, Winnipeg, Manitoba originally granted me full access to utilize these interviews in 1992. I thank then manager Donna Huen for her assistance. This archives has moved to the University of Manitoba Archives and Special Collections, and will be known as the Winnipeg Gay and Lesbian Archives Collection. Thanks to archivist Graham Stinnett for providing access to these documents while they are processed.

20   Jerry Walsh, *Backward Glances: A Compilation of his Remembrances of a By-Gone Era in the Gay Community of Winnipeg*, n.d., pp. 4–5. This twenty-seven-page self-published document was sent to me by Mike Giffin. Mr. Giffin believes that Walsh produced it in the 1990s. Jerry Walsh died in 2000 so I never had the opportunity to interview him about his histories of Winnipeg.

21   Out of the twenty-two interviews, only five were conducted with women. There are restrictions on many of these files, which further impedes writing detailed histories of Winnipeg's lesbian experiences prior to the early 1970s. However, despite the fact that a number of the informants did not wish to be named nor have their materials directly cited without their permission, it is permissible to note the popularity of the Mount Royal Hotel.

22   Mark Turner, *Backward Glances: Cruising the Queer Streets of New York and London* (London: Reaktion Books, 2003), 43.

23   See Valerie J. Korinek, "Activism = Public Education: The History of Public Discourses of Homosexuality in Saskatchewan, 1971-93" in *I Could Not Speak My Heart: Education and Social Justice for Gay and Lesbian Youth*, ed. J. McNinch and M. Cronin (Regina: Canadian Plains Research Center, 2004).

Ties Across the Border

Elizabeth Jameson

SYLVIA VAN KIRK HAS INFLUENCED THE WRITING of American history as have few Canadian historians. Her influence is most evident in histories of the U.S. fur trade, women in the U.S. West, and in histories of Native-Newcomer relations. The frameworks of these fields shifted in the 1980s through Van Kirk's influence and that of other path-breaking scholars who placed American Indian women and other women of colour at the centres of history, and whose scholarship established the intertwined significance of race and gender as analytical categories.

Sylvia Van Kirk first made her mark in the United States, as in Canada, in histories of the fur trade. The U.S. fur trade was smaller than the Canadian trade; it covered a shorter time span and occupied a less central place in narratives of U.S. development and westward expansion than has the fur trade in Canadian history. More than most U.S. scholars, American fur trade historians have been familiar with the work of their Canadian colleagues, and, in the 1970s and early 1980s, joined a rare cross-border cohort of fur trade scholars that included Arthur Ray, John Foster, Jennifer S.H. Brown, William Swagerty, Sylvia Van Kirk, and Jacqueline Peterson.[1]

This transnational conversation was probably easier because the fur trade preceded state formation: cross-border historical perspectives are easier to imagine before there was in fact a border, and before national narratives erased cross-border economies, social networks, and ecologies. It is worth considering, then, how Sylvia Van Kirk reached U.S. historians beyond the circles of fur trade history, to become widely read among historians of American Indians, western women, and of the American West in general. Although some U.S. historians know the full body of Van Kirk's work (I am particularly fond of "A Vital Presence: Women in the Cariboo Gold Rush, 1862–1875"), Van Kirk is best known in the American profession, and by thousands of American history students, for *"Many Tender Ties"*.[2] That Van Kirk became better known in the United States than other excellent Canadian scholars, like Ray and Brown, had to do at least partly with the power of her interpretive framework to inform western, women's, and ethnic histories in the 1980s. It owed something as well to the power of a U.S. narrative of western expansion, which, in the 1980s, became a target for new western histories and for emerging scholarship in western women's history. Van Kirk's narrative disrupted a mythic West that had marginalized women and people of colour.

Van Kirk's impact owed much, as well, to the ways that her scholarship entered the U.S. academic mainstream. *"Many Tender Ties"* found a U.S. co-publisher, and Van Kirk herself participated in the nascent network of western women's historians as it formed in the early 1980s. The University of Oklahoma Press published a U.S. edition of *"Many Tender Ties"* in 1980, the same year that Watson and Dwyer published the Canadian edition.[3] A prominent academic press in the field of western history, the University of Oklahoma Press took a leading role in the early 1980s in publishing new work about western women. Editor-in-Chief John Drayton, an Alberta native, was more prepared than many American publishers to understand the path-breaking significance of Van Kirk's work.

"Many Tender Ties" appeared at a fortuitous moment, as historians generated an intellectual agenda for the new western women's history, articulated in 1980 in a formative essay, "The Gentle Tamers Revisited," by Joan Jensen and Darlis Miller. The new field took form at two conferences, the Women's West Conference, held in Sun Valley, Idaho in summer 1983, and Western Women: Their Land, Their Lives, held in Tucson, Arizona in 1984.[4] Van Kirk attended both.

In "The Gentle Tamers Revisited," Jensen and Miller achieved two critical tasks. Their astonishingly abundant footnotes obliterated the tired claim that women could not be included in western history because there were simply no sources, no evidence, and no scholarship. And Jensen and Miller set the agenda for a developing field, insisting that it be inclusive, that it be multicultural, that it not be based in the assumptions of white pioneers or a triumphalist western narrative. Their multicultural agenda de-centred normative eastern models of gender based in the role prescriptions of an urban elite, and the black/white binary of race based in the experience of slavery in the U.S. South. Neither fit the realities of class or the complex racial ethnic hierarchies of the North American West.[5]

Van Kirk offered a framework that could powerfully challenge the metanarratives of both Canada and the United States. Few U.S. women's historians were aware of Canadian historiography, or of the significance for Canada of a book that placed Aboriginal women at the centre of the fur trade, and thus at the centre of Harold Innis's staples thesis.[6] For historians of race, gender, and the U.S. West, the problematic founding narrative was Frederick Jackson Turner's frontier thesis, which located American democracy, opportunity, and national character on a series of westward-moving frontiers defined by male resource economies. Turner's frontiers, the dividing lines between "savagery and civilization," progressed upward through a nineteenth-century hierarchy of civilizations, from hunting to trading to ranching or mining to farming.[7] Turner did not imagine women on these economic frontiers: there was no hide-tanners' or pemmican makers' frontier, no egg and butter frontier, no teachers' or canners' frontier.[8] The Turnerian paradigm erased all women. It doubly erased American Indian women, as "savages" and as women. And because Turner had so formatively influenced the writing of American history, challenges to the Turnerian paradigm were particularly unsettling to uninterrogated premises of who and what had made the nation.

Western women's historians in the United States contested the androcentric and Eurocentric assumptions of the Turnerian narrative that had so influenced American national imagination. They challenged, too, the women's histories that privileged as normative the experiences of white, eastern, middle-class and literate women. Those challenges found a forum at the first Women's West conference in Sun Valley, where many American historians met Sylvia Van Kirk and heard her speak.

The conference opened with Susan Armitage's challenge to a mythic historical terrain that Armitage dubbed "Hisland," an imagined place, where under perpetually cloudless western skies, a cast of heroic characters engages in dramatic conflict, sometimes with nature, sometimes with each other. Occupationally, these heroes are diverse; they are mountain men, cowboys, Indians, soldiers, farmers, miners, and desperadoes, but they share one distinguishing characteristic—they are all men. It seems that all rational demography has ended at the Mississippi River: all the land west of it is occupied only by men. This mythical land is America's most enduring contribution to folklore: the legendary Wild West.

"The problem with Hisland," Armitage continued, "is that many people believe it is history, and some of those people are historians."[9]

If Armitage had been a Canadian historian, she could not have omitted fur traders from her list of mythic western characters. But that omission was corrected during the plenary that followed her keynote.

Susan Armitage, Melissa Hield, and I had served as the Steering Committee for the Women's West conference. Paula Petrik and Patricia Albers did an extraordinary job as program co-chairs, but left the plenaries to the Steering Committee, and at Armitage's suggestion, we invited Sylvia Van Kirk to speak at the opening plenary. Van Kirk delivered a summary of *"Many Tender Ties,"* outlining the three stages of Aboriginal women's pivotal roles in fur trade society: the first stage, when Aboriginal women were valued as intimate and economic partners; the second stage, when their Métis daughters became favoured marriage partners in the trade because they could negotiate both European and Native cultures; and the third stage, when the arrival of white women reinscribed racial boundaries. Some historians were introduced to Van Kirk's scholarship through her article in *The Women's West*, the anthology that published many of the conference papers.[10]

Just as Jensen and Miller had proved that there were sources for western women's histories, Van Kirk demonstrated that it was possible to "read through" the documents of European men to tease out Native women's essential roles in the social organization of the fur trade and in providing its material requirements. She offered a model for how to use unlikely sources to find women in unexpected places. Her work broke new ground as well in its focused attention on the intimate relationships between European men and Native women that were so central to fur trade society. Van Kirk's skill with sources, her attention to domestic labour as the infrastructure for resource industries, and her focus on intimacy all impacted U.S. scholarship on the fur trade and beyond.

Van Kirk herself occupied a position as cultural intermediary for U.S. and Canadian historians, a role that paralleled the position of Aboriginal and Métis women as women "in between" the First Nations and Europeans. The first two conferences (The Women's West and Western Women: Their Lives, Their Land) were especially important for the professional networks they generated. The fact that Van Kirk attended both conferences established her formative influence in western women's histories.[11] She in turn introduced many American historians to other Canadian colleagues and to their scholarship. In my own keynote for The Women's West conference, I ended by quoting Nellie McClung, about whom I in fact knew very little. I had been introduced to her in *A Harvest Yet to Reap*, one of the few Canadian texts I had then read, and liked the challenge of McClung's words from *Clearing in the West* that appeared as the epigraph: "I grew indignant as I read the history and saw how little the people ever counted.... When I wrote I would write of the people who do the work of the world and I would write it from their side of the fence."[12] After I spoke, Sylvia told me that she had appreciated that I included Canadian women in my talk, and especially McClung, for whom, she said, she felt particular fondness. Her warm encouragement in fact shamed me into reading further, and I remain grateful to her for prodding my way to Canadian history.

Van Kirk's work and her collegiality have, from those early beginnings, continued to influence U.S. scholars. She had already, by the late 1970s, influenced new research on marriage in the much smaller U.S. fur trade. But Van Kirk's influence extended further, as historians worked to place race and gender at the centres of historical inquiry, and to locate women of colour and the arenas of domesticity and intimacy at the centres of change.

Van Kirk first entered American scholarly discourse through the work of U.S. fur trade historians who were influenced by her dissertation and early articles. Some U.S. historians first learned of her work in William Swagerty's footnotes to his important article, "Marriage and Settlement Patterns of Rocky Mountain Trappers and Traders," which appeared in April 1980. The smaller U.S. western fur trade developed in the early nineteenth century, conducted largely by Euro-American men who themselves worked as fur trappers and often lived with American Indians. As in Canada, many formed marriages according to Native custom. Swagerty used Leroy Hafen's biographies of American fur traders to compile an overview of fur trappers' biographies and their marriages. In his first footnote, he introduced five studies that "when published" promised to "help balance the disparity between the Rocky Mountain Fur Trade and that of other regions." These included three completed dissertations (by John Foster, Sylvia Van Kirk, and Jennifer Brown), one dissertation in progress (by Jacqueline Peterson), and Carol Judd's study in progress of Hudson's Bay Company employees after 1821.[13]

From Hafen's biographies, Swagerty teased out a demographic portrait of Rocky Mountain fur traders: their ethnic and national backgrounds, the lengths and numbers of their marriages, and the ethnicities of their partners. An estimated 80 percent of the men married during their years in the trade; over half married Indian women, one-quarter married Hispanic women of the northern

Spanish borderlands, and one-quarter European women. Approximately 70 percent of trappers' marriages with Native women lasted until one partner died—fifty-two marriages lasted an average of twenty-six years. As with the Canadian fur trade marriages that produced the Métis, countless Native women literally mothered new peoples throughout the Americas. Swagerty concluded that the men's most enduring legacy was "their mixed blood children, whose history is yet to be written." What that meant for their mothers is harder to discern because, as with Van Kirk's sources, most of Swagerty's evidence concerned the men.[14]

The most powerful treatment of women in the U.S. fur trade came more recently, from Susan Sleeper-Smith, whose research on women in the Great Lakes fur trade pushed many of the conceptual questions and implications that Van Kirk had raised in *"Many Tender Ties." Indian Women and French Men* probed strategies for Indian and Métis persistence in the Great Lakes through three centuries of colonization and well into the nineteenth century.[15] Sleeper-Smith explored Native women's adaptive strategies as they married fur traders, merged Catholicism with Native practices, and mobilized far-flung Catholic kin networks. Like Van Kirk, Sleeper-Smith demonstrated the central importance of women's work and their trade networks, focusing, for instance, on how Potawatomi agriculture supplied the fur trade. In *Indian Women and French Men*, and in her 2005 article "'[A]n Unpleasant Transaction on this Frontier': Challenging Female Autonomy and Authority at Michilmackinac," Sleeper-Smith presented the life stories of individual women who forged their own power bases, and whose control in turn was challenged by new national and androcentric systems of power.[16]

Sleeper-Smith's careful attention to both persistence and to the erosion of Native and Métis women's authority paralleled Van Kirk's scholarship after *"Many Tender Ties."* In "What if Mama Is an Indian?," "Tracing the Fortunes of Five Founding Families of Victoria," and "A Transborder Family in the Pacific North West," Van Kirk focused, like Sleeper-Smith, on particular fur trade families to explore the differential losses of power of fur trade wives, sons, and daughters as colonial power solidified.[17]

Van Kirk documented Native women's agency during crucial periods of transition. Just as importantly, she demonstrated the limits of that agency as racial lines hardened. Nuanced attention to persistence and decline became part of her intellectual legacy in U.S. scholarship. Here I can only suggest the contours of that impact through the work of some exemplary scholars who acknowledged Van Kirk's influence. We begin a brief tiptoe through their footnotes with the work of Albert Hurtado, one of the leading historians of race and intimacy in the American West, who was among the first to apply Van Kirk's insights beyond the fur trade. In *Indian Survival on the California Frontier*, Hurtado probed how Indian women's vulnerability jeopardized their people, and also their active agency in Indian survival strategies. Rapes, prostitution, venereal disease, and the epidemics that ravaged Native populations all jeopardized women and disrupted cultural practices. By the mid-nineteenth century, the remaining minority of California Indian women experienced dramatically lowered fertility, which further compromised Indians' survival.[18] Hurtado acknowledged the importance of Van Kirk's work for his own focus on women. He wrote in 2008 that "Van Kirk's *Many Tender Ties* greatly influenced my own thinking about Native American history. She was one of the first to write about the importance of Indian and white marriages and kinship ties in the trade. She placed women at the centre of her work and showed me how Indian women, even though they were usually anonymous, could be a big part of the story in *Indian Survival*. Her book was a pioneering attempt to link Indian history with the sensibilities of social and women's history. It remains an important work today."[19]

Hurtado extended his explorations of gender and cultural exchange in *Intimate Frontiers*, which explored how power operated in intimate encounters on successive California frontiers: in the Spanish missions, Mexican California, in the journeys of white Americans toward the gold fields, and during the Gold Rush.[20] Efforts to control marriage, sexuality, reproduction, and inheritance illuminated social power and the limits of women's historical agency. Hurtado's intimate frontiers could be brutally unequal. The violent bounds of intimacy delineated a rapists' frontier, established in practice against conquered and subordinate women. Hurtado vividly etched that violent frontier in the chapter "Amelia's Body," about Amelia Kuschinsky, an adolescent servant in Shasta County, California. Probably impregnated by her employer, Amelia died an excruciating death in 1860, the result of a forced abortion, her mute body defining the limits of women's agency in systems of unequal power.[21] Amelia Kuschinsky, like the "turned off" country wives of the fur trade, cautioned historians about the power relationships that limited women's agency, even when they acted creatively to adapt and survive.

The conceptual power of Van Kirk's work thus informed scholarship that extended far beyond the temporal, geographic, and topical boundaries of the fur trade. Beginning with the papers from the first Women's West conference, I have co-edited three anthologies of western women's histories, and was privileged to publish articles by Sylvia Van Kirk in two of them: in *The Women's West* (1987) and the most recent, *One Step Over the Line: Toward a History of Women in the North American Wests* (2008).[22] The breadth of her influence, though, is most evident in the middle volume, *Writing the Range: Race, Class, and Culture in the Women's West* (1997), in which seven articles mapped her significance for American scholarship.[23] They provide a rough index of Van Kirk's influence on the development of multicultural histories, histories of American Indian women, and histories of intercultural relations.[24]

Two historiographic surveys in *Writing the Range*, Marian Perales' survey of histories of women of colour in the American West and Ramona Ford's overview of changing interpretations of American Indian women, recognized Van Kirk's formative influence on scholarship on the fur trade and intermarriage.[25] Van Kirk's influence was most evident in the articles about Native women. James Brooks' "'This Evil Extends Especially to the Feminine Sex'" addressed the complex practices of captivity and kinship among Native Americans and Hispano/as in New Mexico from 1700 to 1846, and particularly women captives' cultural adjustments and survival strategies. Brooks wrote that Van Kirk provided evidence of another cultural borderland "where patterns of cultural accommodation appear beneath colonial structures of conflict, as the exigencies of day-to-day survival promote periods of relatively peaceful coexistence."[26] In "When Strangers Met: Sex and Gender on Three Frontiers," Albert Hurtado located three California frontiers within a cosmopolitan eighteenth- and nineteenth-century West where people "who met as strangers came to live in close association for decades and often entered into sexual relationships—marriage, long-term cohabitation, and briefer connections as well." His first citation was to Van Kirk's work, which had led him to those intimate frontiers.[27] Van Kirk was cited yet again in Coll-Peter Thrush and Robert H. Keller, Jr.'s article, which used the murder trial of Xwelas, a S'klallam woman, as a lens through which to explore the varieties of intercultural intimacy in the Pacific Northwest. Van Kirk, they said, presented "the mixing of trade and personal life, as well as the active economic role of native women in the early Northwest."[28] Lisa Emmerich's article on the early-twentieth-century campaign by the Bureau of Indian Affairs to improve the health of Indian babies again cited Van Kirk for documenting the impact of colonization on Native women. Even in "situations where their work as trade partners did support continued economic power," Emmerich wrote, "the concurrent destruction of tribal social and political networks frequently led to their subordination."[29] These six articles sketched the contours of Van Kirk's significance for histories of Native women and American Indian peoples: they spanned three centuries, a geographic sweep from the southwestern borderlands through the Pacific Northwest, and historical arenas ranging from sexual intimacy, to trading partnerships, to American courtrooms, and the imperfect projects of well-meaning reformers that historian Peggy Pascoe dubbed "relations of rescue."[30]

Van Kirk's conceptual significance was most evident in work, like Hurtado's and Brooks', that probed intercultural intimacy to illuminate power and to clarify Indian women's active agency in adapting to disempowering situations. That paradigm was developed most powerfully by Peggy Pascoe, represented in *Writing the Range* by her article, "Race, Gender and Intercultural Relations: The Case of Interracial Marriage." Interracial marriage, Pascoe asserted, "involves the making and remaking of notions of race, gender, and culture in individual lives as well as at the level of social and political policy. The vast majority of studies have been carried out by social scientists who search for laws of social behavior that might either predict or account for the incidence of interracial marriage. The handful of historians who have taken up the topic use their insight into change over time to expose flaws in nearly every theory the social scientists have proposed."[31] Sylvia Van Kirk was one of this creative handful, according to Pascoe, who had disrupted social science orthodoxy. Pascoe herself probed the history of intermarriage to unsettle received categories of race and gender, and to suggest that U.S. legislation to ban intermarriage had everything to do with controlling wealth and inheritance. Pascoe extended this work in her prize-winning book, *What Comes Naturally: Miscegenation Law and the Making of Race in America*, an extraordinary contribution to histories of race and gender that probes how control of intimacy underlay larger systems of social power.[32]

Just as the first Women's West conference shook old paradigms by adding new actors to the tired terrain of frontier history, the New Western History announced its challenge to the Turnerian paradigm in Santa Fe in 1989 at the conference "Trails: Toward a New Western History." The furor that the Trails conference provoked among some western historians and journalists offered eloquent testimony to the seductive power of the frontier myth. The fervent defence of a mythic past also affirmed the disruptive power of new narratives. The energetic debates in the late 1980s and early 1990s about new western histories help explain why western women's histories became more prominent and unsettling in the United States than in Canada. Much of the New Western History, however, paid greater attention to race and the environment than to gender, and the trailblazing conference offered only one paper on women's history. But that one, by Peggy Pascoe, offered a paradigm designed to shake the Turnerian narrative from its foundations.

Pascoe powerfully shaped western women's history through the framework she suggested that would focus on women of colour to clarify power relations in the American West. In her influential address to the Trails conference, Pascoe urged historians of western women to "replace the current emphasis on frontierswomen—mythic or real—with a new definition of our field" and "to see our task as the study of women at the cultural crossroads."[33] Placing women of colour at the centre of cross-cultural relationships would illuminate the intertwined axes of race, class, and gender that forged inequalities throughout the West. The most promising work in the new western women's history, Pascoe suggested, focused "on women who were intercultural brokers, mediators between two or more very different cultural groups. Because this approach is grounded in all women's behaviors rather than in white women's attitudes, it brings to centre stage a wide variety of women who have acted as cultural intermediaries."[34]

Two particular groups, Pascoe wrote, had been featured in such studies: the Indian women whose marriages to white men birthed Métis communities around the Great Lakes or ensured Indian survival in California, and Hispanic women whose marriages and business contacts shaped the unique society of the American Southwest. "Perhaps the best-known study of this type," she continued, "Sylvia Van Kirk's *'Many Tender Ties'* ...focuses on Indian women in Canada who, along with their white fur trader husbands, created a unique and rather precarious fur trade society, the dynamics of which shifted when white women entered the area sometime later. In this approach, women's lives become microcosms of the contradictions of conquest—embodiments of the relations of rebellion, cooperation, and subordination that underlay the massive changes conquest brought to the region."[35] As Pascoe eloquently testified, *"Many Tender Ties"* became a founding text for much larger analyses of race, colonialism, conquest, and of strategies of adaptation and endurance. The "ripple effect" of its influence illuminated the subsequent work of James Brooks, Albert Hurtado, and Peggy Pascoe. Brooks' masterful *Captives and Cousins: Slavery, Kinship and Community in the Southwest Borderlands* broke new ground by exploring how captivity and slavery wove new kinship networks that linked a southwestern multiracial society long after European and American conquest. It won the Bancroft Prize in 2003, the equivalent of a Nobel Prize or Academy Award in U.S. History, or perhaps of the Harold Adams Innis Prize in Canadian Social Sciences.[36] Hurtado's scholarship placed Native women at the centres of power, and probed the limits of their agency in the interracial societies of California during successive "frontiers" of European and American settlement. Hurtado redefined frontiers from the perspectives of women of colour, as places characterized by an excess of men—an excess that did not promise opportunity but rather limited the options for the outnumbered women.[37] And Pascoe's theoretical influence demonstrated the power of interracial unions to clarify systems of social inequality.

Focusing on interracial marriage, however, shifted the emphasis from the experiences of Native women themselves, most of whom did not intermarry, and from their sons, who were not favoured marriage partners in the new fur trade society. It is therefore regrettable that Van Kirk's subsequent scholarship has not become as widely known in the United States as *"Many Tender Ties."* It has proven difficult to keep women, and especially women of colour, at the historical centres after the subject of the narrative turns to the nation state. The pattern has unfortunately followed another less heralded strand of the Turnerian frontier paradigm: "Complex society," according to Turner, was "precipitated by the wilderness into a kind of primitive organization based on the family." History progressed as "primitive peoples" became "new nations" and moved from "families into states."[38] Western historians have been willing to add women of colour to the frontier narrative as intimate partners on resource frontiers. But to engage their histories independently and apart from their contacts with Europeans, or to follow them past the birth of the nation, has proven more difficult; to do so would disrupt the settler-to-nation trajectory of most history texts.

It remains to be seen whether historians can follow the Native women who centred Van Kirk's narrative back to their sisters who did not intermarry and forward to a present that continues to marginalize them. Van Kirk's later work has bridged national and conceptual boundaries in new transnational histories of gender that illuminate how regional particularities and national policies refracted relationships of race and gender throughout the post-national North American Wests. That promise was evident at a third conference, the Unsettled Pasts conference held in Calgary in 2002, and the scholarship it produced.[39]

The first major conference on the history of women in western Canada, and the first to bring together significant numbers of historians from the United States and Canada, "Unsettled Pasts" featured Sylvia Van Kirk's luncheon address about one trans-border fur trade couple, Charles and Isabella Ross, and the fates of their children as racial boundaries hardened in two new nations. Van Kirk extended her analysis and time frame beyond the fur trade to the era of colonial settlement, after the new international border along the forty-ninth parallel separated two Hudson's Bay Company (HBC) forts, placing Fort Nisqually in Washington State and Fort Victoria in British Columbia.[40]

The Rosses' ten Métis children faced very different options than their parents had in a region in considerable social and political flux, as race became increasingly important in defining who could possess land and inherit it. Van Kirk illuminated those changes through the shifting marital and economic fortunes of the widowed Isabella Ross and her children, some of whom settled in British Columbia, and some south of the forty-ninth parallel. The children's class status, marital choices, and the racial ethnic identities that they could claim on either side of the border depended partly on where they settled, and partly on gender. With the surplus of male European immigrants, fur trade sons found it difficult to secure an independent economic niche for themselves. The daughters fared better, so long as they remained valued marriage partners, until the arrival of European women erected new racial hierarchies.[41] Their racial status and what it meant depended, too, on national policies that defined Aboriginal rights through racialized and gendered categories.

The marriages of the Ross children reflected the social flux of mid-nineteenth-century Oregon Country. The marriages of some of the older Ross children (Elizabeth, John, and Victoria) cemented ties with other Métis families in Oregon. Charles Ross, Jr., married Catherine Toma (Tumalt), whose mother, Quatan, was Nisqually, and whose father was a French-Iroquois who had come west as an HBC *engagé*. The rapid influx of white settlers into Oregon Country during the 1840s brought a brief period when Métis daughters married incoming white farmers. Catherine Ross married an Englishman, Henry Murray, in 1851. By the mid-1850s, however, attitudes toward interracial marriages became increasingly hostile. The deteriorating racial climate, and outright war with the Indians in 1855, led Charles and Catherine Toma Ross, John Ross, and Victoria Ross and her Métis husband John Wren to move to Vancouver Island, which seemed to offer a more hospitable community.

However, the social and economic options for Métis children rapidly narrowed north of the border as well. The changing social climate drew some of the Ross children back to the United States. One of the younger daughters, Mary Amelia, married her brother-in-law, Charles Wren, after Victoria died in 1859. The Wrens moved back south of the border, to Washington State, as did Charles Ross, Jr., and his family. Through Catherine Toma Ross's rights as a Nisqually, the family took a homestead on the Nisqually Indian Reservation in 1884. Their descendants retain membership in the Nisqually Indian band.

If Catherine Toma had been an Aboriginal Canadian, she and her children would have lost their Indian status, because under the Indian Act an Aboriginal woman who married a white man or a non-status Indian lost her legal status as Indian and her right to live on a reserve. The U.S. racial system differed in that it did not recognize Métis as a category, so that the Ross descendants became "Indian" in the U.S. racial binary. But neither did women automatically lose their Indian identities and entitlements if they married out of the tribe.[42]

The fortunes of the Ross children, both north and south of the 49th parallel, were embedded in how settler societies in the United States and Canada defined race and their differing policies regarding Native and Métis peoples. The Ross family's cross-border migrations illustrated how social networks and kinship might cross national boundaries but were nonetheless affected by those borders and the social boundaries that states constructed.

Van Kirk's scholarship has long bridged the worlds of interpersonal intimacy and state power, and the historical discourses of Canada, the United States, and beyond. It now promises to help clarify the complex projects of new transnational and borderlands histories, directing attention to the individual lives that crossed national boundaries, the social ties that transcended national identities, and the power of state policies to construct different relationships of race and gender on either side of a border. Sylvia Van Kirk's scholarship has compelled us to examine human connections across differences of race, gender, and nationality, and to explore how difference and inequality have been historically constructed and contested. That is no small legacy. It holds the power to place daily life and intimacy at the centres of North American history, where people's daily accommodations forged collective histories. Those histories can chart and illuminate the spaces between private life and public history, and between the nations where Van Kirk's scholarship still resonates.

Notes

1. See for instance Arthur J. Ray, *Indians in the Fur Trade: Their Role as Trappers, Hunters, and Middlemen in the Lands Southwest of Hudson Bay, 1660–1870* (Toronto: University of Toronto Press, 1974); Jennifer S.H. Brown, *Strangers in Blood: Fur Trade Company Families in Indian Country* (Vancouver: University of British Columbia Press, 1980); *The New Peoples: Being and Becoming Métis in North America*, ed. Jacqueline Peterson and Jennifer S.H. Brown (Winnipeg: University of Manitoba Press, 1985); William R. Swagerty, "Marriage and Settlement Patterns of Rocky Mountain Trappers and Traders," *Western Historical Quarterly* 11, 2 (April 1980): 159–80; John Elgin Foster, "The Country-born in the Red River Settlement: 1820–1850" (PhD diss., University of Alberta, 1973).

2. Sylvia Van Kirk, "A Vital Presence: Women in the Cariboo Gold Rush, 1862–1875," in *British Columbia Reconsidered: Essays on Women*, ed. Veronica Strong-Boag and Gillian Creese (Vancouver: University of British Columbia Press, 1992), 21–37.

3. American edition, Sylvia Van Kirk, *Many Tender Ties: Women in Fur-Trade Society, 1670–1870* (Norman, OK: University of Oklahoma Press, 1980).

4. Joan M. Jensen and Darlis A. Miller, "The Gentle Tamers Revisited: New Approaches to the History of Women in the American West," *Pacific Historical Review* 492 (May 1980): 173–213. Each conference generated a book: *The Women's West*, ed: Susan Armitage and Elizabeth Jameson (Norman, OK: University of Oklahoma Press, 1987) and *Western Women: Their Land, Their Lives*, ed. Lillian Schlissel, Vicki Ruiz, and Janice Monk (Albuquerque, NM: University of New Mexico Press, 1988).

5. Jensen and Miller, "Gentle Tamers Revisited."

6. First published in 1930, Harold A. Innis, *The Fur Trade in Canada: An introduction to Canadian economic history*, is best known in Canada through the revised edition (Toronto: University of Toronto Press, 1962). In 1999, the historical geographer Arthur Ray introduced a new edition, also published by the University of Toronto Press.

7. Frederick Jackson Turner, "The Significance of the Frontier in American History," in *History, Frontier, and Section: Three Essays by Frederick Jackson Turner*, ed. Martin Ridge (Albuquerque, NM: University of New Mexico Press, 1993), 62–71. Turner first delivered "The Significance of the Frontier" as a paper at the American Historical Association meeting in Chicago, 12 July 1893.

8. This critique that defining frontiers in terms of male economies immediately skewed the scholarship to marginalize women is cogently developed in William Cronon, Howard R. Lamar, Katherine G. Morrissey, and Jay Gitlin, "Women and the West: Rethinking the Western History Survey Course," *Western Historical Quarterly* 17, 3 (July 1986): 269–90.

9. Susan Armitage, "Through Women's Eyes: A New View of the West," *The Women's West*, ed. Armitage and Jameson, 9–18.

10. Sylvia Van Kirk, "The Role of Native Women in the Creation of Fur Trade Society in Western Canada, 1670–1830," in *The Women's West*, ed. Armitage and Jameson, 53–62.

11. Van Kirk also participated as a commentator at the "Western Women, Their Land, Their Lives" conference. See Sylvia Van Kirk, "Commentary," in *Western Women: Their Land, Their Lives*, ed. Schlissel, Ruiz, and Monk.

12. Elizabeth Jameson, "Women as Workers, Women as Civilizers: True Womanhood in the American West," in *The Women's West*, ed. Armitage and Jameson, 145–64, quote 161, from Nellie McClung, *Clearing in the West*, epigraph Linda Rasmussen, Lorna Rasmussen, Candace Savage, and Anne Wheeler, *A Harvest Yet to Reap: A History of Prairie Women* (Toronto: Women's Press, 1976).

13. Swagerty, "Marriage and Settlement Patterns," 159. Swagerty cited: Foster, "The Country-born in the Red River Settlement"; Sylvia Van Kirk, "The Role of Women in the Fur Trade Society of the Canadian West, 1700–1850" (PhD diss., University of London, 1975); Jennifer Brown, "Company Men and Native Families: Fur Trade Social and Domestic Relations in Canada's Old Northwest" (PhD diss., University of Chicago, 1976); Jacqueline Peterson, "Ethnogenesis: Intermarriage and the Emergence of a Métis Class in the Great Lakes Region, 1690–1835" (PhD diss., University of Illinois, Chicago Circle, in progress), and Carol Judd, Parks Canada, who was "preparing a study of Hudson's Bay Company employees after 1821." For background on the Canadian fur trade, he referred readers to Harold A. Innis, *The Fur Trade in Canada* (New Haven: Yale University Press, 1930) and Arthur J. Ray, *Indians in the Fur Trade: Their Role as Trappers, Hunters, and Middlemen in the Lands Southwest of Hudson Bay, 1660–1870* (Toronto: University of Toronto Press, 1974). See Swagerty, 162, for comparisons of the Canadian and U.S. Rocky Mountain trades.

14. Ibid., esp. 164–74, 180.

15. Susan Sleeper-Smith, *Indian Women and French Men: Rethinking Cultural Encounter in the Western Great Lakes* (Amherst: University of Massachusetts Press, 2002).

16. Susan Sleeper-Smith, "'[A]n Unpleasant Transaction on this Frontier': Challenging Female Autonomy and Authority at Michilimackinac," *Journal of the Early Republic* 25 (Fall 2005): 417–43.

17. Sylvia Van Kirk, "'What if Mama is an Indian?': The Cultural Ambivalence of the Alexander Ross Family," *The Developing West*, ed. John Foster (Edmonton: University of Alberta Press, 1983), 123–36; revised version in *The New Peoples*, ed. Peterson and Brown, 207–17; "Tracing the Fortunes of Five Founding Families of Victoria," *BC Studies* 115/116 (Autumn/Winter 1997–98): 149–179; "A Transborder Family in the Pacific North West: Reflecting on Race and Gender in Women's History," *One Step Over the Line: Toward a History of Women in the North American Wests*, ed. Elizabeth Jameson and Sheila McManus (Edmonton: University of Alberta Press and Athabasca: Athabasca University Press, 2008), 81–98.

18. Albert L. Hurtado, *Indian Survival on the California Frontier* (New Haven: Yale University Press, 1988).

19. E-mail from Albert L. Hurtado to Elizabeth Jameson, 16 August 2008.

20. Albert L. Hurtado, *Intimate Frontiers: Sex, Gender, and Culture in Old California* (Albuquerque: University of New Mexico Press, 1999).

21. Ibid., Chapter 5, "Amelia's Body: The Limits of Female Agency in Frontier California," 115–28.

22. Sylvia Van Kirk, "The Role of Native Women in the Creation of Fur Trade Society," in *The Women's West*, ed. Armitage and Jameson; Sylvia Van Kirk, "A Transborder Family in the Pacific North West," in *One Step Over the Line*, ed. Jameson and McManus.

23. Elizabeth Jameson and Susan Armitage, eds., *Writing the Range: Race, Class, and Culture in the Women's West* (Norman, OK: University of Oklahoma Press, 1997).

24. The seven articles are: Marian Perales, "Empowering 'The Welder': A Historical Survey of Women of Colour in the West," in *Writing the Range*, 21–41; Ramona Ford, "Native American Women: Changing Statuses, Changing Interpretations," in ibid., 42–68; Peggy Pascoe, "Race, Gender, and Intercultural Relations: The Case of Interracial Marriage," in ibid., 69–80; James F. Brooks, "'This Evil Extends Especially to the Feminine Sex': Captivity and Identity in New Mexico, 1700–1846," in ibid., 97–121; Albert L. Hurtado, "When Strangers Met: Sex and Gender on Three Frontiers," in ibid., 122–42; Coll-Peter Thrush and Robert H. Keller, Jr., "'I See What I Have Done': The Life and Murder Trial of Xwelas, a S'Klallam Woman," in ibid., 172–87; and Lisa E. Emmerich, "'Save the Babies': American Indian Women, Assimilation Policy, and Scientific Motherhood,

1912–1918," in ibid., 393–409. Peggy Pascoe's article first appeared in *Frontiers* 12, 1 (1991): 5–18; Thrush and Keller's first appeared in the *Western Historical Quarterly* 26, 2 (Summer 1995): 169–83.

25. Perales, "Empowering the Welder" and Ford, "Native American Women."

26. Brooks, "'This Evil Extends Especially to the Feminine Sex,'" 108.

27. Hurtado, "When Strangers Met," 123.

28. Thrush and Keller, "'I See What I Have Done,'" 186.

29. Emmerich, "'Save the Babies,'" 398, 407.

30. Peggy Pascoe, *Relations of Rescue: The Search for Female Moral Authority in the American West, 1874–1939* (New York: Oxford University Press, 1990).

31. Pascoe, "Race, Culture, and Intercultural Relations," 69.32. Peggy Pascoe, *What Comes Naturally: Miscegenation Law and Making of Race in America* (New York: Oxford University Press, 2009).

33. Peggy Pascoe, "Western Women at the Cultural Crossroads," *Trails: Toward a New Western History,* ed. Patricia Nelson Limerick, Clyde A. Milner II, and Charles E. Rankin, (Lawrence; University Press of Kansas, 1991), 40–58, 42–3.

34. Ibid., 55.

35. Ibid.

36. James F. Brooks, *Captives and Cousins: Slavery, Kinship, and Community in the Southwest Borderlands* (Chapel Hill: University of North Carolina Press, for the Omohundro Institute of Early American History and Culture, 2002).

37. Hurtado, *Indian Survival* and *Intimate Frontiers.* For the definition of frontiers, see *Intimate Frontiers,* xxvii.

38. Frederick Jackson Turner, "The Significance of the Frontier in American History," in *History, Frontier, and Section,* ed. Martin Ridge (Albuquerque, NM: University of New Mexico Press, 1993), 82; Frederick Jackson Turner, "The Significance of History," ibid., 49. This essay was originally published in the *Wisconsin Journal of Education* in 1891.

39. The conference generated two books: *Unsettled Pasts: Reconceiving the West through Women's History,* ed. Sarah Carter, Lesley Erickson, Patricia Roome, and Char Smith (Calgary: University of Calgary Press, 2005) and *One Step over the Line,* ed. Jameson and McManus.

40. Van Kirk, "A Transborder Family."

41. Ibid.

42. Ibid., 84–92.

Historiography that Breaks Your Heart: Van Kirk and the Writing of Feminist History[1]

ADELE PERRY

IN A SLIM VOLUME OF ESSAYS, Cuban-American feminist anthropologist Ruth Behar argues for a located, embodied, and empathetic scholarly practice. Scholars, she writes, should be—and perhaps cannot and should not try not to be—vulnerable observers. Behar explains:

> In the midst of a massacre, in the face of torture, in the eye of a hurricane, in the aftermath of an earthquake, or even, say, when horror looms apparently more gently in memories that won't recede and so come pouring forth in the late-night quiet of a kitchen, as a storyteller opens her heart to a story listener, recounting hurts that cut deep and raw into the gullies of the self, do you, the observer, stay behind the lens of the camera, switch off the tape recorder, keep pen in hand? Are there limits—of respect, pity, pathos—that should not be crossed, even to leave a record? But if you cannot stop the horror, shouldn't you at least document it?[2]

The challenge that this presents to scholarly standards that remain premised on some version of ideals of scholarly remove and objectivity is considerable. To Behar, this is a risk worth taking. "Call it sentimental, call it Victorian and nineteenth-century, but I say that anthropology that doesn't break your heart just isn't worth doing any more," she concludes.[3]

Historians are not anthropologists. Few of us work with living people or in the midst of storms. Most historians work in archives, with documents written by people who, for the most part, lived a long time ago. Even the increasing numbers of historians who use material objects, spoken words, or the land as their source material have been trained in and circulate within a scholarly culture where the archive continues to adjudicate what constitutes a good history and a good historian. Antoinette Burton explains that the archive, "conventionally understood as an institutional site in a faraway place that requires hotel accommodation and a grueling nine-to-five workday," continues to function as the arbiter of historical authority, the site where "the hands-on, hard work of history evidently takes place and that historians get their professional credibility."[4] Historians sometimes regret the hold the archive has on us. But historians can also relish the hold the archive has on us, in part because what Karen Dubinsky calls " telling stories about dead people,"[5] offers us a powerful way to speak to the present through the past, about our current lives, communities, and aspirations through those that came before us.

These are some of the reasons that Behar's plea to think of scholars as vulnerable (and scholarship as heartbreaking) resonates in particular ways for historians—or at least for me. Historians have long struggled with singular openness about the complicated relationship between the past we study and the present we necessarily occupy. We have been less ready to broach difficult questions about method, discipline, and practice that go beyond the pedestrian recognition that every history is, "in a sense, a form of autobiography and an essay in self-knowledge."[6] Some historians are going beyond this to rupture the presumed distinction between biographical and historical writing.[7] Historians still write very little about the research process in general and archival research in particular, especially given the critical role "archive stories" occupy in our informal professional culture. Historians have left it largely to literary critics to parse "the archive" and its fevers.[8] It is ethnographers like Behar who have found ways to critically integrate the research process into their analyses. The research trip, the unyielding archive, the perplexing informant are taken from the footnotes and appendixes and rearticulated as part of, rather than predicate to, the analysis.[9]

This essay uses Behar's remarks and the considerations about historical scholarship they prompt as points of departure for a discussion of Sylvia Van Kirk's 1980 book *"Many Tender Ties": Women in Fur-Trade Society in Western Canada, 1670–1870* and the politics of writing feminist history. The essay proceeds in two parts. I begin by locating *"Many Tender Ties"* as a simultaneously ambivalent and inspiring intervention into women's, Aboriginal, and fur trade historiography. I then turn to the reverberations of this for my own ongoing research on the family histories of James Douglas (1803–1877) and Amelia Connolly (1812–1890). By reading conventional archives in unconventional ways and puncturing presumed distinctions between private and public, Van Kirk provides us with an enduring example of the possibilities as well as the risks, of historiography that breaks your heart.

I

There are a number of scholarly contexts in which Van Kirk's work can be located. In some respects it spans and bridges two scholarships on the western Canadian fur trade. *"Many Tender Ties"* began as a PhD thesis at the University of London, and is very much a part of a postwar scholarship on the Canadian fur trade tied to British institutions. Rooted in research in British archives, including those of the Hudson's Bay Company (HBC) before they were patriated to Winnipeg in 1974, this work is attentive to imperial structures, maritime connections, and a wider Pacific history.[10] Van Kirk's other historiographical foot is planted in the vibrant interdisciplinary scholarship on the fur trade that developed in North America in the 1970s and '80s. Authored by anthropologists, historians, and geographers like Irene M. Spry, Olive Dickason, Arthur Ray, John Foster, and Robin Fisher, this work brought into conversation renewed interest in local Indigenous peoples and "history from below" that was revolutionizing how historians understood the peasants and workers of European society.[11] Through these lenses the western Canadian fur trade was re-figured—it was no longer a story of the British Empire, or of national heroism, but a history of labour performed, goods traded, and lands enclosed. In many ways, this scholarship continues to serve as the central available perspective on the history of eighteenth- and nineteenth-century western Canada and the fur trade.[12]

"Many Tender Ties" is as much a contribution to women's history as it is to fur-trade or Aboriginal history. It was published, as Catherine Hall notes, "when women's history was in its infancy."[13] Canadian women's history was inspired by the revitalization of feminist activism in the late 1960s and more so the early 1970s. It aimed to historicize women's experiences and identities and to "rethink Canada," or reinterpret narratives of national development through the optics of women's experience.[14] *"Many Tender Ties"* substantiated the promise of women's history to not simply treat women as historical actors, but to use their history to leverage a reinterpretation of the past writ large. At a moment when historians

of women were urged to tap new archives like diaries, material culture, and oral history, *"Many Tender Ties"* found them in that most conventional of archives, the records of a powerful imperial enterprise, the HBC. This was the very place where we had been told that women could not be found. Betty Joseph argues that colonial archives constitute their authority in part by constituting the work of the imperial state as a genteel and manly affair.[15] By unearthing rich details about women's lives and work in these most officious of colonial records, Van Kirk shows the masculinity of the HBC records to be a sleight of hand. In doing so, Van Kirk showed us how making women historically visible allows us to recast the most canonical of historical events and topics. In this sense *"Many Tender Ties"* is an example *par excellence* of contrapuntal feminist scholarship. In this volume, Robert Innes' reevaluation of the work of kinship in one multicultural prairie Indigenous community reminds us of the power of new analytics to reframe old questions—in this case using kinship to reframe how scholars have understood nation and 'tribe' in the Aboriginal past.

But *"Many Tender Ties"* is not simply a representative text—it helped inspire careful and revealing reinterpretations of long-submerged family histories and showed (and continues to show) how Canadian history can be fruitfully read in wider, global terms.[16] Selections from it have been routinely (if sometimes awkwardly) included in collections on "American" women's history.[17] Indeed, *"Many Tender Ties"* has had a remarkably international career. Van Kirk's work continues to receive attention, if perhaps insufficient genuine engagement, in a flourishing international scholarship on gender, intimacy, and colonialism.[18] Recent research on mixed-race marriage in New Zealand by Angela Wanhalla and in Australia and America by Katherine Ellinghaus provide only two good examples of how Van Kirk's work has crossed borders.[19]

For all of this, Van Kirk's book is a complicated intervention into the writing of history, and more particularly Aboriginal women's history. Its publication in book form in 1980 and continuing circulation in footnotes and class syllabi are sure signs of the new authority being accrued by both women's history and Aboriginal history. What this institutionalization means for women's history and its connection to feminism remains an issue of some debate.[20] The relationship between Aboriginal history as a sub-discipline and Aboriginal peoples as communities, constituencies, and scholars likewise prompts discussion. In the past decade or so, much of this has concerned historians' formal roles in contemporary Indigenous struggles, especially around land claims.[21] Recent work by Mary Jane Logan McCallum reminds us the extent to which history as a discipline and Aboriginal history as a sub-discipline have ironically worked to marginalize Aboriginal historians.[22]

"Many Tender Ties" begins with a caveat about the limits of the archival records upon which it depends to explain Aboriginal women's motivations and experience. Van Kirk explains that the "paucity of sources, in particular those written by native women" forces the historian to rely on "snippets of information from the extensive collections of traders' journals, letters and wills which have survived."[23] The book proceeds to do just that, finding in the fur trade archive evidence that Aboriginal women sought out (and in some respects, benefitted from) their intimate partnerships with European men. This reflects Van Kirk's concern to acknowledge her subjects as "active agents" who made choices about their own lives and histories, a concern she shared with many social historians writing in the 1970s and '80s. But locating agency in fur trade marriages can rub readers attenuated to the complex and enduring legacies of colonialism, sexuality, and gender the wrong way. The extent to which *"Many Tender Ties"* was wedded to a liberal feminism and grounded in a positivist naïveté that falls on particularly rough ground in the messy context of the colonial archive would increasingly be registered in the 1990s.[24] In the 1990s and 2000s, a wave of feminist historical scholarship on the nineteenth-century Canadian west took Van Kirk's work in new directions. Whether this scholarship—a category into which my own work squarely falls—has meaningfully addressed these critiques remains up for debate.[25]

II

Van Kirk was not my professor, but she was the outside examiner on my 1998 York University PhD thesis. In this critical role she was engaged and gracious about my wanting to make different sense out of marriage, colonialism, and race in mid-nineteenth-century western Canada than she had twenty years earlier. In ways that I did not then anticipate my research has continued to overlap with Van Kirk's. I am now working with the archive that was the source of some of the most enduring material in *"Many Tender Ties"* and has sustained Van Kirk's recent work on fur trade families in nineteenth-century Victoria.[26] My reasons for working with this archive are not the same as Van Kirk's—for me, the family histories of James Douglas and Amelia Connolly provide an excellent opportunity for an exercise in transnational, feminist imperial history. Over the nineteenth century their histories played out in Britain, northwestern North America, and the Caribbean. This movement reminds us of how empire moved and circulated, tying together colonized places as well as metropole and colony. It also prompts us to rethink the shifting politics of race and nation over the long nineteenth century, and ties together the different modes of intimacies and different configurations of imperial economies. But however different my historiographical cues and goals might be from Van Kirk's, I find myself returning to some of the textual references that *"Many Tender Ties"* mined to such effect: James Douglas' fond recollections of the kind bonds of family life in the fur trade or his admonition to his daughter Martha that she not tell her English schoolmates that the Cree stories she knew were her mother's.

I am not always sure what to make of these documents. I was trained primarily as a social historian and I continue to find many of the lessons of contrapuntal "history from below" salutary, particularly when read alongside postcolonial and feminist scholarship.[27] How do the sources that historians continue to heavily rely upon occlude those histories that might be called ordinary or subaltern? How might we seek new archives and read the old ones in new ways that will provoke different understandings of the past—ones that might serve and speak to alternative interests, agendas, and visions? These were some of the questions that informed the dissertation that became my 2001 book, *On the Edge of Empire*. Here I tried to read an archive of fragmentary, sometimes unattributed records produced by the public sphere of mid-nineteenth-century British Columbia—newspapers, state correspondence, court documents, and missionary records—'against the grain' to learn about the lived experience of gender and imperialism. I used whatever memoirs, letters, and journals I found in the archives, but ultimately they were few and relatively unyielding about the categories and questions I had foremost in mind.

Much of the archive that my newer research on the Connolly-Douglas family relies on comes from the same time and place—namely British Columbia in the 1860s and '70s. Yet this archive is very different. What I shorthand as the Douglas-Connolly archive is of course neither singular nor coherent; it includes the records produced and kept by the HBC, the Colonial Office, the governments of British Columbia and Vancouver Island, and a number of private individuals and families tied to this extended kin group. Most significant here are the journals and letters written in the last third of the nineteenth century by Douglas, followed by the records left by his physician and politician son-in-law, John Sebastian Helmcken. Douglas' wife Amelia Connolly left no written archive beyond a handful of perfunctory notes declining invitations or acknowledging gifts. Douglas and Connolly's daughter Martha produced a modest written archive, but her four sisters and one brother left much less.

The records of the Connolly-Douglas family were created by people who were marginal in imperial terms but enormously powerful within the local context of nineteenth-century Victoria. They were canonized as founding fathers—and later (and less often) mothers—of British Columbia, and given secure places in provincial iconography, public culture, and popular historiography. The preservation of Douglas and Helmcken's records in the British Columbia Archives, sometimes transcribed from troublesome nineteenth-century handwriting to accessible typeface, reflects the local significance and authority of the family. These records are not unattributed newspaper articles or correspondence between different and distant levels of an imperial state, but personal documents: journals, memoirs, and the vivid (and at times disarmingly intimate) letters of fathers, daughters, and sons. The danger of becoming what Jill Lepore memorably dubs "a historian who loves too much"[28] is a real one here.

So are the dangers of registering only the events and experiences described in the letters, journals, and memoirs preserved in the archive. The methodological questions that vexed Van Kirk's research haunt this work as well. Archives are simply one heuristic device, and they are a limited one. Working with what is contained within the Connolly-Douglas archive necessarily gives short shrift to important parts of this complicated, transnational family history. Much of what I know about this history comes from occasional glimpses in family records, from scattered records created by contemporaries of Douglas and Connolly, from careful archival research done by historian Charlotte Girard, research that I have tried but not always succeeded in replicating. It is in these places that we learn of Douglas' early history in Demerara, his free Black mother and his likely absent Scottish father, and his schooling in Scotland.[29] It is from fragmentary archival sources, secondary fur-trade scholarship, and one spectacular legal archive that we learn of Amelia Connolly's history as the daughter of a Canadian fur trader and a Cree mother.[30]

These histories—African-Caribbean histories, female histories, Cree and Métis histories, early nineteenth-century histories—surface only intermittently, and then obliquely, in the archive upon which my work primarily relies. In part, the gaping silences in the Douglas-Connolly archive reflect the geographical distances and communicative disconnects in the nineteenth-century British Empire. This was a mobile world that the ship, the letter, and later the telegram traversed slowly, episodically, and with difficulty. People could and did reinvent themselves as they moved from one part of the empire to another, sometimes voluntarily and sometimes because they knew little about where they came from and who they were.[31] The silences that mark the Connolly-Douglas archive were also critical to actively constituting the family as respectable bourgeois subjects of nineteenth-century Empire. This identity was predicated in no small part to overlapping claims to whiteness and active affiliations with the metropole. Despite their considerable wealth and unmatched local authority in mid-nineteenth-century British North America, the Douglas-Connolly family could lay claim to these identities and ties only with considerable difficulty. Securing and defending their status as elites was hard and unremitting work for mixed-race elite families like the Douglas-Connolly's, and the archive was one of the terrains where their struggle was waged.

For any number of different reasons, my analysis has gone in different directions from that taken by Van Kirk in 1980. Yet it has also returned me not only to some of the same records, but to her innovative and enduring approach to those records. And this is where Van Kirk's work connects, if indirectly, to Behar's argument for an engaged scholarly practice. The history of the Douglas-Connolly family is a story of empire, dispossession, migration, state formation, gender, kinship, race, nation, and a spate of local histories. It is history best approached as history that breaks your heart. Certainly it broke theirs; James Douglas' personal archive is shot through with multiple and overlapping layers of loss and dispossession. Some of the losses are literal and pervasive: the death of seven of thirteen children born to him and Amelia as babies and young children and, later, the loss of a daughter and niece in childbirth. "God knows what a sore trial it is, for a Parent to lose a beloved child," Douglas sympathized to a bereaved relation in 1869.[32]

Douglas' losses were also the less literal ones accrued in the mobile geographies and shifting identities of the far-flung nineteenth-century British empire. Douglas had a bourgeois "imperial life"[33] that both traversed and was defined by racial, national, and class boundaries. He began in the fur trade as an indentured servant in the ambiguous position of 'clerk' and eventually became the dominant HBC official on the Pacific coast. Early nineteenth-century records describe Douglas as "mulatto" or "Scotch West Indian."[34] In the middle years of the century, racial discourse proliferated and hardened. At the same time, a string of imperial happenstance led to Douglas' appointment as governor of Vancouver Island in 1851 and of the adjacent colony of British Columbia in 1858, a double post he held until he retired and was named to the Order of the Bath in 1864.[35] As Governor, Douglas developed a pragmatic, localized method of addressing or not addressing Indigenous title to the land, one that would have enormous implications for the fractious land politics that has characterized British Columbia's past and present.[36] For all of these connections, Douglas' history as a son, husband, father and grandfather has been treated as largely separate from his career as a fur trader and colonial administrator.

As Douglas accrued credentials, authority, and wealth, his blackness no longer became a topic of polite discussion, and became submerged in coy and thinly allusive terms.[37] Douglas spent his later childhood and early adolescence in Scotland and his working adult life in Lower Canada, Rupertsland, and Oregon Territory before settling down in Victoria, Vancouver Island. He made one substantial adult trip to Europe following his retirement in 1864–5 and another shorter trip in the 1870s. Douglas owed his remarkable upward mobility to his famous hard work, sharp mind, and abstemious habits, but also to the vagaries of the British Empire at its margins and his multiple geographic mobilities. The distances of empire may have allowed Douglas to operate in very different local racial geographies, but it also separated him from his kin, his birthplace, and knowledge of both. Douglas lost his connection to his mother and his birthplace of Demerara when he was about eight years old, and maintained only sketchy links to Scotland and his kin there until he was in his sixties. He avoided discussing his past whenever possible, and struggled to narrate his own history when compelled to do so.[38] The imperial breaches of Douglas' life were replicated when his own children traversed the British Empire in the hope of securing their place in a shifting bourgeoisie. Douglas insisted that his youngest two children, James Jr. and Martha, be educated in England but worried constantly about them there and feared that they might never return. His daughter Jane followed her husband, another colonial official and merchant with roots in the Caribbean to Scotland, and Douglas despaired that his grandchildren were so far from home. After visiting them in 1864 he wrote that it was "impossible to repress the painful feeling, that it may be for the last time, that we may never meet again on this side of eternity."[39]

Losses and disconnects also shaped Amelia Connolly's life, even if it was lived entirely within northwestern North America. Connolly was born in 1812 at Fort Churchill, and died in Victoria in 1890.[40] Her lifetime coincided with (and was necessarily marked by) massive changes and dislocations for Indigenous peoples in the territories between the Pacific Ocean and the Great Lakes. To reel off a few of the massive changes wrought by the consolidation of British merchant capitalism and settler colonialism in this part of the nineteenth-century world is sufficient: violent conflict within (and eventual consolidation of) the fur trade; the creation of the British colonies of Vancouver Island, British

Columbia, and Red River; the transfer of Oregon territory to the United States; non-Indigenous settlement in significant numbers; the arrival of European missionaries; massive epidemics of European "crowd diseases" (and with them Indigenous depopulation on an unprecedented scale); the transfer of Rupert's Land from the HBC to Canada; the end of the buffalo hunt; the rise (and then dispersal) of Métis community; the signing of the first numbered treaties between Cree, Assiniboine, and Salteaux peoples and the Canadian government; the passage of the first *Indian Act* in 1876 and the beginnings of reserve life.[41]

The changing status of Indigenous women with kin connections to the fur trade reveals much about the impact of these changes. In 1980, Van Kirk argued that there were three main phases in relations between fur traders and Indigenous women: in the first period men in the fur trade partnered primarily with Indigenous women, in the second period they tended to couple with women of mixed origins (many of them themselves daughters of traders), and in the third period fur traders (especially upwardly mobile ones) tended to marry white women who functioned as powerful status symbols. Connolly and Douglas' lives followed some of this trajectory and departed from it in important ways. Her mother, Miyo Nipay, was Cree, and her father, William Connolly, was a Canadian-born fur trader. Their 1803 marriage *a la façon du pays* fits squarely within Van Kirk's characterization of the first period of fur trade marriage.[42] Similarly, the 1828 customary marriage of Amelia, their daughter, to Douglas, her father's direct inferior at Fort St. James, is a fine example of Van Kirk's second phase. Connolly and Douglas' lives fit poorly with the third phase described by Van Kirk. They married by Anglican custom in 1837, and Connolly functioned as the "first lady" of Fort Victoria (and then the Governor's wife), and in 1864 became Lady Douglas. Van Kirk's more recent research makes clear that Connolly and Douglas were hardly alone. In the city of Victoria they joined an intimate circle of elite, mixed-descent families tied to the fur trade.[43]

The intimate histories of this circle confirm what Durba Ghosh has recently argued for nineteenth-century India: the apparent downward trajectory of mixed-race relationship was neither linear nor consistent.[44] Yet as much as Connolly and Douglas' lives were not determined by the shifting and highly gendered politics of race and respectability in late nineteenth-century northwestern North America, they were indelibly marked by them. William Connolly left Miyo Nipay to marry his much younger cousin in 1832. With this his six surviving children, Amelia included, lost their father. In the late 1860s her brother, the Montreal-based solicitor John Connolly, successfully challenged the validity of their father's second marriage and in doing so shifted the public discourse on race, respect-ability and recognition in British North America.[45] This case secured Amelia a portion of her father's considerable estate, but it could not protect her from the criticism of the Anglican missionary posted at Fort Vancouver in the 1830s who publically condemned customary wives, Connolly included.[46] Nor did the fact that Connolly and Douglas wed by Anglican custom in 1838 or accrued so many tangible properties of whiteness insulate them from brittle race-thinking.[47] Mid-nineteenth-century observers routinely commented on Connolly's indigineity and linked it to the perceived shortcomings of her husband's administration.[48]

But I do not know what Connolly made of the shifting politics of race in the nineteenth century or her place within it. The past two decades of reflective femi-nist post-colonial scholarship reminds us that all archives have particularities, limitations and politics.[49] It also reminds us of the critical role played by schol-arly subjectivities. I am white, and the history I am producing would likely look different if I were not. To say that the extent to which a historian working with written records can speak decisively about (let alone "for") Amelia Connolly is limited is something of an understatement. Beyond a handful of brief written notes that survive amongst Douglas' papers, the historian reliant on written re-cords have only Connolly's husband's and children's representations of her. These portrayed her as a strong mother and grandmother who struggled against the fragmentation of her family and worked to keep them literally in one place. Con-nolly did not want her two youngest children to go to England. When Martha first left, Douglas found Amelia "in a burst of incontrollable grief."[50] Amelia was happiest, James explained, when her daughters and grandchildren were nearby.[51]

III

Why does *"Many Tender Ties"* remain an enduring influence on this work and that of so many others? It is in part because, to borrow Behar's phrasing, the history Van Kirk offers breaks our hearts. It is not because *"Many Tender Ties"* broaches the autobiographical. Beyond the brief and tender acknowledgement of her grandparents Van Kirk tells her readers nothing about herself, at least not directly. The footnotes testify to an arduous research process, but readers are not told about the archive and its requirements. We do not learn about what it took to be a young, white Canadian woman researching a PhD dissertation in Britain in the 1960s and '70s, or returning to Canada to teach at a major university.[52] Yet Van Kirk's career reflects significant shifts and persistent patterns in history as a discipline. In the postwar Canadian history beginning to be established as a legitimate sub-discipline in English-speaking Canada—and in the 1970s, '80s, and '90s—women, immigrants, homosexuals, the working-class and Aboriginal people all have established relatively secure places as legitimate subjects of historical inquiry in Canada. Yet women and people of colour continue to occupy marginal and embattled spaces as practitioners and authorities within the sub-discipline of Canadian history.[53]

It is the history Van Kirk offers and the methodology that produced it that both compels and prompts significant questions. *"Many Tender Ties"* shows us how to read a conventional, imperial archive in unconventional ways. Van Kirk finds love and loss amongst the lists of goods traded, labour performed, and dispatches sent to London. In doing so she puts into motion metaphors and links that tie heterosexual intimacies to national formations, and it is here that Van Kirk offers her most conventional and least satisfying reading. *"Many Tender Ties"* presents intimacy between European men and Indigenous woman in terms that Mary Louise Pratt might call a "transracial love plot."[54] Van Kirk further situates these relationships within a liberal interpretation of the western Canadian fur trade as a point of plural, consensual possibility. In doing so, she freights both heterosexual relationships and the fur trade with more interpretative weight than either can rightly bear.

Yet even as she falters, Van Kirk offers us an example of the historian as a teller and analyst of vulnerable histories. What endures about *"Many Tender Ties"* is its insistence on the mutual constitution of the private and the public, the domestic and the political, and the formal and informal economies. To say that the personal is political seems unforgivably trite. But in this shop-worn feminist claim is an observation that not only alerts us to the politics of everyday life but to the familial, intimate, and gendered character of the high politics that form the stuff of conventional historical scholarship. *"Many Tender Ties"* demonstrates that by examining this quotidian world—pemmican made, marriages brokered, children worried about and friendships made and lost—we can leverage new understanding of state and politics. I am working to read the family archive left by the Connolly-Douglas family in new ways that reflect critical scholarship on women's and Indigenous histories. What I continue to draw from Van Kirk's work is her ability to read conventional archives in unconventional ways and to puncture the gendered distinctions of liberal, capitalist modernity. *"Many Tender Ties"* reminds us that we cannot separate the history of women, gender, and the family from that of lands "explored," proclamations made, wars fought, colonies governed, goods traded, and treaties signed or resisted. If this history doesn't break our hearts, it surely should.

Notes

1   I would like to thank Jarvis Brownlie and Valerie Korinek for their help with this paper. Mary Jane McCallum and Jill McConkey offered critical and useful observations. Robert Innes shared his work in progress with me, and Sylvia Van Kirk, Charlotte Girard, John Adams, Jennifer Brown, and Anne Lindsay helped me locate primary documents. I acknowledge the support of the Canada Research Chairs Programme.

2   Ruth Behar, *The Vulnerable Observer: Anthropology that Breaks Your Heart* (Boston: Beacon Press, 1996), 177.

3   Ibid., 2.

4   Antoinette Burton, *Dwelling in the Archive: Women Writing House, Home, and History in Late Colonial India* (New York: Oxford, 2003), 139.

5   Karen Dubinsky, "Telling Stories about Dead People," in *On the Case: Explorations in Social History*, eds. Franca Iacovetta and Wendy Mitchinson (Toronto: University of Toronto Press, 1998).

6   Carl Berger, *The Historical Profession in Canada: Aspects of English-Canadian Historical Writing since 1900*, 2nd edition (Toronto: University of Toronto Press, 1986), 113.

7   See, for examples, Carolyn Steedman, *Landscape of a Good Woman* (Rutgers: N.J., Rutgers University Press, 1987); contributions by Richard White, Philip J. Deloria, Kareen Halttunen, Laurel Thatcher Ulrich, Michael O'Brien, John Demos, and Jacquelyn Dowd Hall, "Round Table: Self and Subject," *Journal of American History* 89, 1 (June 2002): 17–53; Ann Curthoys, *Freedom Ride: A Freedom Rider Remembers* (Sydney: Allen and Unwin, 2002); Catherine Hall, "Introduction," *Civilizing Subjects: Colony and Metropole in the English Imagination, 1830–1867* (Chicago: University of Chicago Press, 2002); Maya Jasanoff, "Border Crossings: My Imperial Routes," in *History Workshop* 64 (Autumn 2007): 372–381; Elizabeth Jameson, "This Bridge Called Women's Stories: Private Lore and Public History," in *Journal of the Canadian Historical Association*, online edition, 2 (2007): 255–75.

8   This point is made by Antoinette Burton in "Introduction: Archive Fever, Archive Stories," in *Archive Stories: Facts, Fictions, and the Writing of History*, ed. Burton (Durham, NC: Duke University Press, 2004).

9   See, for different examples, Nancy Scheper-Hughes, *Death Without Weeping: The Violence of Everyday Life in Brazil* (Berkeley and Los Angeles: University of California Press, 1993); Nancy Rose Hunt, *A Colonial Lexicon of Birth Ritual, Medicalization, and Mobility in the Belgian Congo* (Durham, NC: Duke University Press, 1999); Luise White, *Speaking with Vampires: Rumor and History in Colonial Africa* (Berkeley and Los Angeles: University of California Press, 2000).

10   See, on this context, *Pacific Empire: Essays in Honour of Glyndwr Williams*, eds. Alan Drost and Jane Samson (Melbourne: Melbourne University Press, 1997).

11   Some of their critical work was printed and reprinted in Jennifer S.H. Brown and Jacqueline Peterson, eds., *New Peoples: Being and Becoming Métis in North America* (Winnipeg: University of Manitoba Press, 1985). Two recent festschrift volumes attest to the impact of this work: *From Rupert's Land to Canada: Essays in Honour of John E. Foster*, eds. Ted Binnema, Gerhard Ens and R.C. Macleod (Edmonton: University of Alberta Press, 2002), and *New Histories for Old: Changing Perspectives on Canada's Native Pasts*, eds. Ted Binnema and Susan Neylan (Vancouver: University of British Columbia Press, 2008).

12   Marxist and post-colonial work by Ron Bourgeault, for instance, provided an alternative analysis. See his "Race, Class and Gender: Colonial Domination of Indian Women," *Socialist Studies* 5 (1989): 87–115.

13   Catherine Hall, "Commentary," in *Haunted by Empire: Geographies of Intimacy in North American History*, ed. Ann Laura Stoler (Durham and London: Duke Universities Press, 2006). 455.

14   Veronica Strong-Boag, "Raising Clio's Consciousness: Women's History and Archives in Canada," *Archavaria* 6 (Summer 1978): 70–82.

15   Betty Joseph, *Reading the East India Company, 1720–1840: Colonial Currencies of Gender* (Chicago, University of Chicago, 2003). Durba Ghosh picks up on some of these questions in her "Decoding the Nameless: Gender, Subjectivity, and Historical Methodologies in Reading the Archives of Colonial India," in *A New Imperial History: Culture, Identity, Modernity, 1660–1840*, ed. Kathleen Wilson (Cambridge: Cambridge University Press, 2004).

16   Christine Welsh, *Women in the Shadows* (National Film Board of Canada, 1992).

17   For example, see *Unequal Sisters: A Multicultural Reader in U.S. Women's History*, eds. Vicki L. Ruiz and Ellen Carol Du Bois (New York: Routledge, 1994); *The Women's West*, eds. Susan H. Armitage and Elizabeth Jameson (Norman, OK: University of Oklahoma Press, 1987). Susan Armitage discusses the American context in "Turner's Ghost: A Personal Retrospective on Western Women's History," in *The Practice of U.S. Women's History: Narratives, Intersections, Dialogues*, eds. S. Jay Kleinberg, Eileen Boris and Vicki L. Ruiz (Rutgers, NJ: Rutgers University Press, 2007). Ruth Pierson critiques this in her "Colonization and Canadian Women's History," *Journal of Women's History* 4, 2 (Fall 1992): 134–56.

18   Ann Laura Stoler, "Tense and Tender Ties: The Politics of Comparison in North American History and (Post) Colonial Studies," *Journal of American Studies* 88, 3 (December 2001), reprinted in *Haunted by Empire*, ed. Stoler provides the most prominent international example.

19   Angela Wanhalla, "One White Man I Like Very Much": Intermarriage and the Cultural Encounter in Southern New Zealand, 1829–1850," *Journal of Women's History* 20, 2 (2008): 34–56; Katherine Ellinghaus, *Taking Assimilation to Heart: Marriages of White Women and Indigenous Men in Australia and the United States, 1887–1937* (Lincoln: University of Nebraska Press, 2006); Patricia Grimshaw, "Interracial Marriages and Colonial Regimes in Victoria and Aotearoa/New Zealand," *Frontiers: A Journal of Women Studies* 23, 3 (2002): 12–28.

20   See, for a transnational analysis, Joan Wallach Scott, "Feminist Reverberations," *differences* 13, 5 (2002): 1–23.

21   See the special issue of *Native Studies Review*, 6, 2 (1990).

22   See Mary Jane Logan McCallum, "Indigenous Labor and Indigenous History," *American Indian Quarterly* 33:4 (Fall 2009): 523–544.

23   Sylvia Van Kirk, *"Many Tender Ties": Women in Fur-Trade Society in Western Canada, 1670–1870* (Winnipeg: Watson and Dwyer, 1980), 6.

24   See, for different but equally critical readings, Pierson, "Colonization and Canadian Women's History"; Julia V. Emberley, "'A Gift for Languages': Native Women and the Textual Economy of the Colonial Archives," *Cultural Critique* 17 (1990–1): 21–50.

25   See Sarah Carter, *Capturing Women: The Manipulation of Cultural Imagery on the Prairie West* (Montreal: McGill-Queens University Press, 1997); Elizabeth Vibert, *Traders' Tales: Narratives of Cultural Encounter on the Columbia Plateau, 1807–1846* (Norman, OK: University of Nebraska Press, 1997); Adele Perry, *On the Edge of Empire: Gender, Race, and the Making of British Columbia, 1849–1971* (Toronto: University of Toronto Press, 2001); Myra Rutherdale, *Women and the White Man's God: Gender and Race in the Canadian Mission Field* (Vancouver: University of British Columbia Press, 2003); Myra Rutherdale and Katie Pickles, ed., *Contact Zones: Aboriginal and Settler Women in Canada's Past* (Vancouver: University of British Columbia Press,

2005); Sheila McManus, *The Line Which Separates: Race, Gender, and the Making of the Alberta-Montana Borderlands* (Lincoln, NB: University of Nebraska Press, 2005); Sarah Carter, *The Importance of Being Monogamous: Marriage and Nation-Building in Western Canada until 1915* (Alberta: University of Alberta Press, 2008).

26　Sylvia Van Kirk, "Tracing the Fortunes of Five Founding Families of Victoria," *BC Studies* 115/116 (Autumn/Winter 1997/98): 148–79; Sylvia Van Kirk, "Colonised Lives: The Native Wives and Daughters of Five Founding Families of Victoria," in *Pacific Empires*, eds. Frost and Samson; Sylvia Van Kirk, "A Transnational Family in the Pacific North West: Reflecting on Race and Gender in Women's History," in *One Step Over the Line: Toward a History of Women in the North American Wests*, eds. Elizabeth Jameson and Shelia McManus (Edmonton: University of Alberta Press, 2008). For a more general reassessment, see her "From 'Marrying-In' to 'Marrying-Out': Changing Patterns of Aboriginal/Non-Aboriginal Marriage in Colonial Canada," *Frontiers*, 23, 3 (2002): 1–11.

27　See, for related arguments, Antoinette Burton, "Thinking Beyond the Boundaries: Empire, Feminism, and the Domains of History," *Social History* 26, 1 (2001): 60–71; Victoria Heftler, "The Future of a Subaltern Past: Towards a Cosmopolitan 'History From Below,'" *left history* 5, 1 (Spring 1997): 65–84.

28　Jill Lepore, "Historians Who Love too Much: Reflections on Microhistory and Biography," *Journal of American History* 88, 1 (2001): 129–144. Thanks to Allen Greer for this reference.

29　Charlotte S. M. Girard, "Sir James Douglas' School Days," *BC Studies* 35 (Autumn 1977): 56–63; Charlotte S.M. Girard, "Sir James Douglas' Mother and Grandmother," *BC Studies* 44 (Winter 1979/90): 25–31. Charlotte S.M. Girard, "Some Further Notes on the Douglas Family," *BC Studies* 72 (Winter 1986–7): 3–27; also see W. Kaye Lamb, "Some Notes on the Douglas Family," *British Columbia Historical Quarterly* 17, 1 and 2 (1953): 41–51; John Adams, *Old Square Toes and His Lady: The Life of James and Amelia Douglas* (Victoria: Horsdal and Shubart, 2001).

30　See, for instance, Van Kirk, "*Many Tender Ties*"; Margaret Ormsby, "Douglas, Sir James," Bruce Peel, "Connolly, Suzanne," and "Connolly, William," *Dictionary of Canadian Biography,* found at http://www.biographi.ca. Research on the Connolly family is being done by Jennifer Brown, Anne Lindsay, and Allison Brown, and I thank them for sharing Henry Connolly's memoir with me.

31　See Kirsten McKenzie, *Scandal in the Colonies: Sydney and Cape Town, 1820–1850* (Melbourne: Melbourne University Press, 2004).

32　James Douglas to Edith [Cameron Doughty], 18 October 1869, "Private Letter Book of Sir James Douglas," British Columbia Archives [hereafter BCA], Add Mss B/40/2.

33　See, on these patterns, *Colonial Lives Across the British Empire: Imperial Careering in the Long Nineteenth Century*, eds. David Lambert and Alan Lester (Cambridge: Cambridge University Press, 2006); Tony Ballantyne, *Orientalism and Race: Aryanism in the British Empire* (London: Palgrave, 2002); Alan Lester, *Imperial Networks: Creating Identities in Nineteenth Century South Africa and Britain* (Routledge: London and New York, 2001); McKenzie, *Scandal in the Colonies.*

34　See Simpson's "Character Book," reprinted in Thomas Thorner, "*a few acres of snow*": *Documents in Canadian History, 1577–1867* (Peterborough, ON: Broadview, 1997), 304; Letitia Hargrave to Mrs. Dugald Mactavish, December 1842, in *The Letters of Letitia Hargrave*, ed. Margaret Arnett Maclead (Toronto: The Champlain Society, 1947), 132 (emphasis original).

35　Margaret Ormsby, "Douglas, Sir James," *Dictionary of Canadian Biography*, http://www.biographi.ca.

36 See, most notably, Cole Harris, *Making Native Space: Colonialism, Resistance, and Reserves in British Columbia* (Vancouver: University of British Columbia Press, 2004), Part 1.

37 See Matthew Macfie, *Vancouver Island and British Columbia: Their History, Resources, and Prospects* (London: Longman, Green, Longman, Roberts and Green, 1865), 379.

38 I make these points in "'Is your Garden in England, Sir?' Nation, Empire, and Home in James Douglas' Archive," *History Workshop Journal*, fall 2010, 69:1, 1–19.

39 "Journal of Sir James Douglas' Trip To Europe, May 14, 1864 to May 16, 1865," transcript, BCA B/20/1864, 54.

40 See Nellie de Bertrand Lugrin, John Hosie, ed., *The Pioneer Women of Vancouver Island, 1843–1866* (Victoria: Women's Canadian Club, 1928), Chapter 2.

41 See, for the best overview, Sarah Carter, *Aboriginal Peoples and their Colonizers in Western Canada to 1900* (Toronto: University of Toronto Press, 1999).

42 See, on them, Bruce Peel, "Connolly, William," *Dictionary of Canadian Biography*, Volume 7, and Bruce Peel, "Connolly, Suzanne," *Dictionary of Canadian Biography*, Volume 9, both at http://www.biographi.ca.

43 See Sylvia Van Kirk, "Tracing the Fortunes of Five Founding Families of Victoria," *BC Studies*, 115/116 (Autumn/Winter 1997/98): 148–179; Sylvia Van Kirk, "Colonised Lives: The Native Wives and Daughters of Five Founding Families of Victoria," in *Pacific Empire*, eds. Drost and Samson. Also see Adams, *Old Square Toes and His Lady*.

44 Durba Ghosh, *Sex and the Family in Colonial India: The Making of Empire* (Cambridge: Cambridge University Press, 2005), Introduction.

45 See, on this case, Sarah Carter, *The Importance of Being Monogamous: Marriage and Nation Building in Western Canada to 1915* (Edmonton: University of Alberta Press, 2008), Chapter 4; Sydney L. Harring, *The White Man's Law: Native People in Nineteenth-Century Jurisprudence* (Toronto: University of Toronto Press, 1998), 169–186; Constance Backhouse, *Petticoats and Prejudice: Women and Law in Nineteenth-Century Canada* (Toronto: Osgoode Society and the Women's Press, 1991), 11–13.

46 See *Reports and Letters of Herbert Beaver 1836–1838, Chaplain to the Hudson's Bay Company and Missionary to the Indians at Fort Vancouver*, ed. Thomas E. Jesset (Portland, OR: Champoeg Press, 1949).

47 See, on this idea, Cheryl I. Harris, "Whiteness as Property," *Harvard Law Review* 106, 8 (June 1993): 1710–94.

48 See, for examples, Annie Deans to Brother Sister, 29 February 1854, "Annie Deans Outward Correspondence," BCA, Add Mss E/B/D343A, transcript; Dorothy Blakey Smith, *Lady Franklin Visits the Pacific Northwest: Being Extracts from the Letters of Miss Sophia Cracroft, Sir John Franklin's Niece, February to April 1861 and April to July 1870* (Victoria: Provincial Archives of British Columbia, 1974); *Vancouver Island Letters of Edmund Hope Verney, 1862–1865*, ed. Allan Pritchard (Vancouver: University of British Columbia Press, 1996), 74–77.

49 The most cited article dealing with these and related questions remains Gayatri Spivak, "Can the Subaltern Speak?," reprinted in *Colonial Discourse and Post-Colonial Theory: A Reader*, eds. Patrick Williams and Laura Crissman (New York: Columbia University Press, 1994).

50 James Douglas to Martha Douglas, 13 August 1872, in James Douglas, "Letters to Martha Douglas," 30 October 1871 to 27 May 1874, Transcript, BCA B/40/4A.

51 James Douglas to Jane Dallas, 22 February 1869; James Douglas to James Douglas Jr., 4 February 1869; Private Letter Book of Sir James Douglas" transcript, BCA, Add Mss B/40/2.

52   See Antoinette Burton, "Archive Stories; Gender in the Making of Imperial and Colonial Histories," in *Gender and Empire,* ed. Phillipa Levine (New York: Oxford, 2004)

53   See Donald Wright, *The Professionalization of History in English Canada* (Toronto: University of Toronto Press, 2005), Chapter 5; Ruby Heap, "The Status of Women in the Historical Profession in Canada: Results of 1998 Survey," *Canadian Historical Review,* 81, 3 (September 2000): 436–451; Franca Iacovetta, "Towards a More Humane Academy? Some Observations from a Canadian Feminist Historian," *Journal of Women's History* 18, 1 (Spring 2006): 141–146; McCallum, "Indigenous Labor"; Alan MacEachern, "F is for Faculty," *University Affairs* 10 (October 2006).

54   Mary Louise Pratt, *Imperial Eyes: Travel Writing and Transculturation* (New York: Routledge, 1992), Chapter 5. See Hazel Carby's autobiography in progress for a discussion of why we should resist the temptation to see a cross-race relationship, in this case that of the author's parents, as inherently radical and or liberating. See Hazel V. Carby, "Lost (and Found) in Translation," *Small Axe* 13, 1 (March 2009): 27–40.

Beyond the Borders: The "Founding Families" of Southern New Zealand

Angela Wanhalla

SYLVIA VAN KIRK'S ANALYSIS OF INTERRACIAL MARRIAGE and mixed-race peoples in the western Canadian fur trade has influenced a generation of scholars working on Native women's history, the fur trade, Métis communities, and post-colonial history in Canada and the United States. But Sylvia's work has also reached beyond the borders of North America, shaping the scholarship and approaches of those working on the history of interracial marriage, gender, and colonialism in other former frontier societies like Australia and New Zealand. Southern New Zealand has a distinctive history of hybridity where male newcomers entered into interracial relationships, contributing to the development of a hybrid population that was welcomed and celebrated by officials and Aboriginal peoples. But this history of intermixing is not as well-known as the social worlds and societies created out of the North American fur trade. I explore this social world, taking Van Kirk's scholarship and methodology as a point of reference and extending it to the resource economies and frontier space of southern New Zealand while inviting connections with the histories of gender and colonialism in western Canada.[1]

Southern New Zealand refers to what is known as Otago, Southland, and Stewart Island today, and is the tribal territory of Ngāi Tahu (Figure 1). Fostered by the arrival of the shore-whaling industry, Ngāi Tahu encountered newcomers on an extensive and sustained scale in this region from the 1820s. Unlike deep sea or bay whaling, shore whalers targeted the right whale for its oil and whalebone during a season that lasted from May to October. The long whaling season necessitated the establishment of semi-permanent on-shore settlements, often located near Ngāi Tahu villages. On shore, whalers established a social and economic infrastructure in the form of houses, gardens, boats, landing sites, and stations. Shore whaling, along with sealing and the timber and flax trade, formed the key economic sites of cross-cultural engagement in New Zealand during the first half of the nineteenth century. All three industries (and the newcomers they attracted) were aligned with, and depended upon, Māori communities, but in southern New Zealand shore whaling was the predominant industry, drawing significant numbers of male newcomers from a range of ethnic and religious backgrounds to the region on a permanent basis.

In order to gain access to the land on which to establish a station, newcomers engaged in customary marriage with Ngāi Tahu women. A marriage alliance was usually undertaken with the strong encouragement of Ngāi Tahu leaders, often with a woman of high status so as to gain the protection of the local chief, and access to the resources required to establish a whaling operation. Unlike the early history of the fur trade in the Canadian west, marriage was not limited to the elite, such as owners and managers. Interracial relationships, including customary marriages, were engaged in by all members of the whaling station, from managers to servants such as coopers, carpenters, sailors, and clerks. Status and rank coincided in the marriage market of the Canadian west, and as interracial marriage became more common, a hierarchy of marriage partners emerged that correlated with the Hudson's Bay Company rankings: officers were encouraged to marry European women, those of medium rank were encouraged to marry mixed-blood women, and the lowest-ranked men engaged in intimate encounters with Aboriginal women.[2] Marriage and rank also coincided in the context of shore whaling. While all employees had access to marriage, and there were indeed no restrictions placed on such relationships by station owners, Ngāi Tahu leaders intervened in and mediated the marriage market, identifying men of rank and status with whom to align. Daughters of chiefs, as Atholl Anderson has noted in his social and demographic survey of interracial marriage in southern New Zealand, occupied the top tier of women who married "in" the whaling elite like the Wellers, owners of numerous stations along the southern coast.[3] This marriage hierarchy would shape and influence the fortunes of many mixed-race families.

Interracial relationships were mutually beneficial. Ngāi Tahu welcomed newcomers because the whaling industry fostered new economic conditions and trade relationships, bringing wealth to communities and to chiefly families, and marriage drew whalers into a network of economic, political, and social obligations. But the interracial relationships formed out of shore whaling were more than economic in nature. While they may have been contracted within the context of new trade conditions, what emerged out of the shore-whaling era were permanent, rather than temporary, interracial relationships, and the production of a mixed-race population.

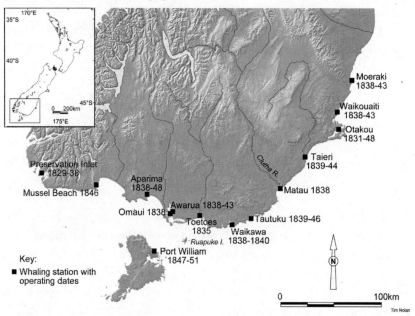

FIGURE 1: Location of shore-whaling stations in southern New Zealand and their years of operation.

In southern New Zealand shore-whaling stations operated as central sites for cross-cultural exchange. Shore whaling, like the Canadian fur trade, was, as Van Kirk has noted, "not simply an economic activity, but a social and cultural complex" based on physical hybridity, as well as cultural, economic, and technological intermixing.[4] What emerged in Canada (and in other frontier regions such as the Great Lakes of the United States) was a set of relationships based not on "casual, promiscuous encounters but the development of marital unions which gave rise to distinct family units."[5] Unlike North America, where there has been a strong interest in the mixed-race communities created out of the fur trade, New Zealand scholars are just beginning to engage with the lives and experiences of the mixed-descent children from relationships formed in the whaling and trading era, which reached its height between the 1820s and the 1840s. Historians of the family and demographers have long noted the presence of interracial marriage and mixed-race peoples in New Zealand's colonial past, but have hesitated to investigate this phenomenon in light of colonial policy and practices until recently. New Zealand historians of colonialism, race, and gender can learn much from Van Kirk's approach, because studies "of families of dual descent will enlarge our understanding of the multiplicity of the colonial experience."[6]

Many of New Zealand's earliest interracial families and communities were formed around shore-whaling stations. This is a statement common to New Zealand scholarship, but thus far the extent to which shore whalers, Māori women, and their mixed-race children formed an identifiable and distinctive community has yet to be thoroughly analysed. Few New Zealand scholars have traced the history of interracial families in detail. The first to do so was Atholl Anderson, who traced the demographic trends of interracial marriage in southern New Zealand across several generations, arguing that the "study of hybridisation, at least in the first instance, has to be built upon detailed regional analyses of historical data."[7] Anderson's 1991 challenge was not taken up until 2006 when Judith Binney, who traced the lives and experiences of mixed-descent children in the Bay of Plenty, noted the presence of elite families in this region, many of whom were Anglican and, in the context of interracial conflict during the 1860s, asserted their loyalty to the Crown.

In recent years Anderson's call for detailed regional and community studies—in order to better understand the complexities of the interracial experience—has been taken up by scholars who have located their research with the context of settler colonialism. Binney signals the importance of religion and class in tracing the fortunes of mixed-descent families within an emerging settler society of the mid-nineteenth century. Binney's families, for instance, lived within the context of war, a brutal policy of land confiscation, and aggressive assimilation policy, and those who professed their loyalty achieved some social and economic prominence. The success of interracial families, some of whom profited materially during an era in which many Māori suffered great loss, needs to be understood in terms of class and its intersection with race and colonial policy. In her finely drawn and sensitive study of the interracial families of southern New Zealand, Kate Stevens demonstrates the value of focused regional studies of hybridity. The mixed-race families of this region were numerous, and their social and economic success often depended upon access to land, itself a product of a good marriage alliance. An elite class of families emerged in the region by the 1860s, just as

Binney found for the Bay of Plenty, but they were small in number. Most southern families lived on the economic margins and within Ngāi Tahu communities, sharing with their relatives a colonial experience of land dispossession.[8]

The rich complexity of the interracial experience, as Binney, Anderson, and Stevens demonstrate, "must now be studied in the distinct localities where Maori and Pakeha [Europeans] inter-married" so the "extent [to which] these mixed marriages created a distinctive New Zealand family," community, or cultural identity can be examined.[9] One of these distinct localities is southern New Zealand, where 140 male newcomers fathered 596 mixed-descent children by the mid-nineteenth century. Because of the extensive and sustained nature of interracial contact amongst Ngāi Tahu, southern New Zealand offers "an important case study in intermarriage and the production of 'half caste' children."[10] Through marriage, the first generation of mixed-race children formed a kinship network that connected Ngāi Tahu and newcomers into a social world of family and community obligations.[11] Marriage was an assimilatory tool for the tribe, and it continued to function in this way well after the whaling trade died out in the late 1840s, as evidenced by the use of marriage to tie together an established network of interracial families across the generations.

Ngāi Tahu and the mixed-descent population

In the late 1840s, when shore whaling was in decline and agricultural development was becoming established, newcomers had already altered the demographics of the Ngāi Tahu population.[12] On his 1844 journey through the South Island, Edward Shortland, the Sub-Protector of Aborigines, noted the "number of half-caste children is, as yet, very trifling; probably little more than three hundred."[13] This was hardly a trifling number within a population that hovered around 2000. What is most interesting about Shortland's journey is the evidence of extensive economic and social interracial interaction around shore-whaling stations, something early settlers in northern New Zealand had noted in the 1830s. Joel Polack, a Jewish trader at the Hokianga, claimed there were "innumerable" Europeans living in the South Island by 1838, who were mostly comprised of "old men [who had been] living there for the last forty years on the coast."[14]

Interracial communities thrived near shore-whaling stations along the coastline of southern New Zealand. In 1844, twenty newcomers, thirteen Māori women and twelve "half-caste" children lived at Aparima, now the settlement of Riverton. A similar-sized community of whalers and Māori resided at the Tautuku whaling station. In 1844 surveyor Frederick Tuckett found the men living at Tautuku had "erected some good houses," and William Palmer, one of the leaders of the community, had a wife of "very prepossessing appearance and manners, the mother of two or three fine children."[15] The Otakou station was home to eighteen newcomers—ten of these men had Māori wives, and had fathered nine children. Sizeable interracial communities also existed at the settlements of Waikouaiti and Moeraki in Otago, both sites of large whaling stations.[16] In total, Shortland identified 170 male newcomers living amongst Ngāi Tahu in 1844.[17]

Johannes Wohlers, the Lutheran missionary located on Ruapuke Island, noted the considerable number of European men "on the shores of this region [southern New Zealand] and more and more remain here." "All of them amalgamate with the natives" and co-habit "in marriage according to the New Zealand way."[18] By December 1845 the southern coast was "crowded with fisheries and many whaling ships are cruising around here."[19] Economic activity was constant, and permanent settlement was emerging out of the whaling industry, reflected in the mixed-race families arising. At the close of 1845, The Neck, the major settlement on Stewart Island, was "inhabited by Europeans who are married to New Zealand women" who had fathered, claimed Wohlers, at least 100 "half-caste" children.[20] Just two months later, Wohlers claimed 150 such children lived "in the surroundings of Foveaux Strait."[21]

Numerous interracial families settled on Stewart Island in the 1840s and 1850s. Indeed, in 1844 72 percent of the mixed-descent population resided in the Foveaux Strait region and 28 percent lived in Otago.[22] While seasonal mobility characterised the shore-whaling industry and the lifeways of its employees, Stewart Island came the closest to developing a distinct mixed-race community primarily because former whalers and their families settled on the island permanently. Many of these men were still residing there in 1864, when surveyor and Land Commissioner Theophilius Heale visited. He described the ex-whalers as "aged men, but they are generally surrounded by half-caste families, who constitute a little community which has grown up entirely without aid or care from the Government, and which is remarkable for the general good conduct of its members."[23]

Alexander Mackay, Native Commissioner, recorded 94 "half-castes" living at or near The Neck, the main settlement on Stewart Island in 1867, most of whom "are grown up, and have families."[24] Moss, Davis, Cooper, Chaseland, Antoni, Goombs, Joseph, Thomas, Brown, Goodwilly, Watson, Leech, Owen, Newton, Wybrow, Cross, Lowry, Anglem, Gilroy, Parker, Joss, Bragg, Honor, Whitelock, Lees, and Bates were just some of the mixed-race families living on the island in 1864. By the 1880s the mixed-race population near the Foveaux Strait had grown substantially and was largely located at the mainland settlements of Riverton and

Bluff as well as on Stewart Island. In 1881, 111 (37 percent) of the 295 people living on Stewart Island were "half-caste," representing one of the largest mixed-race populations in southern New Zealand.[25] By 1896, 88 percent of the Ngāi Tahu population living there was of Māori-European ancestry.

But how does the Ngāi Tahu experience compare on a national scale? Very little is known about the extent or size of the mixed-race population in nineteenth-century New Zealand. It is statistically difficult to account for the mixed-race population because of inconsistent enumeration in the national census. Enumeration of the Māori population began on a national basis in 1874, but the Māori census was held separately to the general population and was not comprehensive, with officials initially preferring estimates rather than precision.[26] To confuse matters, under the Census Act 1877 the mixed-race population was classified as "half-castes living as European" in the general census and "half-castes living as Maori" in the Māori census. Separating "half-castes" along these lines drew upon a much longer tradition amongst officials in the 1840s and 1850s, who defined the population into those recognised by the father as opposed to those "brought up in Maori fashion by the Maori mother." When he claimed a population of 500 individuals of mixed race residing in the city of Auckland in 1857, former Attorney General William Swainson was referring to those acknowledged by their fathers, and therefore living in settler society.[27]

The decision to categorise an individual as "half-caste" in the census was not evenly applied by officials, because individuals of mixed race were not enumerated on the basis of "race" alone. Local enumerators drew upon visual appearance, dress, as well as manner of living when categorising the population. In 1891 persons of mixed race in Otago were, the enumerator decided, not "living as members of a Maori tribe" and omitted them from the Māori census, including them in the general schedule instead.[28] While the census was not precise, the nineteenth-century enumerations do give a general indication of the size of the location of the population. Individuals of mixed race living within European society were recorded in the national census in 1871, totalling 1,465. In 1874, 1,860 "half-castes" were "living as Europeans," which increased to 2,004 "living as Europeans" in 1881.[29] In 1886 "half-castes living as Maori" entered the lexicon of the Māori census, allowing us to gain a much fuller picture of the total population across the two enumerations. Combining the two categories of "half-castes" in the census produces a total mixed-descent population of 4,212 in 1886, 4,828 in 1891, and 5,762 in 1896.[30]

Census statistics also demonstrate that interracial marriage was experienced largely in Māori communities, with many tribal groups absorbing the mixed-race population. From 1886 to 1896 the total mixed-race population represented 0.7 to 0.8 percent of the non-Māori population, but a much larger proportion amongst Māori. In 1886, for instance, mixed-race persons comprised 5.3 percent of the Māori population.[31] For Māori the interracial experience was also characterised by tribal differentiation, which replicates the extent of interracial contact in these regions historically. Individuals of mixed race comprised a much larger proportion of the Māori population in the Bay of Islands, the Bay of Plenty, and the lower South Island, where whaling and trading stations were clustered in far greater numbers than elsewhere in New Zealand. Analysed by tribal group, it is clear that some regions experienced interracial marriage on a more extensive scale than others. According to the 1891 census, 32 percent of the Ngāi Tahu population was mixed race, followed by Ngāti Maniapoto at 11.1 percent. Mixed-race individuals made up a much smaller proportion of Arawa (4.8 percent), Ngāti Porou (6.8 percent), Ngāti Kahungungu (5.2 percent), Ngā Puhi (4.9 percent), and Waikato (3.9 percent). By 1896, the mixed-race population lived increasingly amongst Māori, with 2259 (39 percent) recorded "living as Europeans," compared to 45 percent in 1891. All tribal groups experienced an increase of the mixed-race population: Arawa increased to 5.1 percent, Ngāti Porou to 10.3 percent, and Ngā Puhi rose to 7.4 percent. The largest mixed-race population within Māori tribal territory was located in the South Island, at 48 percent.

While statistics are problematic, they do confirm the Ngāi Tahu population was increasingly comprised of persons of mixed race, and that a sustained pattern of interracial marriage was central to their colonial experience. Like Ngā Puhi in the Bay of Islands, or Ngāti Porou on the East Coast of the North Island, Ngāi Tahu encountered newcomers from the early nineteenth century. What differentiates them from northern groups is that these newcomers remained in tribal territory on a permanent basis, producing a largely mixed-race population by the late nineteenth century. Culture contact in the South Island was not only very different to what was experienced elsewhere in New Zealand, but the extent of interracial relationships in the south also played a significant role in shaping Ngāi Tahu identity during the nineteenth century and beyond.[32] To many outsiders Ngāi Tahu are the "white tribe."

Given the concentration of individuals of mixed race in the far reaches of southern New Zealand from the 1840s, an identifiable mixed-race community with a separate identity could have potentially developed. But a population akin to the Métis in Canada did not eventuate for several reasons. Whalers were a highly mobile group during the 1830s and 1840s, lacking a centre of settlement like Red River or Batoche. As a result, they fathered a mixed-race population in the South Island that was dispersed across Otago, Southland, and Stewart Island. There were small pockets of the country where mixed populations were concentrated, but they were living alongside, and often absorbed by, the Māori population, taking on tribal affiliations and identity.

An identifiable ethnic identity based on distinct cultural and religious values as well as social practices gained little purchase when the newcomers in the southern regions were from diverse origins. In the main, the 140 "founding fathers" of southern New Zealand were European, but they came from a wide range of metropolitan and colonial spaces in Australia, the United States, England, Ireland, and Scotland. William and Edwin Palmer were born to English parents in Australia, as was Nathaniel Bates. George Newton was Scottish, and John Kelly was Irish.[33] American whalers like Lewis Acker settled permanently in the southern regions too, as did Thomas Chaseland, of mixed Aboriginal Australian descent, William Apes, a Native American, and the Portuguese whaler Joseph Antoni. Religious affiliation is also likely to have been diverse, which is something the sole missionary present in the southern region had to grapple with as he attempted to draw newcomers and Ngāi Tahu into the bonds of Christian marriage.

The meaning of marriage

The arrival of missionaries in southern New Zealand ushered in a new phase of interracial contact, in which baptism and marriage were central to the conversion of Māori and newcomer to Christianity and to the creation of a civil and ordered society. Wesleyan missionaries James Watkin, Charles Creed, and William Kirk were stationed at Waikouaiti, north of the Otago Peninsula. But it was Johannes Wohlers (Figure 2), a Lutheran, who had the most extensive contact with southern Māori. Wohlers arrived in the South Island in 1843 with three trainees of the North German Missionary Society. With the encouragement of Ngāi Tahu paramount chief Tuhawaiki, Wohlers established a mission station on Ruapuke Island, in the Foveaux Strait, in May 1844. Ruapuke was the headquarters of southern Ngāi Tahu, but as Wohlers explained, it had certain advantages for a mission site "because it is a sort of gathering place, where everybody, native or European who crosses through these waters comes ashore."[34] He lived at Ruapuke for forty years, ministering to a population on the island and dispersed settlements on the mainland.

FIGURE 2: Johannes Wohlers, the German-born Lutheran missionary based at Ruapuke Island from 1844 until 1885. (Alexander Turnbull Library)

Like whalers, missionaries lived in close proximity to Ngāi Tahu, and the relationships they developed were often ambiguous. A lack of social distance brought the missionary into constant danger of physical and spiritual transgressions. Recognising the isolation of his mission station and the lack of social distance between him and his flock, Wohlers announced, "I am not the man to civilize them, on the contrary the natives uncivilize me."[35] Several cases of New Zealand missionaries, married and single, transgressing stringent nineteenth-century moral and racial boundaries through sexual relationships with Māori women underline the tensions inherent in the missionary encounter.[36] Wohlers was not unaware of these dangers. In May 1845 he noted, "it is not quite without danger for such an old bachelor as me to come into such close contact with the young New Zealand women who are not invariably amiable."[37] Mrs Sterling, he proclaimed, is "the crown of the women at Foveaux Strait and one cannot at all notice that she is a half-caste. She is so pretty, so friendly, so quick and so clever that one might envy Sterling for her."[38] Wohlers' solution to the isolation of Ruapuke and the temptations of Māori women was marriage to Eliza Palmer of Wellington in September 1849.

Missionaries introduced the Christian marriage ceremony into southern New Zealand, and were particularly critical of whalers engaged in illicit relationships. Wesleyan missionary James Watkin viewed interracial marriage as a trade relationship, describing it as "the practise of selling"—denying any female agency in such encounters or an interpretation of them as romantic or meaningful connections.[39] Watkin saw the "practise of selling" as central to the demographic decline of Ngāi Tahu in the southern regions during the 1840s, when inter-tribal conflict, introduced disease, and epidemics were more culpable. Wohlers, in contrast, believed the "Europeans with their mixed offspring are going to continue the line of the thin population of this region."[40] Aboriginal depopulation and eventual disappearance dominates colonial musings on Indigenous peoples and is a persistent trope "in the fantasies of contact."[41] Wohlers supported and encouraged interracial marriage, in part, as a temporary solution to depopulation.

Interracial marriage was a reality in colonial New Zealand. Many missionaries recognised such practices could not be eradicated or prevented, and focused instead on encouraging "regular unions" because marriage was central to the extension of civil society to the trading frontier. Ngāi Tahu women were commended for enthusiastically engaging in the practice. Wohlers proclaimed success when he discovered "girls who are lucky enough to get a European fiancé insist on being officially married."[42] Alfred Domett, Civil Secretary in Governor George Grey's administration and a future premier of New Zealand, linked Wohlers' work in bringing Christian marriage to southern Ngāi Tahu with his "efforts to civilize and improve the Natives in that District."[43] In recognition of this, Ruapuke became a Registry Office for marriages in 1849 under the provision of the Marriage Ordinance 1847, ensuring the rule of law and the authority of the church were extended to all southern Ngāi Tahu.

But bringing Christian marriage to Māori was as much about controlling newcomers as it was about celebrating the successful conversion of Māori to Christianity. German naturalist Ernst Dieffenbach noted, "in many cases, however, the missionaries seem to have been actuated by a desire to check the influence of bad characters who may thus connect themselves with a tribe."[44] Exasperated by the behaviour of former whalers, Wohlers claimed they "don't lift a finger to civilise their wives. The most they do is buy them a European women's dress, whether it fits or is becoming or not."[45] Just seven months later, in December 1845, Wohlers recorded some success, claiming the men, "especially those who already have several children," were seeking to have their "families baptised and to get married to their wives in the Christian way."[46]

Marriage practices in the southern regions pursued by newcomers were, in the main, monogamous, and any deviation from this path often attracted censorship from the local missionary who supported and publicly celebrated a certain type of newcomer masculinity: one that encompassed a Christian union, an absence of violence, and the provision of economic security for the family. Kate Stevens argues that the broad acceptance of Christian marriage by newcomer men, even though many of the unions were long-standing and accepted by Ngāi Tahu because they followed the "custom of the country," "was probably influenced in part by the desire to retain social standing within the emerging colonial society."[47] Polygamous relationships certainly did exist, like Joseph Honour, who Bishop Selwyn, the head of the Anglican mission to New Zealand, found living with two Māori women in 1844. Nathaniel Bates, mentioned later in this chapter, also cohabited with two women—his legal wife as well as the wife of another man.[48] These kinds of relationships, however, were the exception rather than the rule.

A "new stock shall arise"

Because Wohlers lived amongst Ngāi Tahu for forty years and produced an extensive written archive (not to mention records of births, deaths, and marriages), his writings suggest much about the development of the mixed-race population in the southern regions as well as the social world they inhabited. For instance, his register of baptism records a common aspect of life amongst whaling families: the adoption of mixed-race children who had lost their fathers. Most importantly, his extensive archive details the transition of whaling stations into colonial settlements, indicating how class and race intertwined in the making of settler society in much the same way that Sylvia Van Kirk identified the interracial alliances of "five founding families" were crucial to Victoria's founding. Many of the whaling stations in southern New Zealand formed the nucleus of colonial settlements. Indeed, Wohlers celebrated the rise of a mixed-race population, and fervently believed this "new stock" would not only slow population decline but also play a prominent part in establishing an orderly and respectable society. Caroline Brown's story is illustrative.

During February 1846 Wohlers undertook a journey to the Ngāi Tahu settlements along the coast of the Foveaux Strait. At the newly formed settlement of

Riverton he encountered Caroline Brown, who he described as "a pretty young woman." She "lost her father when she was a child and, hence she has grown up amongst the natives without any European education. She does not know any English but that which she has learnt during the few months of her marriage from her husband. [John] Howell wants to civilize her and to make her outstanding among the other women. Hence he does not allow her to sit around among the natives, nor to attend the Maori church services which are led by a native teacher."[49]

Aged thirteen when she married John Howell, Caroline Brown (or Koronaki, to use her Māori name) was one of many mixed-race women in southern New Zealand who married "out" from the mid-nineteenth century. Wohlers described Caroline's situation as "somewhat lonely; for she does not know how to behave among the European women, of whom there are three in this place and hence she does not feel comfortable in their company. She is not allowed to keep close contact with the natives. Neither yet is she conscious of her status. Hence I tried to fill her with pride and put it to her that she was superior to the other women of this settlement. She was the wife of a gentleman and hence must not associate with the women who stood far below her."[50]

At their marriage, John Howell was in the midst of establishing Jacobs River, now known as Riverton, as an agricultural settlement as whaling neared an end in the area.[51] In the early stages of her marriage, as Wohlers noted and despaired of, Caroline preferred the company of Māori and the customs and culture in which she was raised. Writing in 1843, Dieffenbach found that while trade generated wealth for Māori and fostered a mixed-descent population, the arrival and settlement of traders and whalers did not foster a new identity. In fact, mixed-race children retain "many of their mother's peculiarities" and "are generally attached to her race, and of course better acquainted with her language than with English."[52] As Caroline Howell's case demonstrates, at least for the 1840s, interracial marriage took place on Māori terms; newcomers lived in Māori communities and the children were raised, as Dieffenbach noted, by Māori.

FIGURE 3: In this undated photograph Caroline Howell stands next to her sister Peti Hurene, also known as Elizabeth Parata. (Hocken Collections)

The visual record of Caroline's life suggests she lived a life of comfort as the wife of a "gentleman" (Figure 3). Howell's wealth was derived from whaling in the 1840s and cattle and sheep farming in the 1850s. His first marriage to Kohikohi, daughter of chief Patu, gave him access to large tracts of land on which to launch his business ventures. Mercantile success is expressed in the three large properties he owned, which were the centre of social life in Riverton. His status as Riverton's leading "gentleman" was consolidated by his political ties as a member of the Southland Provincial Council, while his brother-in-law, Theophilius Daniel (the husband of Howell's half-sister Elizabeth Stevens), was a member of the Southland and Otago Provincial Councils. Daniel also held the title of Mayor of Riverton for two terms (1879 and 1881). Political ties and material wealth marked Howell and his kin as the pre-eminent family of Riverton, and this respectable status was reinforced through education—both Howell's support for its provision to local children, and that of his children. Education marked the social status of Howell's children, who were all sent to Dunedin— the main urban centre in southern New Zealand—to finish their schooling.

Western dress and her class status leaves an impression Koronaki had assumed a new and stable identity as Caroline Howell, but her ancestry and her appearance was something which the acquisition of material goods and status in the European world could not erase. Over the course of her life Caroline's allegiances traversed the landscape of Māori, European, and mixed-descent communities within the southern region. Caroline existed as part of a network of mixed-descent families in the south, with strong ties of kinship and cultural links to Ngāi Tahu. At first glance the photograph of Caroline (Figure 3) suggests assimilation to European social and cultural values, but this is a family photograph. Caroline stands next to her sister Peti Hurene, who married Tame Parata, the son of Koroteke and Thomas Pratt. Parata was immersed in the political world, both tribal politics and in the mainstream New Zealand political system as the representative for the Southern Māori electorate.[53] In this photograph, Caroline and Peti connect the mixed-descent families of Riverton in the far south and Puketeraki on the Otago Peninsula, demonstrating the resilience of cultural and kinship ties across the vast terrain of the southern region.

In pockets of colonial New Zealand the first generation of mixed-race children did form a new class of colonial elite: they were often well-educated and economically successful—farming their own land—or worked in the civil service as clerks and interpreters. In Poverty Bay and eastern Bay of Plenty, a "subculture" of interconnected mixed-race families existed by the 1860s.[54] Economic and social prominence was achieved through land ownership, based on the status of Māori mothers and consolidated by the marriage of mixed-descent daughters into the colonial elite attached to the circle of government: surveyors, resident magistrates, soldiers, and settler politicians. Mixed-descent sons achieved social success through the patronage of government officials, who found them employment in the public service as interpreters. These families moved in very similar circles, and were tied together by friendship and marriage alliances, replicating the social pattern evident in Victoria, British Columbia during the mid-nineteenth century.

Many mixed-race families in the southern regions did not have the same educational or employment opportunities as those located in the northern reaches of New Zealand.[55] What southern families did share with their northern counterparts was a concern for their children's welfare, education, and economic security. Fathers sought official recognition of their interracial relationships from colonial officials in order to secure the land rights of their children, but it was those men who made the best marriage alliances, gained wealth from the whaling trade, made a smooth transition to pastoralism, and diversified their business interests who could afford to educate their children and secure their economic future.

The "founding families" of southern New Zealand were rarely prominent public figures, like either those in Tauranga and the Bay of Plenty (who were connected to the Auckland colonial elite) or those in Victoria, British Columbia. There were a few mixed-race families in the South Island of high social status who circulated amongst the political and social elite, like John and Caroline Howell. Another was English-born Samuel Hewlings, a surveyor and later mayor of the South Canterbury town of Timaru. Hewlings married Nga Hei (also known as Elizabeth), with whom he fathered five daughters and one son. Fathers who could afford it often chose to educate their children overseas, usually Sydney or London—Hewlings was one of these men. He took his two eldest daughters to England for an education in 1861, and his remaining daughters were educated in Sydney.[56] William Barnard Rhodes (Figure 4) made his fortune from bay whaling off the South Island coastline. Rhodes eventually settled in Wellington and took a prominent role in national politics as a member of the House of Representatives, and served on the Wellington Provincial Council. He was also a large landholder, and owned several businesses in Wellington. Rhodes moved in elite circles, but this did not make him a suitable marriage prospect. When Rhodes married Sarah Ann Moorhouse in 1869, sister of the former Superintendent of Canterbury Province, the Moorhouse family opposed the union because his only natural daughter, Mary Ann, was born to a Māori woman whom Rhodes had never married.[57]

FIGURE 4: William Barnard Rhodes with his "first" wife, Sarah King, and his mixed-race daughter, Mary Ann, in 1858. Mary Ann Rhodes married Edward Moorhouse, the younger brother of her stepmother Sarah Ann, in 1883. Mary and Edward raised a family of four children in Lincolnshire, England. (Alexander Turnbull Library)

Marriage, whether Christian or customary, embedded individuals in a social network across all levels of Ngāi Tahu society. Many of the whaling families, just like fur-trade families in the Canadian west, often intermarried. It was not uncommon for the daughters of whalers to marry men who worked in the same industry as their father, like Margaret Antoni, the daughter of Joseph Antoni, a Portuguese whaler. Margaret married Thomas Chaseland, a well-known southern whaler of mixed English-Aboriginal heritage, at Ruapuke in 1850. Former whaler James Wybrow married twice, first to Temuika, with whom he had three sons. In 1853 he married Elizabeth, the daughter of ex-whaler George Newton and Wharetutu.[58] A quarter of the 140 men who fathered mixed-race children entered into a second marriage, often with a mixed-race or European woman.[59] Wybrow was one of these men, as was Lewis Acker, whose second marriage was to Australian-born Jane Stuart. William Palmer's third wife, Ann Holmes, was "half-caste," while William's brother Edwin abandoned his Māori wife for a marriage with the Scottish-born Beatrice Fowler.[60]

The first generation of mixed-race children was tied by marriage into a complex kinship network. Catherine Acker (1842–1885) married Italian boatbuilder John Rissetto in 1860. Her second marriage was to George Printz (1827–1898), formerly an employee at a whaling station. Printz married a second time, to Matilda Gordon, the daughter of John Howell and Caroline Brown.[61] Nathaniel Bates, a Sydney-born whaler and trader, entered into a customary marriage with Hinepu, and they had three children together before Hinepu's untimely death. In 1848 Bates married Harriet Watson, the daughter of Robert and Parure. After eighteen years and eight children, Nathaniel Bates moved Ann Pauley (nee Williams) into his home, which he still shared with his wife, further highlighting the strong interconnections between whaling families. Ann, the mixed-race daughter of a whaler, was already maried to George Pauley; Bates and Ann were together for twenty-three years.[62] Archival records are replete with endless examples of people like Mary Ann Bates, the eldest child of Nathaniel and Hinepu, who married John Lee in 1858. Lee's second marriage was to Jane Dallas, the daughter of William Dallas and Motoitoi.[63] Evidently the web of kinship formed by mixed-race families extended throughout the southern regions, particularly in the decades of the 1840s and 1850s, as the mixed-race children of whalers entered into adulthood and got married.

Marriage tied together families and their resources, but in a context of a history of sustained and extensive interracial relationships, marriage also tied an individual to a tribe. Atholl Anderson has noted that the first generation of mixed-race daughters tended to "marry out," and the marriage records for the Foveaux Strait region suggest this pattern holds true, but outward marriage did not necessarily mean assimilation in the 1840s or 1850s. Class and status is crucial to understanding and interpreting the extent of assimilation to European cultural values in mid-nineteenth-century New Zealand. Many of the mixed-race women who "married out" during the mid-nineteenth-century did so to men of a similar status to that of their fathers: boat builders, sawyers, sailors, carpenters, and labourers, keeping them connected to the social and cultural world in which they were raised. Wohlers recorded very few mixed-race women marrying into a group he referred to as "gentlemen."

Marriage patterns for mixed-descent men in southern New Zealand during the same period were very different. Sons of whalers were more likely to marry mixed-race or Māori women. European women were a rarity in southern New Zealand in the 1840s and 1850s, and there are no cases of white women marrying Māori or mixed-race men in the Ruapuke marriage register. It was through marriage that "half-caste" men—like Caroline Howell's nephew William Brown—could make good connections. William's marriage to Margaret Davis linked the Browns to a number of well-known Ngāi Tahu families of mixed descent such as Moss, Dawson, Wixon, and Owen. Of mixed race too, William Crane's marriage to Charlotte Areta Paipeta consolidated community connections and united resources and families. Most importantly, these marriages connected not only families but also symbolically tied them to Ngāi Tahu identity. Interracial marriage did not always represent loss. Instead, marriage could act to consolidate, confirm, and authenticate an individual and family as Ngāi Tahu, forming an important part of forging and remaking tribal identity, and negating the development of a separate and distinctive cultural identity based on hybridity in southern New Zealand.

Conclusion

Johannes Wohlers was certainly correct to identify a "new stock" arising out of extensive interracial contact, but this "new stock" did not develop a distinctive cultural identity separate from Ngāi Tahu. Marriage alliances developed by whalers ensured they were embedded in a Ngāi Tahu world, and were bound by affective ties to provide for their family and community socially and economically. Uneven social and economic success was experienced by the southern families and was often dependent upon class, status, and wealth, achieved in many respects through a good marriage alliance. John Howell's pastoral wealth was entirely dependent upon the marriage alliance he contracted with Kohikohi because it tied him to a family of high rank with access to vast resources. Interracial marriages like Howell's were conducted as an alliance, but not all were based on trade—many were in fact formed on the basis of "tender ties." Evidence of this is seen in the longevity of the relationships, the willingness by many to have their customary marriage sanctified by the church, and the desire to seek economic and social security for children in a difficult time of southern history—when British colonisation and land purchases were proceeding at pace. Indeed, by 1864, when the tenth and final land purchase of Ngāi Tahu territory was completed by the Crown, the Ngāi Tahu land base was almost entirely eroded. In the context of the establishment of settler society, social and economic success depended greatly upon class, religion, and respectability. In large part, the mixed-race children of the first generation married within their class, and few became a part of the landed southern gentry. A social world connected by a web of kinship and a shared experience of colonialism involving economic marginalisation between Ngāi Tahu and interracial families ensured that a separate ethnic and cultural identity did not develop in the southern region.

Notes

1   The title of my chapter derives from Sylvia's research on the "founding families" of Victoria, British Columbia: see Sylvia Van Kirk, "'What if Mama is an Indian?' The cultural ambivalence of the Alexander Ross family" in *The New Peoples: Being and Becoming Métis in North America*, eds. Jacqueline Peterson and Jennifer S. H. Brown (Winnipeg: University of Manitoba Press, 1985), 207–220; Sylvia Van Kirk, "Tracing the Fortunes of Five Founding Families of Victoria," *BC Studies*, 115/116, (Autumn/Winter 1997/98): 148–179; Sylvia Van Kirk, "A Transborder Family in the Pacific North West: Reflecting on Race and Gender in Women's History" in *One Step Over the Line: Toward a History of Women in the North American Wests*, eds. Elizabeth Jameson and Sheila McManus (Edmonton: University of Alberta Press, 2008), 81–93. I am grateful to the Royal Society of New Zealand Marsden Fund, which enabled me to undertake the research for this chapter and to deliver a presentation based on this research at the Berkshire Conference on the History of Women held at the University of Minnesota, Minneapolis, in June 2008. Material for this chapter is drawn from my book: Angela Wanhalla, *In/visible sight: the mixed descent families of southern New Zealand* (Wellington, NZ: Bridget Williams Books, 2009).

2   Heather Rollason Driscoll, "'A Most Important Chain of Connection': Marriage in the Hudson's Bay Company," in *From Rupert's Land to Canada*, eds. Theodore Binnema, Gerhard J. Ens and R.C. Macleod (Edmonton: University of Alberta Press, 2001), 99–100.

3   See Atholl Anderson, *Race against time: the early Maori-Pakeha families and the development of a mixed race population in southern New Zealand* (Dunedin, NZ: Hocken Library, 1991).

4   Sylvia Van Kirk, *Many Tender Ties: Women in Fur-Trade Society, 1670–1870* (Norman, OK: University of Oklahoma Press, 1980), 2.

5   Van Kirk, *Many Tender Ties*, 4.

6   Judith Binney, "Contested Ground: Australian Aborigines under the British Crown," ed. Ann McGrath. *New Zealand Journal of History* 30, 1 (1996), 87.

7   Anderson, *Race against time*, 40.

8   Judith Binney, "'In-Between' Lives: Studies from within a Colonial Society," in *Disputed Histories: Imagining New Zealand's Pasts*, eds. Tony Ballantyne and Brian Moloughney (Dunedin, NZ: Otago University Press, 2006): 93–118; Kate Stevens, "'Gathering Places': The Mixed Descent Families of Foveaux Strait and Rakiura/Stewart Island, 1824–1864," BA (Hons) Research Essay: University of Otago, NZ, 2008.

9   Erik Olssen, "Where to From Here?' Reflections on the Twentieth-century Historiography of Nineteenth-century New Zealand," *New Zealand Journal of History* 26, 1 (1992): 66; Erik Olssen, "Families and the Gendering of European New Zealand in the Colonial Period, 1840–80," in *The Gendered Kiwi*, eds. Caroline Daley and Deborah Montgomerie (Auckland: Auckland University Press, 1999): 40. Ann Laura Stoler called for a transnational approach to interrogating the intimacies of empire and colonialism in "Tense and Tender Ties: The Politics of Comparison in North American History and (Post) Colonial Studies," *Journal of American History* 88, 3 (2001). Also see *Haunted by Empire: Geographies of Intimacy in North American History*, ed. Ann Laura Stoler (Durham, NC: Duke University Press, 2006), and *Bodies in Contact: Rethinking Colonial Encounters in World History*, eds. Tony Ballantyne and Anotinette Burton (Durham, NC: Duke University Press, 2005).

10   Kate Riddell, A "'Marriage of the Races'? Aspects of Intermarriage, Ideology and Reproduction on the New Zealand Frontier" (MA thesis, Victoria University of Wellington, 1996), 33. Also see Kate Riddell, "'Improving' the Maori: Counting the Ideology of Intermarriage", *New Zealand Journal of History* 34, 1 (2000): 80–97.

11   Work has begun in this direction. On mixed-descent families, see Angela Wanhalla, "Marrying 'In': The Geography of Intermarriage at Taieri, 1830s–1920s" in *Landscape/ Community: Perspectives from New Zealand History*, eds. Tony Ballantyne and Judith A. Bennett (Dunedin, NZ: University of Otago Press, 2005), 73–94. On racial categories see Riddell, "'Improving' the Maori." On the relationship between colonial and imperial policies see Damon I. Salesa, *Racial crossings: race, intermarriage and the Victorian British Empire* (Oxford: Oxford University Press, 2011). The most recent research on the relationship between shore whaling and interracial marriage is Emily V. Owen, "Intermarriage: Its Role and Importance within Early New Zealand Shore Whaling Stations" (MA thesis, Massey University, NZ, 2007).

12   Elizabeth W. Durwood, "The Maori Population of Otago," *Journal of the Polynesian Society* 42 (1933): 49–82.

13   Edward Shortland, *The Southern Districts of New Zealand: A journal with passing notices of the customs of the Aborigines* (London: Longman, Brown, Green and Longmans, 1851), 77–78.

14   Evidence of Joel Samuel Polack, 6 April 1838, Report from the Select Committee of the House of Lords, appointed to Inquire into the Present State of the Islands of New Zealand, *British Parliamentary Papers, 1837–40*, 81.

15   John Hall-Jones, *The South Explored* (Invercargill, NZ: Craig Printing, 1998), 73.

16   Edward Shortland to Robert Fitzroy, 18 March 1844, in *Great Britain Parliamentary Papers [GBPP] 1846–47*, 317.

17   Shortland to Fitzroy, 18 March 1844, *GBPP*, 317.

18   Johannes Wohlers, Travel Report, 1 May 1845, Wohlers Papers, 0428-04A, Alexander Turnbull Library (ATL).

19   Wohlers, Travel Report, 31 December 1845, Wohlers Papers, 0428-04A, ATL.

20   Wohlers, 31 December 1845, Wohlers Papers, 0428-04A, ATL.

21   Wohlers, 19 February 1846, Wohlers Papers, 0428-04A, ATL.

22   Anderson, *Race against time*, 29.

23   Theophilius Heale to Superintendent of Southland, 15 February 1864, in Alexander Mackay, *A Compendium of Official Documents Relative to Native Affairs in the South Island Volume II* (Wellington, NZ: Government Printer, 1872), 56.

24   Alexander MacKay to Under-Secretary, Native Department, 3 June 1868, in *Mackay's Compendium Volume II*, 64.

25   *Results of a Census of the Colony of New Zealand taken for the Night of the 3rd April 1881* (Wellington, NZ: Government Printer, 1882), 12. See John Hall-Jones, *Stewart Island Explored* (Invercargill, NZ: Craig Printing, 1994) and Basil Howard, *Rakiura: A History of Stewart Island, New Zealand* (Dunedin, NZ: Reed, 1940).

26   Riddell, "'Improving' the Maori," 88. For a discussion of the relationship between the census, racial categories, and their material implications for Ngāi Tahu over the nineteenth and twentieth centuries see Angela Wanhalla, "The politics of 'periodical counting': race, place and identity in southern New Zealand" in *Making Settler Colonial Space: Perspectives on Race, Place and Identity*, eds. Penelope Edmonds and Tracey Banivanua Mar (Basingstoke: Palgrave Macmillan, 2010), 198–217.

27   William Swainson, *New Zealand and its Colonization* (London: Smith, Elder and Co., 1859), 28.

28   "Census of the Maori Population" in *Appendices to the Journals of the House of Representatives* (AJHR), 1891, G-2, 8.

29   *Results of a Census of the Colony of New Zealand, taken for the Night of the 27th February, 1871* (Wellington, NZ: Government Printer, 1872), v. *Results of a Census of the Colony of*

New Zealand, taken for the Night of the 1ˢᵗ of March, 1874 (Wellington, NZ: Government Printer, 1875), 11; *Results of a Census of the Colony of New Zealand, taken for the Night of 3ʳᵈ of April 1881* (Wellington, NZ: Government Printer, 1882), 11.

30 *Results of a Census of the Colony of New Zealand, taken for the Night of the 28ᵗʰ of March, 1886* (Wellington, NZ: Government Printer, 1887): 8 and 359; *Results of a Census for the Colony of New Zealand, taken for the Night of the 5ᵗʰ of April 1891* (Wellington, NZ: Government Printer, 1892), 8 and xlv; *Results of a Census of the Colony of New Zealand, taken for the Night of the 12ᵗʰ of April 1896* (Wellington, NZ: Government Printer, 1897), 7 and Appendix B (Māori Population).

31 This statistic is based on the total Māori population census figure of 41,969, and 2,254 "half-castes living as Maori." In total the mixed-descent population was 4,212, which equates to 10 percent of the total Māori population in 1886.

32 See Bill Dacker, *The Pain and the Love = Te mamae me te aroha: A History of Kai Tahu Whanui in Otago, 1844–1994* (Dunedin, NZ: University of Otago Press, 1994); Hana O'Regan, *Ko Tahu, Ko Au* (Christchurch, NZ: Horomaka Press, 2001); M. Jocelyn Armstrong, "Maori Identity in the South Island of New Zealand: Ethnic Identity Development in a Migration Context," *Oceania* 57, 3 (1987): 195–216; Te Maire Tau, "Ngāi Tahu—From 'Better Be Dead and Out of the Way' to 'Be Seen and to Belong,'" in *Southern Capital: Christchurch: Towards a City Biography, 1850–2000*, eds. John Cookson and Graeme Dunstall (Christchurch, NZ: Canterbury University Press, 2000), 222–47; Stephanie Kelly, "Weaving Whakapapa and Narrative in the Management of Contemporary Ngai Tahu Identities" (PhD thesis, University of Canterbury, 2002).

33 For detailed information on the background of these men, and their marriage alliances, see Anderson, *Race against time*, Stevens, "Gathering Places," and Angela Middleton, *Two Hundred Years on Codfish Island (Whenua Hou): From cultural encounter to nature conservation* (Wellington, NZ: Department of Conservation, 2007).

34 Wohlers, Travel Report, 1 May 1845, Wohlers Papers, 0428-04A, ATL.

35 Wohlers, Ruapuke Report, 2 February 1845, Wohlers Papers, 0428-04A, ATL.

36 The famous cases in New Zealand involve Thomas Kendall, lay missionary with the CMS, the CMS printer William Colenso, who fathered a son with his Māori servant, and claims of rape against Wesleyan missionary William White. See Angela Wanhalla, "The 'natives uncivilize me': missionaries and interracial intimacy in early New Zealand," in *Missions, Indigenous Peoples and Cultural Exchange*, eds. Patricia Grimshaw and Andrew May (Brighton: Sussex Academic Press, 2010), 24–36.

37 Wohlers, Ruapuke Report, 1 May 1845, 0428-04A, ATL.

38 Wohlers, Ruapuke Report, 19 February 1846, 0428-04A, ATL.

39 Journal of James Watkin, 8 March 1841, MS-0440/04, Hocken Library, Dunedin (HL).

40 Wohlers, Ruapuke Report 31 December 1845, Wohlers Papers, 0428-04A, ATL.

41 Mary Ellen-Kelm, *Colonizing Bodies: aboriginal health and healing in British Columbia, 1900–50* (Vancouver, BC: University of British Columbia Press, 1998), 15.

42 Wohlers, Travel Report, 30 June–17 July 1846, Wohlers Papers, 0428-04A, ATL.

43 Sheila Natusch, *Brother Wohlers: A Biography of J.F.H. Wohlers*, 2nd ed. (Christchurch, NZ: Caxton Press, 1992), 179.

44 Ernst Dieffenbach, *Travels in New Zealand*, (Christchurch: Capper Press, 1974 edition), 42.

45 Wohlers Report, 1 May 1845.

46 Wohlers, 31 December 1845.

47 Stevens, "Gathering Places," 20.

48 Ibid., 21.

49   Wohlers, Ruapuke Report, 19 February 1846.

50   Ibid.

51   See Eva Wilson, *Hakoro ki te Iwi: The Story of Captain Howell and his Family* (Invercargill: the author, 1976).

52   Dieffenbach, *Travels in New Zealand*, 41.

53   Māori men gained universal suffrage in 1867, twelve years before non-Māori men in New Zealand. The four Māori electorate seats were established under the Maori Representation Act 1867. No European could stand for election in these seats. Māori political power was restricted to the Northern, Southern, Eastern, and Western electorates because Māori men were unable to stand in European electorates.

54   Binney, "In-Between Lives," 95.

55   Joan MacIntosh, *A History of Fortrose* (Invercargill, NZ: Times Printing, 1975), 39–47.

56   Janet Holm, *Caught Mapping: The life and times of New Zealand's early Surveyors* (Christchurch, NZ: Hazard Press, 2005), 253.

57   Don Grady, *Sealers and Whalers in New Zealand Waters* (Auckland, NZ: Reed, 1986), 186. Geoffrey W. Rice, *Heaton Rhodes of Otahuna: The Illustrated Biography* (Christchurch, NZ: Canterbury University Press, 2001), 35–36.

58   MacIntosh, *A History of Fortrose*, 392.

59   Anderson, *Race against time*, 9.

60   For a discussion of Edwin Palmer and his Māori wife, Pātahi, see Angela Wanhalla, "'One White Man I Like Very Much': Intermarriage and the cultural encounter in southern New Zealand, 1829–1850," *Journal of Women's History* 20, 2 (2008), 34-56.

61   Reunion Committee, *Acker Family, 1834–1984* (Invercargill, NZ: Acker Family Reunion Committee, 1984).

62   Linda J. Scott and Finlay P. Bayne, *Nathaniel Bates of Riverton, his families and descendants* (Christchurch: Bates Reunion Committee, 1994), 5.

63   Scott and Bayne, *Nathaniel Bates of Riverton*, 17–20.

Multicultural Bands on the Northern Plains and the Notion of "Tribal" Histories

ROBERT ALEXANDER INNES

AS AN UNDERGRADUATE STUDENT IN HISTORY at the University of Toronto, I enrolled in a fourth-year seminar course in Aboriginal history taught by Sylvia Van Kirk. I was eager to be in a course that focused entirely on Aboriginal people, and this was the only one offered by the department that fit the bill. I was also somewhat excited by the prospect of taking a course from a professor whose work I had actually read ("Women in Between" had been assigned in a Canadian history class that I had taken a couple years earlier). My excitement was justified—Professor Van Kirk's course was as thought-provoking as it was challenging. At one point, she explained that her approach to Aboriginal history was to place herself in her subjects' shoes and try to ascertain the motivations behind their actions—she wanted to access the Aboriginal perspective(s). As someone who regularly sought to write on Aboriginal topics, I had probably been doing just that; however, this approach had never before been clearly articulated to me. Since taking Professor Van Kirk's course, accessing the motivations and perspectives of Aboriginal people has explicitly guided my scholarly research.

While I was a history major as an undergraduate student, I am not a historian. The discussion I raise in this paper emerged from my dissertation research in American Indian Studies at the University of Arizona. In that work, I explored the importance of family ties to contemporary Cowessess First Nation, of which I am a member. Nearly 80 percent of Cowessess members live off-reserve. A significant number left the reserve as early as the 1940s and 1950s, many in search of employment. Women who left subsequently lost their Indian status upon marrying non-status Indians. As a result, there are numerous Cowessess members who have never lived on the reserve. There also many who were not status Indians or band members until the 1985 amendments to the *Indian Act*. The overall response of Cowessess band members to previous disconnected members has been favourable. This is notable because it stands in contrast to frequent news reports of hostility by other First Nations band members towards newly reinstated members. The basis of my research, then, was to ascertain what motivated Cowessess people's positive response to new and disconnected members.

I argued that contemporary Cowessess band members have retained portions of their traditional kinship practices. Historically, kinship practices were fluid, flexible, and inclusive. At the time that Chief Cowessess signed Treaty Four in 1874, his was a multicultural band comprising five major groups—the Plains Cree, Saulteaux, Assiniboine, Métis, and English Halfbreeds—although individuals from other cultural groups were also part of the band. One of my first tasks was to learn how Cowessess and other bands became multicultural. In my examination of the secondary literature, I discovered that the existence of multicultural bands in Saskatchewan was not reflected in the historical and anthropological interpretations. Scholars, I found, emphasized tribal histories that highlighted intertribal contact and relations, yet with distinct tribal boundaries.

A few authors, such as Susan Sharrock and Patricia Albers, have examined multicultural groups, but not to a degree that helps explain the multicultural nature of the Cowessess band.[1] Sharrock discussed the ethnogenesis of the Cree/Assiniboine, and Albers outlined the merger and alliance of the Cree, Saulteaux, and Assiniboine. However, there is no evidence that the Cowessess band developed a singular distinctive culture. Sharrock's and Albers' conclusions also fail to explain how the Métis, a group supposedly culturally and racially distinct from First Nations, became incorporated into bands.

It seemed to me that the tribal history approach masked the importance that kinship played in band formation and maintenance. The tribal historical approach has been useful for understanding general historical trends of specific cultural and linguistic groups, and provides the context for multicultural bands. In contrast to the fluidity of bands, according to Sharrock, "the membership composition of each tribe or aggregation of bands has been equated with the members of an ethnic unit, with the speakers of an interintelligible language, with territorial corresidents, and with a society comprising the carriers of practitioners of a particular culture."[2] Tribes were culturally and politically bound entities.

Extrapolating band-level relations from those at the tribal level has presented a distorted view of Aboriginal societies. As a doctoral student, Neal McLeod, a member of the James Smith First Nation (located just south of Prince Albert, Saskatchewan), wanted to write a history of the Plains Cree. He soon realized, however, that his project would not be as straightforward as he first thought:

> I had always assumed that my Reserve, James Smith, was a part of the "Plains Cree nation" because that is how my family identified. ... However, as I began to talk to various old people from my Reserve, I became very aware of the contingency the label "Plains Cree" had for my band. I became aware of the ambiguous genealogies that permeated my own family tree, as well as the narrative ironies that emerged when one tried to create a "national" discourse. In addition to the discovery of my own family tree, I became increasingly aware that the situation of James Smith was widespread, and the assertion of a pure, essentialized "Cree" identity (or even a Plains Cree identity) was extremely misleading and limiting.[3]

McLeod came to realize that the people on his reserve, like many in Saskatchewan, were of mixed ancestry. He found that the "reserve system solidified, localized and indeed simplified the linguistic diversity [and therefore the cultural diversity] which once existed in Western Canada."[4] McLeod discovered that members of James Smith were descendants of Plains Cree, Saulteaux, Métis, and Dene people. The tribal-specific approach fails to explain the existence of multicultural bands such as Cowessess and James Smith in the pre-treaty period. Contrary to the tribal view, most Aboriginal bands in the northern plains of Saskatchewan were kin-based and multicultural. Plains Cree, Saulteaux (also known as Chippewa or Western/Plains Ojibwe/Ojibwa), Assiniboine, and Métis individuals shared similar cultural kinship practices that allowed them to integrate others into their bands.

To be clear, multicultural bands like Cowessess did not develop a singular hybridized culture, but rather were able to maintain multiple cultures. This is not to suggest that cultural sharing did not occur, but because there were significant numbers from various cultures within the bands, these individuals were not forced to acculturate to another group. A few examples from Cowessess provide insight into its multicultural nature. In 1914, anthropologist Alanson Skinner published an article that described clan systems amongst the Saulteaux of Manitoba and Saskatchewan. During his visit to Cowessess, a band member informed Skinner that the Saulteaux members of the reserve belonged to one of two clans: Blue Jay or Eagle.[5] Thirty years after settling on the reserve, then, the Saulteaux members of Cowessess band were still known to belong to clans. However, the Plains Cree members of the band did not belong to these clans, a foreign concept in their society. Secondly, Skinner also collected a series of Plains Cree trickster/transformer stories;[6] he published these stories as being Plains Cree in origin, but noted that some were collected from Saulteaux members and were about the Saulteaux trickster/transformer. Finally, there is anecdotal evidence to suggest that some cultural sharing occurred between Plains Cree and Saulteaux band members. One band elder once told me that many of the older people (like my grandfather) spoke a "half-breed Cree" language. This language was not, as I had assumed, a mixture of Cree and English or Cree and French, but rather a mixture of Cree and Saulteaux. Although this elder could understand the language, she did not consider it her language, for she was Assiniboine. Individual band members spoke, or at least understood, more than one language—a number of band members also spoke Michif, the Métis language—and Plains Cree and Saulteaux members maintained their own trickster/transformer stories, which is illustrative of the band's multiculturalism.

Individuals from various cultures were able to coexist in the same band because they shared fairly similar cultural attributes—one such central cultural trait was the way in which kinship was practised. The underlying argument presented in this paper, then, is that the scholarly focus on tribal affiliation ignores the importance of kinship ties as the central unifying factor for Aboriginal groups on the northern plains. Group formation, I contend, was played out at a band level, not a tribal level.

This paper is divided into three sections. The first critiques the use of the term "tribe" put forth by scholars since the 1960s. This is followed by an application of the critique to the standard histories of northern plains people. These histories continue to present tribal histories, which overshadow the role of bands as the primary political and social unit in which northern plains people organized themselves; this, in turn, influences how contemporary Aboriginal groups are viewed. The third section explores the ways that scholars have discussed Métis distinctiveness in comparison with First Nations groups, and argues that these discussions have obscured the close relations between Métis and Plains Cree, Assiniboine, and Saulteaux. Scholars and politicians have created and perpetuated a racialized view of the Métis that acts to ignore their kinship links and cultural similarities with First Nations people. J.R. Miller has challenged researchers to think beyond the artificial differences between the two groups: "investigators of both Indian and Metis history topics really must ask themselves how much longer they are willing to allow obsolete statutory distinctions that were developed in Ottawa in pursuit of bureaucratic convenience and economy to shape their research strategies."[7]

That the term "tribe" is problematic is not a new notion; Morton Fried was the first to point out certain flaws. As summarized by Sharrock, Fried identified two important shortcomings of the term: "1) the validity of tribe as a general stage or level of sociopolitical integration is questionable; and 2) tribe, by non-specific definitions, cannot be correlated completely with any extant or historically well documented, bounded sociocultural unit."[8] For Sharrock, the non-specific definitions of "tribe" are problematic because of "the confounded idea that a tribe is at one and the same time, an ethnic unit, a linguistic unit, a territorial corresidence unit, a cultural unit and societal unit. ... Seldom are these units discretely bounded and correlative in membership composition."[9] Albers also questions the use of the term "tribe" and highlights the importance of kinship:

> The historical situation of the Plains Cree, Assiniboine and the Ojibwa did not conform to typical tribal models where territories were divided, claimed and defended by discrete ethnic groups, nor did it fit descriptions in which political allegiances were defined primarily in exclusive ethnic terms. Ethnicity in the generic and highly abstract sense of a "tribal" name did not always function as marker of geopolitical boundaries. Given a pluralistic pattern of land use and alliance making, most of their ethnic categories did not have a high level of salience or any a priori power to organize and distribute people across geographic space. What appears to have been more important in defining the geopolitics of access to land, labor and resources were social ties based on ties of kinship and sodality in their varied metaphoric extensions and expressions.[10]

However, as mentioned above, Albers does not give serious consideration to how Métis fit within this group dynamic. For Ray Fogelson, "tribe" is an inaccurate reflection of Aboriginal societies, and so he prefers the term "community":[11] "[the] idea of communities is preferable to the idea of tribes, since tribes are politico-legal entities rather than direct face-to-face interactive social groups. Furthermore, in aboriginal and neo-aboriginal times there were very few true tribes, in the sense of institutions with clear lines of political authority, chiefs, councils, and strict membership criteria. ... Tribes were not primordial polities but institutions created to facilitate interactions with states."[12]

Regna Darnell further asserts "that 'tribe' is a highly suspect and thoroughly ethnocentric category, particularly when applied to nomadic hunter-gatherer traditions."[13] Theodore Binnema identifies a particular problem with employing the notion of tribe when studying group relations: "By focusing on a single group such as Crees, the Kutenais, or the Crow, we risk overlooking the important network of relationships that existed between ethnic groups."[14] For most Aboriginal people in general (and Plains Cree, Assiniboine, Saulteaux, and Métis specifically), the network of kinship relations was more important than ethnicity for group identity formation.

By the early 1800s, the Cree, Assiniboine, Saulteaux, and Métis bands were making their presence felt on the northern plains. Social, political, military, and economic alliances among bands from these four groups gave them an advantage in asserting their interests in a highly competitive region. Alliances based on kinship were facilitated by similar social organizations that allowed for incorporation of individuals from other cultural groups. All four groups operated as sets of linked bands, which were politically autonomous units lacking tribal level political organization.[15] For example, in 1937 anthropologist David Rodnick described the historic Assiniboine social and political structure, highlighting the role that kinship played in group formation and maintenance:

> The band was the political unit in Assiniboine life. It was autonomous in nature and completely sovereign. Individual affiliation within the band was loose, since it was relatively simple to form new bands, or for an individual to leave one and join another. An individual called himself a member of the band in which his parents had lived at the time of his birth. Upon marriage he could either elect to remain in his own or else join the band of his wife's people. Due to the fact that such affiliation was not too infrequently changed, the members of a band were normally related to one another.[16]

The Plains Cree, Assiniboine, and Saulteaux bands all followed the Dakota-type kinship system, in which a person's kinship role determined their responsibility to others.[17] A dominant part of this structure was the provision for marriages. The cross/parallel and arranged systems formed the basis of marriages for many Aboriginal groups. Peers and Brown describe the cross/parallel system as: "the children of one's father's brother or mother's sister (i.e. of same-sex siblings); cross cousins are the children of one's father's sister and mother's brother (i.e. of siblings of different sex). Concomitantly, all relatives of one's own genera-tion were grouped either as siblings/parallel cousins (for whom the term was the same); or else they were cross cousins, and potential sweethearts and mates."[18]

Opposite sex cross cousins were eligible, but not exclusive, marriage partners. While people were not confined to marrying their cross cousins, they were freed from the taboos and responsibilities imposed on opposite-sex siblings. By con-trast, parallel cousins treated each other as siblings and were therefore compelled to follow social taboos that strictly forbade marriage. Parallel cousins were also obliged to fulfill supportive roles for each other—roles that were not the primary responsibility of cross cousins.[19] Anthropologists, however, have not commented on how cross/parallel cousin regulations applied (if at all) to second cousins.

Arranged marriages were an important component of the Dakota-type kin-ship system. These marriages occurred either through mutual agreement between parents or by purchase, whereby the groom's family bestowed large amounts of gifts on the prospective bride's family.[20] Arranged marriages allowed bands to create political, economic, and social alliances with other cultural groups, in-cluding Europeans.[21] Multicultural, kinship-based bands were part of a strategy to ensure survival. Albers states that "widening the range of contacts and re-sources to which local groups had access was a sensible strategy for accommo-dating the rapid political, economic and demographic changes taking place in their midst."[22] Kinship alliances between Aboriginal groups accomplished the same objective as it did in the fur trade. Van Kirk describes the function of kin-ship in the fur trade: "from the Aboriginal point of view, cross-cultural unions were a way of integrating the Euro-Canadian stranger into Native kinship net-works and enmeshing him in the reciprocal responsibilities that this entailed."[23]

The notion that tribal boundaries were concrete has been facilitated by the way scholars have described kinship patterns.[24] These writers acknowledge that traditional kinship made an individual's acceptance as a new band member a relatively easy process. For example, David G. Mandelbaum states that for Plains Cree bands "any person who lived in the encampment for some time and who traveled with the group soon came to be known as one of its members."[25] Most new members could trace a kinship link to someone in the band, but this was not always the case. In situations where there were no kinship ties, "marriage into the band usually furnished an immigrant with the social alliances neces-sary for adjustment to the course of communal life. Thus the numbers of each band were constantly augmented by recruits from other bands of Plains Cree, or from other tribes."[26] Mandelbaum recognizes that members of other "tribes" were incorporated into Plains Cree bands, but the implication of this was that these outside tribal members became acculturated to the Plains Cree culture, which ensured that the latter's cultural boundaries were maintained. The result of these scholars' treatment of Saskatchewan's Aboriginal peoples has been to essentialize their identities and blur their multicultural composition.

While some scholars have challenged the notion of the term "tribe," others have continued to describe the inter-group relations at a tribal level. An example of this approach has been used to describe relations between the Saulteaux and Assiniboine. According to Laura Peers and Harold Hickerson, the Saulteaux were on good terms with the Cree, but their relations with the Assiniboine were somewhat more tenuous.[27] They suggest that the cause of the less favourable relations between the Saulteaux and the Assiniboine was competition for depleted resources in the region. Peers supports her position by quoting from the autobiography of John Tanner, an American who had been kidnapped by the Shawnee from his Ohio home as an adolescent in 1792 and was later adopted into an Odawa family. Tanner wrote that the Saulteaux saw the Assiniboine as filthy and brutal, and that "something of our dislike may perhaps be attributed to the habitually unfriendly feeling exists among the Ojibbeways" toward the Assiniboine.[28] Peers also cited the explorers Lewis and Clark, who stated in 1804 that there was a partial state of war existing between the Saulteaux and Assiniboine.[29] Yet by the turn of the century Tanner and his family were living with Cree and Assiniboine in the Pembina Mountain region. Interestingly, Hickerson states that the Cree were not happy with the Saulteaux's westward expansion, an aspect of their relations that Peers ignores to perhaps better highlight the closeness of the two groups. Even though the Cree were not happy with the Saulteaux presence, Hickerson nevertheless notes that the three groups set out together to fight the Sioux.[30] That scholars have often used inter-band relations as examples of inter-tribal relations perhaps helps to explain this seemingly contradictory evidence.

Evidence of warfare of any kind between the Saulteaux and the Assiniboine is rather sketchy. For example, the Lewis and Clark reference to a partial war used by Peers is vague. Lewis and Clark provided lists of characteristics of various First Nations groups of the northern plains, and stated that the Red Lake, Pembina, and Portage la Prairie Saulteaux warred with the "Sioux (or Darcotas) (and partially with the Assiniboine)."[31] They referred twice in the same manner to conflicts between the Saulteaux and Sioux but, despite providing detailed descriptions of battles between other groups in their journal, made no references to any actual conflicts between the Saulteaux and Assiniboine.[32] That the Saulteaux and Assiniboine continued joint economic, military, and social activities at a time when they were supposed to be close to war suggests that their relations were more peaceful than usually described. This is not to suggest that there were no tensions, but rather that any tensions probably occurred at a band level and were not strong enough to result in violence at a tribal level.

There is much more evidence to indicate that the Saulteaux and Assiniboine had a very close relationship. For example, in the late 1790s Tanner and his family arrived in Red River from Michilimackinac, and later met with many Cree and Assiniboine. He described the experience with the Cree and Assiniboine: "we were at length joined by four lodges of Crees. These people are the relations of the Ojibbeways and Ottawwaws, but their language is somewhat different so as not to be readily understood. Their country borders upon that of the Assiniboins, or Stone Roasters; and though they are not relations, nor natural allies, they are sometimes at peace, and are more or less intermixed with each other."[33]

In 1804, some 300 Saulteaux and Assiniboine warriors left Red River to Pembina in search of Sioux.[34] The following year, the Saulteaux travelled with the Assiniboine and Cree to Mandan villages to trade for horses. The Saulteaux also acquired horses from the Assiniboine by trading their medicine. Of the Assiniboine, Tanner wrote that "so many Ojibbways and Crees now live among them that they are most commonly able to understand something of the Ojibbway language."[35] That the nature of the inter-group relations was a band consideration—not a tribal one—is highlighted by Tanner's description of one Cree band's threat of violence against his family "on the account of some old quarrel [that they had] with a band of Ojibbways."[36] This threat of violence by one Cree band against a Saulteaux band highlights the political autonomy of the bands. As Hickerson and Peers outline, the Cree and the Saulteaux had a long-lasting relationship, but this does not mean that periodic conflicts between individual bands did not occur. David Rodnick points out that occasional conflicts occurred even between similar cultural groups. He explains that among the Assiniboine, "inter-band feuds of momentary duration took place occasionally. These, however, were conflicts between two large families, rather than actual band affairs."[37] Tanner's experience with that particular Cree band is a clear indication that tensions occurred between bands, but this did not equate to tribal conflict, a notion that scholars have ignored.

The history of Saskatchewan's Aboriginal people during the 1870s and 1880s is commonly portrayed as the history of the Plains Cree.[38] Although the Saulteaux, Assiniboine, and Métis are present in these and other histories, scholars have usually placed them in the background, subordinate to roles played by Plains Cree. For example, Sarah Carter emphasizes the Plains Cree in her study: "Plains Cree bands in the district covered by Treaty Four, concluded in 1874, are the focus of this study. They lived west of the Saulteaux of the parkland and included Saulteaux, Assiniboine, and mixed-bloods among their number."[39] While Carter acknowledges bands comprised of members from other cultural groups, they are nevertheless portrayed as essentially Plains Cree.

This picture painted by historians is somewhat misleading because the designation Plains Cree often masks a reality of multiculturalism among the bands, especially given that many of the prominent chiefs of this period were of mixed ancestry. For example, Little Pine's mother was Blackfoot and his father was Plains Cree.[40] According to Hugh Dempsey, Poundmaker was the son of an Assiniboine man and a Métis woman who had been adopted by Blackfoot Chief Crowfoot.[41] Chief Big Bear's father is considered to have been a renowned Ojibwe medicine man named Black Powder, who was originally from Ontario and the chief of a mixed Cree and Saulteaux band. The exact ethnicity of Big Bear's mother is not known.[42] Piapot, leader of the Young Dogs, was Cree-Assiniboine.[43] According to Doug Cuthand, Sweet Grass, one of the leading spokesmen in the Treaty Six negotiations, was Gros Ventre, and his mother, according to Allan Turner, was a Crow woman.[44] Pasqua was Plains Cree, but he was also chief of a predominantly Saulteaux band.[45] Although most scholars have been aware of the mixed ancestry of these chiefs, they have usually presented most of them as essentially Plains Cree, ignoring both their multicultural background and that of the bands that they led.

Scholars have also gone to great lengths to emphasize the differences and tensions between Métis and First Nations. John Milloy, for example, points to Plains Cree frustrations with Métis buffalo hunting practices. He cites fur trader John McLean, who noted that the Plains Cree responded to incursions into their hunting territory by attacking small groups of Métis and lighting massive prairie fires to dissuade them from utilizing their hunting territory.[46] Peers contends that the "Métis hunts continued to deplete the dwindling bison herds, and, under such conditions, decades-old resentment against them escalated into real hostility."[47] She also states that the Saulteaux presence in large mixed encampments was not resented in the same way that the presence of the Métis was because the Saulteaux "used and indeed emphasized their kinship with the plains [sic] Cree to gain access to the bison."[48] According to Greg Camp, the European cultural influence of the Métis caused friction between them and the Saulteaux in the Turtle Mountain region.[49] Although the Turtle Mountain Chippewa had complained to fur traders and American officials about Métis hunting practices, they had become economically and socially intertwined with the Métis. Nonetheless, Camp states that "the mixed-blood presence south of the [American] border was no less a threat to the food supply of the full-bloods."[50]

Describing relations between the Assiniboine, Plains Cree, Saulteaux, and Métis in the Cypress Hills, Sharrock cites fur trader Isaac Cowie, who mentioned a combined encampment of these group, where the "Indians kept the Métis under constant surveillance, besides subjecting them to many other 'annoyances.'"[51] This action was apparently due to a level of distrust that the other groups had for Métis hunting practices. In describing the relations between these groups, Sharrock states, "based on documentable degrees of interrelatedness, the Assiniboine were most closely interrelated with the Cree-Assiniboine [a new distinct ethnic group that emerged from the interaction of the Cree and Assiniboine], and the Cree with the Saulteaux. The united Assiniboine and Cree-Assiniboine acted as a unit in opposition to the Cree and Saulteaux forces, and the entire northeastern plains grouping acted in opposition to the half-blood Métis."[52]

Sharrock's assessment appears to have been influenced by Cowie's own negative view of the Cree-Assiniboine, known as the Young Dogs. Cowie had had some unpleasant interactions with some Cree-Assiniboine and placed them in contrast to other groups. He wrote, "The Young-Dogs might be most fittingly expressed by calling them the sons of the female canine."[53] In discussing the factors that led to the creation of a distinct Cree-Assiniboine culture, Sharrock outlines the problems with tribal categories, but by privileging Cowie's views in describing the interactions between the Cree-Assiniboine band and other bands, she reifies the very tribal boundaries that she seeks to challenge. Her descriptions disregard the fact that most of the other bands at Cypress Hills were culturally mixed groups, even though they may not have developed a hybridized culture like the Young Dogs. The problem, it appears, is that Sharrock considered bands to be monocultural, not multicultural. This misconception led her to discuss the differences both among First Nations groups as well as between Métis and First Nations groups.

The emphasis on tension between Métis and First Nations' groups belies the fact that these groups were closely related, and is underscored by the actual level of conflict that existed in comparison to other Aboriginal groups. That the Plains Cree, Assiniboine, and Saulteaux fought many battles against other First Nations is well documented. Although there may be references to conflict between the Plains Cree, Assiniboine, and Saulteaux and the Métis, there are no actual accounts of any battles. This suggests that the Plains Cree, Assiniboine, and Saulteaux treated the Métis differently than, say, how they treated the Blackfoot, where stolen horses could spark a violent response. The Plains Cree, Assiniboine, and Saulteaux were concerned about Métis buffalo hunting practices, but they attempted to settle the situation by expressing their concerns to fur traders, keeping the Métis under surveillance and subjecting them to "annoyances," or lighting prairie fires. Considering the central importance of the buffalo to their own economic, social, and spiritual well-being, it is surprising that there are no accounts of the Plains Cree, Assiniboine, and Saulteaux waging war on the Métis. At most, there were only small attacks.

The close relations between First Nations and Métis people meant that Plains Cree, Assiniboine, and Saulteaux bands were unwilling to wage war against the Métis, even though the latter were infringing on an important social and economic resource. These ties help to explain why there were Métis who fought alongside their First Nations relatives in battles against other First Nations groups. The level of tension and the different treatment—vis-à-vis other Aboriginal groups—between Plains Cree, Assiniboine, Saulteaux, and Métis has been glossed over by scholars, whose work has unjustifiably emphasized differences between First Nations and Métis. Any tension that occurred between Métis bands and the Cree, Assiniboine, and Saulteaux bands does not appear to have been any more significant than tensions that occurred between the bands of these First Nations.

The reason for the lack of warfare is likely to have been due to kinship ties between the groups. The close relation between First Nations and Métis is highlighted by the degree of intermarriage. As noted earlier, Chief Poundmaker's mother is reputed to have been Métis. This was not a lone example; Chief Little Bone, or Michel Cardinal, was of Saulteaux/Métis ancestry, and had many wives who were either Saulteaux or Métis, or both.[54] Chief Gabriel Cote, or the Pigeon, was the son of a Saulteaux mother and Métis man.[55] Heather Devine suggests that Chief Cowessess may have been Marcel Desjarlais, who was of Saulteaux and Métis ancestry.[56] The father of another Cowessess chief, Louis O'Soup, was named Michel Cardinal.[57] Although the Métis had developed a separate culture, it contained enough common points that they were able to marry into these bands without any significant disruptions to either group.

The close relations and similar cultural features between the Métis and Plains Cree, Assiniboine, and Saulteaux is illustrated both by the fact that many bands contained Métis members as well as the chiefs' desire to have Métis included in the treaties. During Treaty Four negotiations in 1874, for example, Chief Kamooses (also spelled Kanooses) requested that the Métis be included in the treaty.[58] Two years later, at the Treaty Six negotiations, Chief Mistawasis also requested that his Métis relatives be included in the treaty.[59] In 1881 in the Cypress Hills, Chiefs Lucky Man and Little Pine made similar requests.[60] That same year, the governor-general—the Marquis of Lorne—visited the Northwest Territories and met with First Nations leaders at Fort Qu'Appelle. The spokesperson for the assembled chiefs was Louis O'Soup. Among the list of grievance O'Soup presented to Lorne was a request that the Métis be included in the treaties.[61] Even after the government refused to enter into treaty negotiations with the Métis, many simply joined their relatives in bands that had been recognized as Indian. This would not have been possible were they not closely linked by kinship and culture.

There can be little doubt that the presence of the Métis has added a certain complexity to intra-Aboriginal relations. This complexity has been due in no small part to outsiders' attempts to understand the impact of the racial make-up of the Métis. Since the 1970s, scholars have purported to understand the Métis by concentrating on their cultural rather than racial attributes, the practice of earlier scholars.[62] Nonetheless, the notion of race is still embedded in discussions about Métis people. That is to say, scholars have implicitly categorized Métis as a racial category distinct from First Nations people. For example, Métis are frequently described as cultural brokers, cultural mediators, or bicultural because of their ability to straddle First Nation and European cultures. However, First Nations were also cultural brokers, cultural mediators, and were bicultural or even multicultural. There were many First Nations people and groups who, to varying degrees, acculturated themselves to various European practices and values. These individuals or communities, however, have not usually been viewed as cultural mediators in the same way as have the Métis. The difference is that historical and contemporary outsiders have viewed the Métis and First Nations through racialized lenses.

For many years, scholars' myopic view of the Red River Métis has worked to reinforce the static nature of Métis cultural expression.[63] Although recent scholars of Métis history are beginning to look "beyond Red River" and provide new views of Métis history, many tend to have simply replaced Red River Métis with Plains Métis as representing the prototypical Métis.[64] As Brenda Macdougall states in her study of Île à la Crosse Métis in northern Saskatchewan, "it would seem that Red River myopia has given way to a Plains—whether Canadian or

American—myopia that still constrains our ability to recognize the diversity of the Métis experience in Canada. It is an unwillingness to acknowledge that the ethnogenesis of a new people was dynamic, occurring in different regions at different times as the fur trade expanded and contracted."[65] As a result, the undertaking of massive buffalo hunts, acceptance of Roman Catholicism, French language usage, the wearing of a combination of European and First Nations clothing, and other markers are viewed as cultural standards for all Métis. The presence of such a dominant expression of Métis culture has made it difficult to acknowledge the possibility that a diverse range of Métis cultural forms exists.

The scholarly discussion of the existence of proto-Métis bands also heightens the racial and cultural differences between Métis and First Nations groups. John Foster has identified the processes, later expanded upon by Heather Devine, that allowed mixed ancestry people to move from "proto-Métis" into "full-blown Métis" identities.[66] He asserts that the relationships between European fur traders and First Nations men played a crucial role in this process. Foster claims that the development of a Métis identity occurred in a two-stage process involving independent traders—usually of French origin and known as freemen or, as Foster labels them, outsider adult males. The first stage saw the outsider adult male marry into an Indian band and develop a close relationship with the adult male members of the band and other outsider adult males. After becoming sufficiently assimilated into the band's social and political culture, the freemen would establish their own bands with their Indian wives and children. Foster attributes the ethos of the adult French Canadian males as the motivating factor for leaving their wives' bands and establishing their own. This ethos among French men "emphasized the necessity of being a man of consequence in one's own eyes and in the eyes of one's fellows"—that is, other adult French Canadian males.[67] In this milieu, outsider adult males were characterized as having a large degree of assertiveness, apparently in contrast to First Nations men.

These bands, as Foster and Devine have argued, were proto-Métis—that is, they were still too Indian, yet not European enough to be considered truly Métis. The argument runs that after two or three generations of adopting and adapting European cultural influences with those of First Nations' culture, these proto-Métis developed new expressions that were different than either parent cultures—they became a "new nation."[68]

The flaw in this thinking, however, is that when First Nations groups adopted and adapted European culture, they were not considered anything less than First Nations. Indeed, First Nations' cultures have changed—the difference, however, is that there is an implicit racial component when discussing the Métis that is absent when discussing First Nations' cultural change. The concept of proto-Métis is predicated on the interpretation that there have always been significant differences between Métis and First Nations cultures. It is built on the assumption that the Red River Métis culture is the only Métis culture and those Métis groups who exhibited a higher level of First Nations cultural characteristics than European must therefore not be Métis. This denies not only the diversity of cultural expressions, but any possibility that Métis culture has the ability to change in response to temporal and spatial factors in the same way as First Nations' groups. Depending on the location and period, various Métis groups responded differently to external factors, which means that more than one kind of Métis culture must have emerged.

One challenge to the race-based theories of ethnogenesis is to view the freemen not as "Indianized Frenchmen," as Ruth Swan states, but as actual Métis.[69] Historians do not consider the freemen to be Aboriginal because they were Europeans. However, upon marrying into First Nations bands the freemen became sufficiently culturally competent to gain the confidence of their bands. If they were unable to demonstrate an ability to secure the physical and cultural survival of their wives and children, it is unlikely that the freemen's new relatives would have allowed them to form their own bands. The freemen would have been immersed in First Nations culture, but they would not have expunged their French cultural heritage—they would have become bicultural. They would have passed to their children aspects of their French culture, but they also would have transmitted the cultural norms of their First Nations in-laws to ensure that their children could operate successfully within this social and cultural environment.

While the French freemen brought both their French culture and acquired First Nations cultural knowledge into their marriages, First Nations women continued to pass on their own cultural knowledge to their children. Macdougall describes the role that women had in the development of Métis culture: "as Aboriginal women married outsider adult male fur traders, they brought to their marriages attitudes and beliefs—indeed, a worldview—about family and social life that influenced the creation of a Métis socio-cultural identity. Furthermore, that these families lived in the lands of their maternal relatives and, as was the case of the Île à la Crosse Métis and spoke the languages of those maternal cultures certainly shaped their worldview."[70] Macdougall further states, "far removed from emerging centres of Red River and non-Native settlement, in regions such as northwestern Saskatchewan the reality was that family life, and in particular these female-centred family networks," were central to the advent of Métis culture.[71] It was the women's kinship links that enabled new bands to be established, and it was the maintenance of these links that allowed the bands to survive. By highlighting the role of Aboriginal women, Macdougall not only challenges the emphasis placed on the French freemen, but also sheds light onto the importance that First Nations cultural practices had in Métis cultural development. The weight given to Métis European-ness has unfairly overshadowed First Nations culture in the emerging Métis culture. I suggest that this overshadowing is due to the scholarly tendency to view Aboriginal people at a tribal level—not a band level—and to view the Métis in racial terms instead of cultural terms.

By viewing these new Métis groups from a band-level perspective instead of a tribal level, it becomes apparent that they were culturally different from their parent band because of the bicultural nature of the freemen and, to a lesser extent, their First Nations wives. This cultural difference between the new Métis and First Nations bands may not have been as great as it would become in later years, when some Métis groups underwent significant cultural change. Certainly, this does not mean that all freemen would have been Métis; however, acknowledging the "Métis-ness" of the freemen eliminates the issue of race when discussing Métis culture and allows for change, adaptation, and a range in Métis cultural expression. Viewing Métis from a band perspective also challenges the notion that Métis cultural expressions differed greatly from those of First Nations. Realizing this, perhaps, helps to explain continued political, military, economic, and social alliances between these groups.

Nicole St-Onge has recently suggested that scholars have overlooked Métis/Saulteaux relations during the mid-nineteenth century in St. Paul des Saulteaux, located on the western edge of the Red River colony.[72] St-Onge states that scholars since the early 1980s have accepted the notion that the Métis "had endogamous tendencies by the early and mid nineteenth century with men occasionally bringing native-Indian wives into the community and Métis women also occasionally incorporating Euro-Canadians, white merchants and voyageurs in the fold."[73] However, her examination of church and census records shows that, in contrast to previous research, there was actually a high rate of intermarriage between the two groups. The prominence of a notion of Métis endogamy emphasizes the cultural differences between the Métis and Saulteaux and other First Nations groups. This difference is epitomized by the (mis)characterization of buffalo hunting as belonging to the Métis and fishing, trapping, tapping for syrup, and salt making as to the domain of the Saulteaux. However, as St-Onge points out, Métis women who married Saulteaux men became involved in Saulteaux economic activities. The intermixing of these two groups "indicates that, prior to 1870, ethnic identities were fluid, relational and situational."[74] The Métis and Saulteaux shared sufficient cultural kinship practices to allow for the incorporation of new members: "given the practices of incorporation and inclusiveness of both the Métis and Saulteaux, there was no reason or necessity in the course of their lives for residents of the Northwest to limit themselves to one identity. If mechanisms existed in both Métis and Saulteaux communities to incorporate European outsiders into extensive family networks, it was all the easier for people already closely allied to merge with either or both communities as circumstances dictated."[75]

St-Onge reminds us that First Nations and Métis groups had the social mechanisms to integrate Europeans into their groups, yet the idea that First Nations and Métis could join each other's group has not been considered. Scholars simply have not recognized that the two groups shared similar cultural kinship understandings. However, as St-Onge states, an "initial conclusion advanced here is that converging histories, economic pursuits and kinship ties were blurring the ethnic distinction between the Métis and their close allies, the Ojibwa-Saulteaux, and perhaps others, as the nineteenth century progressed."[76] Scholars' inability to see the cultural similarities is due to a tendency to highlight the cultural differences between First Nations and Métis people. That tendency itself has been fuelled by an implicitly racial view of these groups. St-Onge's findings, then, are significant because they help to explain how Métis individuals could be incorporated into bands and even become leaders.

The legal status of Métis, as Miller has noted, has guided the scholarly agenda and popular conceptions of the Métis. The Métis as a group did not sign treaties with the Canadian government nor are they considered Indian under the *Indian Act*. As a result, the Métis fall under a different legal classification than do First Nations. Unlike First Nations, the Métis are the responsibility of provincial governments. In recent years, there have been legal arguments put forth that the Métis should be considered Indians under Section 91(24) of the Canadian Constitution.[77] However, this argument is greatly undermined because outsiders have viewed the Métis as "not Indian," regardless of close relations or cultural similarities, for over two centuries. Some First Nations people continue to hold the view that Métis are "not Indian"; from this perspective, it follows that Indians are more culturally Aboriginal than Métis and therefore have a stronger claim to Aboriginal rights, thus raising the issue of cultural authenticity. For some First

Nations leaders and First Nations people of Métis ancestry, then, acknowledging the close relationship with the Métis or Métis ancestry could be viewed as detrimental in terms of rights and entitlements. These contemporary tensions are similar to the historic tensions, for access to resources is the central issue.

This is not to suggest that no First Nations leaders have acknowledged their ties to the Métis. In September 2007, for example, comments by Richard John, the former chief of One Arrow First Nation, illustrate that the close ties between First Nations and Métis have not been forgotten by some contemporary First Nations. According to Blair Stonechild and Bill Waiser, the Métis forced Chief One Arrow and other First Nations to participate in armed conflict against the Canadian government at Batoche during the 1885 Resistance.[78] According to John's family history, however, Chief One Arrow willingly joined the conflict. John notes, "There are friendships [between residents of One Arrow and the neighbouring Métis at Batoche] right through to this day. We help each other and it has been that way from prior to 1885."[79]

What is the implication of viewing Aboriginal groups from a band perspective rather than a tribal perspective? Should scholars discard tribal terms completely? There is agreement among some ethnohistorians that tribal designations are a European construction and were applied to Aboriginal groups somewhat haphazardly.[80] Abandoning tribal categories would not only be difficult, it may not even be desirable. Plains Cree, Saulteaux, Assiniboine, and Métis cultural groups did exist; while they shared many similarities, there were undeniable cultural traits that differentiated them. It was these cultural differences that made the bands and the individuals in the bands multicultural. Even individuals who were not of mixed ancestry were multicultural. It will not be an easy task to ascertain how many bands were multicultural, or, if they were, to what degree they were multicultural. In addition, given the colonial imposition of the outsider's definition, many contemporary Aboriginal people have, as McLeod notes, "essentialized" their cultural identities. For many Aboriginal people, cultural affiliation is vital.

However, contemporary kinship patterns—at least among Cowessess people and likely for other First Nations as well—ensure that band members' collective identity survives. Cowessess people's attitudes are shaped within the context of family/kinship connections, not by externally defined tribal or cultural affiliations. A person's family name places that person within the familial reserve context. This is not to claim that cultural affiliation is totally ignored, but rather that it is not the primary identifier that connects people—certainly not in the way that family/kinship does. For Cowessess people, family/kinship ties are of greater importance to identity than place of residence, gender, cultural affiliation, or notions of race. To outsiders, members may say that they are Plains Cree or Saulteaux, but what is really important is to which families they are related. This kinship pattern is historically based and it is what most historians have not fully articulated.

The concept of tribe, with its well-defined cultural boundaries, and the notion of Métis as a culturally and racially distinct group from First Nations does not explain the multicultural composition of many Saskatchewan First Nations. The role and function of kinship practices, however, provide a greater understanding of Saskatchewan First Nations, and help to explain the motivation of historic intra-Aboriginal relations in the northern plains.

Notes

1   Patricia Albers, "Symbiosis, Merger, and War: Contrasting Forms of Intertribal Relations Among Historic Plains Indians," in *The Political Economy of North American Indians*, ed. John H. Moore (Norman: University of Oklahoma, 1993), 94–132; Patricia Albers, "Changing Patterns on Ethnicity in the Northeastern Plains," in *History, Power, and Identity: Ethnogenesis in the Americas, 1492–1992*, ed. Jonathon Hill (Iowa City: University of Iowa Press, 1996), 90–188; and Susan Sharrock, "Crees, Cree-Assiniboines, and Assiniboines: Interethnic Social Organization on the Far Northern Plains," *Ethnohistory* 21, 2 (1974): 95–122.

2   Sharrock, "Crees, Cree-Assiniboines, and Assiniboines," 95.

3   Neal McLeod, "Plains Cree Identity: Borderlands, Ambiguous Genealogies and Narrative Irony," *Canadian Journal of Native Studies* 20, 2 (2000): 437–454.

4   Ibid., 441.

5   Alanson Skinner, "The Cultural Position of the Plains Ojibway," *American Anthropologist* 16, 2 (1914): 314–318.

6   Alanson Skinner, "Plains Cree Tales," *Journal of American Folklore* 29, 113 (1916): 341–367.

7   J.R. Miller, "From Riel to the Metis," *Canadian Historical Review* 96, 1 (1988): 19.

8   Sharrock, "Cree, Cree-Assiniboine, and Assiniboines," 97.

9   Ibid.

10 Albers, "Changing Patterns on Ethnicity," 91.

11 Raymond D. Fogelson, "Perspectives on Native American Identity," in *Studying Native America: Problems and Prospects*, ed. Russell Thornton (Madison: University of Wisconsin Press, 1998), 51.

12 Ibid.

13 Regna Darnell, "Rethinking the Concepts of Band and Tribe, Community and Nation: An Accordion Model of Nomadic Native American Social Organization," in *Papers of the Twenty-Ninth Algonquian Conference*, ed. David Pentland (Winnipeg: University of Manitoba Press, 1998), 93.

14 Theodore Binnema, *Common Contested Ground: A Human and Environmental History of the Northwestern Plains* (Toronto: University of Toronto Press, 2004), 12.

15 Heather Devine, *The People Who Own Themselves: Aboriginal Ethnogenesis in a Canadian Family, 1660–1900* (Calgary: University of Calgary Press, 2004); David G. Mandelbaum, *The Plains Cree: An Ethnographic, Historical, and Comparative Study* (Regina: Canadian Plains Research Center, 1979); Laura Peers, *The Ojibwa of Western Canada, 1780–1870* (Winnipeg: University of Manitoba Press, 1994); David Rodnick, "Political Structure and Status Among the Assiniboine Indians," *American Anthropologist* 39, 3 (1937): 408–416; Laren Ritterbush, "Culture Change and Continuity: Ethnohistoric Analysis of Ojibwa and Ottawa Adjustment to the Prairies" (PhD diss., University of Kansas, 1990).

16 Rodnick, "Political Structure," 408.

17 See, for example, Patricia Albers, "The Plains Ojibwa," in *Handbook of North American Indians, Vol. 13, Part 1*, ed. Raymond J. DeMallie (Washington, DC: Smithsonian Institute, 2001), 652–660; Raymond DeMallie and David Reed Miller, "The Assiniboine," in *Handbook of North American Indians, Vol. 13, Part 1*, ed. Raymond J. DeMallie (Washington, DC: Smithsonian Institute, 2001), 572–582; Robert Lowie, "The Assiniboine," in *Anthropological Papers of the American Museum of Natural History, Vol. IV, Part 1* (New York, 1909); Mandelbaum, *The Plains Cree*; Peers, *The Ojibwa of Western Canada*, Laura Peers and Jennifer S.H. Brown, "There is No End to Relationship

Among the Indians: Ojibwa Families and Kinship in Historical Perspective," *The History of the Family: An International Quarterly* 4, 4 (1999): 529–555.

18 Peers and Brown, "No End to Relationship," 533.

19 Ibid.

20 Raymond DeMallie, "Kinship and Biology in Sioux Culture," in *North American Indian Anthropology: Essays on Society and Culture*, eds. Raymond J. DeMallie and Alfonso Ortiz (Norman: University of Oklahoma Press, 1994), 108–124.

21 Albers, "Symbiosis, Merger, and War"; Jennifer S.H. Brown, *Strangers in Blood: Fur Trade Company Families in Indian Country* (Vancouver: University of British Columbia Press, 1980); Sharrock, "Cree, Cree-Assiniboine, and Assiniboines"; Sylvia Van Kirk, *Many Tender Ties: Women in Fur-Trade Society, 1670–1870* (Norman: University of Oklahoma Press, 1983); Bruce White, "'Give Us a Little Milk': The Social and Cultural Significance of Gift Giving in the Lake Superior Fur Trade," in *Rendezvous: Selected Papers of the Fourth North American Fur Trade Conference*, ed. Thomas S. Buckley (St. Paul, MN: University of Minnesota, 1984), 185–196; Bruce White, "The Woman Who Married a Beaver: Trade Patterns and Gender Roles in the Ojibwa fur trade," in *Expression in Canadian Native Studies*, eds. Ron. F. Laliberte et al. (Saskatoon: University of Saskatchewan Extension Press, 2000), 178–121.

22 Albers, "Changing Patterns on Ethnicity," 114.

23 Sylvia Van Kirk, "'Marrying-In' to 'Marrying-Out': Aboriginal/Non-Aboriginal Marriage in Colonial Canada," *Frontiers* 23, 3 (2002): 4.

24 See, for example, Mandelbaum, *The Plains Cree*; and Peers and Brown, "No End to Relationship."

25 Mandelbaum, *The Plains Cree*, 105–106.

26 Ibid., 106.

27 Peers, *The Ojibwa of Western Canada*; Harold Hickerson, "The Genesis of a Trading Post Band: The Pembina Chippewa," *Ethnohistory* 3, 4 (1956): 289–345.

28 John Tanner, *The Falcon: A Narrative of the Captivity and Adventures of John Tanner* (New York: Penguin Books, 2000), 38.

29 Ibid., 44.

30 Hickerson, "The Genesis of a Trading Post Band," 310.

31 Gary E. Moulton, ed., *The Lewis and Clark Journals: An American Epic of Discovery: The Abridgment of the Definitive Nebraska Edition Meriwether Lewis, William Clark, and Members of the Corps of Discovery* (Lincoln: University of Nebraska Press, 2003), 441–443. Emphasis in original.

32 Ibid., 305, 317.

33 Tanner, *The Falcon*, 31.

34 Peers, *The Ojibwa of Western Canada*, 9.

35 Ibid., 132.

36 Ibid., 79.

37 Rodnick, "Political Structure," 409.

38 For example, see Sarah Carter, *Lost Harvests: Prairie Indian Farmers and Government Policy* (Montreal/Kingston: McGill/Queen's University Press, 1990); John Tobias, "Canada's Subjugation of the Plains Cree, 1879–1885," in *Out of the Background: Readings on Canadian Native History*, eds. Robin Fisher and Kenneth Coates (1982; reprint, Toronto: Copp Clark Pitman Ltd, 1998), 150–176; Michel Hogue, "Disputing the Medicine Line: The Plains Cree and the Canadian-American Border, 1876–1885," *Montana: The Magazine of Western History* 52 (2002): 2–17; and Katherine Pettipas,

Severing the Ties That Bind: Government Repression of Indigenous Religious Ceremonies of the Prairies (Winnipeg: University of Manitoba Press, 1994). Although the focus of the articles by Tobias and Hogue is Plains Cree and Pettipas' book examines prairie First Nations' responses to government religious suppression, many of the bands and individuals whom they discuss were of mixed ancestry. For example, Pettipas' second chapter, "The Ties That Bind: The Plains Cree," places the Plains Cree at the centre of her examination.

39   Carter, *Lost Harvest*, 45.

40   John Tobias, "Payipwat," in *Dictionary of Canadian Biography Online*, http://www.biographi.ca/EN/ShowBio.asp?BioId=41111&query=Payipwat.

41   Hugh Dempsey, "P_tikwahanapiw_yin (Poundmaker)," in *Dictionary of Canadian Biography Online*, http://www.biographi.ca/EN/ShowBio.asp?BioId=39905&query=Poundmaker.

42   Hugh Dempsey, *Big Bear: The End of Freedom* (Lincoln: University of Nebraska Press; Vancouver: Douglas and McIntyre, 1984).

43   John Tobias, "Payipwat," in *Dictionary of Canadian Biography Online*, http://www.biographi.ca/EN/ShowBio.asp?BioId=41111&query=Payipwat.

44   Doug Cuthand, *Askiwina: A Cree World* (Regina: Coteau Books, 2007); Allan R. Turner, "Wikaskokiseyin, also written Wee-Kas-Kookee-Sey-Yin, Called Sweet Grass," in *Dictionary of Canadian Biography Online*, http://www.biographi.ca/EN/ShowBio.asp?BioId=39439&query=Sweet%20AND%20Grass.

45   Kenneth Tyler, "PASKWÜW, Pasquah, "The Plain," in *Dictionary of Canadian Biography Online*, http://www.biographi.ca/EN/ShowBio.asp?BioId=39874&query=PaskwŸw.

46   John S. Milloy, *The Plains Cree: Trade, Diplomacy, and War, 1780 to 1870* (Winnipeg, University of Manitoba Press, 1988), 107.

47   Peers, *The Ojibwa of Western Canada*, 186.

48   Ibid., 187.

49   Greg Camp, "The Turtle Mountain Plains-Chippewa and Métis, 1797–1935" (PhD diss., University of New Mexico, 1987), 42.

50   Ibid., 75.

51   Sharrock, "Cree, Cree-Assiniboine, and Assiniboines," 113.

52   Ibid., 114.

53   Cited in Sharrock, "Cree, Cree-Assiniboine, and Assiniboines," 113.

54   Devine, *The People Who Own Themselves*, 120.

55   John Tobias, cited in Lawrence Barkwell and Lyle N. Longclaws, "History of the Plains-Ojibway and the Waywayseecapo First Nation" (unpublished manuscript, 1996), 95–96.

56   Devine, *The People Who Own Themselves*, 132.

57   Sarah Carter, "O'Soup, Louis," in *Dictionary of Canadian Biography Online*, http://www.biographi.ca/EN/ ShowBio.asp?BioId=41754&query=cowessess.

58   Alexander Morris, *The Treaties of Canada with the Indians of Manitoba and the Northwest Territories Including the Negotiations on Which They Were Based* (Belfords, Clarke and Co., 1880; reprint, Toronto: Prospero Books, 1991), 119.

59   Ibid., 222.

60   Hogue, "Disputing the Medicine Line," 10.

61   Carter, "O'Soup, Louis."

62   See, for example, Brown, *Strangers in Blood*; Jennifer S.H. Brown, "Woman as Centre and Symbol in the Emergence of Métis Communities," *Canadian Journal of Native Studies* 3 (1983): 39–46; Olive Dickason, "From 'One Nation' in the Northeast to 'New Nation' in the Northwest: A Look at the Emergence of the Métis," in *The New Peoples: Being and Becoming Métis in North America,* eds. Jacqueline Peterson and Jennifer S.H. Brown (Winnipeg: University of Manitoba Press, 1985), 19–36; John Foster, "Some Questions and Perspectives on the Problem of Métis Roots," in *The New Peoples,* eds. Peterson and Brown, 73–91; John Foster, "The Origins of the Mixed Bloods in the Canadian West," in *Essays on Western History: In Honour of Lewis Gwynne Thomas,* ed. Lewis H. Thomas (Edmonton: University of Alberta Press, 1976), 71–80; Harriet Gorham, "Families of Mixed Descent in the Western Great Lakes Region," in *Native People, Native Lands: Canadian Indians, Inuit and Métis,* ed. Brian A. Cox (Ottawa: Carleton University Press, 1988), 37–55; Jacqueline Peterson, "Prelude to Red River: A Social Portrait of the Great Lake Métis," *Ethnohistory* 25, 1 (1978): 41–67; Jacqueline Peterson, "Ethnogenesis: Settlement and Growth of a 'New People,'" *Journal of Indian Culture and Research* 6, 2 (1982): 23–64; Jacqueline Peterson, "Many Roads to Red River: Métis Genesis in the Great Lakes Region, 1680–1815," in *The New Peoples,* eds. Peterson and Brown, 37–72; and Van Kirk, *Many Tender Ties.*

63   Miller, "From Riel to the Métis."

64   "Beyond Red River: New Views of Métis History Symposium," Michigan State University, 2006.

65   Brenda Macdougall, "*Wahkootowin:* Family and Cultural Identity in Northwestern Saskatchewan Métis Communities," *Canadian Historical Review* 87, 3 (2006): 439.

66   Foster, "Some Questions and Perspectives"; John Foster, "'Wintering,' the Outsider Adult Male and the Ethnogenesis of the Western Plains Métis," *Prairie Forum* 19, 1 (1994): 1–13; Devine, *The People Who Own Themselves.*

67   Foster, "'Wintering,'" 9.

68   Arthur S. Morton, "The New Nation: The Métis," in *The Other Natives: The/Les Métis, Volume 1, 1700–1885,* eds. Antoine S. Lussier and Bruce D. Sealey (Winnipeg: Manitoba Métis Federation Press. 1978), 27–38.

69   Ruth Swan, "The Crucible: Pembina and the Origins of the Red River Valley Métis," (Ph.D. diss., University of Manitoba, 2003). Swan's use of the term "Indianized Frenchmen" is in reference to individual French Canadian traders who lived among First Nations groups and adopted their customs and culture rather than those freemen who formed their own bands.

70   Macdougall, *Wahkootowin,* 437–438.

71   Ibid., 456.

72   Nicole St-Onge, "Uncertain Margins: Métis and Saulteaux in St-Paul des Saulteaux, Red River, 1821–1870," *Manitoba History* 53 (2006): 2–10.

73   Ibid., 3.

74   Ibid., 9.

75   Ibid.

76   Ibid., 10.

77   Dale Gibson, "When is a Métis an Indian? Some Consequences of Federal Constitutional Jurisdiction over Métis," in *Who are Canada's Aboriginal Peoples?: Definition, Recognition, and Jurisdiction,* ed. L.A.H. Chartrand (Saskatoon: Purich Publishing, 2001), 258–267.

78   Blair Stonechild and Bill Waiser, *Loyal Till Death: Indians and The North-West Rebellion* (Calgary: Fifth House, 1997).

79 John Lagimodiere, "Historians Chided for Misinformation," *Eagle Feather News* 10, 9 (2007): 6.

80 Darnell, "Rethinking the Concepts of Band and Tribe," 97. See also K.A.C. Dawson, "Historic Populations of Northwestern Ontario," in *Papers of the Seventh Algonquian Conference, 1975*, ed. William Cowan (Ottawa: Carleton University, 1976), 157–174; Beryl C. Gillespie, "Territorial Expansion of the Chipewyan in the 18th Century," in *Proceedings: The Northern Athapaskan Conference* (National Museum of Canada, Mercury Series, Publications in Ethnology, No. 27, 1975), 350–388; Adolph Greenberg and James Morrison, "Group Identities in the Boreal Forest: The Origin of the Northern Ojibwa," *Ethnohistory* 29, 2 (1982): 75–102; Dale Russell, *Eighteenth-Century Western Cree and Their Neighbours* (Ottawa: Canadian Museum of Civilization, Archaeological Survey of Canada, 1991); Theresa M. Schenck, *"The Voice of the Crane Echoes Afar": The Sociopolitical Organization of the Lake Superior Ojibwa, 1640-1855* (New York: Garland Publishing, 1997); James E.G. Smith, "On the Territorial Distribution of the Western Woods Cree," in *Papers of the Seventh Algonquian Conference, 1975*, ed. William Cowan (Ottawa: Carleton University, 1976), 414–435; and C.J. Wheeler, "The Historic Assiniboine: A Territorial Dispute in the Ethnographic Literature," in *Actes du 8e Congress des Algoquinists*, ed. William Cowan (Ottawa: Carleton University, 1977), 115–123.

"A World We Have Lost": The Plural Society of Fort Chipewyan[1]

Patricia A. McCormack

Introduction

TWO REMARKABLE BOOKS THAT EXAMINED SOCIAL SYSTEMS of the fur trade were published in 1980: Sylvia Van Kirk's *"Many Tender Ties": Women in Fur-Trade Society in Western Canada, 1670–1870* and Jennifer Brown's *Strangers in Blood: Fur Trade Company Families in Indian Country.* These studies shifted fur trade studies toward greater consideration of the social contexts within which the fur trade occurred, as well as those which developed as an outcome of the trade. Van Kirk argued that "the fur trade generated a distinctive regional way of life,"[2] neither Indian nor European, but which "combined both European and Indian elements to produce a distinctive, self-perpetuating community."[3] While she did not provide a detailed picture of this way of life, she pointed to some of its elements, particularly the economic and mediatory roles played by women. It was clearly neither homogeneous nor a simple synthesis of its different components. It was instead a plural society, in which a multiplicity of residents—Aboriginal and non-Aboriginal alike—operated by means of an over-arching fur trade mode of production. It was therefore a unique form of multiculturalism that predated the much vaunted multiculturalism of the modern Canadian state.

Van Kirk and Brown both ended their study of fur-trade society in 1870, with the establishment of what Van Kirk termed "a modern, agrarian British society" in the Northwest, although that occurred primarily in the parkland and plains, where European settlers took up homesteads and established farms and ranches.

146

In the northern fringes of the parkland and the subarctic forests, lands less suitable for agriculture, the fur trade and its distinctive social configuration persisted well into the twentieth century and arguably still exists in some modest dimension even today. In northern Alberta and adjacent regions, it began to be undermined only after Treaty 8 was signed in 1899. The treaty opened the door to a state-sanctioned capitalist mode of production, accompanied by new land uses and restrictive regulatory structures that were facilitated by systematic racism directed at Aboriginal people. The resistance to these new processes by local people—especially Aboriginal but not exclusively so—provides additional perspectives on the way of life and the relations of power they were trying to protect.[4]

This article builds on the work of Van Kirk and others in detailing the structure of one regional plural society, the fur trade world at Fort Chipewyan, an important trade centre on Lake Athabasca in what is now northern Alberta. One of its goals is to lay the groundwork for the long overdue study of such distinctive plural societies, as opposed to the persistent tendency to reduce the world of the fur trade to simplistic oppositions between colonizers and the colonized and the homogenization of the people of the Northwest into "Indians," "Métis," or "traders." It draws on Mary Louise Pratt's concept of a "contact zone," "the space in which peoples geographically and historically separated come into contact with each other and establish ongoing relations."[5] At Fort Chipewyan and other fur trade regions, these different people learned how to live and interact with one another in ways that persisted for long periods, though not necessarily characterized by the "conditions of coercion, radical inequality, and intractable conflict" that to Pratt characterize classic colonial relations.[6] While the fur trade occurred within a context of expanding global capitalism and colonialism, the integration among different regions and individuals at an international level was fundamentally economic, not political, although it was "reinforced to some extent by cultural links and...political arrangements."[7] Elsewhere, I have argued that true colonialism—"economic exploitation based on the seizure of political power"[8]—did not characterize the Canadian fur trade until processes of internal colonialism began with the expansion of the new Canadian state into the Northwest after 1870.[9] A related argument in this paper is that the Aboriginal people of these plural societies did not become *dependent* on Europeans in the way it has been commonly understood; they did not come under European political or economic domination until true colonialism was imposed. In Fort Chipewyan, that did not occur until the twentieth century, after the signing of treaty and the issuance of Half-breed scrip, when internal colonialism attended the expansion northward of the Canadian nation-state.

This approach challenges popular understandings about the nature of the fur trade. It proposes that fur trade societies were far more dynamic in their interactions than most historians have realized, that European traders were not "in control," that Aboriginal peoples exercised real agency, and that it was the decisions and actions of both Aboriginal and European people that together generated the fur trade society that is described in this paper. This interpretation has been influenced by the growing body of detailed knowledge about the complex histories of Aboriginal and non-Aboriginal women alike, although scholars have yet to realize the full potential of this literature for the ways in which we write our stories about history. As early as 1991, Peggy Pascoe called for scholars to use western women's histories as a vehicle to study "the three central axes of inequality: race, class, and gender," and the distribution of power in the nation. She called for the writing of "multicultural history," finding a way to include all the groups in "a readable story."[10]

This paper is a step in that direction, one component of my long-term research in Fort Chipewyan. The fur trade directly into the Athabasca country began in 1778, when Peter Pond led an expedition to the lower Athabasca River and Lake Athabasca. In 1788, the post of Fort Chipewyan itself was established; it is the oldest, permanently occupied community in Alberta and one of the earliest in the Northwest. The analysis of what happened when Europeans and Aboriginal people met in this region, the creation of the fur trade mode of production that underlay the plural society, rests on multiple sources, including archival documents and published sources, material culture, oral history, and my personal fieldwork in and long-term involvement with Fort Chipewyan and its residents. I was fortunate not only in hearing many stories about what life was like in the past from people who had been part of this distinctive world, but also in having the opportunity to live in Fort Chipewyan and visit many of the bush settlements in the surrounding region, now mostly abandoned.[11]

Building a Plural Society

Fur trade posts such as Fort Chipewyan, Île à la Crosse, Fort Resolution, Fort Edmonton, and other major centres such as Red River and Prince Albert, exemplified the contact zones theorized by Mary Louise Pratt, a concept she preferred to that of the "frontier," a construction that privileges the point of view from Canada and the Grand Narrative of Canadian history.[12] The trading post provided a *place* in which all the people of the region could interact and jointly create a kind of *intersubjectivity*. This term refers to a shared, mutual space, produced through a process of dialogue and communication and characterized by a set of meanings which properly belonged to none of the interacting cultures.[13] It was represented in a new *fur trade* mode of production. In each region, the social and physical community developed as a complex plural society with multiple ancestries and identities, encompassing numerous sub-communities that continued to exist side-by-side. Social boundaries were fluid and defined by interactional spheres as much as they might be by personal or group identities.

Six broad sets of actors were important in constructing and maintaining the new fur trade mode of production and an integrated, plural society. From the earliest days of the trade, there were European and Aboriginal partners in trade and marriage who reached out to one another and learned how to interact successfully across cultural boundaries of custom and protocol. There were other Aboriginal men from the same early period who worked as occasional labour for European companies. As the fur trade moved into the Northwest, so too did mixed ancestry men from the Great Lakes area who were part of the labour force, especially for Montreal-based companies. There were also European men who moved into new areas after learning how to interact appropriately with Aboriginal peoples, men such as James Knight and David Thompson. Last, there were missionaries who followed the fur traders into the Northwest in the mid nineteenth century.

The social community that their interactions produced at Fort Chipewyan was typical of other regions while unique in its specific elements. Physically, it was spatially dispersed, revolving around but not restricted to the trading centre at Fort Chipewyan, which grew into a small town after 1870. In 1902, Hugh Richardson[14] estimated that about 250 people lived in Fort Chipewyan permanently, while 1,250 people lived elsewhere, mostly in small settlements in the "bush," the common term for the lands surrounding residential locales. These settlements, which were the spatial outgrowth of the mobile local bands of the nineteenth century, were oriented to Fort Chipewyan, to one another, and to a lesser extent to settlements in the periphery of other trading posts. They were mostly occupied seasonally, especially in winter, when they provided a base for families engaged in hunting, trapping, and fishing. During the summer, most bush residents travelled across the land, typically in areas of traditional land use, producing food to meet their immediate and long-term subsistence needs. The settlements in the Fort Chipewyan region were usually named after the locality, such as "Birch River" or "Deep Lake," although one particular locality, "Old Fort," took its name from the first North West Company post established on

Lake Athabasca in 1788. The knowledge of names demonstrated the territorial extent of the local plural society. The bush settlements persisted until the decades after World War II, when virtually everyone left the bush as a permanent place of residence and moved to Fort Chipewyan, where they began to constitute a new kind of social community.

From the beginning, the ethnic, cultural, and linguistic profile at Fort Chipewyan was a conglomerate of peoples with different origins, identities, and languages, including Chipewyans, Crees, Highland Scots (including men from the Outer Hebrides), Orcadians, French Canadians, and diverse mixed-ancestry peoples.[15] Elsewhere, I have called it a "rababou," or cultural stew, which was reflected in the linguistic mixing that occurred throughout the Northwest.[16] Some of these mixed-ancestry people arrived as fur trade employees; others were a local population, the result of intermarriage from the earliest days of the local fur trade. Most local "Half-breeds" had Chipewyan mothers or grandmothers.[17] By the end of the nineteenth century, residence choice—whether people lived in Fort Chipewyan or in bush settlements—had become a marker of a broad cultural orientation and related way of life, with its associated occupations. It was at least as important as "ethnic" or "cultural" designations. Many people spoke or understood multiple languages. In turn, occupation and way of life influenced the identities that people embraced, including the generation of new "Half-breed" or "Métis" identities. The people of the town and those of the bush lived separate but connected lives, joined together by ties of kinship, marriage, friendship, and religion. They were two halves of a regional population, and then, as now, nearly every person could trace a genealogical relationship to virtually everyone else.[18]

The fact that these very different peoples came together in a joint endeavour, with some kind of collective commitment, does not imply that it meant the same thing to all parties. Aboriginal and European peoples brought distinctive modes of production and cultural understandings to their interaction in a common social formation at Fort Chipewyan. All the partners in the fur trade contributed to building bridges between their separate systems of domestic and capitalist production and meaning, collectively creating a new space that would allow them to negotiate exchanges of furs, foods, goods, and persons successfully.

Indian involvement in the fur trade has historically been conceptualized as the rapid adoption of "superior" European manufactures and consequent Indian "dependence" on Europeans. It has fostered a notion of the primitive Indian, unwittingly selling his autonomy for trade goods and thereby moving forward in his cultural evolution and eventual integration into the state.[19] Yet in the Canadian fur trade, Europeans relied almost exclusively on Indians to produce furs, and they encouraged this specialization. It was impossible to provision trading posts from remote centres in Britain or Quebec, so Europeans relied heavily on local foods, much of it produced locally by the resident Aboriginal people who knew how to do so. Europeans learned to utilize Aboriginal material culture that was superbly suited to local conditions. Thus, Aboriginal people who trapped also commonly produced food provisions to sell, particularly fresh and dried meat, and occasionally they provided their labour to operate transport systems, work at the post, and manufacture persistent and highly adaptive items of "Indian" technology, such as snowshoes and moccasins. Aboriginal women married to post employees were especially active workers, although their labour is obscured because it was rarely registered in post records. They worked in the fisheries and produced other foods, they prepared hides and furs and sewed clothing, and they bore children, reproducing the local labour force. Brown has described much of this productive labour as "a woman's industrial revolution."[20] Both Brown and Van Kirk have written extensively about European reliance on the labour and knowledge of Indian and Métis women.[21]

In short, dependence was a two-way street. European dependence on local people was probably inevitable, given Indian knowledge of the resource base, which gave them economic control, and the sovereignty they exercised over their traditional lands, which gave them political control. Newly arrived Europeans learned crucial skills and local customs from other employees who had already mastered them and from their Indian and Métis associates. Ironically, to the extent that Europeans and incoming mixed-ancestry people learned how to survive locally and were socially integrated into Aboriginal bands, they themselves became independent of direct control by the traders, much as were the Chipewyans and Crees themselves.

As long as Chipewyans and Crees in the Fort Chipewyan region brought furs and food to trade, the traders did not need to control the labour process directly, and they probably would have found it impossible to do so. Nevertheless, they sought some measure of control over the producers, to try to keep their attention focussed on producing desired commodities and to ensure that furs went to them rather than to a competitor. At the same time, Indians sought to exercise their own control, especially over the terms of trade, the quality of goods available to them, and the extent to which economic relations needed to be mediated by social relations.[22]

This discussion suggests several points of articulation between the domestic mode of production of the Chipewyans and Crees—a use-oriented system—and the (merchant) capitalist mode of production—a profit-oriented system linked to the growing world economy—of the incoming traders at Fort Chipewyan that would produce the new fur trade mode of production.[23] Chipewyan and Cree men and women were willing to produce furs and provisions to exchange for imported commodities and to work more directly for the traders on an occasional basis, especially as post hunters and fishermen. They were willing for their daughters and sisters to marry European traders and employees. These marriages established the affinal links that facilitated and channelled economic exchanges and created a female labour force at the post. The children they produced became not only part of the local labour force but also the glue that helped integrate the local plural society. To James Clifton, they were "culturally enlarged" men and women, capable of moving seamlessly among the different cultures of the region.[24]

The result was that Chipewyans and Crees added two new components to their economy: independent (petty) commodity production and wage labour, although reimbursed by exchange credits, not cash payments.[25] Along with the regular post employees, Métis and European alike, and their Aboriginal family members, they also manufactured snowshoes, leather, and other commodities required locally, although there is little evidence such items were produced for direct exchange. Thus, the new mode of production was a *mixed economy*, one with three different sectors: domestic production, independent commodity production, and wage labour. It was oriented in many ways to, but not dominated by, capitalist exchanges.

For their part, Europeans were willing to enter into a range of social relations or transactions with the Indians, including marital alliances, which transcended the purely economic aspect of exchanges. Europeans also needed to obtain most of their own food from local resources. Costs incurred in hunting and fishing to support the post were part of the overhead of doing business. The distinction between commercial and subsistence food production narrowed when post employees, both European and mixed-ancestry, lived and hunted with their Indian allies and kinsmen. Such activities were a reversal of the trend among Europeans toward a fully socialized labour force.

While Indians certainly wanted a wide range of European manufactures, which became part of their means of production, it is simplistic to claim that their involvement in the trade as regular producers of fur and food was due primarily to a "seemingly insatiable appetite" for these goods.[26] The fur trade literature contains numerous examples of northern Indians who had little use for most of the trade goods they were offered.[27] Arthur J. Ray pointed out that Indian demand for goods was relatively "inelastic." If prices paid for furs increased, Indians often trapped less, not more.[28] Many Indians had to be induced to produce goods for trade, especially in the volume desired by the traders, and it was an ongoing concern at Fort Chipewyan throughout the nineteenth century.

The methods used by European traders were related to changes in the social formation of the region that occurred as traders and their employees entered into the relations of production of the local Indian bands, in two ways. First, traders and their employees entered into "country marriages," or marriage *à la façon du pays*, with Aboriginal women.[29] As Sylvia Van Kirk explained, "The marriage of a fur trader and an Indian woman was not just a 'private' affair; the bond thus created helped to advance trade relations with a new tribe, placing the Indian wife in the role of cultural liaison between the traders and her kin."[30] Trappers and traders became affinal kinsmen, a relationship with expectations of mutual assistance and reciprocal exchanges.

Indians and Europeans were also linked together by the extension of credit, or debt, to individual trappers, a financing system that became extensive in the nineteenth century in the Fort Chipewyan region and persisted until the 1940s, although diminished in the twentieth century.[31] To Rosemary Ommer, credit was "the mechanism whereby merchant capital delegated the power of production to 'independent' operators on certain terms, with certain strings attached, in order to generate the flourishing of individual enterprise and the expansion of the whole economy."[32] Tanner has explained how credit both defined and mediated the trade relationship: "The obtaining of credit marked an important change in the economic life of a trapper. It indicated a long-term commitment to trapping as the major winter productive activity, and to dealings with a single trader, in order to exchange the results of this activity for some valued end."[33]

Credit was extended to group leaders—trading chiefs or Aboriginal middlemen—in the early years of the fur trade, especially those important leaders who travelled a long way to reach the post. Some were formally outfitted as chiefs, a well-known institution by the time the trade arrived in the Athabasca country. At the Lake Athabasca posts, it appears that credit was more likely to be extended to leaders of local families who were important in the fresh meat trade. Both forms can be found in the earliest direct record, which is Cuthbert Grant's 1786 journal of spring activities at the Athabasca River post, under the direction of Peter Pond.[34] By 1825, when James Keith described the Chipewyans, he noted that there were few men who warranted the elevated title of "Chief": "their influence & authority being little known beyond the circle of their own Family."[35] Cuthbert Grant distinguished between Indians paying their credits and trading furs or provisions; the latter referred to transactions that occurred after the fall debts had been settled.[36] He described Indians *selling* meat, clearly a market transaction.[37]

Post managers kept account books that tracked each trapper's sale of furs and provisions and purchases of goods at the post. A trapper who accepted credit became linked to a particular trading post and was required to travel there at least twice yearly, once to obtain his fall trapping "outfit" on credit and a second time to trade his furs and pay off his debt.[38] Credit stabilized a trapper's relations with the trader. An 1860 Fort Chipewyan report remarked, "Debts are given to Indians who are faithful in paying them."[39] From the trapper's point of view, it was a way to capitalize the coming winter's trapping, by providing the goods he needed from the post, while at the same time allowing him to trap when and how he pleased.[40] On a pragmatic level, it stimulated trapping because trappers had to pay for their purchases in order to obtain more credit, despite the Hudson's Bay Company policy of periodically writing off bad debts. More broadly, it accorded with Chipewyan and Cree ideologies of reciprocity, the need to repay those who have given a gift or otherwise provided assistance.[41] As Adrian Tanner writes, the trader could use credit to limit the sorts of goods available to trappers: "By allowing only certain goods to be purchased on credit a trader was able to do more than just influence the buying habits of Indians along what he thought to be more prudent lines. He was also able to stress the importance of trapping as an activity, allowing only those supplies needed for a trapping expedition on credit. In this way he ultimately could increase the fur harvest of his district, on which most of his profit could be made."[42] Furthermore, Tanner writes, "Credit established personal relations between the trader and his trappers, and gave the trader the advantage of having the trappers under an obligation to him. Through this relationship he was able to directly influence their economic life by personal intervention, and discourage activities which conflicted with trapping."[43]

Country marriages and creditor-debtor relations established the initial social ties which joined together Aboriginal and European peoples. As Marshall Sahlins has suggested, it was "social relations, not prices [that] connect up 'buyers' and 'sellers.'"[44] As Indian involvement in the fur trade became regularized, Indians participated in what are represented on the account books as individual transactions, although it appears that whoever was named was typically acting on behalf of his entire band, which benefitted from the goods he acquired in trade. His trade represented production by his immediate family and possibly a somewhat larger social group. The Chipewyan and Cree bands were no longer marginal to or outside the world system but integrated into it as a periphery. This transformation occurred at Fort Chipewyan after the establishment in 1821 of a monopoly on trade by the Hudson's Bay Company.[45] By the second quarter of the nineteenth century, the Chipewyans and Crees who had become permanent occupants of the Fort Chipewyan region and traded there regularly could no longer be characterized by a "total economy." For Chipewyans and Crees and some people of mixed ancestry, the new mode of production had the following configuration:

Forces of Production

Resources. While the total resource base was initially unchanged, Chipewyans and Crees developed different patterns of resource exploitation, which can be inferred in part from records of fur and food production. They emphasized some fur and game resources that previously would have been little utilized or utilized differently, thereby affecting regional ecosystems in often-significant ways. From the earliest days of the Athabascan fur trade, provisions were important trade items, especially fresh and dried meat.[46] While the earliest fur trade journal mentions trade in moose and caribou, as the trade expanded bison became an important resource for commercial hunting. Northern bison herds (the so-called wood bison) were hunted so intensively that by the 1840s their numbers were in serious decline.[47]

The Chipewyans who chose to relocate to the Fort Chipewyan region shifted from the resources of the transitional treeline zone to those of the boreal forest, which meant that they were mostly hunting bison and moose, not barren-ground caribou, and a different configuration of smaller animals. Ray has suggested that food resources were less plentiful than in their former territory[48] and that Indian economic specialization was accompanied by reliance on a more restricted and less variable resource base, which made their new economy more unstable. Both points are arguable. There is no reason to believe that the resources available in the biome of the Fort Chipewyan region were impoverished compared to those of the transitional treeline region, especially given the role played by controlled burning in managing habitats for game and fur animals.[49] In the late eighteenth and early nineteenth centuries, before bison numbers diminished, there were substantial herds that ranged as far north as Great Slave Lake and east of the Slave River,[50] and bison were plentiful in the Peace River country. According to Samuel Hearne, "Of all the large beasts in those parts the buffalo is easiest to kill."[51] Barren-ground caribou continued to migrate occasionally to the Fort Chipewyan region, woodland caribou lived in the Birch Mountains, and the Peace-Athabasca Delta supported a rich resource complex. Even deer and elk were reported in the region.[52] The 1823–1824 post report remarked, "The hunting grounds of the Indians in that locality are well stocked with large animals."[53] The following year, the report commented that the Chipewyans feed off the "fat...of the land & water of the first of which they are seldom destitute."[54]

While both Chipewyans and Crees established themselves as distinct socio-territorial groups in the Fort Chipewyan region, using clearly defined and segregated areas for subsistence and residence, they continued to travel to other areas suitable for hunting and trapping. This was especially the case for Chipewyans, who were described as relatively independent of Europeans and their goods, despite their "numerous Population," due to their "wandering habits, great attachment and frequent Visits to their lands."[55] Crees, on the other hand, were "more Ltd. Population, stationary habits, & dependent situation on Europeans."[56] Beginning in the mid nineteenth century, strategic Chipewyan-Cree marriages began to erode the restrictive territorial boundaries of particular bands and optimize land-use possibilities.[57] Members of ethnically distinctive local bands thereby began to construct a new multi-ethnic regional band.

Technology. Perhaps the most striking feature of the fur trade mode of production was that an increasingly large portion of Aboriginal technology was obtained through trade. Both Chipewyans and Crees enjoyed access to a wide inventory of imported manufactures, including guns and ammunition, metal goods, textiles, and decorative items. A blacksmith was on hand at the post to make gun repairs, which encouraged reliance on firearms. Some theorists have argued that Chipewyan relocation to this region was possible only because of the new fur trade goods they could obtain, especially guns, which facilitated their hunting of large, solitary animals rather than herds of caribou. However, the frequent references in Cuthbert Grant's 1786 journal to hunters bringing moose meat to the post to trade indicate that by this early date Chipewyans as well as Crees were hunting moose quite capably, although it is not clear whether or not they relied on firearms as opposed to snares or other traditional hunting techniques.[58] The latter seems more likely; firearms and ammunition must have been in short supply in the early days of local trade, and they were far from reliable.

By 1823, the Chipewyans who were "more accustomed to whites" were reported to be copying them in manner and dress.[59] By mid century, all Indians had evidently replaced much of their material culture inventory. Father Taché, writing at Isle à la Crosse in 1851, noted that Chipewyan "Men's clothes are quite similar to those of our peasants; they obtain their clothing in the stores of the Company where it is received ready made from England."[60] In 1859, Robert Campbell, the Hudson's Bay Company factor at Fort Chipewyan, wrote to the director of the new Industrial Museum of Scotland: "You will perhaps be surprised to learn, that even in this Northern District, the "Indians" appreciate the convenience of the articles of civilised usage so much, that hardly a trace now remains of their former dress, domestic utensils, or weapons of war, or the chase; all have already fallen into disuse among them."[61]

Such comments support the popular notion that Indian peoples had become "dependent" on the fur trade. As "trappers," they were believed to have "lost" their original autonomy. Ray referred to Indians as "increasingly caught in the trap of having to buy the tools that they needed"[62] at a time when the resource base was increasingly unstable. Such an interpretation involves a material culture-focussed concept of "autonomy" that is not usually applied to non-Aboriginal peoples. "Dependence" has become established in academic and popular discourse as a term connoting a special kind of Aboriginal subordination. In fact, all peoples who became part of the world system were (and are) "dependent" on exchanges in the market place. Among their ranks were British workers, but the term "dependence" is rarely used to characterize them. Ironically, British workers were probably more dependent on the goodwill of company owners than were northern Indian trappers and hunters, who maintained considerable independence and had to be courted and enticed by Company traders throughout the nineteenth century.[63]

There is no evidence that the less visible aspects of Aboriginal technology were replaced. As Father Taché pointed out in 1951, "All the Indians are better naturalists, not only than our country people, but even than the most learned elements of our populations."[64] They maintained their knowledge of local ecosystems, animal behaviour, and the use of fire to manipulate plant and animal populations. Controlled burning was an important tool to create and maintain the prairies and other early successional habitats on which most species of fur trade and subsistence importance relied.[65] While Crees, many of whom originated in the fire-adapted parkland of the Saskatchewan River basin, were undoubtedly familiar with the principles of fire management and could easily apply them to their new northern homeland, it may have been a new technology to Chipewyans, who would not have used it in the caribou ranges of the transitional treeline. Presumably they learned its use by observing other residents, including the Beaver Indians they displaced, and by trial and error.

An important addition to their technology, and crucial to the development of trapping as a regularized activity, was the dog team. Dogs were hitched in single file to a toboggan or sled, facilitating winter travel among residential settlements, trapping areas, and the fur trade post. While the idea of dog teams seems to have been introduced, perhaps by example, at least some of the implements were homegrown, a synthesis of pre-existing sleds and the carioles and dog harnesses introduced by traders and their employees.[66] People fashioned their own sleds and harnesses from wood and leather. People also continued to use dogs for "packing" furs and other items at other times of year when sleds could not be used.[67] When dog teams were adopted by Chipewyans and Crees at Lake Athabasca is not known, but it may have been related to some measure of increased sedentariness; keeping dogs requires their owners to stockpile meat or fish for their feed. An entry in Cuthbert Grant's journal from the Athabasca River fort, dated 5 April 1786, referred to two Chipewyans arriving from "Lack de Brochet"—Jackfish (Richardson) Lake—with "two trains of meat," possibly the first reference to local dog sled use.[68] In 1801, Mackenzie described Cree women making "their journies [sic], which are never of any great length, with sledges drawn by dogs."[69] However, his reference was not specific to the Crees of Lake Athabasca.

Labour. Labour allocation was similar to that of the domestic mode of production, in that men and women undertook different and complementary fur trade and subsistence activities. Both men and women trapped, though generally for different species and in different localities. Women's traplines were usually in the vicinity of their settlement, whereas men used their dog teams to trap at a greater distance, thereby increasing the productive capacities of the local band. Dog teams provided transport among traplines, kill sites, and winter settlements, and between settlements and trading posts.

There was also a new *regional* division of labour represented by the concentration of some Aboriginal peoples in trapping and subsistence pursuits and others in wage labour. While the former have often been characterized as Chipewyans and Crees, and the latter, as Half-breeds and Métis, these identities were influenced by occupational choices and the social communities to which people belonged. Such specialization was rarely exclusive. People who worked directly for the traders and, in the second half of the nineteenth century, for missionaries, typically enhanced their wages by hunting, fishing, and cultivating small gardens, or by acquiring food from their relatives, thereby reducing both the costs incurred by traders in maintaining the labour force and their otherwise dependent position as labourers. The concept of a regional division of labour, with occupational specialization occurring within immediate social networks— the local bands and their later outgrowths within the town of Fort Chipewyan itself—also marks the mixed economy of the fur trade mode of production.

Relations of Production

The primary goal of Chipewyans, Crees, and most Métis was still survival. That meant that trapping and wage labour were undertaken only to provide themselves with enough exchange value to purchase the items they needed. Not surprisingly, there were few changes from the pre-existing relations of production. The major shift was the intervention of the European trader and his employees in the relations of production, paralleling the intervention of imported manufactures in the forces of production. It was the traders who solicited and encouraged Aboriginal participation in the fur trade and employed them as labourers.[70] They drew upon their social ties with Aboriginal peoples and their control over exchange rates, though not without considerable negotiation and occasional resistance by Aboriginal producers. In many ways they were like "big men," able to motivate Aboriginal subsistence activities but not dictate to them.[71] For example, on 2 October 1868, the chief factor at Fort Chipewyan, William McMurray, "had a conference with the Indians & explained to them his intentions concerning their debts furs &c during the ensuing Winter."[72] Traders did not seek otherwise to alter Aboriginal use of or access to bush resources. All Indian participants had to provide themselves with food and other subsistence items, thereby underwriting their own reproduction costs, which reduced costs that the traders would otherwise have been forced to cover and enhanced the value appropriated by the traders.

Ray has argued that one role of the traders was to encourage Indian trappers to rely upon a less reliable resource base by relying instead on assistance from the Hudson's Bay Company during times of privation.[73] The Company stocked foodstuffs for distribution at such times. This practice, he said, reduced Indian self-sufficiency even further. Indians were therefore vulnerable to low fur returns and shortages of food.[74] They turned to the Company for relief at such times, a situation that Ray has interpreted as a fur trade–based "welfare system."[75] However, Ray himself has pointed out that assistance provided to Indians was drawn from the "excess profits" made by the Company. Conceptualizing it as welfare supports an interpretation of Indian "dependency." It may be better thought of as a return of a portion of the excessive surplus value appropriated by fur trade merchants. Occasional assistance provided by the trading companies was a way of helping the Indians make a "living wage," not equivalent to government support in the twentieth century for peoples displaced from the means of production or the production process. Moreover, at Fort Chipewyan the resource base may have been more reliable than at most posts, and there is little evidence to support the notion that the Company regularly put up extra supplies in case Indians went hungry. In fact, post journals recorded complaints if Indians had to be fed from Company stores during intervals of starvation.

Despite the changes stemming from fur trade involvement, the structure of control within Chipewyan and Cree societies was still vested in the members of the local bands. However, the groundwork had been established for individualized production of and control over furs, provisions, and goods, potentially conflicting with persistent values about sharing. Aboriginal peoples faced new contradictions which related to a mode of production based on a *mixed economy* comprising production for subsistence, production for exchange, and wage labour. There were potential contradictions between internal and external leadership and control and between individual and communal activities in the productive process.

In short, the fur trade mode of production reflected the addition of trapping, production of provisions, and wage labour to the former economy. It was the beginning of a mixed economy that would provide additional flexibility for livelihood. At the same time, Aboriginal peoples were vulnerable to limits that might be imposed on their access to the resources of the bush, to changes in the availability of the species they exploited, and to changes in the structure of the fur trade. While involvement in the fur trade is often seen as making Aboriginal economic structures more fragile and less certain, at the same time the existence of a mixed economy evened out some of the problems by offering new ways of livelihood.

Superstructure

Superstructural elements were an outgrowth of those of the originating modes of production. There is no evidence that Chipewyans or Crees who trapped changed their fundamental value systems in any significant way. Some subtle changes may have resulted from the roles played by Métis and European employees in the fur trade relations of production. Especially in earlier days, they were often sent out to winter with Indian bands, to encourage production of furs and provisions and also to support themselves. Many men married or lived with local women and began families. Fathers transmitted at least some of their values to their children, even when those children were raised in their mother's culture and with her cultural identity. These values supported an acceptance of trapping and trading as legitimate and worthy activities. Yet Aboriginal people did not come to accept the legitimacy of lineal authority, whether by outsiders or their own members. Traders insinuated themselves into the relations of production by manipulating exchange relationships, not by imposing any measure of formal authority.

Roman Catholic Métis and Protestant Scots also taught their families some aspects of their Christianity, paving the way for the arrival of Christian missionaries. They were a less formal but highly important influence in the relations of production. While early missionary accounts show that Aboriginal peoples willingly acquired selected aspects of Christianity, missionaries were often dismayed by the persistence of "Indian" spiritual beliefs and practices. In spirituality, as in all other areas, Aboriginal people adopted elements selectively, reshaping them to accord with their own cultural traditions.

Métis and Europeans and the Fur Trade Mode of Production

While most of this discussion has focussed on Chipewyans and Crees, it is useful to speak explicitly of a shift by many Europeans to a fur trade mode of production as well, and of the special place occupied by Métis, who were born of, and into, the fur trade mode of production.[76] The heart of the fur trade mode of production was a highly flexible, mixed economy. There was a continuum of choice and involvement, ranging from relative isolation to intense engagement with the world system, but marked always by a combination of commercial production and unimpeded access to and control over bush resources, subject only to traditional socio-territorial arrangements. In the Fort Chipewyan region, people who became known as Half-breeds (today, Métis) tended to emphasize the wage labour side, although their economic activities were far broader, especially for gens libres or "freemen," the men who were not regular employees of post or mission. They subdivided into two groups: families with either French or Scottish ancestry and affiliations. After the fur trade stabilized in the nineteenth century, many European traders spent their adult lives as middle managers living in communities such as Fort Chipewyan, marrying local women, raising children, and largely alienated from a European capitalist sphere. Lower-level employees, whether Indian, Métis, or European, even if they received a full-time wage, were never completely separated from the means of production.

New company employees learned essential skills from long-term employees and from their Aboriginal partners and kinsmen. Even if they began as true proletarians from Britain or Quebec, once they were living in the fur trade country, they were able to achieve considerable independence.[77] They learned how to live and travel in the bush, they had social ties to Indian bands, and through their jobs and their kinsmen they enjoyed access to the bush-based means of production and were involved in the kinship-oriented relations of production. For example, at Fort Chipewyan several men spent considerable time during the year, especially in winter, living with their families at fishing camps, putting up fish for post provisions, and feeding themselves at the same time, probably quite well. These camps were conveniently situated for occasional visits from Chipewyans and Crees, and there appears to have been virtually no supervision by Company officers. It is not surprising that Bishop Taché referred to the "unbounded liberty" enjoyed by Half-breeds living in the Northwest.[78]

In terms of superstructure, the flexibility of the mixed economy comprising the fur trade mode of production meant that it could be operated by people with diverse values. There is no evidence that Europeans who embraced a new-found independence abandoned their own fundamental acceptance of lineal authority, although at times they may have held it in abeyance and worked around it when it suited them to do so. It is suggestive of tendencies of European wage labourers to resist unfair treatment and the worst excesses of industrial development, but to accept the legitimacy of the underlying system.

At the same time, the fur trade literature indicates that many European fur trade workers, despite their professed Christianity, learned new expressions of spiritual power from Aboriginal people. For example, David Thompson wrote about how French Canadians shared many beliefs with Indians: both believed that when Thompson made his astronomical observations, he "was looking into futurity and seeing everybody, and what they were doing." His own men believed that he had power over wind.[79] In another example, William Watt wrote to his mother that Orcadian William Rowland "has been so long among half breeds that he has got into all their superstitious notions."[80] But the situation was almost certainly more complicated than Watt indicated. Men from Orkney and Lewis brought their own rich oral traditions with them to the Northwest, where they undoubtedly resonated with the parallels in the Aboriginal traditions they learned from wives, in-laws, and fellow workers.[81]

The Fur Trade Mode of Production: Resilient and Long-Lasting

In the world of the fur trade, neither Aboriginal nor European peoples felt compelled to follow a narrow course in what they chose to adopt or learn from one another. The complex cultural interchange that operated at every level created a broad substrate for the plural society associated with the fur trade mode of production. As Sylvia Van Kirk wrote in 1980, the fur trade society was a distinctive social formation that "combined both European and Indian elements to produce a distinctive, self-perpetuating community."[82] To the extent it was expressed within the plural society of each post and its surrounding region, it reflected different modulations of the same basic fur trade mode of production, in which local people controlled most of the means of production they utilized and were involved in face-to-face social relations and obligations.

The fur trade mode of production was also remarkably stable, persisting at Fort Chipewyan and other northern locations for well over a century, until after World War II. It afforded the region's residents considerable resilience in coping with the dramatic changes forced upon them after Canada was created as a nation-state and embarked on a program of economic development in the Northwest, including the Fort Chipewyan region. At the same time, it continued to articulate with a capitalist mode of production that was engineering radical political and economic changes in Britain, Britain's Canadian colonies, and later the Dominion of Canada. As northern capitalism and government regulatory regimes expanded after World War I, Aboriginal people were steadily displaced from their traditional lands and resource base. Government agents prevented them from exercising control over the lands they had formerly governed, and outsiders produced income from resources that had formerly been exploited solely by local people. Their economic and political autonomy diminished to the point that, by the 1950s and 1960s, they could no longer support themselves from the traditional mixed economy. It was at this time that families abandoned the bush and relocated to Fort Chipewyan, where a new form of plural society began to develop, one in which Aboriginal people were now subordinated to the non-Aboriginal people who created the rules that now governed their lives.

Notes

1   A version of this chapter was first published in *Fort Chipewyan and the Shaping of Canadian History, 1788–1920s: "We like to be free in this country"* © University of British Columbia Press, 2010. The paper was originally presented at a session in honour of Sylvia Van Kirk, "Many Tender Ties," Canadian Historical Association Conference, 27–30 May 2007, Saskatoon.

2   Sylvia Van Kirk, *"Many Tender Ties": Women in Fur-Trade Society in Western Canada, 1670–1870* (Winnipeg: Watson and Dwyer, 1980), 2.

3   Ibid., 5. To preserve the integrity of archival sources and older published works, as well as the usages of community members, this paper employs historic terminologies that today have largely been replaced by "First Nations" and "Métis." The term "Aboriginal" refers to First Nations and Métis collectively; "European," to people from Europe or descended from Europeans; and "Euro-Canadian," to Canadians of European descent. More specific terms of identity are used where appropriate.

4   For further detail on this resistance, see Patricia A. McCormack, *Fort Chipewyan and the Shaping of Canadian History, 1788–1920s* (Vancouver: University of British Columbia Press, 2010).

5   Mary Louise Pratt, *Imperial Eyes. Travel Writing and Transculturation* (London: Routledge 1992), 6.

6   Ibid.

7   Immanuel Wallerstein, *The Modern World-System* (New York: Academic Press, 1974), 15.

8   G. Balandier, "The Colonial Situation: A Theoretical Approach," in *Social Change: The Colonial Situation*, ed. Immanuel Wallerstein (New York: John Wiley and Sons, 1966), 37.

9   McCormack, *Fort Chipewyan*.

10 Peggy Pascoe, "Western women at the cultural crossroads," in *Trails: Toward a New Western History*, ed. Patricia Nelson Limerick, Clyde A. Milner II, and Charles E. Rankin (Lawrence, Kansas: University Press of Kansas, 1991), 52.

11 A more complete discussion of the fur trade mode of production and the ethnohistory of the Fort Chipewyan region can be found in McCormack, *Fort Chipewyan*.

12 Patricia A. McCormack, "Competing narratives: barriers between Indigenous peoples and the Canadian state," in *Indigenous Peoples and the Modern State*, ed. Duane Champagne, Karen Jo Torjesen, and Susan Steiner (Walnut Creek, CA: AltaMira Press, 2005), 109–120, outlines the key points in the dominant narrative about Canada's history, or the "Grand Narrative," and compares it to competing narratives by Aboriginal people.

13 Johannes Fabian, "Time and the Work of Anthropology," in *Critical Essays 1971–1991* (Chur, Switzerland: Harwood Academic Publishers, 1991), 92; Patricia A. McCormack and Arthur J. Sciorra, "Building partnerships: Canadian museums, Aboriginal peoples, and the spirit and intent of the Task Force on Museums and First Peoples," paper prepared for the Canadian Association for the Conservation of Cultural Property, Whitehorse, Yukon, 29–31 May 1998; Richard F. Salisbury, "Transactions or transactors? An economic anthropologist's view," in *Transaction and Meaning: Directions in the Anthropology of Exchange and Symbolic Behavior*, ed. Bruce Kapferer (Philadelphia: Institute for the Study of Human Issues, 1976), 42.

14 Hugh Richardson, Diary, Trip with Annuity Party, Treaty No. 8, Athabasca District, 1902, Library and Archives Canada, MG27II18, 20.

15 On the European side, these ancestries included French and the diverse people from Britain, especially Orcadians and Lewismen; the Aboriginal side included Cree and Ojibwa Algonquian speakers and Iroquois.

16 McCormack, *Fort Chipewyan*, chap. 2.

17 It is important not to overemphasize historic distinctions between Chipewyans or Crees and Half-breeds or Métis at Fort Chipewyan. There is no evidence that the people themselves drew such firm boundaries, especially once people with different cultural identities began to intermarry. Such an emphasis reflects a European racial consciousness, fostered by political situations at Red River and in the Saskatchewan basin, where in the nineteenth century Métis became politically and militarily important. The ethnic distinctions imposed in northern Alberta by government policies at the time of Treaty 8 on a much more fluid condition were consequences of these developments elsewhere.

18 Fictive kinship ties articulated other relationships. For example, men who worked together on the boats called one another *nistow*, the Cree (male-speaking) term for brother-in-law, and one that implies a cooperative relationship. Agnes Deans Cameron observed, "it is the vocative used by the Cree in speaking to anybody he feels kindly toward." Agnes Deans Cameron, *The New North: Being Some Account of a Woman's Journey through Canada to the Arctic* (New York: D. Appleton and Company, 1910), 56. Roman Catholic missionaries were called "Père," "Frère," "Mère," and "Soeur." It was no surprise that when Treaty 8 was negotiated in 1899, Crees and Chipewyans found it easy to extend kinship terms to the Queen and her representatives. Charles Mair, *Through the Mackenzie Basin* (Toronto: William Briggs, 1908); Govt. of Canada, *Treaty No. 8*, facsimile edition (Ottawa: Queen's Printer and Controller of Stationery) ([1899] 1966). Even today, people who establish long-term relationships in Fort Chipewyan are commonly drawn into relations of real or fictive kinship.

19 For example, see Robert F. Murphy and Julian H. Steward, "Tappers and trappers: parallel process in acculturation," in *Theory in Anthropology*, ed. Robert A. Manners and David Kaplan (Chicago: Aldine Publishing Company, [1956] 1968), 393–408.

20 Jennifer S.H. Brown, "Fur trade history as text and drama," in *The Uncovered Past: Roots of Northern Alberta Societies*, ed. Patricia A. McCormack and R. Geoffrey Ironside, Circumpolar Research Series No. 3 (Edmonton: Canadian Circumpolar Institute, University of Alberta, 1993), 83.

21 Jennifer S.H. Brown, *Strangers in Blood: Fur Trade Company Families in Indian Country* (Vancouver: University of British Columbia Press, 1980) and Van Kirk, *"Many Tender Ties."*

22 For example, Van Kirk, *"Many Tender Ties"*; Arthur J. Ray, *Indians in the Fur Trade: Their Role as Trappers, Hunters, and Middlemen in the Lands Southwest of Hudson Bay, 1660–1870.* (Toronto: University of Toronto Press, 1974); Harold A. Innis, *The Fur Trade in Canada* (New Haven: Yale University Press, [1956] 1964), 373.

23 The theoretical structure of *mode of production* is used to represent the internal dynamics of these local worlds. It is a structure of material reproduction that includes the technical components of the forces of production and the social components of the social relations of production. See McCormack 2009 for a longer discussion of mode of production and the domestic and capitalist modes of production that were joined at Fort Chipewyan.

24 James A. Clifton, "Alternate identities and cultural frontiers," in *Being and Becoming Indian: Biographical Studies of North American Frontiers*, ed. James A. Clifton (Chicago: Dorsey Press, 1989), 29.

25 Innis, *Fur Trade in Canada*, 161, 240; Ernest Mandel, *An Introduction to Marxist Economic Theory* (New York: Young Socialist Alliance, 1967), 30, and *Marxist Economic Theory* (London: Merlin Press, 1968), 66.

26 (Murphy and Steward, "Tappers and trappers," 400; Donald F. Bibeau, "Fur trade literature from a tribal point of view: a critique," in *Rendezvous: Selected papers of the Fourth North American Fur Trade Conference, 1981*, ed. Thomas C. Buckley (St. Paul, Minnesota: North American Fur Trade Conference, 1984), 83–91.

27 For example, see Samuel Hearne, *A Journal from Prince of Wales' Fort in Hudson's Bay to the Northern Ocean 1769, 1770, 1771, 1772*, ed. Richard Glover (Toronto: Macmillan, 1958), 50–51, 176; Alexander Hunter Murray, *Journal of the Yukon 1847-48*, ed. L.J. Burpee, Publications of the Canadian Archives No. 4, 1910, 29; Russell George Rothney, "Merchant capital and the livelihood of the residents of the Hudson Bay basin: a Marxist interpretation," (MA thesis, Department of Economics, University of Manitoba, 1975), 63–65.

28 Ray, *Indians in the Fur Trade*, 68–69, 141–2.

29 Van Kirk, *"Many Tender Ties"*; Brown, *Strangers in Blood*.

30 Van Kirk, *"Many Tender Ties,"* 4. In its early years, the Hudson's Bay Company tried, without much success, to prevent marital liaisons between its men and Aboriginal women, fearing that they would interfere with a profitable trade. Van Kirk pointed out how shortsighted such a policy was, in that it was marital relationships that established the personal ties that made trade possible. This point was visually dramatized in *Ikwe*, one of the four "Daughters of the Country" films. *Ikwe: Daughters of the Country*, dir. Norma Bailey (Ottawa: National Film Board of Canada, 1986). By the time the Company had moved inland, it had accepted the reality of widespread "country marriages," many of which persisted, leading to new forms of plural societies (see Patricia A. McCormack, "Lost women: Native wives in Orkney and Lewis," in *Recollecting: Lives of Aboriginal Women of the Canadian Northwest and Borderlands*, ed. Sarah Carter and Patricia A. McCormack (Edmonton: Athabasca University Press, 2011).

31 Cf. Ray, *Indians in the Fur Trade*, 137–8, 196–7; Arthur J. Ray, "Periodic shortages, native welfare, and the Hudson's Bay Company 1670-1930," in *The Subarctic Fur Trade: Native Social and Economic Adaptations*, ed. Shepard Krech III (Vancouver: University of British Columbia Press, 1984), 1–20; Arthur J. Ray, "The decline of paternalism in the Hudson's Bay Company fur trade, 1870–1945," in *Merchant Credit and Labour Strategies in Historical Perspective*, ed. Rosemary E. Ommer (Fredericton, NB: Acadiensis Press, 1990), 188–202; Toby Morantz, "'So Evil a Practice': A look at the debt system in the James Bay fur trade," in *Merchant Credit and Labour Strategies in Historical Perspective*, ed. Rosemary E. Ommer (Fredericton, NB: Acadiensis Press, 1990), 203–222; Adrian Tanner, "The structure of the fur trade" (MA thesis, Department of Anthropology, University of British Columbia, 1965); Rothney, "Merchant capital," 85–86; Patricia A. McCormack, Fort Chipewyan field journals, 1977-78, in possession of the author. Although theoretically synonymous in the fur trade, as traders spoke of extending credit or debt to the Indians, the two terms differ considerably in their connotations and etymologies. Credit is a positive term, implying that an individual is trustworthy, whereas debt is negative, a state of obligation. Together, they represent the duality of credit relationships between traders and trappers.

32 Rosemary E. Ommer, "Introduction," in *Merchant Credit and Labour Strategies in Historical Perspective*, ed. Rosemary E. Ommer (Fredricton, NB: Acadiensis Press, 1990), 9.

33 Tanner, "The structure of the fur trade," 46.

34 Harry J. Duckworth, ed., *The English River Book: A North West Company Journal and Account Book of 1786* (Montreal and Kingston: McGill-Queen's University Press, 1990).

35 HBCA B.39/e/8, fo. 28.

36 Duckworth, *English River Book*, 180n12 and passim.

37 For example, ibid., 12.

38   Once missionaries arrived, it became common for men, at least, to travel to Fort Chipewyan at least four separate times: in late spring, especially after break-up, to sell furs; in fall, before freeze-up, to obtain credit and outfit themselves for the winter season; and at Christmas and Easter, for church services.

39   HBCA B.39/e/10, fo. 1.

40   Tanner, "The structure of the fur trade," 47; Morantz, "So Evil a Practice," 221.

41   E.g., Ray, "Periodic shortages," 11; Morantz, "So Evil a Practice," 221.

42   Tanner, "The structure of the fur trade," 49.

43   Ibid., 47–8.

44   Marshall Sahlins, *Stone Age Economics* (Chicago: Aldine Publishing Company, [1972] 1974), 298.

45   Patricia A. McCormack, "Becoming trappers: the transformation to a fur trade mode of production at Fort Chipewyan," in *Rendezvous: Selected papers of the Fourth North American Fur Trade Conference, 1981*, ed. Thomas C. Buckley (St. Paul, MN: North American Fur Trade Conference, 1984), 155–173.

46   Duckworth, *English River Book.*

47   Theresa A. Ferguson, "Wood Bison and the early fur trade," in *The Uncovered Past: Roots of Northern Alberta Societies*, ed. Patricia A. McCormack and R. Geoffrey Ironside, Circumpolar Research Series No. 3 (Edmonton: Canadian Circumpolar Institute, University of Alberta, 1993).

48   Ray, "Periodic shortages," 9.

49   Patricia A. McCormack, "Deconstructing Canadian subarctic grasslands," paper prepared for the European Environmental History Conference, Amsterdam, 5–9 June 2007.

50   Hearne, *Journal*, 161–4.

51   Ibid., 163.

52   HBCA B.39/e/7, fo. 5.

53   Ibid., fo. 3.

54   HBCA B.39/3/9, 7.

55   HBCA B.39/e/8, fo. 8.

56   Ibid., fo. 7.

57   Patricia A. McCormack, "Chipewyans turn Cree: governmental and structural factors in ethnic processes," in *For Purposes of Dominion: Essays in Honour of Morris Zaslow*, ed. Kenneth S. Coates and William R. Morrison (North York, ON: Captus University Publications, 1989), 128. It is not yet clear how these marriages related to pre-contact Chipewyan-Cree marriages, known from oral traditions and some fur trade records. In the early eighteenth century, Crees raided northern Athapaskans for women and children. Patricia A. McCormack, "The many faces of Thanadelthur: documents, stories, and images," in *Reading Beyond Words: Contexts for Native History*, ed. Jennifer S.H. Brown and Elizabeth Vibert, 2nd ed (Peterborough, ON: Broadview Press, 2003), 329–364. But other marriages may have been the product of an earlier, more peaceful social situation in which at least some Chipewyans and Crees established alliances between their respective bands. It seems that all-Aboriginal plural societies pre-dated the arrival of Europeans, providing a model for their later development.

58   Duckworth, *English River Book.*

59   HBCA B.39/e/6, 3.

60   "Letter from Bishop Alexandre Taché to his mother, concerning his life with the Chipewyan Nation," trans. Father Gaston Carrière, *Prairie Forum* 3, 2 (1978): 146.

61   Royal Museum of Scotland, 5 May 1859.

62   Ray, "Periodic shortages," 4.

63   Similarly, Toby Morantz, writing about Crees of James Bay, has argued that they were neither controlled by debt nor dependent on the Hudson's Bay Company, but "fully in control of their own hunting strategies." Morantz, "So Evil a Practice," 221.

64   "Letter from Bishop Alexandre Taché," 138.

65   Henry T. Lewis, "Maskuta: the ecology of Indian fires in northern Alberta," *Western Canadian Journal of Anthropology* 7, 1 (1977): 15–52; *Fires of Spring*, prod. and dir, Henry T. Lewis, 1978; Henry T. Lewis, *A Time for Burning*, Occasional Publication No. 17 (Edmonton: Boreal Institute for Northern Studies, University of Alberta, 1982); Patricia A. McCormack, Fort Chipewyan field journal, 1975; Fond du Lac River-Black Lake field journal, 1976, in possession of the author; "Deconstructing Canadian subarctic grasslands."

66   Hearne, *Journal*, 213; Alexander Mackenzie, *The Journals and Letters of Sir Alexander Mackenzie*, ed. W. Kaye Lamb (Cambridge: Published for the Hakluyt Society at the University Press, 1970), 154; Patricia A. McCormack, *Northwind Dreaming. Fort Chipewyan 1788–1988*, exhibit catalogue, Provincial Museum of Alberta Special Publication No. 6 (Edmonton: Provincial Museum of Alberta, 1988), 48, 55.

67   McCormack, *Northwind Dreaming*, 49, 57.

68   Duckworth, *English River Book*, 11.

69   Mackenzie, *Journals and Letters*, 135.

70   European missionaries also played a role in encouraging Aboriginal industry, even though they could not realistically change much about the structure of Aboriginal societies. The greatest change may have been the Aboriginal shift to monogamy, but that did not seem to halt the traditional customs of cross-cousin marriage and the sororate.

71   Melanesian "big men" are the classic instances in the anthropological literature (e.g., Sahlins, *Stone Age Economics*, 135–139, 208.

72   HBCA B.39/a/46, fo. 41.

73   Ray, "Periodic shortages," 7–8.

74   Ibid., 10.

75   Ibid., 16–7.

76   Fur trade literature has concentrated on changes to Aboriginal cultures, especially "Indian" cultures, with far less attention paid to mixed-ancestry ("Métis") residents in these plural societies and even less to the Europeans who participated in the trade. In communities such as Fort Chipewyan, where marriages between European men and mixed-ancestry women occurred, it may be more appropriate to consider the non-Indian (non-Cree, non-Chipewyan) community as a reconstituted European community, but with a distinctive Aboriginal twist (see McCormack, "Lost women," for additional discussion on this point).

77   Foster suggested that in the French Canadian tradition, men expected eventually to evolve from "servant" to "master," which in the fur trade context was equivalent to moving from "*engagé*" to "freeman." John E. Foster, "Some questions and perspectives on the problem of metis roots," in *The New Peoples: Being and Becoming Métis in North America*, ed. Jacqueline Peterson and Jennifer S.H. Brown (Winnipeg: University of Manitoba Press, 1985), 81. Hudson's Bay Company employees were willing at times to contest their work or bargain for higher wages. For example, see Barbara Belyea, *Dark Storm Moving West* (Calgary: University of Calgary Press, 2007), 104–6. The restlessness of the worker in a capitalist system was bolstered by the independence they saw all around them.

78   Bishop Alexandre Taché, *Sketch of the North-West of America*, trans. Captain D.R. Cameron, (Montreal: John Lovell St. Nicholas Street, 1870), 108.

79   David Thompson, *Travels in Western North America, 1784–1812*, ed. Victor G. Hopwood (Toronto: Macmillan, 1971), 119, 127. Such power is especially important to people who spend time on large lakes and rivers. I have heard stories at Fort Chipewyan and elsewhere about spiritually powerful individuals who had such power over wind.

80   Wm. Watt, Fort Pitt, to his mother, 16 Jan. 1869; Watt, n.d. I am grateful to Alice King for allowing me to read and quote from this family correspondence.

81   Carolyn Podruchny has discussed similarities among oral traditions of Aboriginal people and French-Canadian voyageurs as points of "cultural conjunction" that were a form of *métissage* outside of the practice of marriage." Carolyn Podruchny, "Werewolves and windigos: narratives of cannibal monsters in French-Canadian voyageur oral tradition," *Ethnohistory* 51, 4 (2004): 678.

82   Van Kirk, *"Many Tender Ties,"* 5.

Others or Brothers?: Competing Settler and Anishinabe Discourses About Race in Upper Canada

ROBIN JARVIS BROWNLIE

SETTLER COLONIALISM IN CANADA, as in other parts of the world, was a cultural and discursive project as well as a material and geopolitical one. Ideas and images were required to justify the wholesale appropriation of other people's land and, as many scholars have shown, there was no shortage of cultural representations to furnish the necessary rationalizations.[1] In Upper Canada, the local First Nations were longstanding allies of the British Crown, whose military actions during the American Revolution and the War of 1812 had helped prevent the territory from falling to the United States. How did settlers and British officials justify the racial hierarchy they established in the lands of these loyal Mississauga, Ojibway, Algonquins, and Six Nations? Of course, there were treaties with the Mississauga and Ojibway, which the British saw as outright purchases of Aboriginal land. But the remaining reserves and other Aboriginal resources were objects of constant encroachment and squatting, while settlers began clamouring for full access to reserve lands as soon as they were established.[2] Claims about race were central to these processes, as settlers adopted and adapted colonial racial discourses to explain why they should have a privileged right to lands and resources that remained in Aboriginal hands. Clearly, only some deep-seated difference from British people could legitimize the logic of dispossession.

Moreover, images of Indians had additional discursive functions, as they served to produce whites, Anglo-Saxons, and Canadians at the same time.[3] Discussing the political representation of Native Americans in the early days of the United States, Helen Carr has observed, "in each of these texts the production of a certain kind of American (and there may be different kinds of Americans) is accomplished through the production of a certain kind of Indian (and there are then inevitably different kinds of Indians)."[4] A similar argument may be made for the British-claimed territory north of the U.S. Given the differing class, ethnic, and religious affiliations of the newcomers in British North America, dichotomizing ideas about Indian-ness and whiteness could serve to unify the disparate settlers by forging a common identification with a "white race."

There is a well-developed literature in Canada and beyond about images of the Indian that underpinned the colonial enterprise in the Americas.[5] British imperial ideology, of course, had been elaborating complex discourses about Indians since early in its colonial North American career. Thus, texts produced in Upper Canada drew on a set of conventional colonial gendered and racialized understandings that circulated within the larger British imperial world. These understandings proceeded from several assumptions: that a category such as Indian was meaningful; that there were real differences—in character, morality, and intelligence, for example—between Indians and whites; and that Euro-Canadian commentators could observe and explain the inherent nature of the Indian. There were many and conflicting strands of thought within these discourses, which could be selected and reconfigured to suit each author's purposes. How were such discourses taken up in Upper Canada and tailored to its circumstances, particularly to its relatively unusual situation of long-term military alliance and extensive treaty relations with Indigenous people? While a good deal has been written about the settlement and development of Upper Canada[6] and another important field examines First Nations people in the period,[7] there are still few historical writings that analyze the interaction between the two. More particularly, historians have not yet examined the role of Upper Canadian settlers in promoting a Canadian discourse about First Nations people, settlement, and race. As historian Cecilia Morgan has commented, "to date we have only a rudimentary understanding of British and Anglo-American immigrants' dependence on Aboriginal peoples for legitimization and justification. ... the processes whereby the former developed their own identities and subjectivities by gazing and commenting on those of the First Nations and attempting to change them require further study."[8] In this chapter, I begin to map the elaboration of racial discourses about Indian-ness and whiteness in Upper Canada.

The concerns of this chapter mirror some of those that Sylvia Van Kirk pursued in her work. *Many Tender Ties* examined the fur trade rather than the settlement era, but Sylvia was among the path-breaking scholars who took Aboriginal participation in historical events and processes seriously and sought to recover Aboriginal perspectives. She also investigated the impact of colonial racial ideology, tracing the breakdown of the integrated, multicultural fur trade society as white supremacy came to dominate the upper echelons of the traders' world.[9] My study connects as well to the work of Cecilia Morgan, who has made important contributions to the understanding of gendered colonial discourses and Aboriginal responses.[10] Like Van Kirk and Morgan, I am interested in tracing the effects of race and gender in the colonization of northern North America and, in attempting to look at both sides of that encounter, ensuring attention to Aboriginal agendas and perspectives as well as those of colonials. Like Sylvia Van Kirk and many who followed, I have investigated the voluminous archive produced by the colonizers, looking for the scattered evidence of Aboriginal actions and, occasionally, voices.

Thus, this chapter is based on two disparate sets of written records produced by individuals stemming from both sides of the colonial divide. On the one hand, there is the large archive of documents produced by colonizers, from which I have selected Upper Canadian newspapers published between roughly the 1820s and the 1850s, specifically those published in communities located near Indian reserves. Newspapers offered local perspectives aimed largely at a local market, even if most of them reprinted textual material from all over North America and the British Empire. These publications, then, can be seen as reflective of editors living in Upper Canada and speaking primarily to the settlers of that colony. On the other hand is the small archive of written documents from Aboriginal authors, from which I selected the main Aboriginal published texts of the period as well as a set of written addresses from several First Nations orators recorded in 1840–41. All these texts are from the same time period and broadly the same colonial context, but they differ considerably in their purposes and intended audiences. While it is difficult to know precisely who read the newspapers, it is clear that these publications were partly advertising vehicles, primarily for small local businesses, partly "booster" publications that sought to advance British-style settlement and development, and were also often outlets for the expression of political views. Content was determined by three main purposes: the need to attract readers, the need to attract advertisers, and the political interests of the editor. The intended audience was local settlers and clearly did not include First Nations people, most of whom could not read or speak much English.

The Aboriginal-authored documents analyzed here consist of two published books and a set of addresses delivered in 1840–41; they concern the rebuilding of the monument to fallen war hero Sir Isaac Brock. The books were written by two Ojibway men who had converted to Methodism and become Methodist preachers, Peter Jones and George Copway; the addresses were authored by leaders of several First Nations in Upper Canada who had sent men to fight in the War of 1812 and had known Sir Isaac Brock. In all cases, the intended audience was non-Aboriginal people in the British colonial world. The Brock Monument addresses were delivered to British officials of the Indian Department, and suggest an attempt to appeal to the British settler population. The books were aimed at the Christian reading public in Upper Canada as well as Britain and the United States. All the texts show clear evidence of an effort to touch the hearts and minds of settlers in the interest of evoking sympathy with First Nations people. The books, being much longer, were particularly explicit in their intent to address the negative effects of colonization and suggest new approaches, while the speeches limited themselves to suggesting a common humanity, valour, and patriotism that linked First Nations and British men.

This chapter juxtaposes these settler texts and Indigenous counter-discourses in order to examine the interaction of ideas about race, colonization, and settlement in the formative period of Upper Canada. This juxtaposition facilitates some larger conclusions about the discursive strategies of both parties. While the settler newspapers almost always emphasized difference and disconnection, the Indigenous writings were much more inclined to suggest connection and continuity, pointing to similarities, common values, and a shared past to bolster their claim to a place in the new society. In sermons, writings, and speeches, the Haudenosaunee and Anishinabeg constructed self-images that were designed to break down racial barriers, stressing their commonality with the newcomers over their differences. While critical of the discrimination, dispossession, and social harm they had experienced at the hands of many newcomers, they underlined their long-standing military alliance and solidarity with Britain and spoke to universal human qualities. In particular, they utilized gendered concepts of male valour and national defence to construct a shared history and masculinity, and thereby to envision a shared, cooperative future.

By contrast, the settlers drew clear lines of exclusion based on race and posited a future of Indigenous disappearance. Despite the polyvalent voices and emphases of the Upper Canadian newspapers, some distinct themes and patterns emerge. For one thing, their representations of nearby First Nations generally displayed a certain sympathy and often expressed a sense of responsibility for their problems. Contemporary local Indigenous people were portrayed either in relatively positive terms or as a group whose difficulties were largely caused by whites. At the same time, the most familiar negative images of Indian-ness—of moral failure and unprovoked violence—were also common in the colony's press. Such images were purveyed almost entirely with reference to faraway Indigenous groups who were demonized partly by borrowing cultural productions from the United States. Thus, the newspapers were in effect able to "have it both ways": to view their Indigenous neighbours as safe and human, and simultaneously to dehumanize Indians as a group and present the sensational stories of Indian aggression and depravity that helped justify the colonial project. A final pattern that sidestepped the whole issue of responsibility was to erase Indigenous people entirely, manufacturing settler histories that depicted colonization occurring in an empty land.

Settler Discourses about Race

The newcomers who settled in Anishinabe and Haudenosaunee territory north of the Great Lakes were a heterogeneous group with differing class, ethnic, and religious affiliations. They were Scots, Irish, English, and U.S.-born; Catholic and Protestant; middle-class and working-class. These distinctions and rivalries divided them in important ways. Discourse about race was one obvious tool to overcome such divisions by superimposing upon them an overriding white/British/Anglo-Saxon identity that trumped the other categories, at least in the presence of the racial other. The notion of racial superiority was also a convenient way to explain the justness of the colonial project. Yet race was a blunt tool, racial notions were often contradictory, and colonial actors with different agendas offered competing interpretations of the whole idea. Thus, the ways in which ideas about race were combined and enacted in this particular place and time indicate something about prevailing social relations and about the political and social aspirations among the colonists.

In settler newspapers, a variety of factors combined to produce a consistent tendency to present local First Nations in a neutral or positive light. For one thing, until at least the 1840s, settlers in Upper Canada were usually acquainted with some actual Anishinabe, Haudenosaunee, Delaware, or Wendat people.

The colony never experienced the frontier warfare with Indigenous people that was such a prominent feature of U.S. settler expansion, instead enjoying a peace maintained largely through treaties and the tradition of military alliance. In fact, Upper Canadians boasted of their situation of relative peace, contrasting it with the open conflict of the colonization process in the United States. As one writer put it in the midst of the rebellions of 1837–8, Upper Canadians were "a people living in peace and security under the faith of special treaties, and of the law of Nations."[11] The same writer complained about Americans assisting Upper Canadian rebels who had fled across the border, asserting that the U.S. should "eschew the monstrosity of conspiring with fugitives from justice" when it had so many race problems of its own, including "fifty thousand Indians eager for vengeance, for multitudinous aggressions." Canadian newspapers also criticized the maintenance of slavery and other brutalities, such as the use of bloodhounds to track down the last Seminoles fighting forced relocation: "'THE MOST FREE AND ENLIGHTENED NATION' on earth exterminating a wretched handful of poor Indians in Florida, with the aid of BLOODHOUNDS!!!"[12] Here it is obvious that racial discourses served the process of Upper Canadian identity formation, using the U.S. as a convenient foil for the assertion that the colony pursued a kinder, gentler, more enlightened policy towards racialized groups within its claimed borders.

Practical and psychological needs also helped shape the discourses of settlement. Most settler authors were intent on encouraging further immigration. Threatening images of local Indigenous people might have frightened off potential new settlers, the necessary reinforcements in the battle against the wilderness. The newcomers also had to maintain a sense of their own security, living dispersed among Indigenous peoples. These considerations militated against the most unfavourable characterizations of local groups. At the same time, the need to justify the colonial project and explain the settlers' right to this land taken from others dictated a steady refrain of anti-Indigenous rhetoric. These contradictory requirements seem to have produced a strategy that preserved Indians as a negative referent in racial representations, while avoiding the spread of anxiety about their proximity. The newspapers managed this by re-circulating negative depictions of Indians from the U.S., while ensuring that reports on nearby Indigenous groups made them appear harmless. Moreover, republished British images of natives from all over the world, particularly India, functioned as a further set of negative referents and foils for whiteness without raising the spectre of the deadly savage in one's own backyard.

Thus, the newspapers show a direct correlation between the proximity of the Indigenous group in question and the sympathy with which it was presented. While nearby groups were portrayed neutrally or in positive terms, more distant ones were subject to characterizations conforming to colonial fears and fantasies about the racial other. There was a preponderance of articles emphasizing savagery, treachery, cruelty, and vengefulness among Indians, but such characteristics were never attributed to local groups. The negative stereotype was thus effectively built and reinforced, while maintaining a sense that Canadian Indians were safe. The items that dealt with local groups focused almost entirely on benign political activities such as friendly addresses to key government officials or chiefs journeying to Europe to discuss land claims and other grievances. In 1829, for example, the *Brockville Gazette* reprinted an item from the *Quebec Gazette* briefly describing some activities of the local Wendat (Huron) and Haudenosaunee (Six Nations). Both groups were said to be sending deputations to England to press grievances about land and other economic matters. The chief of Sault St. Louis (Kahnawake) was travelling with his nephew, another chief, and an interpreter "to claim the other half of their seignory of St. Regis, which they have been refused." At the same time, "Kotska," said to be a chief of the Hurons of Lorette, had been "empowered by the tribes in both provinces, to make complaint of the diminution of their government supplies of guns and ammunition, cloathing [sic], &c. and to claim lands."[13] The item also noted that the local Indians (of unspecified nation) had set out for a hunting expedition but abandoned the excursion upon encountering foot-deep snow. These items appear of suspect reliability—the colonists were liable to call any Indigenous spokesperson a chief, and it seems rather unlikely that Indigenous people out hunting in December could be surprised (much less prevented from hunting) by a foot of snow! Nevertheless, the tone of friendly interest was typical.

Examples of negative imagery were more numerous, however, and they usually referred to Indians from south of the border—except those items addressing alcohol-related violence, which will be discussed below. The newspapers reported on hostilities among First Nations, especially those forcibly relocated west, and also between Indians and settlers or soldiers. In 1828, for example, the *Gore Gazette* reprinted an article from the *Arkansas Gazette* entitled "Disturbances among the Indians." The article reported on conditions in the Indian Territory, the region to which many eastern tribes had been moved to make way for the expanding United States. "It seems that peace and tranquility cannot be maintained in this section of the Territory, where so many Indian tribes are crowded together, possessing such various habits, and labouring under the influence of revengeful and warlike dispositions." The item recounted how the killing of an Osage man by a group of Indians, later described as "one white man, two half breeds, and two Indians," was avenged by the pursuing friends of the murdered man. The Osage were said to be under the influence of missionaries and "partially engrossed in agricultural pursuits," which of course meant they were partially "civilized." They pursued the five men and killed them all; the army was then called in to ensure there were no more hostile parties.[14]

An item in the *Brockville Gazette* entitled "Indian Hostilities on our Frontier" reported on violence in Missouri caused by settlers squatting on Indigenous land. The article, reprinted from the *Missouri Intelligencer*, overtly took the settlers' side, opening thus: "On Sunday morning last, our citizens were thrown into considerable consternation and excitement on the arrival of news that a number of respectable citizens of this country had been killed by a band of the Ioway, Sioux or Winnebagoe Indians … a few days previous." The incident was sparked by local settlers occupying new land for stock-raising several months before, to the alarm of the Indigenous group that hunted in the area (they called themselves Iowas, according to the article, but the settlers believed they were Winnebago or Sioux/Dakota). This group "ordered the settlers off, pretending that the land belonged to them, and threatening to kill them if they refused," following up this threat with visits, then harassment, and finally a "whipping" delivered to a settler named Myrtle. Myrtle then collected a group of settlers, twenty-seven in total, who "proceeded with him to try and arrange matters with the Indians or drive them off," resulting in a confrontation with the Iowa in their camp. An Iowa man cocked and levelled a gun, his adversary responded with a shot to his head, and then the general firing began, leaving eleven or twelve Iowa and three settlers dead. A large military response followed: "The Governor of Missouri has called out a thousand militia for the protection of the frontier, and has requested of Brigadier General Atkinson the aid of the U. States' troops in that quarter, and Brig. Gen. Leavenworth has already marched for the frontier with the disposable force stationed at Jefferson Barracks, amounting to fourteen companies." This piece from a U.S. paper appears to have been reprinted verbatim, including the title that referred to "our" frontier, thus reproducing rhetoric from the U.S. context without comment or alteration. In part, of course, this practice was a way of acquiring text to fill the newspaper's pages. Nevertheless, its effect was to broadcast the original author's perspective on the conflict and reinforce views of Indians as violent adversaries who wrongly opposed the taking of their land. Such accounts of armed conflict with Indigenous people consistently located the Indigenous adversaries far from Upper Canada.[15]

The pattern of differentiation between local and distant First Nations may be productively analysed through the use of literary theorist John Barrell's concept of "this/that/the other," developed in his examination of English Romantic writer Thomas de Quincy and the psychopathology of imperialism. Barrell finds in de Quincy's writing not only a self and an other, but a third party, "way over there, which is truly *other* to them both." Through the interpolation of this third party, an "absolute other," the first other can be "made over to the side of the self—to a subordinate position on that side," subsuming difference by emphasizing commonalities that set them both apart from the absolute other.[16] Barrell investigated this triangulation process as one of the mechanisms used by the British imperial power to construct a national identity that overcame differences such as class—a process that was extended to overseas colonies like Canada as well. But it appears to be at work also in the Upper Canadian journalistic treatment of Indians that distinguished between local groups and those at a significant distance, especially those in the path of the expanding United States. By displacing the negative traits of Indian-ness onto faraway groups and printing examples of the Christian, anglicized political rhetoric of the Anishinabeg and Haudenosaunee in Upper Canada, the newspapers preserved all-important colonial racial distinctions and simultaneously alleviated local anxiety about the proximity of Indians to new settlers. The otherness and outsider status even of nearby Indigenous people were not placed in question, and they remained as boundary markers of civilization that confirmed the superior, civilized status of the British newcomers. But their inherent savagery was diminished by contrast with the alleged misdeeds and character flaws of the "absolute other" American tribes.

Rhetorical Strategies of Whiteness

The racial discourses circulated in Upper Canada were not only about Indianness. Indeed, rhetorical strategies of whiteness and British-ness were a more prominent feature of the texts in which Upper Canadians represented themselves. The values and institutions they defined as quintessentially British—particularly British liberty, justice, morality, and self-control—were often primary themes in material relating to the United States and also in anecdotal references to Indigenous people. As a colony in the process of becoming, Upper Canada needed a set of justifications for the particular institutions and policies it was developing and for the order it was establishing in this once-foreign land. The settlers began immediately to develop a history that explained the presence of

British-ness far from Britain and that attempted simultaneously to indigenize settlers of British descent.[17]

One important discursive strategy visible in the newspapers is the representation of history as a story of civilization and progress in which Indigenous people by definition did not participate. Assigning Indigenous people to "anachronistic time," a position outside of history and historical process,[18] the settlers used poems and descriptions of recently settled districts to establish white origin histories that erased first peoples and dated history from the arrival of the first white settler (sometimes only a few months earlier). Whiteness was thus shown to be foundational to the colony—the necessary condition of its coming into being—which was equated with the land's progress from unpopulated wilderness into civilization. As one writer expressed this process in an 1835 description of the Midland District, "thirty years ago, this tract of country was a howling wilderness, and now it resembled a well-kept garden."[19] Or consider these words from 1828: "Indeed, when we reflect that but a few months ago, this spot, now so replete with life and enjoyment, was one vast wilderness—its sole inhabitants the savage beasts of the forest—we are almost led to question the reality of such a change."[20] Such representations appear highly ironic when one considers the nearby presence of Haudenosaunee farmers who had been growing corn, beans, and squash in the area for centuries, as had their Wendat predecessors. But this is characteristic: the settlers' discourses about history were founded on a profound disregard for the life that preceded them. "Life and enjoyment" were coterminous with British civilization and incompatible with wilderness, the place on whose disappearance the colony was predicated. In this sense, there was ample reason to associate Indians with wilderness, both being conceptual devices that registered colonial advancement through the displacement of the inferior other.

The newspapers' constructions of land and history racialized space in a simple binary, opposing white civilization to the Indigenous or simply bestial wilderness. Newspaper writers were fond of such phrases as "regions where but a short time ago howling wolves and savages trod."[21] Indigenous people did not count as "peopling" an area, an activity that was reserved for whites. For instance, one article describing the Midland District and Kingston asserted "this rich and highly cultivated tract of country, was first peopled by a bold and enterprising set of men, to whom toil was a pleasure, and danger a sport."[22] (The context makes clear that these words referred to European settlers, not First Nations.) Often the pre-settlement era was depicted as lacking humans entirely.

For instance, an 1828 poem about the town of Guelph rhapsodized about the nearby river, "and gave its sweet murmurs unheard of by man;/ No foot pressed its bank, save the deer stalking by,/ Or when wild ones of forest in thirst to it ran."[23] In this case Indigenous existence was entirely suppressed, since the river was "unheard of by man." In other instances Indigenous people could potentially be included in terms such as "wild ones."

In praising the progress of civilization and the destruction of the wilderness, the historical constructions presented in newspapers foresaw and implicitly celebrated the disappearance of Indigenous people, who would be eliminated along with the wilderness they both symbolized and depended upon. In keeping with this expectation, the newspapers enacted a powerful, insistent association of Indians with violence, war, and death. This association is particularly noteworthy given the absence of warfare in the transfer of Upper Canada from Indigenous to British hands. In the late 1840s, Goderich's paper the *Huron Signal* ran a number of items about Indigenous death, with the following titles: "The Indian's Death Song," "The Grave of the Indian King," and "The Dead Squaw." "The Grave of the Indian King" talked a good deal about living Six Nations people, but placed them far in the past and centred on the death of the key figure, a "king" of the Six Nations.[24] The other two items painted pictures of unnamed, iconic Indian figures—one of each sex—lying dead, and used these constructions to emphasize their difference from the European ideal. In many other newspaper items at least one Indigenous person ended up dead, often in a romantically tragic scene.

Linking Indigenous people with death was, in a sense, the ultimate resolution to the contradictions and dilemmas of colonization. In this context, the constant talk of the wilderness falling under the woodman's axe was also a coded reference to the disappearance of Indians, anticipating the institutionalization of the "Vanishing Race" concept. Though the seeds of this idea were visible in the discourses of the 1820s to 1850s, the time was not ripe for its full unfolding in Upper Canada. There were still too many Indigenous people, exercising too much active resistance to colonization, to envisage their complete disappearance or, more importantly, to paint their extinction as a tragic moment. For now, the melodramatized deaths of individuals stood in for the later tragic expectation of annihilation. Perhaps most important at this point was to exonerate whites in the passing of Indigenous people, portraying their deaths largely as the result of their own failings or internal violence, or as the unfortunate but inevitable result of the clash with the advanced British civilization.

Indigenous Discourses about Race

Much as settler discourses were directed to a colonial and imperial audience, at least some Indigenous people were aware of them and concerned about their impact. In order to examine the Indigenous side of the story, this chapter uses two sets of texts to make a preliminary exploration of Indigenous strategic responses to settler exclusions and to consider the discourses of self, race, and gender they produced in the process. On the one hand, there are the relatively well-known publications of the two Anishinabe (Ojibway) Methodists who published books in the period, Peter Jones and George Copway. On the other hand, there are the speeches and written addresses delivered by representatives of the Anishinabeg and other Indigenous groups in 1840 and 1841, on the occasion of the destruction of Sir Isaac Brock's monument.

Common themes and approaches are evident in these records. In particular, these spokesmen addressed themselves to Britons and Euro-Canadians as friends, compatriots, and participants in common undertakings. The speakers of 1840–41 emphasized the war experiences they shared with Euro-Canadians and their part in defending Canada during the War of 1812. They made financial contributions to the reconstruction of the Brock Monument and in so doing stressed their unity of purpose with their "white brethren," not only in rebuilding the monument but also in safeguarding their common country.[25] Peter Jones and George Copway placed more emphasis on the Christianity they shared with their reading public, but both also alluded to the history of military alliance—in fact, some of the Brock Monument addresses were printed in Jones' book *History of the Ojebway Indians*. Through an appeal to Christian solidarity as well as military cooperation, Jones and Copway hoped to influence public opinion and Indian policy in more favourable directions. In all these instances, the emphasis was on common experiences, values, and goals.

An examination of gendered self-representation in these texts reveals another area in which these spokesmen sought to build bridges of understanding. While the notion of race served to separate them from the settlers, gender was a commonality that Indigenous men could manipulate to suggest sameness, equality, and unity. In their speeches and writings, they constructed images of Anishinabe and Haudenosaunee men with which British and Euro-Canadian men of influence could identify. Most of the Brock Monument addresses expressed Indigenous notions of masculinity that valued military prowess, valour, and the male role of national self-defence—traits they knew were equally admired among the British. Similarly, in his book *Traditional History and Char-*

acteristic Sketches of The Ojibway Nation, George Copway devoted considerable space to accounts of war and the Anishinabeg's successes in territorial expansion. Copway and especially Jones also stressed masculine virtues prescribed by Christianity, such as temperance, hard work, missionary zeal, and chivalrous treatment of women. Pointing to their history as British allies and to the cooperative efforts of Euro-Canadian and Anishinabe missionaries, the Anishinabeg suggested a racial order based on equality and common purpose rather than conflict and defeat. By constructing a shared history and masculinity, these men endorsed a common, cooperative future.

The Brock Monument addresses of 1840–41 focussed on the shared experience of invasion and offered a subtly gendered Indigenous understanding of the War of 1812 and its place in their history. Reaching across the racialized borders of colonial interaction, the speakers emphasized the suffering and loss they had shared with whites during the war and their common determination to defend the country that was their home. They also stressed the male role of warrior and defender that their men shared with the white men. The speaker for the Walpole Island Anishinabeg declared of Sir Isaac Brock, "that chief led us as well as you to victory; on that Hill which we conquered, his blood was mingled with ours."[26] He asked that the new monument acknowledge the Indigenous war effort: "Father, when the passerby gazes on the Monument of Brock let him see written: 'The red man struck the foe by the side of the dead, he lives in their hearts, and their hand has here placed one Stone to his memory.'"[27] The Mississauga of Rice Lake stated, "some of us fought on the same field, on which the gallant General fell.—We then felt the same sorrow in our hearts, that our loyal brothers in arms, the white men, felt; and we still unite with them in the deepest regret at our common loss."[28] Through the financial contributions they made, these groups sought to transform the monument into a symbol not only of their joint victory in the War of 1812, but also of the common cause of rebuilding the monument itself. The structure would then stand as a material reminder of a shared present as well as a shared history.

This moment in 1840–41 represents only one incident in a sustained practice of Indigenous people's self-representation (and action) as defenders of Canada and the British crown. Only a few years earlier, during the Upper Canada rebellion, First Nations had offered military support for the Crown to help put down the insurrection (in fact, some preparations were made to mobilize their warriors, though it never became necessary). George Copway asserted "the Indian population of Canada have ever manifested a strong friendly feeling towards the

British government."[29] In 1855, the Ojibways of New Credit sent money from their band funds to be donated to the Patriotic Fund in England for the Crimean War; the Six Nations of the Grand River donated money to the fund and also offered to send some of their young men to fight for Britain.[30] When the Boer War broke out, the Six Nations of the Grand River again offered to send a contingent of men to assist the British, noting that this action was "in accordance with the customs, usages, and treaties of their forefathers, who have in the past always fought in the defence of the Crown and British flag."[31] This approach united Indigenous men with settler males in a shared role of national defence, continuing an Indigenous diplomatic practice that stressed mutual military aid as a key feature of cooperation and friendship between nations. Moreover, Indigenous self-representation as defenders of the British Crown, particularly in the decades after the War of 1812, tapped into a discourse about loyalty and patriotism that had strong currency in the colony. Since the late eighteenth century, declarations of attachment to the British connection and loyalty to crown and empire were utilized as "an important way of legitimating and validating claims to various kinds of political power."[32] The gendered implications of these discourses similarly resonated with the themes Indigenous men had emphasized: "The meaning of the war and of loyalty itself was fixed in language that celebrated masculine military struggle and sacrifice."[33] Through repeated allusions to their loyalty and military support, First Nations people sought to keep alive a relationship of goodwill and mutual protection between themselves and the crown that became increasingly important as their own numerical significance and political power declined.

Gender and race also figured prominently in two publications: George Copway's *Traditional History and Characteristic Sketches of the Ojibway Nation*, which appeared in 1850, and Peter Jones' *History of the Ojebway Indians*, published posthumously in 1861. Both books were clearly designed to construct a counter-discourse to British and American constructions of Indians. Jones and Copway presented images of their people that emphasized qualities they believed their white audiences would identify with and value. In Copway's case this meant asserting the superiority of some aspects of Anishinabe culture, while for Jones it entailed denouncing the old ways and asserting the Anishinabeg's aptitude for embodying Christian virtues once they had accepted the gospel. Gendered representations were central to each man's discursive strategy.

Inevitably, both books were haunted by the image of the savage, the colonial invention that so powerfully underpinned the British imperial project. Copway's book unequivocally adopted the figure of the Noble Savage, while Jones embraced a belief in the Ignoble Savage. Both texts assumed that these figures were to disappear through a process of acculturation and Christianization. But in Copway's presentation, Anishinabe ways should not disappear entirely, since the whites had things to learn from them, especially their non-coercive forms of law, government, and social control, which were based on an appeal to reason rather than on threats and punishments. In keeping with this positive reading of Anishinabe culture and critical approach to European ways, Copway also mounted a much more explicit colonial critique, though there were moments of critique in Jones' text as well. In Jones' narrative, Anishinabe ways were almost entirely depicted as cruel, sensuous, indolent, and unjust, and the men's treatment of women played a significant role in this portrayal.

Copway's *Traditional History and Characteristic Sketches* focused almost entirely on the past, presenting a romanticized version of the Anishinabeg's history and portraying them as natural Christians whose government was based on reason rather than force. He depicted a whole, harmonious, happy society that embodied many of the Christian virtues even before Christianity entered their lands. In Copway's words, "peace and happiness entwined around the fire-side of the Indian once. Union, harmony, and a common brotherhood cemented them all."[34] The book praised the Anishinabeg for their physical hardihood and beauty, and for their superior rationality—revealed, for instance, in their form of government. Copway remarked about their means of obtaining social consensus without resort to force, "they would not as brutes be whipped into duty. They would as men be persuaded to the right."[35] Given the centrality of reason in British claims to moral superiority, Copway's words were aimed straight at the heart of the "civ-sav" dichotomy.[36]

Copway began his text with a detailed description of the Anishinabeg's country in a format obviously drawn from travel narratives. The text effectively reclaimed and symbolically repossessed the lands of the Anishinabeg, almost all of which had been appropriated by the colonizers by this time. The various sections of this chapter bore subheadings such as "Their Lakes" and "Their Rivers," citing as the main Anishinabe rivers the St. Lawrence, the Mississippi, and the Red River—watercourses that white readers would certainly have identified as their own, not Anishinabe property. At the same time, Copway deployed an idealizing description of the country itself to exalt the Anishinabeg, especially the men. After lavishly describing the land's beauty, Copway wrote the Anishinabeg themselves through the landscape, not in order to reduce them to wildlife but to endow them with the rugged splendour of their own country. As he wrote, "it is not much to be wondered at that in such a climate, such a strong, athletic, and hardy race of men should exist, as the Ojibways are generally acknowledged to be."[37] It is most instructive to juxtapose this approach with the Upper Canadian narratives of landscape described above, in which Indigenous people were similarly equated with the natural features of the land. Copway seems to have adopted the same terms, but inverted them by expressing admiration for the land, rivers, and forests in their natural state, and by defining them as a home, not a wilderness. "The mountains, rivers, lakes, cliffs, and caverns of the Ojibway country, impress one with the thought that Nature has there built a home for Nature's children."[38] By pairing the Romantic movement's idealization of nature and the colonial equation of Indigenous people with wilderness, Copway was able to produce a positive image of his own people. Similarly, he expressed a nationalism that his settler readers could recognize: "I love my country; and will any of my readers condemn a child of the forest for loving his country and his nation?"[39]

Copway had much more to say about men than women. Anishinabe men were depicted first and foremost as the essence of masculine power, as heroic warriors who triumphed over their enemies, expanded their territory, and bravely aided the Europeans in their wars. Copway devoted several whole chapters to accounts of the Anishinabeg's wars with the Haudenosaunee and the Dakota, recounting how the Anishinabeg united with other tribes to drive the mighty Haudenosaunee out of the lands north of Lake Ontario, which they then claimed as their own. While the cruelty of war was not absent from his narrative, the central thrust was to emphasize his people's military prowess. Even in the large sections of the book that did not deal with war, Anishinabe men appeared as masters of their environment; in Copway's words, "ruler(s) of the forest world."[40] Asking his readers to picture an Anishinabe man standing on a mountain, he called him "one of Nature's sons standing in her own battlements,"[41] a military image that again invoked the warrior role.

The corollary to this positive depiction of Anishinabe culture was an outspoken critique of colonialism. Copway criticized Yankee commerce and enterprise for their insatiable appetite for Indigenous lands and their willingness to obtain them unjustly. He was particularly critical of the way alcohol was used by white traders and others to destroy Indigenous people for their personal profit. He also mounted a broader critique of white policies and civilization, calling into question the colonizers' implementation of their own Christian and civilizing rhetoric. Copway pointed out that European institutions such as prisons and poor-houses were indications of a society's failure to obtain its goals ration-ally and effectively, and he contrasted these harsh, punitive methods with the old Anishinabe system which used persuasion and reason rather than force to achieve social order. Finally, Copway addressed the accusation of savagery that whites made against Indigenous people, reversing the direction of condemna-tion. He cited the North American wars between whites as one cause of the massive decrease in the Indigenous population, and added, "during these wars the Indian has been called from the woods to show his fearless nature, and for obeying, and showing himself fearless, it is said of him that he is 'a man without a tear.' He has been stigmatized with the name—'a savage,'—by the very people who called for his aid, and he gave it."[42] White people were censured here for their ingratitude, and the courage and military prowess of Indigenous men was once again highlighted—with a subtext, perhaps, of superior bravery. At the same time, the passage reminded readers of the crucial role First Nations had played as military allies in Europe's North American wars.

Peter Jones took a very different tack in his work, published eleven years after Copway's. Jones seemed concerned with debunking romantic portrayals of Indigenous life such as those offered by Copway—in fact, he may have been responding partly to Copway's depictions. One of his goals was to counter the claims of those who opposed missionization and assimilation programs on the grounds that Indigenous people were better left to themselves, a position that was detrimental to his own project of universal Christianization and Europe-anization. His tactic for countering opposition to missionization was to paint Indigenous life in the most negative terms, and he focussed particularly on men to represent the worst features of Anishinabe culture as he saw it. Thus the Ig-noble Savage (clearly gendered male) stalked the pages of *History of the Ojeb-way Indians*. Jones painted a picture of squalor and alcohol abuse in Indigenous communities, reflecting some of the experiences he had as a child.[43] He claimed that First Nations people in their uncolonized state were never happy, assert-ing: "from experience of my early life, I can truly say, that their imaginary bliss is so mixed up with everything that is abominable and cruel, that it would be vain to look for real happiness among savage tribes."[44] Jones's text, then, repro-duced many of his era's negative colonial stereotypes and discourses of other-ness, though from time to time he also disrupted them.

Jones's gendered representations posed a marked contrast to those offered by Copway. His book reproduced the classic stereotype of Indigenous women as mistreated drudges who performed all the labour while their husbands lounged in camp.[45] Only Christianity could save women from this fate by turning their men into gentle, upstanding Christian farmers who relieved women of the outdoor work so they could tend the domestic realm. While Jones's depiction of Anishinabe men did not deny them their masculinity, it was clear from the text that the forms of masculinity defined by their own culture—especially the emphasis on becoming a warrior—were among the first things to be changed by a rescuing Christianity. They would instead adopt the virtues of Christian masculinity, among which Jones foregrounded Christ-like qualities such as gentleness and solicitousness towards women. Jones also argued that many Indigenous people were sufficiently educated and acculturated to exercise full civil rights and to "use the rights of British subjects as judiciously as many of their white neighbours."[46] This assertion—claiming rights that were pre-eminently male in the Euro-Canadian context of the time—was Jones's way of quietly laying claim to the rationality that Copway also claimed for the Anishinabeg, the difference being that Copway constructed that rationality as an Anishinabe quality while Jones attributed it to the influence of whites. Thus, in Jones's work, Indigenous masculinity was to be remade in Christ's image, again for the purpose of creating commonality among all of Upper Canada's inhabitants. Ultimately, he intended this process to serve as a vehicle for access to the rights and privileges of non-Indigenous settlers in order to prevent further dispossession and marginalization of his people.

Interestingly, there were some areas of confluence between settler discourses and those of Indigenous people. Perhaps the most obvious relates to alcohol—both settlers and Indigenous spokespersons not only deplored the baneful effect of alcohol on Indigenous communities, but also blamed white whisky-sellers for the harm the drug caused. For all parties, this reality called into question the claimed moral superiority of whites. For instance, in an 1843 story entitled "An Indian Tragedy," a young Potawatomi woman in Michigan was said to have killed her alcoholic husband after he sold her favourite pony for drink. According to the story, her father, the chief, was then required by tribal law to pronounce a death sentence on her. The story focussed largely on a melodramatic account of the father's suffering at being required to condemn his daughter, as well as a gory account of her execution. But it ended with a moral about the alcohol trade: "Thus perished, says my informant, the best Indian and handsomest squaw of their tribe, the victim of the whisky seller, who is far more guilty than either of the others of a moral wrong."[47] In a similar vein, an 1857 letter in the *Grand River Sachem* headed "The Murder near Lindley's" blamed liquor-sellers for the death of an Indigenous man. The author, "Spectator," noted that the man had been killed by another Indigenous man when both were intoxicated. Pointing out that the law against selling alcohol to Indians was routinely flouted with impunity, Spectator concluded, "let me ask, Mr. Editor, which is the greater criminal, the Indian who in a fit of drunkenness, cimmits [sic] murder, or the white man who, in his sober senses, is daily violating the law, and that too when he knows that such violation of law will naturally lead to crime and bloodshed?"[48] An 1856 letter in the *Caledonia Advertiser* adopted a similar tone of reproach, beginning with some rhetorical questions about the claimed superiority of whites: "Where is that enlightenment, that social order, that high state of civilization which we profess to have attained? Where that purity of morals, that as British subjects we attribute to ourselves?" The author went on to cite two examples of Indigenous people being abused by whites while intoxicated, one a scene that occurred opposite Young's Saloon "between a couple of Indians, in a beastly state of intoxication." According to the letter-writer, there was "a party present, who set them to fight, then set his Dog upon them; and then, by way of winding up the affair, knocked their heads together."[49] Instead of blaming the liquor-sellers, this writer was concerned to expose a broader pattern of settlers abusing Indigenous people made vulnerable by alcohol.

Indigenous authors were equally concerned about the liquor problem. George Copway repeatedly condemned the introduction of alcohol, at times linking it explicitly with a colonial campaign to destroy Indigenous peoples: "The pale face says that there is a fate hanging over the Indian bent on his destruction. Preposterous! They give him liquors to destroy himself with, and then charge the great Good Spirit as the author of their misery and mortality."[50] Copway argued that the introduction of alcohol had brought the most deadly effects of colonization, greater even than the impact of disease. He also noted that the liquor-sellers had profited from their wrong-doing: "The fire-water has done its work of disaster. By it the glad shouts of the youth of our land have died away in wails of grief! Fathers have followed their children to their graves. ... around the cheering fires of the Indian, the white man has received the gain of avarice. ... Wave after wave of destruction has gone on—the raven-wings of the angel of death have covered their fires, and still unsatisfied, it screams for more victims— all, all,—yes, all for '*model New England rum*.'"[51]

Peter Jones, too, spoke repeatedly about the curse of alcohol, citing it as the primary cause of Indigenous people's numerical decline. Characteristically, he parcelled out the blame equally, arguing that the "savage passions" and lifestyle of Indigenous people were central to the problem: "Of all the causes which have contributed to the rapid decrease of the Indian tribes, the abuse of ardent spirits, while following their native mode of life, is, in my opinion, the primary and the most important. For when an Indian is intoxicated, all the savage passions of his nature assume the entire control, often leading him to commit the most barbarous acts of cruelty and even murder."[52] Despite this emphasis on Indigenous responsibility, the preacher also included in his published works a number of passages delivering an evangelical warning for the whites involved in liquor-selling, including these words: "What an awful account must the wicked whites give at the great day of judgement, when the blood of those Indians slain and ruined by strong drink will be required at their hands! May the Lord have mercy upon the poor white heathens!" [53]

For both Indigenous and settler commentators, the practice of urging liquor on Indigenous people highlighted the failure of Euro-Canadians to abide by Christian principles. Their denunciations were usually not aimed at whites in general, but at liquor-sellers or "the worst classes of pale faces,"[54] or sometimes frontier settlers as a group. Un-Christian behaviour was the problem, and Christianity was deemed to be the solution. The overall message, then, was that some whites were sinful, while Indigenous people *as a group* were weak, lacking in self-control, and often "savage" (which implied a lack of self-control, but also a heightened capacity for violence and immorality). No one mentioned that only some Indigenous people chose to drink, nor did anyone attempt to analyse the underlying social causes of alcohol abuse. Thus, while such narratives appeared on the surface to denounce whites, in the end they can be seen as part and parcel of the larger discourse of Indigenous deficiency and white superiority.

Conclusion

Historian James Axtell has pointed out that, in initial encounters, Europeans expected Indigenous peoples to be different and mostly inferior, while Indigenous peoples expected "others" to be similar and equal or superior to themselves.[55] After centuries of contact, vestiges of this pattern were still refracted in the racial discourses of Upper Canada, a reflection of the two parties' differing needs and positions as well as their cultural frameworks. In negotiating their era's ideologies of difference, George Copway and Peter Jones both made strategic accommodations, acknowledging difference while proposing a future of similarity and equality. The Brock Monument speakers of 1840–41 evoked the themes of common struggle, loss, victory, and love of country to underline their shared humanity and solidarity with the white newcomers. The larger goal for all these

Indigenous men was to surmount the barriers erected by colonial racial ideologies—partly through the use of gender—in order to re-establish more reciprocal relations. By this time, they were obviously the weaker party in the colonial encounter, and they had little left but words with which to fight for their remaining lands and a place in the new society. Until 1860, Britain was the arbiter between First Nations and settlers in Upper Canada, and Indigenous men addressed its officials and its public in the language of loyalty and attachment, but also of masculine sacrifice and valour.

For their part, the settlers were intent on elaborating difference as a strategic weapon against the inclusion and equality Indigenous people sought, and as a unifying device to help create a homogeneous, distinctly British colony. Their discourses about race included not only references to Indians, but also a whole collection of imperial subjects within the British Empire, whose alleged customs and actions contrasted with the upright, civilized behaviour of Britons in Canada and elsewhere.[56] Most importantly, racial representations served to create images of whiteness that both unified the disparate settlers and justified their continuing expansion into new Aboriginal territories. Much as they might welcome the declarations of loyalty and solidarity offered by Aboriginal spokespersons, British settlers in Upper Canada were determined to maintain racial divides that served so effectively to uphold their own territorial claims, their privileged political status, and their social dominance.

Notes

1   See, for example, Edward W. Said, *Culture and Imperialism* (New York: Knopf, 1993); Mary Louise Pratt, *Imperial Eyes: Travel Writing and Transculturation* (London: Routledge, 1992); *Tensions of Empire: Colonial Cultures in a Bourgeois World*, eds. Frederick Cooper and Ann Laura Stoler (Berkeley and Los Angeles: University of California Press, 1997); Catherine Hall, *Civilising Subjects: Metropole and Colony in the English Imagination 1830–1867* (Chicago: University of Chicago Press, 2002); *Race, Space, and the Law: Unmapping a White Settler Society*, ed. Sherene Razack (Toronto: Between the Lines, 2002); *Unsettling Settler Societies: Articulations of Gender, Race, Ethnicity, and Class*, eds. D. Stasiulis and N. Yuval-Davis (London: Sage, 1995); Sara Mills, *Discourses of Difference: An Analysis of Women's Travel Writing and Colonialism* (New York: Routledge, 1991); Anne McClintock, *Imperial Leather: Race, Gender, and Sexuality in the Colonial Conquest* (New York: Routledge, 1995); Reginald Horsman, *Race and Manifest Destiny: The Origins of American Racial Anglo-Saxonism* (Cambridge: Harvard University Press, 1981).

2   See Sidney L. Harring, *White Man's Law. Native People in Nineteenth-Century Canadian Jurisprudence* (Toronto: University of Toronto Press, 1998).

3   For the sake of readability, I have chosen to avoid lumbering the text with quotation marks, but I should emphasize that I understand terms like "Indian," "white," "Anglo-Saxon," and "Canadian" to be problematic constructions, not self-explanatory descriptors. The term "Indian" is used here only in reference to racial constructions, not to refer to actual people.

4   Helen Carr, *Inventing the American Primitive. Politics, Gender and the Representation of Native American Literary Traditions, 1789–1936* (New York: New York University Press, 1996), 11.

5   See, for example, Deborah Doxtator, *Fluffs and Feathers. An Exhibit on the Symbols of Indianness. A Resource Guide* (Woodland Cultural Centre, 1992); Daniel Francis, *The Imaginary Indian: The Image of the Indian in Canadian Culture* (Vancouver: Arsenal Pulp Press, 1992); Sarah Carter, *Capturing Women: The Manipulation of Cultural Imagery in Canada's West* (Montreal/Kingston: McGill-Queen's University Press, 1997); J.E. Chamberlin, *The Harrowing of Eden: White Attitudes Toward North American Natives* (Toronto: Fitzhenry and Whiteside, 1975); Olive Dickason, *The Myth of the Savage and the Beginnings of French Colonialism in the Americas* (Edmonton: University of Alberta Press, 1984, reprinted 1997); Terry Goldie, *Fear and Temptation: The Image of the Indigene in Canadian, Australian and New Zealand Literature* (Kingston: McGill-Queen's University Press, 1989); Carole Gerson, "Nobler Savages: Representations of Native Women in the Writings of Susanna Moodie and Catharine Parr Traill," *Journal of Canadian Studies* 32, 2 (Summer 1997): 5–21; Elizabeth Vibert, "Real Men Hunt Buffalo: Masculinity, Race, and Class in British Fur Traders' Narratives," in *Gender and History in Canada*, eds. J. Parr and M. Rosenfeld (Toronto: Copp Clark, 1996); Elizabeth Vibert, *Traders' Tales: Narratives of Cultural Encounters in the Columbia Plateau, 1807–1846* (Norman: University of Oklahoma Press, 1997); Julia Emberley, *Defamiliarizing the Aboriginal: Cultural Practices and Decolonization in Canada* (Toronto: University of Toronto Press, 2007); James Clifton, *The Invented Indian: Cultural Fictions and Government Policies* (New Brunswick: Transaction Publishers, 1990); Robert F. Berkhofer Jr., *The White Man's Indian: Images of the American Indian from Columbus to the Present* (New York: Vintage Books, 1979).

6   John Clarke, *Land, Power, and Economics on the Frontier of Upper Canada* (Montreal/Kingston: McGill-Queen's University Press, 2001); E. Reginald Good, "Mississauga-Mennonite Relations in the Upper Grand River Valley," *Ontario History* 87, 2 (June 1995); *Colonial Leviathan: State Formation in Mid-Nineteenth-Century Canada*, eds. Allan Greer and Ian Radforth (Toronto: University of Toronto Press, 1992); Patricia Jasen, *Wild Things: Nature, Culture, and Tourism in Ontario, 1790–1914* (Toronto:

University of Toronto Press, 1995); Douglas McCalla, *Planting the Province: The Economic History of Upper Canada, 1784–1870* (Toronto: University of Toronto Press, 1993); Cecilia Morgan, *Public Men and Virtuous Women: The Gendered Languages of Religion and Politics in Upper Canada, 1791–1850* (Toronto: University of Toronto Press, 1996); Carol Wilton, *Popular Politics and Political Culture in Upper Canada, 1800–1850* (Montreal/Kingston: McGill-Queen's University Press, 2000); Julia Roberts, *In Mixed Company: Taverns and Public Life in Upper Canada* (Vancouver: UBC Press, 2009); Jane Errington, *Emigrant Worlds and Transatlantic Communities: Migration to Upper Canada in the First Half of the Nineteenth Century* (Montreal/Kingston: McGill-Queen's University Press, 2007); Jane Errington, *The Lion, The Eagle, and Upper Canada: A Developing Colonial Ideology* (Kingston/ Montreal: McGill-Queen's University Press, 1987).

7   Carl Benn, *The Iroquois in the War of 1812* (Toronto: University of Toronto Press, 1998); David Calverley, "Who Controls the Hunt? Ontario's *Game Act*, the Canadian Government, and the Ojibwa, 1800–1940" (PhD thesis, University of Ottawa, 1999); Janet E. Chute, *The Legacy of Shingwaukonse. A Century of Native Leadership* (Toronto: University of Toronto Press, 1998); Sidney L. Harring, *White Man's Law; Nin.Da.Waab. Jig. Gin Das Winan. Documenting Aboriginal History in Ontario* (Toronto: Champlain Society, 1996); *Aboriginal Ontario: Historical Perspectives on the First Nations*, eds. Edward S. Rogers and Donald B. Smith (Toronto: Dundurn Press, 1994); Peter S. Schmalz, *The Ojibwa of Southern Ontario* (Toronto: University of Toronto Press, 1991); Donald B. Smith, *Sacred Feathers: the Rev. Peter Jones (Kahkewaquonaby) and the Mississauga Indians* (Toronto: University of Toronto Press, 1987); Elizabeth Graham, *Medicine Man to Missionary. Missionaries as Agents of Change among the Indians of Southern Ontario, 1784–1867* (Toronto: P. Martin and Associates, 1975).

8   Cecilia Morgan, "Turning Strangers into Sisters: Missionaries and Colonization in Upper Canada." In *Sisters or Strangers? Immigrant, Ethnic, and Racialized Women in Canadian History*, eds. M. Epp, F. Iacovetta, and F. Swyripa (Toronto: University of Toronto Press, 2004), 24.

9   Sylvia Van Kirk, *"Many Tender Ties": Women in Fur-Trade Society in Western Canada, 1670–1870* (Winnipeg: Watson and Dwyer, 1980). For the impact of racial ideology on fur trade society, see 173–244.

10   See, for instance, Cecilia Morgan, "'A Wigwam to Westminster': Performing Mohawk Identity in Imperial Britain, 1890s-1900s," *Gender and History* 25, 2 (Aug. 2003): 319– 41; Cecilia Morgan, "History, Nation, Empire: Gender and the Work of Southern Ontario Historical Societies, 1890–1920s," *Canadian Historical Review* 82, 3 (September 2001): 491–528; Cecilia Morgan, "Private Lives and Public Performances: Aboriginal Women in a Settler Society, Ontario, Canada, 1920s–1960s," *Journal of Colonialism and Colonial History*: Special issue, Colonialism in Settler Societies 4, 3 (2003): 1–16.

11   *Cornwall Observer*, 4 January 1838, 2.

12   "Bloodhounds," *Cornwall Observer*, 6 February 1840, 2 (emphasis in original).

13   *Brockville Gazette*, c. December 1829.

14   "'Disturbances among the Indians,'" *Gore Gazette*, vol. II, no. 26, Saturday, 23 August 1828, 2 (N12 R1p). Reprinted from the *Arkansas Gazette*.

15   "Indian Hostilities on our Frontier," *Brockville Gazette*, 28 August 1829, 2. Reprinted from the *Missouri Intelligencer*.

16   John Barrell, *The Infection of Thomas de Quincy: A Psychopathology of Imperialism* (London: Harvard University Press, 1991), 10–11, 18–19, quoted in Catherine Hall, *Civilising Subjects: Metropole and Colony in the English Imagination 1830–1867* (Chicago: University of Chicago Press, 2002), 19.

17   For a thorough discussion of indigenization as a goal of English-Canadian literature, see Terry Goldie, *Fear and Temptation*.

18   For useful analyses of this process, see Maureen Konkle, *Writing Indian Nations: Indian Intellectuals and the Politics of Historiography, 1827–1863* (Chapel Hill and London: University of North Carolina Press, 2004), 6, 36; and Colin M. Coates and Cecilia Morgan, *Heroines and History: Representation of Madeleine de Verchères and Laura Secord* (Toronto: University of Toronto Press, 2002), 257–74.

19   "Travels in Upper Canada, No. XIII. Midland District—Kingston," *British Whig*, c. June 1835. Reprinted from *Montreal Gazette*.

20   "Guelph Anniversary," *Gore Gazette*, Saturday, 23 August 1828, 2.

21   "Agriculture," *Cayuga Sachem*, Friday, 18 August 1854, 1.

22   "Travels in Upper Canada, No. XIII. Midland District—Kingston," *British Whig*, 14 July 1835, 2. Reprinted from *Montreal Gazette* (emphasis added).

23   James Keough, "Guelph," *Gore Gazette*, Saturday, 15 November 1828.

24   Goderich, *Huron Signal*, Friday, 16 June 1848, 1, and Friday, 23 June 1848, 1.

25   The expression "white brethren" was used in the addresses from the Walpole Island, Saugeen, Chippewa, and Six Nations speakers. Archives of Ontario, F1151, MU296, Brock Monument Papers 1840–1857 VI Indian Papers.

26   Archives of Ontario, MU 296, F1151, Folder VI, Indian Papers, "Address of the Walpole Island Indians."

27   Ibid.

28   Archives of Ontario, MU 296, F1151, Folder VI, Indian Papers, "Address of the Mississauga Indians of Rice Lake, dated at Rice Lake Mission, Otonabee, Jan. 7, 1841,—signed by George Paudash, John Crow, John Copoway, and John [illegible]."

29   George Copway (Kahgegagahbow), *The Traditional History and Characteristic Sketches of The Ojibway Nation* (Toronto: Prospero Canadian Collection, 2001; orig. London: C. Gilpin, 1850), 201.

30   Peter Jones, *History of the Ojebway Indians; with especial reference to their Conversion to Christianity* (London: A.W. Bennett, 1861), 214, also reported in "The Indian Subscription to the Patriotic Fund," *Cayuga Sachem*, 8 June 1855.

31   Canada, *Sessional Papers*, Annual Report of the Department of Indian Affairs, 1899 (Ottawa: 1900), xviii.

32   Morgan, *Public Men and Virtuous Women*, 23.

33   Ibid., 52.

34   Copway, *Traditional History and Characteristic Sketches*, 264.

35   Ibid., 144.

36   Native Studies scholar Emma LaRocque developed the expression 'civ-sav' in her article "The Métis in English Canadian Literature," *Canadian Journal of Native Studies* 3, 1 (1983): 86.

37   Copway, 10.

38   Ibid., 3.

39   Ibid., 14.

40   Ibid.

41   Ibid.

42   Ibid., 263.

43   Donald B. Smith, *Sacred Feathers*, 38, 67–8.

44 Jones, *History of the Ojebway Indians*, 28.

45 Jones, *History of the Ojebway Indians*, 60. For an analysis of the "squaw drudge" in colonial mythology, see David D. Smits, "The 'Squaw Drudge': A Prime Index of Savagism," *Ethnohistory* 29, 4 (1982).

46 Jones, *History of the Ojebway Indians*, 218.

47 Ibid.

48 Spectator, "The Murder near Lindley's," *Grand River Sachem*, 17 June 1857.

49 Watchman, "To the Editor of the Advertiser," *Caledonia Advertiser*, Wednesday, 21 May 1856, 2.

50 Copway, *Traditional History and Characteristic Sketches*, 93–4.

51 Ibid., 264.

52 Jones, *History of the Ojebway Indians*, 30.

53 Peter Jones, *Life and Journal of Kah-ke-wa-quo-na-by (Rev. Peter Jones), Wesleyan Missionary* (Toronto: Missionary Committee, Canada Conference, 1860), 29.

54 Copway, *Traditional History and Characteristic Sketches*, 255.

55 James Axtell, *Beyond 1492: Encounters in Colonial North America* (New York: Oxford University Press, 1992), 30–33.

56 See, for instance, Morgan, *Public Men and Virtuous Women*, 87.

Attitudes Toward "Miscegenation" in Canada, the United States, New Zealand, and Australia, 1860–1914[1]

VICTORIA FREEMAN

IN 1863 A NEW WORD WAS ADDED TO THE LANGUAGE OF RACE.[2] Coined in London for a social phenomenon that the general public found both troubling and titillating, the word "miscegenation" —interbreeding between members of what were presumed to be distinct "races"—coupled the most intimate act of inclusion with an idea promoting social exclusion. In so doing, it epitomized what Ann Stoler has identified as a fundamental contradiction of colonialism—that it must simultaneously incorporate and distance the colonized to maintain the boundaries of colonial rule.[3]

Sylvia Van Kirk brilliantly documented this tension in her work on intermarriage in the fur trade and in early colonial society in Canada. In *"Many Tender Ties"* and subsequent articles, notably "From 'Marrying-In' to 'Marrying-Out': Changing Patterns of Aboriginal/Non-Aboriginal Marriage in Colonial Canada," she noted the increasingly racist discourses directed toward Native and mixed-blood women upon the arrival of white women in the British North American colonies as the latter evolved toward colonies of settlement.[4] Although her own work has focused primarily on an earlier period of Canadian history than that considered in this article, Van Kirk drew attention to the colonial attitudes to intermarriage and miscegenation in the settler society of late nineteenth-century Upper Canada so searingly described in the short stories of early twentieth-century Mohawk/British author Pauline Johnson.[5] The present article was inspired by Van Kirk's foundational work and is an exploration of such attitudes within a broader comparative and theoretical framework.

In a 2001 article in the *American Historical Review*, Patrick Wolfe put forward the proposition that discourses of miscegenation in colonial societies vary depending on whether the colonizing power's relationship to the colonized centres on land or labour. In franchise colonies (such as the Netherlands East Indies) or slave colonies (such as the American South), where colonizers extracted surplus value by mixing a subjugated people's labour with the natural resources of the colonized land, miscegenation discourses were such that they promoted an increase in the size of the labour force available to the colonizers.[6] Settler colonies, by contrast, seek to replace the Indigenous population on its own land. Thus miscegenation discourses in settler colonies have supported territorial expropriation and elimination or absorption of the competing presence. When outright extermination is not possible or desirable, Wolfe argues, settler colonialism attempts in various ways to distance or neutralize the Indigenous inhabitants, whose land use, modes of production, and governance are incompatible with that of the colonizers. Wolfe posits three phases of settler colonialism: confrontation, carceration (including removal), and assimilation (both biological and cultural), which could coexist temporally within a single nation-state. The term "settler colonialism," in Wolfe's usage, is not a description of a nation's origins, but rather an assertion about its structure.[7]

Wolfe's article provides a convenient springboard for a comparison of attitudes toward miscegenation in late nineteenth-century and early twentieth-century Canada, the United States, Australia, and New Zealand. Although these nations were all settler societies and their nineteenth-century colonizers shared a common ethnic heritage, there are intriguing differences in attitudes, discourses, and practices related to "racial" mixing during this period. These differences suggest that there may be other factors influencing attitudes to miscegenation in addition to the interests of settler capitalism. For example, European judgments of the stage of civilization of various Indigenous cultures appear to have affected the nature and virulence of the dominant discourses, as did the previous history of interaction between the two peoples.

A crucial dynamic that Wolfe does not explore is the relationship between dominant discourses and actual practices. While Wolfe considers only the colonizers' discourses and deals only with those that were dominant, such attitudes were never monolithic, even among the ruling elites who articulated these discourses.[8] There were always alternate and minority viewpoints and regional differences with which the ruling elites had to contend. Furthermore, the working-class European men who were the foot soldiers of colonial expansion frequently thought and behaved differently than their upper-class employers might have wished. Thus the actual forms of so-called racial mixing in late nineteenth-century Canada, New Zealand, Australia, and the United States were determined by the interaction of numerous factors, including the attitudes, strategies, and customary practices of those "on the other side of the frontier."[9] The practice of "miscegenation," in turn, had various consequences that affected attitudes and discourses among both colonized and colonizing groups.

An additional consideration that Wolfe does not directly address is that these nation states, with the exception of the United States, coalesced in the late nineteenth and early twentieth centuries, when anti-miscegenation discourses were at their height (and one could argue that the American Civil War was also a nation-defining event). The intersection of pro- or anti-miscegenation discourses and national self-definition and settler-colonial identity merits further study.

These, then, are some of the issues to be considered in this exploration of the similarities and differences in attitudes toward miscegenation in these four countries. Given the huge scope of this topic, and the fact that, at present, I am working from secondary sources, my analysis will be suggestive and preliminary, rather than comprehensive.

An essential feature of settler miscegenation discourses in Canada, New Zealand, Australia, and the United States was that they did not exist in isolation from one another. Rather, they were part of a pan-European debate about human difference that was intimately connected to the global spread of empire. Indeed, by the late nineteenth century, most of the world was ruled by a small number of European nations and the United States; the British Empire was the largest and most successful. The coronation of a new British king in 1902, for example, was celebrated by Britons around the world "as a symbol of the world-wide domination of their race."[10] Most Europeans—and most people of British ancestry, whether in the United States, British colonies, or Britain itself—shared a sense of racial superiority over non-white colonized peoples, taking for granted that there was a fundamental difference between those of European (and especially Anglo-Saxon) descent and the rest of the world's peoples. Some believed that this difference reflected different stages of cultural development, while others attributed the differences to fundamental biology. The word "race"

itself reflected this confusion: sometimes it referred to supposed biological difference, sometimes to nation, and sometimes to culture.

An earlier Enlightenment discourse still promoted by humanitarians argued
that all humans had common origins, and that any differences were the result of
cultural evolution. But by the late nineteenth century, the Indian mutiny of 1857,
the Métis uprisings of 1869–70 and 1885 in Canada, the Waikato war in New
Zealand, the wars with the Sioux and other tribes in the United States, and other
resistances by Indigenous peoples fed fears of Indigenous violence and reinforced
European disillusionment in the possibility of "civilizing" others. New racial discourses offered supposedly scientific, biological explanations for why attempts
at civilizing Indigenous peoples had failed. Significantly, these racial discourses
were also gendered. Because science was considered a masculine sphere, "racial
dominance became an expression of masculine virtue and humanitarianism belonged to the sphere of women's work and feminine weakness."[11]

The writings of nineteenth-century racial theorists such as the American J.C.
Nott, the Frenchman Arthur de Gobineau, and the Scot Robert Knox articulated
supposedly scientific theories establishing the biological superiority of the white
race. These theories were later buttressed by social Darwinism and the Victorian
pseudo-sciences of phrenology and eugenics. Although there were variations
and numerous contradictions, the essence of these theories was that there was a
natural evolutionary hierarchy of the races, with Africans and Aboriginal Australians at the bottom—the missing link, some said, between apes and humans.
Native North Americans were a little higher up the scale, then Asians and Poly-
nesians (including Maoris), with Eastern and Southern Europeans higher still.
Western Europeans were at the top, with Anglo-Saxons, according to the British,
at the very pinnacle of human evolution.[12] Because of this hierarchy of ability
and morality, some peoples were meant to rule, others to be ruled or improved.
Civilization was thought to be a creation of the white race, and racial purity
deemed necessary for the survival of civilized nations.

Polygenists such as Nott argued that the different races were, in fact, different
species, with different biological origins, and that these permanent racial differences set limits on the possibilities for cultural change. While such extreme poly-
genist arguments do not appear to have become the dominant discourse in any of
these countries, they nevertheless influenced popular opinion as racial attitudes
hardened and the views of humanitarians became increasingly marginalized.[13]

Perhaps more than at any other time, then, the colonizing populations in
late nineteenth-century Canada, the United States, New Zealand, and Austra-

lia shared a racial (and, in the case of the British colonies, a cultural) identity. Yet none of these nations, although imagined as white and Anglo-Saxon, were "racially" or culturally homogenous at all; this homogeneity had to be constructed.[14] Preventing interracial contact, including miscegenation, came to be seen by many white citizens in these and other nations as necessary to protect racial purity and thus social order—racial mixing, conceived of as an adulteration of the blood, supposedly led to national degeneration. Some theorists associated racial degeneration with both heredity and the environment; thus, an unhealthy or immoral way of life (such as sexual relations without Christian marriage) caused physical and mental defects that could be passed on to children, degrading racial and national essences. Mixed unions were believed to result in infertility or unstable offspring, inferior to both parent stocks in vitality, intelligence, and morality—though some theorists said that the offspring were superior to Indigenous races and more amenable to civilization because they carried more white blood.[15]

In Canada, Australia, and the United States, late nineteenth-century anti-miscegenation discourses became an element of larger processes of national self-definition on the basis of race. As the *Oxford History of the British Empire* notes regarding Australia and Canada, "exclusion and restraint seem to have provided the cement of federation."[16] At Confederation, Canada was constituted as having two founding "races"—French and English—as if Aboriginal people had never existed, thus constituting the national essence in terms of "whiteness" more than a single culture,[17] a construction that was challenged by the Métis in the Red River Resistance of 1870.[18] The White Australia policy (which had more covert cousins in New Zealand and Canada) coincided with national federation and kept out immigrants on the one hand and isolated Australia's "black problem" on mission stations and reserves on the other.[19]

The American Civil War highlighted that nation's deep divisions on the issue of race. While a minority of Abolitionists openly advocated "amalgamation" with Native Americans and blacks to create a new American people, the abolition of slavery also resulted in heightened anti-miscegenation rhetoric and the development of new techniques (such as Jim Crow laws) to maintain racial boundaries, while Americans' belief in "manifest destiny" resulted in a second series of wars that subjugated and dispossessed Indigenous peoples in the West.[20]

New Zealand took a somewhat different course than the other three societies in this process of national self-definition. Perceiving Maoris to be less different than other Indigenous peoples and unable to exclude them from public life because of their relatively large numbers, their military strength, and the small size of the north and south islands, Maoris were increasingly constructed as an exception to prevailing racial discourses. "Owing to his exceptional character-istics," a leading newspaper announced in 1901, "the Maori interferes in no way with our national homogeneity. His position is…unique."[21] Maoris were accord-ed the rights of full citizens, at least in theory, while other races such as Asians were considered inferior and excluded. Thus, the discourses used and the nature of the exclusions deemed necessary for nation-building varied from country to country, but attitudes to miscegenation were inevitably part of this process.

Although the ultimate aim of institutionalizing settler colonialism was simi-lar in all four societies, the differing racial assessments of Australian Aboriginals, Indigenous people in North America, and Maori also contributed to different attitudes toward miscegenation in each country. Aboriginal peoples in Australia were perceived to live an anarchic, animal-like existence as small groups wan-dering aimlessly over the land without government, agriculture, or even mate-rial belongings. Many Europeans described them as the most primitive people known, as living fossils from a previous phase of human evolution, and inca-pable of progress.[22] Some believed that Aboriginal society was not merely primi-tive but degenerate, reflecting not the original condition of humankind but "the ultimate depths of human degradation."[23] Extinction was the conclusion of this degenerative process. Australian Aboriginals, therefore, were a doomed race;[24] relegated to the very bottom of the colonial racial hierarchy, they had no rights, and certainly were not owners of the land.

Given these attitudes, it is not surprising that intermarriage was less frequent in Australia than in Canada or New Zealand, where Indigenous peoples were more highly regarded. Intermarriage (as opposed to concubinage) presupposes conditions of relative equality between the families of the two partners. An ad-ditional factor was that Australians were not only seen as Indigenous but also as black, sharing the projection of subhuman intelligence, base instincts, and uncontrolled sexuality attributed to Africans and African-American slaves. Ab-original women were routinely considered to be prostitutes, and the myth of the Black Peril or Black Beast Rapist, so common in relation to African men in both the United States and white settler colonies in Africa, was also used against Ab-original men—though somewhat less virulently.[25] According to Daisy Bates, a prominent white commentator on Aboriginal Australians in the early twentieth century, the unrestrained licentiousness of Aboriginals was a prominent cause of their extinction.[26]

The Indigenous peoples of North America were also considered uncivilized savages, but they were seen as more intelligent and more socially organized (particularly peoples like the Haudenosaunee or Iroquois, who formed political confederacies), and were more often recognized as nations. In the United States, they were constructed racially in contrast to African slaves. As Brian Dippie has noted, the independence and love of freedom of North American Indigenous peoples resonated with deeply held American values, and was often contrasted with the supposed submission of Africans to slavery.[27] There was considerable debate about whether Native peoples were fundamentally akin to Anglo-Americans or radically different, as African-Americans were perceived. This was an essential question, as some racial theorists endorsed miscegenation between races that were similar or related to each other, but opposed it if they were highly divergent.[28] According to Wolfe, Native Americans' susceptibility to imported diseases (as opposed to the Africans' apparent immunity to both tropical and European diseases) was seen as proof by many Americans that the former were a doomed race that would soon die out, while blacks were meant to labour.[29] Such fates had different implications for racial mixing.

The American preoccupation with black sexuality led some to conclude that "the entire interracial sexual complex did not pertain to the Indian,"[30] but, as Wolfe has shown, the most distinctive feature of American miscegenation discourses was that they were different for African slaves and for Native Americans.[31] According to a theory popular in late nineteenth-century America, the supposed differences between blacks and whites were absolute and essential, an indelible characteristic that would survive any amount of mixture (hence the American one-drop rule that identified anyone with "black blood" as black). The Indigenous peoples of the United States (and Canada), meanwhile, were seen by humanitarians as more culturally adaptive and, hence, marriageable. They believed that the Native American race could be diluted out of existence.[32] Even some Americans who considered Native Americans unimprovable advocated intermarriage. They believed that only racial or genetic mixing—not cultural change—could incorporate Indigenous peoples.[33] As a result, American attitudes to intermarriage between Anglo-Americans and Native peoples could best be described as ambivalent—racial mixing was reviled by many, tolerated by others, and occasionally advocated.[34]

Of all the Indigenous peoples in these four nations, the Maori of New Zealand were considered the most advanced because they lived in substantial houses in well-populated villages, were agriculturalists, and had forms of social, political, and military organization recognizable to Europeans. Furthermore, they actively engaged with European culture from first contact—initiating trade, developing new economic activities in response to changing opportunities, and readily adopting elements of Christianity—and thus were believed to be the most capable of being civilized. Because of this perception of greater kinship with European societies, there was far less hostility to intermarriage, which was generally accepted throughout New Zealand's post-contact history.[35]

European perceptions of the differences between Indigenous cultures explain some of the reasons for these different attitudes to racial mixing, but there were also other factors. In general, there appears to have been more intermarriage where the Indigenous group had large numbers, military power, and something other than land that Europeans coveted and that the Indigenous peoples were willing to trade. Intermarriage was common in colonies or regions where mercantile relationships, rather than white settlement, were the rule.[36] This was certainly the case in earlier phases of the history of Canada, New Zealand, and some regions of the United States (e.g., the Northwest). In Australia, where trading relationships did not develop to the same extent, intermarriage was far less common.

One of the main features of this form of intermarriage was that it was desired by Indigenous peoples as much as it was by European traders. In New Zealand, there was an early period of trading before white settlement began in earnest in which marriage alliance was the predominant form of relationship. According to James Belich, virtually every non-missionary station—trading, timber, sealing, or whaling—and every individual trader was soon linked to the Maori by marriage, a deliberate strategy of Maori chiefs to maintain control over "our Pakeha." (Pakeha is the Maori word for the non-Maori inhabitants of New Zealand.) Pakeha did not have much choice in taking these wives because, as one British man put it, " it is not safe to live in the country without a chief's daughter as protection."[37]

Similarly in Canada, widespread intermarriage, based largely on Indigenous traditions, incorporated French and, to a lesser extent, British men into Indigenous kin and trading networks in the *pays d'en haut* for more than two centuries.[38] The fur trade was at least initially a cooperative exchange where reciprocity and mutuality was essential. Aboriginal women were not merely a sexual substitute for absent European women; they provided essential services, such as the preparation of pelts and access to trade networks, that European women could not have furnished, while Native peoples gained preferential access to European trade goods through their familial ties to Europeans. Indeed, of all the societies under discussion, Canada had the longest period of initial ethnic mixing because Canada was a predominantly mercantile colony until the late eighteenth century; settlement was limited in extent until after the American Revolution.[39] In Canada, Native peoples and Europeans developed "a symbiotic relationship that is without parallel in the colonial history of North America"[40] based on the fur trade and military alliance.

This mercantile pattern of intermarriage in Canada, New Zealand, and some parts of the United States changed when white settlement increased and the balance of power between Indigenous and newcomer populations shifted. It was largely obsolete by the 1880s, if not earlier, depending on region. Subsequent intermarriage was more a matter of sentiment between individuals than arranged unions linking families and cultures. Yet the history of intermarriage in Canada, New Zealand, and the American Northwest left a significant portion of the population with mixed ancestry and a personal stake in a more positive view of Indigenous peoples.

In all four societies, white attitudes to racial mixing changed as European women arrived in increasing numbers and as Indigenous populations, decimated by wars and disease, moved from a condition of exteriority to incorporation as small minorities in settler nation-states. In Canada, anti-miscegenation discourses became more influential as it became a British settler colony. Although intermarriage was never banned, even men in the fur trade began to prefer women of mixed ancestry to Native wives. When white women arrived in fur-trade country in the 1820s and 1830s, mixed-blood women were increasingly considered unsuitable spouses for officers and were frequently ostracized.[41] Intermarriage became a marker of class, regarded as more acceptable among the voyageurs and lower-ranked employees of the Hudson's Bay Company than officers. Country marriages—those solemnized by Indigenous tradition—were the most common form of marriage in mixed relationships, but were increasingly frowned upon over the course of the nineteenth century. In 1886, these marriages were denied legal recognition, meaning that respectable society considered the progeny of such relationships bastards and the Native or mixed-ancestry wives of dubious morality.[42]

In the first half of the nineteenth century, women of British/Native descent who could display appropriate class markers had been able to attain a privileged white racial identity in fur-trade country and some centres such as Victoria (something rarely possible for their brothers), but by the late nineteenth century anyone known to carry Native blood was at risk of exclusion from "respectable" society.[43] According to Peter Jones, there were relatively few mixed marriages after 1830 in the more settled areas of Upper Canada.[44] The Red River Resistance in 1870 and Northwest Rebellion in 1885 reinforced Euro-Canadian views that the progeny of such marriages were violent and degenerate.

However, sexual and marital practices at the centre of power were often notably different than those on the periphery. White men in the remaining frontier regions, notably British Columbia, continued to marry or live with Aboriginal women. Such men were increasingly deemed lower class and degenerate; they were considered to have "gone Native," and some lost their settler status socially, if not legally.[45] Significantly, contact with white men was not seen to civilize Aboriginal women—the men were regarded as having been polluted and corrupted by their Aboriginal partners.[46]

The Canadian government became involved in regulating intermarriages through the Indian Acts of 1869 and 1876. Consistent with gendered citizenship legislation in many other nations, the Indian Act maintained Euro-Canadian men's nationality regardless of their choice of partner, and established that a woman assumed her husband's citizenship. Native women who married non-Native men lost their status as Indians, as did their children, while white women who married Native men acquired Indian status. Since the former situation was far more common than the latter, intermarriage became a means of removing Indigenous women from their own cultures.[47] The Act reduced the number of people eligible for Indian status and hence the need for reserve land and government spending on Indians.

This legislation marked a new phase in the assimilatory agenda of Canadian settler colonialism. The perception of Indigenous people as a vanishing race was crucial to this policy, for as the number of Indigenous people dwindled to 2.5 percent of the overall population by the end of the nineteenth century,[48] "racial" mixing posed less of a threat to the dominant Canadian culture. The demographic imbalance ensured quick dilution of any supposedly contaminating effects of Indigenous blood. Yet while the official government discourse promoted social assimilation by legal means, intermarriage was frowned upon in the court of public opinion, and people of mixed ancestry were generally not accepted into the mainstream unless they could convincingly "pass" as white.[49] The great majority of mixed marriages resulted only in the loss of Native status and consignment of the progeny to a social limbo. What is clear is that Canadian settler society used miscegenation discourses "not only to contain whiteness but also to maintain strict boundaries around Indianness."[50]

In the Australian colonies, Aboriginal segregation was emphasized far more than assimilation. The stated government policy was assimilation, but it was promoted with far less enthusiasm than in the United States or Canada. For example, education of Aboriginal people was never a major objective.[51] Indeed, from the beginning of British settlement, the logic of elimination was inherent in the doctrine of *terra nullius*, which was used to dispossess Aboriginal people and deny any form of Aboriginal title,[52] and in the indiscriminate killing of Aboriginals in many frontier regions. Middle-class mixed marriages were rare, partly because of the strong class consciousness brought to Australia from England; it was often asserted that only the "lowest" white men had sex with Aboriginal women.[53] However, working-class mixed marriages involving either Aboriginal men or Aboriginal women were tolerated, if infrequent.

Although intermarriage was never widely advocated or practised, it was increasingly prohibited as racial attitudes grew more extreme over the late nineteenth and early twentieth centuries. In most Australian states, Aboriginal people were required to obtain permission to marry. In the early twentieth century, marriages between Aboriginal and non-Aboriginal people could not take place without the permission of the Chief Protector of Aborigines or his equivalent.[54] In most jurisdictions, when an Aboriginal woman married a non-Aboriginal man, she could no longer live on an Aboriginal reserve or receive any of the benefits provided for Aboriginal people.[55] Some states also discouraged marriages between full-blood Aboriginals and people of mixed ancestry.[56] State policies were also introduced around the turn of the century to remove people of mixed ancestry (especially children) from Aboriginal communities and incorporate them into white society, thus preventing further miscegenation with Aboriginal people.[57]

The case of late nineteenth-century America illustrates the complexity of determining dominant racial attitudes, for in this time period several very different discourses concerning intermarriage with Native Americans contended for supremacy. That fourteen states in the United States prohibited intermarriage between Native and white people[58] is ironic, to say the least, given that the story of Pocahontas, in which a Native "princess" saved a Euro-American man by marrying him, was a foundational American myth and intermarriages had actually been infrequent throughout most American history.[59] Such ambivalence or confusion is probably a reflection of the fact that, from the beginning, America encompassed several different societies with very different attitudes toward miscegenation.[60] The early settler colonies on the eastern seaboard coexisted with the fur trade in the northwestern regions formerly controlled by the

French, then with African slave plantations in the southern colonies, as well as a large Spanish[61]/ Native mestizo population in the Southwest. After the Civil War, most northern states repealed anti-miscegenation laws, but they were still enforced in the West and South through much of the twentieth century.[62]

The different racial constructions of African-Americans and Native Americans are evident in the fact that many more states directed anti-miscegenation laws against blacks.[63] Native Americans were mentioned less frequently because legislators were far more worried about non-white men who might marry white women (and thus usurp white male privilege) than about white men who might marry non-white women, as was the usual form of intermarriage involving Native Americans.[64] Nonetheless, intermarriage with Native women was increasingly frowned upon over the course of the nineteenth century, especially after the establishment of reservations in the West. In contrast to attitudes in Australia and some parts of Canada, working-class white men who married Native women were scorned as "squaw men"—freeloaders who lived off the resources of the reservations.[65]

Humanitarians also had a strong presence in late nineteenth-century American discussions of race because of the large and well-organized antislavery movement. A number of abolitionists were in favour of intermarriage with both blacks and Native people. Many humanitarians advocated intermarriage because it would promote total assimilation and absorption of the dwindling Indigenous race into the dominant majority, thus providing a more humane solution than frontier violence to the problem of what to do with Indigenous peoples in a settler society.[66]

This was the continuation of an alternative discourse present in both Canada and the United States that had at various times promoted miscegenation as an instrument of empire. French officials in New France had fitfully promoted intermarriage as a means to create a new people ideally suited for the new colony, and had occasionally offered dowries for Native women. Similarly, the British authorities in colonial Nova Scotia were instructed to offer various incentives to promote intermarriage, although these were never actually implemented.[67] In the United States, Thomas Jefferson, among others, had advocated miscegenation with Native Americans to create a new, unified American people.[68] Some late nineteenth- and early twentieth-century anthropologists advanced similar discourses, contending that racial mixing would improve humankind and create a new, more vigorous race of Americans. This ideal of peaceful amalgamation has been characterized by

Ann McGrath as "a nationalist fantasy of harmonious land takeover with a benign marriage of cultures and a reassuring confirmation of ownership."[69]

While such discourses were usually framed in terms of the classic form of intermarriage between white men and Indigenous women, during this period a number of American social activists and public figures propounded an alternative view. Surprisingly, their solution to "the Indian Problem" was intermarriage between Native men and white women, which they believed would be the key to civilizing Native American society.[70] (Historically, such couples had faced considerable hostility.) This argument was based on the fact that a number of Indigenous men had become acculturated and educated professionals, and had married middle-class Anglo-American women. It drew on American ideals of equality, opportunity, and social mobility, and the view of white women as the chief custodians and promoters of civilized values. It was also class-based—such marriages were only acceptable when the men were acculturated professionals.[71]

There was no consensus on racial mixing in the United States. In the early twentieth century, according to Gary Nash, "racial intermingling dropped precipitously as a new white orthodoxy depicted mixed-race people as degenerate and racial amalgamation as a prescription for national suicide."[72] Yet, while extreme anti-miscegenation opinion was strong, it was counterbalanced by the many prominent individuals in frontier regions who were of mixed ancestry themselves or in mixed relationships. Also, as America increasingly defined itself as "the great melting pot," to totally condemn such mixing meant repudiating American national identity.[73]

In contrast, the New Zealand government was not able, and perhaps did not wish, to regulate intermarriage as Australian and American authorities did. Assimilation through racial mixing was always the main policy. Maori women who married well-to-do settlers were often able to move into the Pakeha middle class.[74] Yet intermarriages apparently became less frequent in the late nineteenth century as settlers increasingly swamped the Maori and gained control over land.[75]

The chief factor affecting attitudes to miscegenation in turn-of-the-century New Zealand was Maori population decline, both in absolute and relative terms. A population that was 100 percent Maori in 1769 had declined to 5 percent in 1896.[76] Many settlers did not believe that the Maori would survive, and attributed this expected extinction to the "fatal impact" theory. Yet, as appropriated Maori cultural symbols and New Zealand's relatively good relations with Indigenous peoples (as compared with Australia) were an increasingly important element of national identity,[77] and as humanitarians had considerable influence in New Zealand, there was concern that the Maori should not become extinct. It was believed that Maoris could be saved and improved through intermarriage, as half-castes were considered to be the healthiest and most non-degenerative aspect of Maori society. A new people—intermediate between Pakeha and Maori—would be born, which Pakeha assumed would be more Pakeha than Maori.[78]

This positive spin on intermarriage was reinforced by new theories of Maori racial origins. In 1885, Edward Tregear, a surveyor, scholar, and civil servant, published *The Aryan Maori*,[79] in which he argued that the Maori were a branch of the Caucasian race and shared an ancient origin with northern Europeans. Both British and Maori were members of an Aryan master race, but had gone in different directions after leaving their homeland of India and were now reunited. Although the book was often ridiculed for its poor science, James Belich argues the book ranks with the Treaty of Waitangi as a key text of Maori-Pakeha relations.[80]

By constructing Maori as racially homogenous with Pakeha, their assimilation became more palatable, and Pakeha ownership of the land could be legitimized through racial mixing. Yet this public discourse did not fully counteract more negative covert attitudes toward Maori. James Bennett speaks of the "fundamental disjuncture between public or institutional recognition of Maori equality and private prejudice."[81] Furthermore, the Pakeha plan for Maori redemption required Maori cooperation. There was Maori opposition to the ideology of assimilation through intermarriage and a parallel discourse of a separate Maori vision for their future. Nonetheless, some Maoris believed that equality lay in affirming their imagined racial status as "honorary whites,"[82] and joined whites in opposing immigration by Asians. Others thought that intermarriage with whites could strengthen the Maori and provide a stronger, yet still Maori, race.[83]

Thus far, attitudes to intermarriage have been the main focus of this article, but intermarriage was by no means the only form of miscegenation in Canada, the United States, New Zealand, or Australia. While public discourses might be pro- or anti- intermarriage in various colonial circumstances, there were clearly other, more covert attitudes determining interracial sexual contact. Kay Schaffer has commented that the "sexual exploitation of [Indigenous] women was endemic to British imperialism—the romance between dusky, dark-haired maidens and pioneering heroes was at the core of the colonial adventure tale."[84] It was tacitly understood that "so long as European women were absent, Indigenous women could be used to satisfy what were perceived to be natural needs."[85] While anti-miscegenation legislation frequently targeted both interracial sex and intermarriage, the latter was usually most strongly prohibited, likely because marriage also involved issues of property and inheritance.[86]

Even when white women were present, the late nineteenth-century cult of true womanhood (which encouraged British and American women to be pure, pious, domestic, and basically uninterested in sex except for procreation) and the construction of European males as having naturally coarse instincts ensured that illicit "interracial" sex took place in all four societies, even though it contradicted public moral standards.[87] Myrna Tonkinson suggests that the traditional prerogative of aristocratic men to engage in sex across class lines provided the basic rule of conduct, allowing British men to have extramarital sex with Indigenous women in Australia with little sense of responsibility for any offspring that might ensue.[88] Similar notions of "the casual use of a social inferior for sexual pleasure"[89] appear to have been operative elsewhere; for example, a number of prominent Pakeha leaders in New Zealand had white wives and Maori mistresses.[90] White women, on the other hand, were usually considered "deeply depraved" if they had sex with social inferiors. In fact, to some colonials such relationships appear to have been literally inconceivable.[91]

The colonial construction of Indigenous women as prostitutes was common in many colonial societies around the world since, by definition, "savages" could not restrain their passions, and in many Indigenous societies women enjoyed more sexual freedom than European women.[92] By the mid-nineteenth century, according to Jean Barman, "Europeans perceived all female sexual autonomy to be illicit, especially if it occurred in the public sphere, which was considered exclusively male."[93] Colonizers often used the charge of prostitution as justification for intervention in Indigenous—and especially Indigenous women's—lives.[94] With the exception of Australia, where rapes by Aboriginal men sometimes triggered hysteria in the white community and the advocacy of lynching, colonizers rarely viewed Indigenous men as sexual threats to white women.[95] As Kathryn McPherson notes elsewhere in this volume, Indigenous women were generally viewed as a far greater sexual threat to white society.

Sex for remuneration was indeed a fact of life for some Indigenous women, particularly in regions or countries where there was a radical imbalance of power between colonizers and Indigenous peoples, and where rapid white settlement proceeded without an initial trading phase or any recognition of Indigenous rights or treaties. In these regions, interracial relationships appear to have focused more on sex because there was no need to establish social or economic relations with Indigenous communities. The rapid destruction of Indigenous self-sufficiency in such areas forced larger numbers of Indigenous women to exchange sexual services for necessities, including food.[96]

In Australia, California, and mid-nineteenth-century British Columbia, for example, prostitution and non-marital sexual arrangements were far more prevalent than intermarriage.[97] Relationships in such areas were usually shorter and appear to have been more exploitative, with fewer counterbalancing interests to encourage respectful treatment of Indigenous women. In Australia, illicit, casual contact was the norm, with prostitution the most tolerated pattern. In British Columbia, shorter-term live-in relationships became prevalent in the mid-nineteenth century as the economy shifted to mining and lumber extraction. Large numbers of white men entered the province, a marked change from the earlier fifty-year period of the fur trade, when intermarriage was more common.[98] In the Yukon, the contrast between the behaviour of trappers and miners is illustrative of the economic underpinnings of these relationships. Many non-Native trappers became "squaw men," living with Native women and joining Natives in the harvest economy (though many eventually abandoned their families and returned south), whereas more transient non-Native miners scorned the squaw men and were generally interested in short-term sex only, often in the context of drinking parties.[99] As Robert Young has commented, "the forms of sexual exchange brought about by colonialism were themselves both mirrors and consequences of the modes of economic exchange that constituted the basis of colonial relations."[100]

That rape was part of the miscegenation complex in such areas can be verified by the fact that white men were rarely prosecuted or received only light sentences for raping Indigenous women.[101] Indeed, it has been suggested that in some circumstances Native groups offered women's sexual services as a way of reducing the incidence of random and violent rape and exerting some control over interracial sexual encounters.[102] Rape and abuse of Indigenous women sparked much of the violence between Indigenous men and settlers in many frontier regions. Ironically, the retaliatory violence of Indigenous men only reinforced European notions of Indigenous peoples as savages.[103]

Indigenous peoples in these four societies often had very different ideas than Europeans about sexuality, cultural and biological differences, and sexual mixing with "others," though their attitudes to sexual relations between Europeans and Indigenous peoples are far less well-documented and have been the subject of much less study. Further research is needed to understand the concepts of human difference held by the Indigenous groups in question and to determine if any of these were in any way analogous to the European concept of "race," an endeavour well beyond the scope of this article.[104] However, it can be stated that, like Europeans, their beliefs and practices concerning sex in general and with strangers or ethnic others varied significantly from group to group,[105] as well as within groups, and changed over time. Indigenous discourses were usually not dominant because sexual relations with Europeans generally took place under conditions of inequality, except in some situations where Indigenous people were numerically superior or their cooperation was required.

Many of the taboos central to the construction of European sexuality of the day simply did not exist in Indigenous cultures prior to contact. In many societies, divorce was easy, and polygyny, premarital sex, and in some cases homosexuality were generally accepted. Among some peoples, ritual and public sexual practices were conducted.[106] Because the group, rather than the nuclear family, was the main social unit, and many societies were matrilineal, establishing paternity was often less important to Indigenous peoples.[107]

True prostitution—sex as a purely commercial transaction—appears to have been rare or non-existent before contact, and practices that Europeans perceived as prostitution were often understood differently by Indigenous peoples.[108] For example, the common payment of a bride price was an exchange between families rather than the outright buying of women, as portrayed by Europeans. In many Indigenous societies in Australia and New Zealand (and a significant number in North America), husbands might lend their wives to visitors or trade their sexual services for goods, either with or without the women's consent. This, however, was thought of as a matter of hospitality or gift-giving, part of the continuous reciprocal exchange that cemented relationships and ensured social order. Furthermore, wife exchange was not uncontrolled sexuality, as Europeans often thought. In the case of Australian Aboriginal peoples, it was conducted in keeping with strict kin classifications and reciprocal obligations, something that went unrecognized by European men.[109] Some Indigenous groups believed that coitus with the same woman transferred power from one man to another, as in the Mandan buffalo-calling ceremony. These practices were sometimes extended to white men, who were also seen as powerful.[110]

A form of sexual exchange or temporary marriage between European whalers and Indigenous women in New Zealand in the first half of the nineteenth century is an example of significant differences between Europeans and Indigenous peoples with respect to sexuality, and a reminder of Indigenous people's agency in "interracial" relationships. Unlike the indiscriminate and temporary brothel sex common in most European port encounters, the usual pattern was a sexual contract with a single Maori woman for a sailor's entire three- to five-week stay at the port. In exchange, the tribe of the woman received a gun and the woman herself typically received a dress for her services. Because premarital sex was acceptable before marriage and such "temporary marriages" were variations on Maori traditions of sexual hospitality, there appears to have been no sense of immorality on the part of Maoris. Maori women entered willingly into such contracts with the approval and involvement of Maori men, who considered ex-ship girls to be very desirable wives.[111] Another variation was reported in 1825 among the Chinook on the west coast of North America, where "even high status women would sell their bodies to Europeans if the price was right, in spite of the severe punishment their husbands might inflict on them."[112] These examples are from an earlier period before widespread white settlement, but they are indicative of profoundly different cultural attitudes to sexuality that likely persisted in some form in the period in question.

Similarly, in Australia, where the frontier persisted in some areas into the twentieth century, Aboriginal women enjoyed a high degree of control over their own lives in marriage, sex, and reproduction. According to some historians, many willingly entered sexual relationships with white men;[113] others have said that the bestowal of women may have been a major source of men's secular power in pre-contact Aboriginal societies.[114] Aboriginal women may have offered sex to barter for food or favour, indulge in sexual variety, escape harsh camp conditions, steal weapons, learn English, and acquire knowledge that could be passed on to men.[115] According to Kay Schaffer, "Aboriginal men may have offered their women to white invaders for a variety of reasons: to promote peace and hospitality; to exercise diplomacy and maintain status within traditional societies and between white and black men; to establish relations of reciprocity and kin affiliations; and to survive as their lands were decimated."[116]

In other societies, or even under different circumstances in the same societies, Indigenous women were not free to engage in interracial sexual relations as they chose, but were compelled to have sexual relations with white men. Some Indigenous women in Canada were encouraged or forced by relatives to provide sex to white men.[117] The Mandans, Maoris, Dene, Australian Aboriginals, and others sold slave women captured from other tribes to European men for sexual purposes.[118] Certainly, in these contexts, such practices reinforced male authority in both cultures.[119] In many circumstances, it is possible that male and female attitudes to sexual relations with Europeans were quite different.

Sexual relations between Indigenous women and European men altered gender relations in Indigenous societies, and this undoubtedly affected what both sexes thought about such practices, particularly over time. Intermarriage could be a route to increased status, wealth, or leisure for Indigenous women. Sylvia Van Kirk asserted that intermarriage was attractive to many eighteenth- and early nineteenth-century Native women in Canada because access to time-saving European tools reduced their workloads. Susan Sleeper-Smith has documented how, through intermarriage, Native and Métis women became the backbone of mixed fur-trading networks in the American Northwest.[120] Intermarriage could also offer a refuge from maltreatment by Indigenous males, particularly in Indigenous societies where women did not have equal status with men, such as among the Chinook or Dene.[121] In Australia, Aboriginal women acted as intermediaries in frontier areas, and as a result their status and power increased relative to that of Aboriginal men.[122] On the South Island of New Zealand, nineteenth-century Maori women apparently preferred to take Pakeha husbands—perhaps, as James Belich suggests, to increase their status, gain material advantages, or in the hope that European blood would help immunize children against European diseases. This pattern shifted after 1900, apparently as a result of a policy by southern Maori chiefs to preserve chiefly bloodlines and solidify land claims.[123]

Indigenous women's involvement in relationships with white men also meant greater exposure to diseases—including sexually transmitted diseases—and possibly decreased fertility, which may have exacerbated Indigenous population decline. In Australia, there was a considerable gender imbalance, with one-third more Aboriginal men than women, making it increasingly difficult for men to obtain wives and thereby complicating marriage practices such as polygyny. Aboriginal men from some groups reacted by abducting women from neighbouring clans, which sparked increased warfare between clans. Some Aboriginal men requested that white male Protectors of Aborigines assist them in securing the return of their wives from white men.[124] Similarly, in British Columbia in the 1880s and 1890s, petitions signed by Indigenous men (perhaps at the instigation of missionaries) called on the federal government to bring women back to Native communities, by force, if necessary.[125]

As Albert Hurtado has commented, "Interracial sexuality [and marriage] provided a way to incorporate strangers in tribal life and created kinship ties with newcomers, yet it also put women at risk, subverted traditional gender roles, infected reciprocity with marketplace ethics, aggravated population decline, and thus weakened tribal society."[126] Given such consequences, it is likely that there was considerable debate within Indigenous societies about its merits.

This preliminary survey suggests that while the relation to land was the underpinning of the dominant discourses of racial mixing in these settler societies, and that these discourses were grounded in an international pan-European discussion of social and physiological difference, constructions of sexuality, class, race, gender, and national values—as well as previous experiences of inter-ethnic contact—all played roles in determining attitudes and policies toward racial mixing in any particular circumstance.[127] The actual forms of mixing that took place, and to a certain extent the discourses about them, were shaped by Indigenous as well as European attitudes and agency, and in some instances were shaped as much by male patriarchal authority and male gender solidarity across cultures as by the interests of settler colonialism. As Patrick Wolfe has argued, the fundamental issue "is not race or sexuality *per se* but the maintenance of social divisions"—"holding the line when it comes to power, privilege and access to resources."[128] Attitudes, practices, and discourses concerning miscegenation, then, could be various and contradictory even within the same territory. They did not reflect a set of fixed beliefs, but were means to various ends, and hence infinitely adaptable to local circumstances.

Notes

1   This paper was previously published in *Native Studies Review* 16, 1 (2005) and has been slightly revised for inclusion in this anthology. I would like to thank Sylvia Van Kirk, Anne Keary, the audience at "Natives and Newcomers: A Comparative Perspective," and the *Native Studies Review* anonymous reviewers for their helpful comments on earlier versions of this paper.

2   Patrick Wolfe, "Land, Labor and Difference: Elementary Structures of Race," *American Historical Review* 106 (June 2001): 867n5. It is exceedingly difficult to talk about the concepts of race and miscegenation without inadvertently reproducing racial thinking. In this essay, it is to be understood that "race" is a construct rather than an essence, and that "miscegenation" is a racialized word for the production of children as a result of sexual relations between members of certain ethnic groups. For a full discussion of the development of the concept of miscegenation, see Robert Young, *Colonial Desire: Hybridity in Theory, Culture and Race* (London: Routledge, 1995).

3   Ann Laura Stoler, "Sexual Affronts and Racial Frontiers: European Identities and the Cultural Politics of Exclusion in Colonial Southeast Asia," in *Tensions of Empire: Colonial Cultures in a Bourgeois World*, eds. Frederick Cooper and Ann Laura Stoler (Berkeley and Los Angeles: University of California Press, 1997): 199, 202.

4   Sylvia Van Kirk, *"Many Tender Ties": Women in Fur-Trade Society in Western Canada, 1670–1870* (Winnipeg: Watson and Dwyer Publishing Ltd., 1980); "Colonized Lives: The Native Wives and Daughters of Five Founding Families of Victoria," in *Pacific Empires: Essays in Honour of Glyndwr Williams*, eds. Alan Frost and Jane Samson (Melbourne University Press, 1999), and "From 'Marrying-In' to 'Marrying-Out': Changing Patterns of Aboriginal/Non-Aboriginal Marriage in Colonial Canada," *Frontiers* 23, 2 (2000): 1–11.

5   See, for example, E. Pauline Johnson, "As It Was in the Beginning," in *The Moccasin Maker* (Toronto: William Briggs, 1913), and other stories, discussed in Sylvia Van Kirk, "From 'Marrying-In' to 'Marrying-Out,'" 9. Van Kirk introduced me to this work in 2003, when she was my PhD supervisor.

6   Similarly, in the case of mercantile colonies like New France, miscegenation served the economic interests of the colonizers by securing access to furs for the fur trade and Indigenous labour to prepare and transport the pelts.

7   Wolfe, "Land, Labor and Difference," 871.

8   For example, missionary discourses were different from those of chief traders. The views on miscegenation articulated in the Colonial Office were frequently different from those of settlers and their political leaders.

9   This was the title of a groundbreaking book by Australian historian Henry Reynolds.

10 Eric Hobsbawm, *The Age of Empire, 1875–1914* (New York: Vintage Books, 1989): 70, quoted in Peter Russell, "The Distinctive Foundations of Australian Colonialism," in *Friends Long Estranged*, eds. Margaret MacMillan and Francine Mckenzie (Vancouver: UBC Press, 2003), read in ms. p. 90.

11 Catherine Hall, *White, Male, and Middle-class: Explorations in Feminism and History*, quoted in Douglas A. Lorimer, "Race, science and culture: historical continuities and discontinuities 1850–1914," in *The Victorians and Race*, ed. Shearer West (Aldershot, Hants.: Scolar Press; Brookfield, Vt.: Ashgate Publishing Co., 1996), 28.

12 Lorimer, "Race, science and culture," 22; Wolfe, "Land, Labor and Difference," 876. See Young, *Colonial Desire*, for an extended discussion of British, French, and American racial theories.

13 Robert E. Bieder, "Scientific Attitudes Toward Indian Mixed-Bloods in Early Nineteenth Century America," *Journal of Ethnic Studies* 8, 2 (1975): 26. See also Russell McGregor,

Imagined Destinies: Aboriginal Australians and the Doomed Race Theory 1880–1939 (Victoria: Melbourne University Press, 1997), Chapter One; James Belich, *Paradise Reforged: A History of the New Zealanders from the 1880s to the Year 2000* (Honolulu: University of Hawai'i Press, 2001): 207.

14   Daiva Stasiulis and Radha Jhappan, "The Fractious Politics of a Settler Society: Canada," in *Unsettling Settler Societies: Articulations of Gender, Race, Ethnicity and Class*, eds. Daiva Stasiulis and Nira Yuval-Davis (London: Sage, 1995), 98. Canada's United Empire Loyalists, supposedly the epitome of British racial purity, actually included such diverse peoples as Germans, Highland Scots, Abenaki, Six Nations Iroquois, and 3000 free blacks. See also Wolfe, "Land, Labor and Difference," 883, James Bennett, "Maori as Honorary Members of the White Tribe," *Journal of Imperial and Commonwealth History*, 29, 3 (Sept. 2001): 33–53; McGregor, *Imagined Destinies*, 169–170.

15   See Young, *Colonial Desire*, and Owen White, *Children of the French Empire: Miscegenation and Colonial Society in French West Africa 1895–1960* (Oxford: Oxford University Press, 1999), chapter 4, for a discussion of pan-European discourses.

16   Andrew Porter, "Introduction: Britain and the Empire in the Nineteenth Century," in *The Nineteenth Century*, ed. Andrew Porter, Vol. 3 of *Oxford History of the British Empire*, ed. Wm. Roger Louis (Oxford: Oxford University Press, 1999), 22.

17   Porter, "Britain and the Empire," 21.

18   This point was made by Sylvia Van Kirk, who argues that Louis Riel "saw Metis people (the product of a unique Western Canadian experience of miscegenation) as the rightful centre of a developing Canadian West." Personal communication.

19   James Bennett, "Maori as Honorary Members of the White Tribe," *Journal of Imperial and Commonwealth History*, 29, 3 (2001): 35.

20   See David D. Smits, "'Squaw Men,' 'Half-Breeds,' and Amalgamators: Late Nineteenth Century Anglo-American Attitudes Toward Indian-White Race-Mixing," *American Indian Culture and Research Journal* 15, 3 (1991): 29–61; Margaret D. Jacobs, "The Eastmans and the Luhans: Interracial Marriage between White Women and Native American Men, 1875–1935," *Frontiers* 23, 2 (2000): 34–35.

21   As quoted in Belich, *Paradise Reforged*, 208–9.

22   Wolfe, "Land, Labor and Difference," 869; K.R. Howe, *Race Relations: Australia and New Zealand, A Comparative Study 1770s–1970s* (Wellington: Methuen, 1977), 19.

23   McGregor, *Imagined Destinies*, 9.

24   Ibid., 58.

25   Patricia Grimshaw, Marilyn Lake, Ann McGrath, Marian Quartly, *Creating a Nation, 1788–1990* (South Yarra [Aus]: McPhee Gribble Penguin Books, 1994): 147–8; Myra Tonkinson, "Sisterhood or Aboriginal Servitude? Black Women and White Women on the Australian Frontier," *Aboriginal History* 12 (1988): 34.

26   McGregor, *Imagined Destinies*, 121.

27   Smits, "Squaw Men," 55.

28   Ibid., 32–33.

29   Wolfe, "Land, Labor and Difference," 877n35.

30   Winthrop Jordan quoted in ibid., 871–72.

31   Ibid., 886, 892. See also Smits, "Squaw Men," 43–44, 46–47. The dominant anti-miscegenation discourses applied to blacks eventually also seep into discourses about Native Americans.

32   Wolfe, "Land, Labor and Difference," 885. Smits, "Squaw Men," 43–46. A topic for further investigation is how the absence of plantation slavery affected discourses of miscegenation in Canada.

33 Roger Nichols, *Indians in the United States and Canada: A Comparative History* (Lincoln: University of Nebraska Press, 1998), 184.

34 Wolfe, "Land, Labor and Difference," 892; Smits, "Squaw Men," 57.

35 Howe, *Race Relations*, 77; Patricia Grimshaw, "Interracial Marriages and Colonial Regimes in Victoria and Aotearoa/New Zealand," *Frontiers* 23, 2 (2002): 21; Robin Fisher, "The Impact of European Settlement on the Indigenous Peoples of Australia, New Zealand, and British Columbia: Some Comparative Dimensions," *Canadian Ethnic Studies* 12 (1980): 8.

36 Wolfe, "Land, Labor and Difference," 868n9.

37 Quoted in James Belich, *Making Peoples: A History of the New Zealanders, from Polynesian Settlement to the End of the Nineteenth Century* (Auckland, N.Z.: Allen Lane, 1996), 172.

38 See Van Kirk, *Many Tender Ties*. For the experience in the American Northwest, see Susan Sleeper-Smith, *Indian Women and French Men: Rethinking Cultural Encounter in the Western Great Lakes* (Amherst: University of Massachusetts Press, 2001).

39 Even though the French established a settler colony on the shores of the St. Lawrence, it was small and was established on land claimed by no Indigenous group at the time of settlement.

40 Olive Patricia Dickason, "From 'One Nation' in the Northeast to 'New Nation' in the Northwest: A look at the emergence of the métis," in *The New Peoples: Being and Becoming Métis in North America*," eds. Jacqueline Petersen and Jennifer Brown (Winnipeg: University of Manitoba Press, 1985), 29.

41 Van Kirk, *Many Tender Ties*, 95, 186.

42 Ibid., 241.

43 Van Kirk, "Colonized Lives," 231. See also Johnson, "As it Was in the Beginning."

44 Donald B. Smith, *Sacred Feathers: The Reverend Peter Jones (Kahkewaquonaby) & the Mississauga Indians* (Toronto and London: University of Toronto Press, 1987), 130.

45 Adelle Perry, *On the Edge of Empire: Gender, Race, and the Making of British Columbia 1849–1871* (Toronto: University of Toronto Press, 2001), 54, 71.

46 Ibid. See also Jean Barman, "Taming Aboriginal Sexuality: Gender, Power, and Race in British Columbia, 1850–1900," *BC Studies* 115/115 (Autumn/Winter 1997/1998): 237–266.

47 Sylvia Van Kirk, "From 'Marrying-In' to 'Marrying-Out,'" 5.

48 *Encyclopaedia of Aboriginal Australia*, 1299, and Royal Commission on Aboriginal Peoples, *Report*, vol.1, 14, quoted in Russell, "Australian Colonialism," 99.

49 Van Kirk, "Colonized Lives," 232. This was especially true in urban areas and southern Canada.

50 This quote was taken from a remark by Renisa Mawani about British Columbia in "Between and Out of Place: Mixed Race Identity, Liquor, and the Law in British Columbia, 1850–1913," in *Race, Space and the Law: Unmapping a White Settler Society*, ed. Sherene H. Razack (Toronto: Between the Lines, 2002), 58, but is equally applicable to Canada as a whole under the impact of the Indian Act.

51 Katherine Ellinghaus, "Margins of Acceptability: Class, Education and Interracial Marriage in Australia and North America," *Frontiers* 23, 2 (2002): 59; Russell, "Distinctive Foundations," 72; McGregor, *Imagined Destinies*, 94.

52 Wolfe, "Land, Labor and Difference," 869. See also Henry Reynolds, *The Law of the Land* (Melbourne: Penguin Books, 1987).

53 Tonkinson, "Sisterhood," 32.

54 Ann McGrath and Winona Stevenson, "Gender, Race, and Policy: Aboriginal Women and the State in Canada and Australia," *Labour/Le Travail* 38 (Fall 1996)/*Labour History* 71 (November 1996): 47.

55 Ibid., 43.

56 Grimshaw, "Interracial Marriages," 19.

57 Wolfe, "Land, Labor and Difference," 872; Suzanne Parry, "Identifying the Process: The Removal of 'Half-Caste Children from Aboriginal Mothers,' *Aboriginal History* 19, 2 (1995): 146.

58 Jacobs, "The Eastmans," 32.

59 Peggy Pascoe, "Race, Gender and Intercultural Relations: The Case of Interracial Marriage," in *Writing the Range: Race, Class and Culture in the Women's West*, ed. Elizabeth Jameson and Susan Armitage (Norman, OK: University of Oklahoma Press, 1997): 70.

60 British North America and later Canada was also comprised of regions with different colonial histories, such as Newfoundland, New France, Nova Scotia, Upper Canada, the *pays d'en haut*, the Red River Colony (and Rupertsland more generally), and British Columbia. To my knowledge there is as yet no comparative study of attitudes to miscegenation in these varying colonial situations during the time period under consideration.

61 Spanish attitudes to sexuality and interracial relationships appear to have been different from those of Anglo-Americans. See Albert L. Hurtado, "When Strangers Met: Sex and Gender on Three Frontiers," in *Writing the Range: Race, Class and Culture in the Women's West*, 126.

62 Jacobs, "The Eastmans," 32.

63 In the mainland United States, forty-two states, colonies, or territories passed laws against marriage between "races." Jacobs, "The Eastmans," 32.

64 Pascoe, "Race, Gender and Intercultural Relations," 71.

65 Jean Barman, "What a Difference a Border Makes: Aboriginal Racial Intermixture in the Pacific Northwest," *Journal of the West* 38, 3 (1999): 18; Smits, "Squaw Men," 48. According to Ken Coates in *Best Left as Indians: Native-White Relations in Yukon Territory, 1840–1973* (Montreal and Kingston: McGill-Queen's University Press, 1991), 82, "squaw men" were also denigrated and marginalized in the Yukon. As Wolfe points out, this attitude is consistent with his general theory of miscegenation discourses under settler colonialism, because "assimilation of whites into the Indian population was anathema to the logic of elimination." Wolfe, "Land, Labor and Difference," 893.

66 Smits, "Squaw Men," 43; Ellinghaus, "Margins of Acceptability," 58.

67 Olive Dickason, *Canada's First Nations: A History of Founding Peoples from Earliest Times* (Toronto: McClelland & Stewart, 1992): 168–172; J.B. Brebner, "Subsidized Intermarriage with the Indians: An Incident in British Colonial Policy," *Canadian Historical Review* 6, 1 (1924): 33–6.

68 Thomas Jefferson, quoted in Bieder, "Scientific Attitudes," 19.

69 Ann McGrath, "White Brides: Images of Marriage across Colonizing Boundaries," *Frontiers* 23, 2 (2000): 88.

70 Jacobs, "The Eastmans," 34.

71 Ellinghaus, "Margins of Acceptability," 63, 69.

72 Gary Nash, "The Hidden History of Mestizo America," in *Sex, Love, Race: Crossing Boundaries in North American History*, ed. Martha Hodes (New York and London: New York University Press, 1999), 22.

73 Smits, "Squaw Men," 56.

74 Grimshaw, "Interracial Marriages," 22.

75 Belich, *Making Peoples*, 252.

76 Kate Riddell, "'Improving the Maori': Counting the Ideology of Intermarriage," *New Zealand Journal of History* 34, 1 (2000): 80.

77 James Bennett, "Maori as Honorary Members of the White Tribe," *Journal of Imperial and Commonwealth History* 29, 3 (2001): 34; Belich, *Paradise Reforged*, 209.

78 Riddell, "'Improving the Maori,'" 82–83. This assumption proved to be incorrect. Historically, most people of mixed ancestry have chosen a Maori identity regardless of blood quantum. According to Riddell, the proportion of people identifying as Maori had risen to 14 percent by 1971.

79 Edward Tregear, *The Aryan Maori* (Wellington: George Didsbury, 1885).

80 Belich, *Paradise Reforged*, 208.

81 Bennett, "'Improving the Maori,'" 37, 39.

82 Ibid., 46; Belich, *Paradise Reforged*, 210–11.

83 Riddell, "'Improving the Maori,'" 85, 88, 95.

84 Kay Schaffer, "Handkerchief Diplomacy: E.J. Eyre and Sexual Politics on the South Australian Frontier," in *Colonial Frontiers: Indigenous-European Encounters in Settler Societies*, ed. Lynette Russell (Manchester and New York: Manchester University Press, 2001), 134.

85 Barman, "Taming Aboriginal Sexuality," 240; Tonkinson, "Sisterhood," 30.

86 Pascoe, "Race, Gender and Intercultural Relations," 70.

87 Hurtado, "When Strangers Met," 126; Belich, *Making Peoples,* 252–253; Tonkinson, "Sisterhood," 32–33; Perry, *Edge of Empire*, 59–66. See also Sarah Carter, *Capturing Women: The Manipulation of Cultural Imagery in Canada's Prairie West* (Montreal and Kingston: McGill-Queen's University Press, 1997).

88 Tonkinson, "Sisterhood," 31.

89 Philip Mason, *Patterns of Dominance*, quoted in Barman, "Taming Aboriginal Sexuality," 240.

90 Belich, *Making Peoples*, 253.

91 Tonkinson, "Sisterhood," 31. Van Kirk, "'Marrying-In,'" 6. "Aboriginal men were seen to be usurping Euro-Canadian male prerogatives; and it was not acceptable for a white woman to be subordinate to an Aboriginal man" (Ibid., 7).

92 Hurtado, "When Strangers Met," 123–128; Barman, "Taming Aboriginal Sexuality," 241; Ann McGrath, "Black Velvet: Aboriginal Women and their Relations with White Men in the Northern Territory, 1910–40" in *So Much Hard Work: Women and Prostitution in Australian History*, ed. K. Daniels (Sydney: Fontana Books, 1984); Kathryn Rountree, "Remaking the Maori Female Body: Marianne Williams's Mission in the Bay of Islands," *Journal of Pacific History* 35, 1 (2000): 57–58; Perry, *Edge of Empire*, 59–66. Missionaries sometimes saw Indigenous women as passive and vulnerable objects of degradation by European men. At other times, sexually active Indigenous women were characterized as lascivious or shameless.

93 Barman, "Taming Aboriginal Sexuality," 241. Independent female sexuality threatened the foundation of the patriarchal family because children were considered to belong to their father, who had to be certain of his parentage.

94 Ibid., McGregor, *Imagined Destinies*, 63–80.

95 Grimshaw et al., *Creating a Nation*, 147–8. In the Australian case, this may have been because Aboriginal men were also seen as black. While North American captivity narratives sometimes portrayed Native American men as sexual threats, on the whole

they were not associated with rape to nearly the same degree as were black men. For Canadian attitudes, see Perry, *Edge of Empire*, 175; Carter, *Capturing Women*; Barman, "Taming Aboriginal Sexuality," 241. A different dynamic was evident in colonial New Mexico, where hundreds of Spanish women and children were captured by Comanches and Navahos and incorporated into long-term conjugal and family relations in Indigenous communities. This was part of a broader captive-exchange system that had roots in the Spanish slave trade and Indigenous traditions of exchanges and captures of women. See James F. Brooks, "'This Evil Extends Especially to the Feminine Sex': Captivity and Identity in New Mexico, 1700–1846," in *Writing the Range: Race, Class, Culture and the Women's West*, 98. Belich notes that Maori resented that white women seldom married Maori men, but I am not aware of evidence of fear of Maori men as sexual threats to white women. Belich, *Making Peoples*, 253.

96 See, for example, McGrath, "Black Velvet," 249; Hurtado, " When Strangers Met," 134.

97 Tonkinson, "Sisterhood," 31; Hurtado, "When Strangers Met," 128; Perry, *Edge of Empire*, 58.

98 Perry, *Edge of Empire*, 58.

99 Ken Coates, *Best Left as Indians: Native-White Relations in Yukon Territory, 1840–1973* (Montreal and Kingston: McGill-Queen's University Press, 1991), 82.

100 Young, *Colonial Desire*, 181.

101 Grimshaw et al., *Creating a Nation*, 147–8; Perry, *Edge of Empire*, 67.

102 Hurtado, "When Strangers Met," 130.

103 Schaffer, "Handkerchief Diplomacy," 135. Reynolds, *The Other Side of the Frontier: Aboriginal Resistance to the European Invasion of Australia* (Victoria, Australia: Penguin Books, 1982), 57; Hurtado, "When Strangers Met," 128; Perry, *Edge of Empire*, 64.

104 According to Van Kirk, some Native people thought that mixed bloods had superior physical attributes that made them better hunters and braver warriors. Van Kirk, *Many Tender Ties*, 46.

105 For example, while premarital sex was acceptable for women in many Indigenous cultures such as many Plains Indians of North America and others, premarital and extramarital sex among men was generally tolerated, but chastity was expected of women. Hurtado, "When Strangers Met," 124.

106 Hurtado, "When Strangers Met," 131; Barman, "Taming Aboriginal Sexuality," 243; Schaffer, "Handkerchief Diplomacy," 135–6; A.J. Ballantyne, "The Reform of the Heathen Body," in *When the Waves Rolled in Upon Us: Essays in Nineteenth Century Maori History*, eds. Michael Reilly and Jane Thomson (University of Otago Press, n.d.), 39.

107 Barman, "Taming Aboriginal Sexuality," 243.

108 Hurtado, "When Strangers Met," 124; Belich, *Making Peoples*, 152–153; Barman, "Taming Aboriginal Sexuality," 232–43.

109 Schaffer, "Handkerchief Diplomacy," 135–6.

110 Hurtado, "When Strangers Met," 131.

111 Belich, *Making Peoples*, 152–153. Similarly, Inuit women at Herschel Island appear to have willingly climbed on board American whaling ships to engage in sex for remuneration. Coates, *Best Left as Indians*, 79.

112 David Peterson-del Mar, "Intermarriage and Agency: A Chinookan Case Study," *Ethnohistory* 42, 1 (1995): 6.

113 Diane Bell, *Daughters of the Dreaming*, 2nd ed. (Minneapolis: University of Minnesota Press, 1993): 42.

114 Schaffer, "Handkerchief Diplomacy," 135–37.

115 McGrath, "Black Velvet," 249.

116 Schaffer, "Handkerchief Diplomacy," 137.

117 Barman, "Taming Aboriginal Sexuality," 245; Kerry Abel, *Drum Songs: Glimpses of Dene History*, Montreal and Kingston: McGill-Queen's University Press, 1993, 23; Coates, *Best Left as Indians*, 79.

118 Belich, *Making Peoples,* 153–4; Tanis Thorne, *The Many Hands of My Relations: French and Indians on the Lower Missouri* (Columbia: University of Missouri Press, 1996); Lyndall Ryan, "The Struggle for Recognition: Part-Aborigines in Bass Strait in the Nineteenth Century," *Aboriginal History* 1, 1 (1977): 30–31; Abel, *Drum Songs*, 78–79. The kidnapping of women from each other's culture is another variant. See Brooks, "'This Evil Extends Especially to the Feminine Sex,'" 97–121.

119 Sometimes the slave-owners were women. In the 1820s, several slave-owning Native wives of Hudson Bay employees also kept prostitutes at Fort George in the Columbia district. Peterson-del Mar, "Intermarriage and Agency," 6.

120 Van Kirk, *Many Tender Ties*, 75; Sleeper-Smith, *Indian Women, French Men*. Was intermarriage less attractive in matrilocal societies where women wielded considerable power, such as the Haudenosaunee?

121 Peterson-del Mar, "Intermarriage and Agency," 4–6; Abel, *Drum Songs*, 22–23.

122 Grimshaw et al., *Creating a Nation*, 139–40.

123 Belich, *Making Peoples*, 256.

124 Grimshaw et al., *Creating a Nation*, 139–40.

125 Barman, "Taming Aboriginal Sexuality," 253.

126 Hurtado, "When Strangers Met," 137.

127 The discourses of white women, the attitudes of Indigenous peoples to "others," and attitudes toward (and treatment of) individuals and populations of mixed ancestry by both Europeans and Indigenous peoples are but three of the many topics that merit further research and discussion.

128 Wolfe, "Land, Labor and Difference," 904, 894.

Home Tales:
Gender, Domesticity, and Colonialism in the Prairie West, 1870–1900

KATHRYN MCPHERSON

SYLVIA VAN KIRK'S LANDMARK STUDY *"Many Tender Ties": Women in Fur-Trade Society in Western Canada, 1670–1870* grapples with the many ways that gender and sexuality shaped colonial economies of western North America. Her narrative concludes in the mid-nineteenth century, when the arrival of elite, white women to Red River was reconfiguring social hierarchies. As European traders adopted the new racial ideology that marked white women as signifiers of civilization, many men abandoned their Aboriginal-ancestry wives and children, leaving those families without economic, legal, or social support. Van Kirk's story ends with newly articulated racial cleavages rupturing relations between European and Aboriginal women just as agricultural settlement was about to supplant the fur trade as the dominant economy of western Canada.

In recent decades, feminist historians have extended Van Kirk's analysis to consider how relations of race and gender underpinned the colonialization of, and colonial societies in, western Canada after 1860. Scholars such as Carter, Perry, Rutherdale, and Burnett have explored the spatial and legal constraints placed on First Nations women; the diverse genres of masculinity possible on colonial frontiers; the work of Euro-Canadian missionaries, teachers, and nurses in Aboriginal communities; and travellers' tales of "exotic" Indigenous women and men.[1] Such research has drawn on feminist and post-colonial theory to place Canada's "white settler" societies within the international scholarship on gender and imperialism.[2]

This article contributes to the rethinking of women's experiences and relationships by analyzing Euro-Canadian settler women's accounts of their interactions with Aboriginal peoples during the early years of agricultural settlement in the prairie west. In particular, the analysis presented here explores settler women's encounters with Indigenous women and men to interrogate how white women in the Canadian "frontier" came to understand their own place in the colonizing process. Working with Pratt's concept of gendered "contact zones" in colonial locales, this article interrogates the possibility that "woman to woman" contact might have reconfigured the nature of relations between European/Indigenous people, producing a different colonial encounter among women than among men.[3]

In the decades after 1850, the northwest interior of Canada—the territory bounded by the 49th parallel on the south, the Rocky Mountains on the west, and the Canadian shield at the north and east—was transformed as the fur trade economy was supplanted by an agricultural one, eventually dominated by "King Wheat." Heralded as the last great agricultural frontier, the federal government's land legislation (Dominion Lands Act of 1872), treaties with Aboriginal people, and an aggressive new immigration policy combined to bring the prairie west into Confederation, economically and socially as well as politically. Only the "Second Riel Rebellion" of 1885, in which Métis resistance to Canadian annexation was defeated, disrupted the smooth transition from resource to agricultural frontier on the prairie west. By 1914 the prairie west was a multi-ethnic region—the breadbasket of the British Empire.[4]

The place of Euro-Canadian women in this dramatic transformation is, in many ways, well-trod scholarly ground. We have an extensive body of scholarship focusing on prairie farm and rural women in the late nineteenth and early twentieth centuries. Yet most of that literature focuses on women's economic, cultural and political contributions to community building, and assesses white women's lives against those of their male kin-folk.[5] The fact that those women were building homes, farmsteads, and community institutions on Native land is, by and large, missing from those analyses. How did white women on the prairie west interact with local First Nations people?[6]

That such interaction occurred seems possible—even logical—given the work patterns of Native and white women alike. First Nations women in plains communities made vital contributions to their families' economies through activities like berry-picking, fishing, foraging for firewood, and selling baskets and other goods at local markets. These economic activities depended upon Native women's geographic mobility and their knowledge of the local ecologies.[7] Likewise, farm women spent a good deal of time working in the garden, gathering firewood, herding the animals, preparing dairy products and foraging in local fields and bushes for berries or herbs to supplement their diets. Settler houses—whether the near-mythic sod hut or the wooden structures that replaced the soddie—were small and it is thus unlikely that the physical space of the household would have loomed large in the daily labours of homesteading women. Rather, one would think, white women would have spent much of their day working outside—much like their Aboriginal counterparts—thereby producing a "contact zone" in which white women might come into direct contact with First Nations women or men.[8]

The likelihood of such contact was increased by the fact that in the first generation of agricultural production, most homesteads had very little land actually under cultivation, leaving open the possibility for Native people to continue to use traditional transportation routes, forested areas, or streams.[9] Only when settler families brought a significant amount of land and cultivated/fenced it did shared use become impossible. For Native people, then, the establishment of these early farms did not immediately disrupt established Native land-use patterns. Indeed, diaries of Euro-Canadian settlers from the 1880s describe Native people travelling along well-worn trails from the Turtle or Pembina Mountains near the 49th parallel up to Lake Winnipeg or Winnipegosis for the winter. Given this proximity to each other and the distance settlers had to travel to markets, the likelihood of Euro-Canadian women interacting with their Native neighbours seemed great.[10]

Yet oral and written accounts from the 1870s to 1900s contain little evidence of white women encountering their Native neighbours in the fields and berry patches of the prairie west. Rather, most primary sources document female settler-Aboriginal encounters within white women's domestic space. Sometimes this contact occurred when white women hired Aboriginal women as domestic servants, laundresses, or cooks, and other times when Aboriginal women traded baskets or leather goods on settler women's doorsteps. Other times, contact occurred when Euro-Canadian women had surprise "visits" from their Native neighbours. Indeed, stories of these visits—often recounted in memoirs or community histories of the later nineteenth century—share a common structure that I have come to call a "reverse captivity narrative" or "domestic intrusion narrative." In these narratives, white settler women recount being trapped in their own homes by uninvited and usually unwanted Aboriginal guests seeking food, trade, warmth, or to satisfy their curiosity.

Let me provide some examples of these "domestic intrusion" narratives. Ella Routley's memoir of her childhood years in the early 1880s in the Carberry, Manitoba area included a section that explained how "those Indians were a source of worry." The Routley farm was located close to a Cree or Assiniboine encampment; as Routley remembers, "there would often be thirty or forty of them about forty rods from the house." These neighbours visited. In Routley's words:

> [T]hey would come for water then they would want milk and butter. They were so sneakish. They would not come in the lane but when you least expected them they would be at the dore. [sic] And several times when we were away they would burst the dore [sic] open but the only things they took was a pepper and salt shaker. They lit the lamp and left it burning and the glass was all smoked up.

> One time they were passing the house in the winter as the rode [sic] went through our field and passed the house. I was alone with the Children and had pulled down the blinds when I saw them coming and when I thought they would all be gone I peaked out the key hole and a big Indian was just peaking in. He left when he saw me but I guess I was the worst frightened of the two.[11]

A similar encounter was reported in Gertrude Quelch's memoir published in the *Manitoba Free Press*. Entitled "An Immigrant to Manitoba in 1882," it explained to readers that the First Nations people living five miles from the Quelch homestead were "quite friendly and used to visit us."

> Of course they generally came for something. They did not knock but would glide in and sit down and never say a word till you spoke to them. Most of them could understand English and speak it enough to make themselves understood; if they were at a loss for a word they would make signs…. In olden days the squaws [sic] never visited, but later they did, and would bring beadwork etc for sale and they always looked for a meal; but you had to be careful what you put on the table for when they had eaten all they wanted they would gather up the remainder and take it home with them. One day a friend of mine put all the butter she had in the house on the table, when she was giving a squaw a meal, and the squaw wrapped it up and took it away in her

bundle, leaving my friend a sadder and wiser woman. They did it quite openly. I have had them ask me for a paper to wrap up what they took.[12]

In a similar vein, Lucy Eleanor Irvine, Mrs. Charles Musgrove, of Boissevain, Manitoba recalled that the "Indians" who travelled from North Dakota to south-western Manitoba "were harmless, though their habits of wandering about peering in windows, entering & squatting on the floor were disconcerting to settlers who had recently experienced the Riel Rebellion. Supplies such as tea, sugar & flour were none too plentiful but whites gladly handed them over on request."[13] Likewise, V.H. Lawrence's "Pioneer Recollections" include his memories from the 1890s of Cree neighbours who would "wander round outside the house peeking in through the windows. My mother did not appreciate that one day when she was in bed with the newest baby."[14] Or we can turn to Shelagh Nolan's "A Young Girl in the Old West," the 1986 *Beaver* article about her grandmother's recollections of her girlhood in and around Calgary. Nolan reported that Mary Elizabeth Lee, or Minnie, and her younger sister Flora "found the Indians very friendly." According to Minnie, "at the house the squaws would paste their noses against the windows to see us. Fair haired children were a novelty to them and one Indian offered Mother many ponies for Flora."[15]

The Cree, Assiniboine, Ojibway, and Blackfoot people of the prairie west had strong economic and cultural reasons for visiting Euro-Canadian homes. Trade was a vital element in the economies of plains people.[16] First Nations women and men came to settler homes with beadwork, woven baskets and mats, fish and small game, and berries—as Mary Higginson of Manitoba's Portage la Prairie district wrote to her grandmother in 1874, "we get any amount" of "high-bush cranberries" from local Native women.[17] First Nations women and men also traded their labour, working as domestics, washerwomen or in seasonal harvests, digging potatoes or harvesting wheat.[18] In return, Native peoples sought butter, milk, tea, flour, and even laudanum—commodities produced or procured through Euro-Canadian economies and considered valuable by Native and non-Native commentators alike.[19] Acquiring such commodities was particularly urgent in the 1880s and 1890s, when First Nations families were facing economic crisis. As scholars like Maureen Lux have shown, many plains communities faced poverty and disease in these decades, when traditional forms of economic sustenance were undermined through the decimation of plains bison, the establishment of reserves, and the expansion of agricultural settlement.[20] In the words of leading historian J.R. Miller, "the three decades following the treaty negotiations [of the 1870s] were among the most difficult western Indians faced."[21]

Yet trade of goods and labour reflected not only material need but also longer-standing cultural strategies and beliefs. Native women's participation in trade, for example, spoke to Aboriginal gender roles, wherein women's substantial economic responsibilities included initiating trade and other economic transactions. Women's arrival at the doorsteps of settler homes was rooted in First Nations women's role in securing food and provisions for their families. In an era when many western Canadian towns were limiting Aboriginal women's presence, First Nations women may have sought out trade ties at settler women's homes precisely because they were being barred from selling wares at local markets.[22]

And not all visits revolved around trade; First Nations women were present in settler women's homes when they shared their substantial midwifery skills with settler women in labour.[23] Aboriginal people might also celebrate settler children's births; Augusta Boulton received a visit from a Cree neighbour who, after the birth of Boulton's son George, "took the child…bent gravely over it and kissed its forehead. Then he took 25 cents, opened his little fist and closed it upon it. Giving the baby back, he turned and left the house without a word."[24] Local First Nations might also visit settler homes on New Year's Day to wish their white neighbours well.[25] Such exchanges cemented social and political relations among those co-habiting the Canadian plains. Some of those relations may have been familial; census data from the 1880s and 1890s reveals the persisting presence of mixed-ancestry families in many prairie communities, and thus First Nations people could well have had kin ties with settler households.[26] On other occasions, First Nations guests may have been "returning a call"—stopping in on a neighbour just as Euro-Canadian men had done on their travels across the region. Gertrude Quelch's father took a wrong turn walking home one day and, having "wandered quite a long way out of his path," came upon a Cree family. The family invited Mr. Quelch to sit by their fire, have a smoke, and enjoy a meal; in subsequent years, the family visited the Quelch homestead in return.[27]

Numerous scholars have assessed the cultural values that shaped trade and gift giving among First Nations peoples. Historian Paul Thistle notes that for western Canadian Cree "the reciprocal exchange of food continued to be a central part of the social relationship which, from the Cree standpoint, was inherent in the trade system itself."[28] Indeed, anthropologist Mary Black-Rogers has pointed out that in Native requests for food, claims they were "starving" might have functioned literally (in that people were dangerously hungry), or metaphorically or manipulatively—as in when First Nations traders "asked" for what their cultural traditions deemed necessary for trade to occur.[29] Bruce White takes this analysis further; in his work on the Lake Superior Ojibway of the early nineteenth century, White argues that gift giving was an important mechanism through which the Ojibway organized familial obligations and relations, with parents giving gifts to children as a sign of parental responsibility and authority. Family might include biological children, nieces and nephews, and adopted kin. White argues that Ojibway trade with Europeans extended this familial model, structuring relations of trade according to long-standing patterns of gift giving. Sometimes the Ojibway considered European traders as brothers or children, literally or symbolically "adopting" traders and giving gifts accordingly. Other times Ojibway leaders positioned European traders as "fathers," granting European crowns paternal responsibility and trust.[30] The Ojibway, Cree, Assiniboine, and Blackfoot people of western Canada held similar views; the First Nations people who signed treaties with the Canadian government in the latter third of the nineteenth century believed they were establishing a "family relationship with the Queen and her people." Accordingly, settlers—the "fathers"—were obliged to provide the food and supplies specified in Treaties to represent the government with whom the Treaties had been signed.[31] In other instances, First Nations people assumed the status of "father" giving gifts to "adopted" children, or sought a cup of tea as a precursor to trade, or were visiting neighbours, wishing them well with a new child or for a new year.

Aboriginal peoples' motivations for visiting their neighbours were complicated and complex. Yet in settler women's retelling, such complexities were rarely acknowledged; rather, encounters were cast as strange, frightening, and fraught with misunderstanding. Often told many years after the "pioneer" era had ended, these tales structured Native-white encounters as chapters of a bygone era. Most accounts about the 1880s and 1890s were recorded in the twentieth century, captured as part of community history projects or written down by children or grandchildren. For instance, in the 1950s the Historical and Scientific Society of Manitoba initiated a project "assembling information of community and historical value" pertaining to "Pioneer Days and Ways in Manitoba".[32] Even primary sources allegedly written "at the time" were really memoirs. Such was the case for Emma Averill's "A Journal from Liverpool to the Far West of Manitoba, 1880." The author confesses that although she had begun to record her experiences before travelling west, the "journal" had been completed many years later. Averill explained, "before laying down my pen I must own that my journal was not continual after we left Lakefield [Ont]." Rather, "the latter part of this is written entirely from memory, excepting that I referred to my husband's short diary for the exact dates and hours of our journey from there to Winnipeg." Attrill's alleged journal was really a retrospective account, written years later "from a log shanty 16' x 14' where four children are doing their lessons and with my attention constantly divided between baking, churning, cooking, washing, and every other domestic duty and that which now lies before you."[33]

Settler women, then, retold their tales of encounters with "Indians" as they looked back on a world which had passed and which they now tried to understand. Carol Gerson makes this argument about narratives produced by colonizers in Upper Canada in the mid-nineteenth century. Gerson examines the "anecdotes" about First Nations people contained within the published work of Catharine Parr Traill and Susanna Moodie to argue that in "texts intended for public consumption" narratives "may be shaped as much by discursive conventions and ideological concerns as by the desire to document lived experience."[34] For women narrating western Canadian settlement of the 1870s and 1880s, one of the "discursive conventions" at play was what literary critic Elizabeth Thompson has coined the "archetypal pioneer woman." Thompson analyzes the "pioneer woman" as a "literary character type" that appears in Canadian fiction from the 1840s right through to the 1970s. Thompson modestly disclaims that "no direct causal link can be established between various generations of Canadian writers,"[35] yet historical evidence suggests otherwise. Female settlers in the Northwest were aware of the "pioneer archetype" made famous by early nineteenth-century writers like Parr Traill and Moodie. For example, one anonymously authored and handwritten manuscript from the early 1890s sought to debunk promotional pamphlets and immigration recruitment material of the 1880s. Its title, "My four years experience in the North West of America: Roughing it in the far West," purposely played on Moodie's *Roughing it in the Bush*. Gertrude Quelch's memoir stated that her neighbours were the Moodies: "Mrs. Moodie was the grand-daughter of the Mrs. Moodie that wrote 'Roughing It in the Bush.'"[36] Harriett Traill—daughter-in-law of Catharine Parr Traill—recorded her experiences as the wife of Hudson's Bay Company employee Thomas Traill. Emma Averill migrated west from her home in Lakefield, Ontario, a village close to the homes of the Strickland Sisters. Such clues from western Canadian documents suggest that the colonists of the late nineteenth century were well-versed in the earlier generation of pioneer tales, and familiar with the "pioneer woman" persona.

Within the "discursive convention" of early nineteenth-century contact narratives was a version of the domestic visit tales. For instance, Catharine Parr Traill's 1836 publication *The Backwoods of Canada* included stories of Aboriginal neighbours visiting her home for trade or tea. In one of Parr Traill's dramatic tales, the author retells a story she had heard about a pioneer woman a generation earlier. In that tale, a widow, raising her children in a sparsely settled district, was startled one night when an Aboriginal man suddenly entered her cabin. The man "had entered so silently that it was not till he planted himself before the blazing fire that he was perceived by the frightened widow and her little ones, who retreated, trembling with ill-concealed terror to the furthest corner of the room." The silent intruder did not seem to notice the fear of his hostess or her family. Rather, he "proceeded to disencumber himself from his hunting accoutrements" and made it clear that he planned to shelter himself from the cold and stormy night within the warmth of the woman's cabin. The terrified woman held her children to her as they watched their "unwelcome" guest. "Imagine their horror," wrote Parr Traill, "when they beheld him take from his girdle a hunting-knife, and deliberately proceed to try its edge. After this his tomahawk and rifle underwent a similar examination." Terrified, the widow watched as her visitor moved toward her. "What then was her surprise and joy when he gently laid the rifle, knife, and tomahawk beside her, signifying by his action that she had nothing to fear at his hands."[37]

The widow, who according to Traill was feeling akin to a "condemned criminal" that received a reprieve "at the moment previous to his execution," was " eager to prove her confidence and her gratitude...[to] the now no longer dreaded guest." Assisted by her elder children, she prepared her guest food and drink, and readied a comfortable bed replete with clean bedding. In a lighthearted twist, Parr Traill described the man's curious appraisal of the soft bed: "After a mute examination of the bed-clothes for some minutes, with a satisfied laugh, he sprang upon the bed, and curling himself up like a dog, in a few minutes was sound asleep." The story concludes with the stranger departing at dawn as silently as he had arrived, reappearing occasionally in the neighbourhood. "The children, no longer terrified at his swarthy countenance and warlike weapons, would gather round his knees, admire the feathered pouch that contained his shot, finger the beautiful embroidered sheath that held the hunting-knife, or the finely-worked moccasins and leggings; whilst he would pat their heads, and bestow upon them an equal share of caresses with his deer-hounds."[38]

In this tale, Parr Traill suggests the possible sexualization of Aboriginal visitors. The widow's initial fears—explicitly defined as fear of physical violence—were abated when the man removed his weapons, which were described in phallic terms, implicitly speaking to the threat of sexual violence. Relieved of this fear, the widow fulfilled her domestic role by making him a bed, on which her Aboriginal visitor curled up and went to sleep. The man made no demand on the widow except for a warm place to sleep, and when he subsequently appeared he behaved like a good father figure, patiently enduring the children's inquisitive hands. It is tempting to suggest the man is degraded by his absence of sexuality, but the fact that the widow made a bed for him could symbolize the possibility of consensual sexual relations. Indeed, the story itself is told in sexual terms, with the "climax" of fear (and coercive male sexuality) replaced by the persisting presence of this attractive male character in the widow's domain.

Late nineteenth-century stories never suggested that Native men might be sexually potent or dangerous, but like Parr Traill incorporated the romanticized image of the noble savage and the dying race, made popular by writers like Wordsworth and Fenimore Cooper. In Parr Traill's words, "the race is slowly passing away from the face of the earth." [39] As Gerson notes about Parr Traill and Moodie, "the elegiac tone sometimes adopted by both sisters invests First Nations people, as remnants of the past, with romantic quality akin to the nostalgia felt by their European counterparts for architectural ruins."[40] Western Canadian commentators too mobilized images of the "noble savage"; Augusta Boulton described one regular visitor who she claimed was a chief named Cakequas. She describes this "particularly fine-looking man" as follows: "I remember once his coming in the door, tall, silent, impassive. Indians never speak to woman."[41]

Most tales, though, minimized complimentary descriptions, stressing instead the strangeness of domestic guests and the tension produced by white women's innocence and ignorance, which in turn produced fear. This tension was resolved in one of three ways. In some stories, women were rescued by male aid—anxiety over the unknown guests was managed by the arrival of more "knowing" male kinfolk. For example, August Boulton's chivalrous visitor was patiently waiting for Mr. Boulton to come into the house so the two men could consult a map.

Often the tension was resolved through knowledge acquisition, as Euro-Canadian women came to "understand" that Native people were not a threat. Emma Averill's memoir includes a story that is remarkably like Traill's, without the weary widow or the unsheathing of knives. Still, "we frequently had a visit from an Indian, who with his gun or spear for killing the rats would open the door and walk in, seat himself by the stove and generally try to carry on a little conversation." Emma's efforts to discourage the guest one day failed, and she subsequently concluded that "our Indian visitors have behaved so pleasantly that I have quite lost my fear of them and do not in the least mind their unceremonious style of coming and going."[42]

In many stories, the tension was resolved through humour, with the Native characters being as shocked or scared as the whites. In all cases, of course, the protagonist persists and survives, ensuring that the story and its retelling served as testimonial to the cultural victory of Euro-Canadian settlers. As such, they are the stories of colonizers. Indeed, the humour suggested by many stories was premised upon the unneeded anxiety that novice pioneers felt when confronted for the first time by their Aboriginal neighbours. The anxiety was unneeded precisely because, in hindsight, First Nations people were no threat to Euro-Canadian agricultural society.

These "domestic intrusion" stories offered white women a particular location in the larger set of memories about colonization. Such accounts served to legitimize these historical actors as "authentic" pioneer women, distinct from their sisters in imperial centres or more recent immigrants to the region.[43] Interactions with Aboriginal peoples underscored the fact that however humble their domestic abodes—however hard their conditions of life and labour or however far from family and friends—pioneer women struggled with and overcame obstacles that would have defeated a lesser gal. Regardless of the fear that First Nations people might strike in the hearts of women, at the end of the day the women were victorious in protecting their infants and their homes; indeed, in no case did the female protagonist respond to their "domestic intrusion" by abandoning their household and leaving their own homes.

By celebrating white women's survival in the face of unwanted Aboriginal guests, reverse captivity narratives served to emphasize white settler women's claim to domesticity. Such claims were significant in settler economies where women spent much of their time outside the home. Houses themselves were small and sparse: Emma Attrill wrote her narrative from within the walls of her 14' x 16' log cabin. Maria Owens's 1880 letter to her sister Maggie described her nearest neighbour, whose "house is not any bigger than your dining room, no sellar [sic] nor upstairs."[44] In Toronto, or Montreal, or London, the only women who occupied such meagre homes or performed such heavy labour were unskilled working-class women whose class denied them any claim to gentility or respectability. But on the "frontier," stories of domestic privation signified the respectable work of empire. In their rhetorical defence of the domestic realm, white settler women were entitled to bourgeois respectability that would have been denied to urban women living and working in similarly deprived circumstances.

There is a further class dimension to these stories. The white women who narrated the tales often claimed they were puzzled by what their visitors wanted; settler women represented themselves as novices, taken by surprise by the economic or social contact being initiated. Reading the accounts of negotiations between white- and brown-skinned women, one wonders whether the resourceful working-class women of Bettina Bradbury's Montreal or the inventive women of east-end London that Ellen Ross described (pawning their husbands' dress pants for the week) might not have boasted better bartering skills than did the farm women who settled in southwestern Manitoba.[45] Farm women in the prairie west seemed remarkably uncreative, negotiating only around domestic labour and baskets: berries, game, herbs, mushrooms, and moccasins were rarely offered and never requested. By contrast, the Aboriginal women clearly desired items like butter and milk—items that would subsidize the meagre rations government agents were providing.

Certainly the stories underscored the sexual respectability of white settler women. Even when First Nations men penetrated the heart of domestic and family life in these tales, they did not threaten the sexual respectability of settler women and their families. Representations of women living in uncharted territory did not leave those women vulnerable to sexual conquest. In fact, by rendering the white female protagonist spatially fixed within the domestic sphere, these narratives served to emphasize the geographic mobility of Aboriginal women. As Sarah Carter has clearly shown, Aboriginal women had to be mobile if they were to support their families, yet it was that very mobility that fuelled white authorities' beliefs that Native women were socially and sexually dangerous.[46] In leaving their own families to "visit" Euro-Canadian households, the Aboriginal female characters in domestic intrusion narratives are rhetorically located outside the feminized domesticity the stories celebrate.

If these tales inscribed settler women in the historical narrative of pioneer, they did so without tainting white women's class or racial or sexual status. At the same time, these stories could also be deployed to write women into the creation of nation, a goal that was particularly important for early twentieth-century narrators committed to gaining political rights for white women. An episode retold in Nellie McClung's 1935 memoir *Clearing in the West* illustrates the political ends to which intrusion narratives could be utilized.[47] In the chapter entitled "Trouble in the Northwest," McClung recalls the fear that rippled through her southwestern Manitoba community when news of the 1885 Rebellion broke out. It is not surprising that McClung, a well-known literary figure, was fully versed in the tales of Mrs. Delaney and Gowanlock, who published their memoirs of being held hostage by Big Bear for two months after the North West Rebellion.[48] In McClung's 1935 story about the Rebellion, neighbours were preparing for Native unrest to spread among the local Sioux people, but her own mother "stood firmly by her belief that the Indians would not hurt the women." In fact: "Women are safer with Indians than they would be with some white men," proclaimed the mother of Canada's most vocal feminist. McClung's sister Hannah shared her mother's views. Hannah declared, "I'm not afraid of Indians; especially our own Indians who come selling baskets. They're friendly and they don't know anything about the trouble in Saskatchewan. They can't read and the trouble is three hundred miles away." When the youthful Nellie had nightmares about "savages" attacking, she calmed herself with the knowledge that her sister would "talk" angry Natives down, while "mother would make tea for them and feed them currant buns and get them persuaded to go back and make their baskets and behave themselves."[49]

Such confidence in the civilizing power of white women was soon tested when rumours spread about a caravan of carts wending its way north. Nellie and Hannah rushed home to see three carts and ponies in their farmyard. The girls were struck by fear, "but nothing could be more peaceful than the farm yard that moment. Hens and chickens circled the space in front of the horse stables, the hens scratching and calling... every aspect of the day and the place spoke of peace." McClung followed her sister into the house:

> When we opened the kitchen door the room seemed to be full of Indians; at least the floor was covered by them, for with their blankets and shawls, one squaw, with a papoose can cover much space; the acrid smell of burned willow roots and tanned hide filled the air. On the other side of the stove with the oven open Mother sat in a rocking chair, with a flannel on her knee on which lay an Indian baby, a poor little wrinkled thing with a face like an old monk, whimpering softly like a sick puppy. She was rubbing its chest with goose-grease. [50]

Invoking Christian symbolism, McClung then described the young Sioux mother on her knees at Mrs. Moody's feet "watching with impassive face." With the baby out of danger, the other Aboriginal women also sought various medical treatments from the capable Mrs. Moody—Mrs. Moody had laudanum, so her Sioux neighbours may well have been correct in turning to her for some short-term comfort for their pains. [51]

As in other such tales, the settler women (or girls in this case) found their initial fear was erased when they realized the simplicity of their visitors' needs, and the story concluded with an ironic twist. McClung reported that the Sioux group made the rounds of the neighbourhood "and were so well fed and showered with gifts of flour, potatoes, eggs and butter that they must have wondered, if Indians do wonder, at the sudden warming of hearts that had taken place. Houses that had been closed and locked to them from behind the edge of factory cotton blinds, now were opened hospitably and kettles were boiled and meat was fried for the visiting delegates." Thus, concluded the reminiscing McClung, the conflict in Saskatchewan prompted a positive outcome in relations between the races in Pelican Lake, Manitoba.[52]

In this instance, Mrs. Moody's domestic skills facilitated relations between whites and the local First Nations people at a critical point in the nation's history. In their successful handling of their domestic invasion, women like Moody were not just experiencing part of the pioneer experience but also assuming heroic status. Indeed, McClung suggests that Moody's management of her Native visitors suggested that the military conflict in the North West (an act which a committed pacifist like McClung could not endorse) might have been averted by some sensible food and health care. In McClung's retelling, the domestic sphere was a metaphor for the political sphere much like maternal feminists saw the successful homemaker as a ready and needed participant in civic public life—one whose private domestic skills would benefit civic public society.

While they were true colonizers who helped reduce conflict, such women were nonetheless not the victims of the colonial venture. They were able to serve the fledgling nation without sacrificing their fundamental claim to respectable femininity, a claim that was predicated on Victorian women remaining in (and succeeding at) maternal domesticity. Most intrusion narratives included children: Shelagh Nolan's grandmother was a young girl when Aboriginal neighbours offered to "trade" for her fair-haired sister Flora, and Ella Routley was caring for her younger sisters when she experienced her first uninvited guests.[53] That children signified familial domesticity was evident in an 1885 drawing of the McLean women included in the *Family Herald and Weekly Star* coverage of the North West Rebellion. Titled "Noble Women on the Defensive," the drawing depicted three generations of McLean women standing by the interior wall of their house or barn, looking out a window. As Gillian Poulter's study shows, most images of women in the Rebellion emphasized women's powerlessness. By contrast, the 1885 *Family Herald and Weekly Star* drawing permitted women military agency, albeit exercised from the safety of the domestic realm. The two women are holding rifles, with a large axe sitting nearby, as they look out the "loophole" ready to repel prospective intruders. Their adherence to Victorian codes of morality is suggested in their hair and dress: an older woman in black, a younger woman wearing an apron. The milk stool is tipped over behind them, signifying that their domestic chores have been interrupted by the need to take up arms. Published in June 1885, this image managed to give these women agency, but from within a safe realm—defending their home or homestead.[54]

The narrative device of domestic intrusion and temporary captivity served to illustrate settler women's pioneering adventures in ways that implicitly and explicitly reinforced the pioneer woman's claim to class, racial, and gendered respectability. Claims to this gendered status not only served the individual women as they wrote themselves into their family histories—it also helped produce a collective identity that located white settler women at the heart of the narrative of colonization, and through that narrative at the core of nation building. Like the captivity narratives analyzed by Carol Smith Rosenberg for early American history, the "reverse captivity tales" of late-nineteenth-century western Canada made white women authorial voices on the nature of national and colonial histories, "authorizing themselves as writers and citizens" by using a "distinctly New World device."[55] This "new world" was gendered, locating female domesticity and sexual respectability as the foundation for women's claim to building white settler nations. The intrusion tales of western Canada reflected the dual vision between "old world and new" that Marilyn Lake has eloquently identified. Lake argues that the collective identities of new-world nations were forged in opposition to the old civilized order of Europe and in opposition to "primitive" Indigenous cultures.[56] Domestic intrusion narratives foregrounded the primitive conditions necessitated by pioneering, but distanced such domestic hardship from the failed domesticity of First Nations guests. The female iconography produced by and for white settler women produced a space of "woman to woman contact" that named and celebrated pioneer women's contributions to building settler society, while dismissing the complex economic and cultural strategies that brought First Nations neighbours to settler women's doors.

Notes

1   Sarah Carter, *Capturing Women: The Manipulation of Cultural Imagery in Canada's Prairie West* (Montreal: McGill-Queen's University Press, 1997); Adele Perry, *On the Edge of Empire: Gender, Race and the Making of British Columbia, 1849–1871* (Toronto: University of Toronto Press, 2001); Myra Rutherdale, *Women and the White Man's God: Gender and Race in the Canadian Mission Field* (Vancouver: University of British Columbia Press, 2002); Kristin Burnett, *Taking Medicine: Colonialism, Settlement and Women's Healing Work in Southern Alberta, 1880–1930* (Vancouver: University of British Columbia Press, 2010).

2   Katie Pickles and Myra Rutherdale, *Contact Zones: Aboriginal and Settler Women in Canada's Colonial Past* (Vancouver: University of British Columbia Press, 2005); Sarah Carter, Lesley Erickson, Patricia Roome and Char Smith, *Unsettled Pasts: Reconceiving the West Through Women's History* (Calgary: University of Calgary Press, 2005).

3   Mary Louise Pratt, *Imperial Eyes: Travel and Transculturation* (London: Routledge, 1992), 6–7.

4   For a survey of western Canadian history see Gerald Friesen, *The Canadian Prairies: A History* (Toronto: University of Toronto Press, 1987).

5   Kathryn McPherson, "Was the Frontier 'Good' for Women? Historical Approaches to Women and Agricultural Settlement in the Prairie West, 1870–1900," *Atlantis* 25, 1 (Fall 2000): 75–86.

6   Very few studies explore the ways that "ordinary" settler women encountered Aboriginal people. Patricia Roome considers Henrietta Muir Edwards's relations with local Blood women, and with Aboriginal communities in western Canada more generally, although Muir Edwards was not an "ordinary" farm woman. Patricia A. Roome, "'From One Whose Home Is among the Indians': Henrietta Muir Edwards and Aboriginal Peoples" in *Unsettled Pasts.*

7   Sarah Carter, "Categories and Terrains of Exclusion: Constructing the 'Indian Woman' in the Early Settlement Era in Western Canada," *Great Plains Quarterly* 13 (Summer 1993): 147–61.

8   Pratt, *Imperial Eyes.*

9   A.M. Armitage of Virden recorded in his family memoir that as late as 1908, "There were also quite a few Indians traveling between the Birdtail and Griswold reserves" (Archives of Manitoba [AM], MG8 B105). A.M. Armitage collection. See also recollections such as Alexander McGillvray, who travelled west in 1878. McGillvray recalls that in the 1880s Aboriginal people still trapped in the area around Manitou, Manitoba, and when they "travelled west they stayed on the south part of his quarter. About one half-mile south was a flat spot where the Indians held a pow-wow" (Alexander McGillvray, AM, MG8 B62 "Panting Collection," file 37).

10   Irene Spry calls this era of shared use one of "open commons," one that by the end of the century would give way to private ownership and loss of common use. Irene Spry, "The Great Transformation: The Disappearance of the Commons in Western Canada" in *Man and Nature on the Prairies*, ed. Richard Allen, (Regina: Canadian Plains Research Center, 1976) and "The Tragedy of Loss of Commons" in *As Long as the Sun Shines and the River Flows: A Reader in Canadian Native Studies*, ed. Ian A.L. Getty and Antoine Lussier (Vancouver: University of British Columbia Press, 1983).

11   Memoir of Ella Routley (Carberry Archives), 94–87.

12   Gertude Quelch, "An Immigrant to Manitoba in 1882," *Manitoba Free Press*, 28 August 1926 (AM, MG8 B70).

13   "Reminiscences of C.C. Musgrove" (AM, MG14 C17).

14   Valentine Laurence "Diary" (AM, P3756 f2).

15 Shelagh Nolan, "A Young Girl in the Old West," *The Beaver* 66, 4 (July 1986): 49–54.

16 On the importance of trade see Arthur J. Ray, *Indians in the Fur Trade: Their Role as Hunters, Trappers and Middlemen in the Lands Southwest of Hudson Bay* (Toronto: University of Toronto Press, 1974) and Laura Peers, *The Ojibwa of Western Canada, 1780–1870* (Winnipeg: University of Manitoba Press, 1994).

17 Mary Higginson to Grandmother, 6 December 1874 (AM, P5905, Byers Family Papers, file 1).

18 "What Women Say of the Canadian North-West," 43–45, includes settler women's responses to the question "Do you experience any dread of the Indians?" Very few women responded to the affirmative. Many women reported no interactions with local First Nations people. Others reported hiring local women and men, trading with them, and receiving visits from them. See also, Robert Bartleman of Morden, Manitoba interview, "Those [Indians] in the vicinity were peaceable and sold baskets" (AM MG28 B62 Panting Collection, file 6).

19 Diaries, letters, and autobiographical accounts often refer to the value of butter. See for example Maria Owens's 1882 letter to her sister Maria: "butter s .40c now but I have none to sell, got .25c for all I sold but the cows did not do very well calved too early in Feb and March," 18 December 1882 (AM, MG8 B104); or Mary Higginson to Grandmother, 6 December 1874, "butter is very scarce out here and is 35c a pound will be glad when we get cows of our own but must wait till we get a location first. We all missed the butter very much at first" (AM, P5905, Byers Family Papers, file 1).

20 Maureen Lux, *Medicine that Walks: Disease, Medicine and the Canadian Plains Native People, 1880–1940* (Toronto: University of Toronto Press, 2001).

21 J.R. Miller, "'I Will Accept the Queen's Hand': First Nations Leaders and the Image of the Crown in the Prairie Treaties," in *Reflections on Native-Newcomer Relations: Selected Essays* (Toronto: University of Toronto Press, 2004), 260.

22 See Carter, "Categories and Terrains of Exclusion."

23 Kristin Burnett, "The Healing Work of Aboriginal Women in Indigenous and Newcomer Communities" in *Place and Practice in Nursing History*, ed. Jayne Elliott and Meryn Stuart (Vancouver: University of British Columbia Press, 2008). See also Reverend E. Ben Johnson's reminiscences of his years as a Methodist missionary in the Swan River Valley, which includes stories of Native women helping European woman in childbirth. Reverend E. Ben Johnson "Journal" (AM, MG7 C17).

24 "Reminiscences of Augusta Boulton in 1880" (AM, MG 14 B20 Box 2, file 63).

25 Mrs. Mary Brown, family history, 1952, 11 (AM, MG9 A81).

26 The Census of Canada, 1881 (DBS). South Western Extension sub-district of Manitoba lists several households where the original listing of families as "half-breeds" was corrected by the supervisor to read "French." Across western Canada, Aboriginal women sometimes lived in the same community as neighbours to their (unacknowledged) former partner and his new wife. See for example, Perry's discussion of Susan Moir Allison and John Allison's former partner Suzanne. See also, Burnett, *Taking Medicine*.

27 Quelch, "An Immigrant to Manitoba in 1882."

28 Paul C. Thistle, *Indian-European Trade Relations in the Lower Saskatchewan River Region to 1840* (Winnipeg: University of Manitoba Press, 1986), 83.

29 Mary Black-Rogers, "Varieties of 'Starving': Semantics and Survival in the Subarctic Fur Trade, 1750–1850," *Ethnohistory* 33, 4 (Fall 1986): 353–383.

30 Bruce M. White, "'Give Us a Little Milk': The Social and Cultural Meanings of Gift Giving in the Lake Superior Fur Trade," in *Rendezvous: Selected Papers of the Fourth North American Fur Trade Conference*, ed. Thomas C. Buckley (St. Paul, MN: The North American Fur Trade Conference, 1984).

31   Miller, "'I Will Accept the Queen's Hand,'" 259.

32   The Historical and Scientific Society of Manitoba "Pioneer Days and Ways in Manitoba" 1953 in the Panting Collection at Manitoba's Provincial Archives (AM, MG 28 B62). Retrospective accounts are also included in published sources such as Mrs. H. McCorkindale's memoirs "Homesteading at Indian Head" as recounted by her daughter, Mrs. Jean McCorkindale Thomas of Summerside, PEI, *Saskatchewan History*, 1951.

33   ELA (Emma Averill), "A Journal From Liverpool to the Far West of Manitoba" (AM, P267 MG8 A24).

34   Carole Gerson, "Nobler Savages: Representations of Native Women in the Writings of Susanna Moodie and Catharine Parr Trail," *Journal of Canadian Studies* 32, 2 (Summer 1997): 11.

35   Elizabeth Thompson, *The Pioneer Woman: A Canadian Character Type* (Montreal: McGill-Queen's University Press, 1991), 59.

36   Indeed, two of Catharine Parr Traill's sons worked in the west for the Hudson's Bay Company, and William's wife Harriet wrote a diary, now preserved at the Glenbow Museum and Library (Glenbow Archives [GA] Traill Fonds).

37   Catharine Parr Traill, *The Backwoods of Canada: Being Letters from the Wife of an Emigrant Officer* (London, England: Nattali and Bond, 1836), 218.

38   Parr Traill, *The Backwoods of Canada*, 219.

39   Gerson, "Nobler Savages," 11. James Fenimore Cooper, *The Last of the Mohicans* (H.C. Carey and I. Lea, 1826).

40   Gerson, "Nobler Savages," 14.

41   "Reminiscences of Augusta Boulton."

42   Averill, "A Journal From Liverpool."

43   After 1896, the number of eastern-European migrants to the Canadian west grew dramatically, undermining the "English" character of the region's "white" population. See, for example, Frances Swyripa, *Wedded to the Cause: Ukrainian-Canadian Women and Ethnic Identity, 1881–1891* (Toronto: University of Toronto Press, 1992).

44   Maria Owens to Maggie, 14 July 1880, in Thomas Higginson Collection (AM, MG8 B104).

45   Bettina Bradbury, *Working Families: Age, Gender, and Daily Survival in Industrializing Montreal* (Toronto: University of Toronto Press, 1993); Ellen Ross, *Love and Toil: Motherhood in Outcast London, 1870–1918* (New York: Oxford University Press, 1993)

46   Sarah Carter, "First Nations Women of Prairie Canada in the Early Reserve Years, the 1870s to the 1920s: A Preliminary Inquiry" in *Women of the First Nations: Power, Wisdom, and Strength*, ed. Marie Smallface Marule, Brenda Manyfingers, and Cheryl Deering (Winnipeg: University of Manitoba Press, 1996).

47   Nellie McClung, *Clearing in the West: My Own Story* (Toronto: Thomas Allen, 1935).

48   For a full analysis of Gowanlock and Delaney's narratives see Sarah Carter, *Capturing Women: The Manipulation of Cultural Imagery in Canada's Prairie West* (Montreal: McGill-Queen's University Press, 1997).

49   McClung, *Clearing in the West*, 184–5.

50   Ibid., 188.

51   Ibid., 189.

52   Ibid.

53   Nolan, "A Young Girl in the Old West," and "Memoir of Ella Routley."

54   See Gillian Poulter's fine analysis of eastern Canadian media coverage of the North West Rebellion in *Becoming Native in a Foreign Land: Sport, Visual Culture and Identity in Montreal, 1840–85* (Vancouver: University of British Columbia Press, 2009), especially Chapter 5.

55   Carol Smith-Rosenberg, "Captured Subjects/Savage Others: Violently Engendering the New American," *Gender and History* 5, 2 (1993): 177–95 shows how Sarah Rollandson's captivity narrative wrote herself into the centre of the colonizing venture of Puritan society.

56   Marilyn Lake, "Between 'Old World Barbarism' and 'New World Primitivism': The Double Difference of the White Australian Feminist" in *Australian Women: Contemporary Feminist Thought*, ed. N. Grive and A. Burns (Melbourne: Oxford University Press, 1994).

"I am a proud Anishinaabekwe": Issues of Identity and Status in Northern Ontario after Bill C-31[1]

KATRINA SRIGLEY

"THE NORTH WAS ALWAYS PART OF ME...IT SHAPED WHO I AM," said Alice Desjarlais during her 2006 interview in North Bay, Ontario. As a young woman in the 1960s, Desjarlais wanted to leave the North behind, to escape her family and everything associated with it.[2] Born in 1949 on a trapline in northwestern Quebec, Desjarlais was the youngest in a family of six children. She remembered little happiness in her childhood. Her mother carried a deep and intractable hatred of 'white' people, having lost four of her sons to the residential school system. First it was their physical absence, then their emotional distance when they returned, filled with distaste for their culture and their parents' way of life.[3] One of them sexually abused Desjarlais, who recalled that "a negative spirit" entered her from this violence, one that took her years to face and extricate. Desjarlais' parents tried to keep her out of the school system, withdrawing her whenever possible to educate her in the bush. Despite these efforts, at sixteen Desjarlais was sent to North Bay to attend high school. This did not last long; as soon as she had a chance, she quit and fled to Toronto. "I hated my own culture. I wanted to hide that part of me...I wanted to be a white person," explained Desjarlais, adding with infectious laughter, that she hoped to "pass as an Italian." For Desjarlais, this self-hatred initiated a twenty-year cycle of addiction and abuse that only ended when she decided to come home to northern Ontario and allow the elders to help her understand her parents and respect her culture. "I realized that I

241

had to go up North again and reconnect with my identity." Today, Dejarlais says with conviction and calmness, "I am a proud Anishinaabekwe. When I found it I hung on to it and didn't want to let go."[4] At this point, her Aboriginal identity, once a source of alienation, became a powerful foundation for belonging.

Desjarlais' story and the stories of nine other Aboriginal women from northern Ontario provide an opportunity to consider the connection between identity and belonging in the years after Bill C-31 (1985), An Act to Amend the Indian Act.[5] By restoring status to generations of women who had lost it by marrying non-Aboriginal men or Aboriginal men without status, Bill C-31 initiated profound transformations in the lives of Native women.[6] It altered relationships to indigeneity, families, communities, and the Canadian government. While examining how women negotiated these shifts, this article also reflects on the multiple ways in which women like Desjarlais strengthened their self-identities to heal, participate in, and initiate remarkable cultural and political change in their communities. The women who share their stories here range in age from 38 to 81, and have spent most or all of their lives in northern Ontario.[7] All of them identify as Aboriginal women, though three of them do not have official status. They are women of varied backgrounds and ways of life: Anishinaabe, Cree, and Métis, middle and working class, traditionally and formally educated, lesbian and heterosexual, Roman Catholic, atheist, and observing the traditions of Native spirituality. Together their stories, along with issues explored in this volume by Victoria Freeman, Rob Innes, and Angela Wanhalla, expose issues central to our understanding of the history of Aboriginal women in twentieth-century Canada. The colonial agendas of Canada's past, particularly the desire to assimilate or destroy First Peoples, continues to create violence, alienation, and sadness in women's lives.

Challenging these legacies has taken many forms. Through political organizations at the international, national, provincial, and band level, women have raised awareness and fought for change. By demanding that the Canadian government fulfill status entitlements, women have secured better economic futures for themselves and their children. Through cultural reclamation, connections to land and community, and the guidance of elders, women have healed wounds and forged different paths. Most specifically, these women's stories reveal how landmark decisions like Bill C-31 influenced the lives of Aboriginal women by reminding us—with anger, sadness, and tremendous humour—that a sense of belonging rooted in positive individual and cultural identity and the fulfillment of historical obligations on the part of the Canadian government is the surest way to heal the insidious and lasting violence of colonialism.[8]

Historiographically, this article speaks to the ongoing need for more research on Native women in Canadian history. In 1980, Sylvia Van Kirk placed Aboriginal women within the history of the Northwest fur trade. She did so to tell the stories of women, but also to remind us, through "*Many Tender Ties*" and her subsequent research on the five founding families of Victoria, that we must look for women in places we do not expect to find them. In an equally important sense, Van Kirk's scholarship reminds us that we should not presume all Aboriginal women are the same; instead, we must recognize what is both unique and typical about their experiences and voices.[9] Despite this research, along with that of Jennifer Brown and more recent scholarship in the field (including a significant number of local and community studies in the fields of anthropology, geography, Native studies, and sociology), there continue to be profound gaps in our sense of the experiences and place of Aboriginal women in the history of Canada.[10]

This silence is particularly significant with regard to the twentieth century. For a long time, the argument that contact, settlement, and other forms of "fatal impact" had made Aboriginal peoples irrelevant by the beginning of the twentieth century, ensuring that Indigenous history in this period would be limited.[11] If Aboriginal peoples had been assimilated and their cultures destroyed, what else would there be for social historians to say about this tragic story? The traction of this argument, John Lutz contends in his book *Makúk: A New History of Aboriginal-White Relations,* is bound to the sources and methodologies historians have employed. These approaches to the past have limited the ability of historians to find and to hear Aboriginal voices.[12] Van Kirk, Lutz, and other scholars developing an Indigenous-centred historiography suggest we need to think differently about source material. Wills, marriage records, newspapers, organizational documents, and photographs are among the many sources in which we can find Aboriginal people's experiences.[13] Doing so requires more fluid and varied methodological approaches which take inspiration from historians and non-historians alike. The scholarship of Kathy Absolon, Julie Cruikshank, Bonita Lawrence, Linda Tuhiwai Smith, Winona Wheeler, Shawn Wilson, and others offers abundant examples of how employing Indigenous methodologies and views of history—widening our understanding of the role of storytelling in memory, shifting our periodization, or thinking differently about concepts such as economy, or gender, or the life of glaciers—fundamentally alters our understanding of the past.[14] When we think in these terms—when we listen well to one another—we enrich our history and multiply our options for a positive way forward. "History is power," explains Maori scholar Linda Tuhiwai Smith, and when we challenge omissions and overcome silences in the historical record we contribute to the recovery of language and culture, to healing, and to relationship-building that is essential to a sustainable future.[15] This article forefronts the experiences and perspectives of Anishinaabe, Cree, and Métis women from the North Bay area through interview-based research relationships (or, in the words of Winona Wheeler, "Indigenous oral histories") to expand our understanding of the impact of government policy on women, their families and communities in late twentieth-century Canada.[16]

Irrespective of historiographical silences, Aboriginal women and issues of importance to them have been present in public discourse since the mid-twentieth century. The visibility of women as political activists has been central to this trend. After 1951, when amendments to the *Indian Act* eliminated restrictions on women's political leadership, Aboriginal women claimed political roles, including leadership positions as chiefs and on band councils.[17] They were visible as protestors and community leaders at conflicts like the 1990 Oka crisis. They demanded that their voices be heard through organizations such as Indian Rights for Indian Women, the Ontario Native Women's Association, and the Native Women's Association of Canada (NWAC). Through policy papers, participatory action research, and reports (such as Kathleen Jamieson's 1978 paper for the Canadian Advisory Council on the Status of Women, "Indian Women and the Law in Canada: Citizens Minus"), these women showed that Aboriginal women faced unique challenges that were a consequence of their disenfranchisement through the *Indian Act*, including extreme violence inside and outside their communities.[18] Local and community studies published in Aboriginal newspapers such as *Windspeaker*, as well as volumes such as Silman's *Enough is Enough: Aboriginal Women Speak Out* and Kim Anderson's *A Recognition of Being*, provide equally compelling evidence of the place of Aboriginal women in twentieth-century Canada.[19] These crucially important studies give voice to women's experiences. Indeed, they make clear that Aboriginal women are the most visible but ignored group of women in Canadian history.

Bill C-31—Issues of Identity and Status

When the Canadian Parliament passed Bill C-31, An Act to Amend the Indian Act, many Aboriginal women celebrated. It was, after all, a hard-won victory with a lengthy history. By this time, efforts to erode the power of Aboriginal women in their communities had been ongoing for hundreds of years. For Muriel Sawyer, the ultimate purpose of the Indian Act was to "Get rid of those Indians" by attacking the cultural position and legal rights of women.[20] Sawyers' perceptions are well-supported when we consider how identity and status have been used to disenfranchise women. In the Canadian context, the concept of "Indian" used in government discourse is the creation of the colonizing society.[21] It has changed over time as a reflection of the perceptions and needs of that society, from images of the "noble savage"—violent warrior, primitive child—to that of the "environmental steward," and has become inseparable from the political, legal, and economic rights covered by status.[22] Rooted in legislation from the nineteenth century, government definitions of "Indians" were initially wide-sweeping, and included people who were adopted or lived within a Native community. By 1851, however, this definition was limited to those who were of "Indian" blood or could prove that their father was "Indian." This latter requirement introduced patriarchal relations of power that were foreign to many Aboriginal communities, and certainly the Anishinaabe people of Lake Nipissing.[23] Later in the 1850s, conceptualizations of "Indianness" were gendered more explicitly, when the colonial government determined that women whose husbands became enfranchised lost their status.[24] The *Indian Act* of 1876 formalized this gender discrimination. Section 12 (1)(b) declared that women who married non-Native men, or Native men who did not have status, lost their own status. This meant they lost treaty annuities, the right to live or own any property on reserve, even through inheritance. Even more frustrating was the provision that granted status to non-Aboriginal women who married Aboriginal men. Until 1951, women were not allowed to participate in community governance as elected officials or as voters in the elections of chiefs and council, an explicit violation of the traditional political and leadership roles women held in their communities.[25] Such policies disrupted the gender order in Native communities and caused significant ruptures in women's lives, dividing them from their families, communities, and the land of their people. Indeed, status was far more than a bureaucratic designation—it documented historical obligations. It was about ancestors and a sense of belonging. It was about identity.[26]

Unsurprisingly, then, the passage of Bill C-31 provided reason to celebrate. Finally, the efforts by Jeanette Corbière-Lavell, Yvonne Bedard, Sandra Lovelace, and organizations such as the Native Women's Association of Canada to eliminate elements of the *Indian Act* that were discriminatory against women had been recognized. After fighting local battles, in 1973 Corbière-Lavell, from Wikwemikong First Nation on Manitoulin Island in northeastern Georgian Bay, brought her case before the federal courts. She had lost status through marriage and was challenging the deletion of her name from the band list. In a similar case, Yvonne Bedard from Six Nations in Brantford, Ontario, challenged her eviction from her home on reserve, which had been willed to her by her mother. Both women argued that the *Indian Act* discriminated against women and violated the *Canadian Bill of Rights*. Though the Federal Court of Appeal agreed with their position, the Supreme Court of Canada reversed this decision, claiming that section 12(1)(b) of the *Indian Act* was not discriminatory.[27] In a highly divisive move, the National Indian Brotherhood sided with the federal government, arguing that 12 (1)(b) protected Native communities from white men. They did not mention the many white women who had married Aboriginal men, gained status, and were living on reserve. Mary Two-Axe Early first shed light on this issue in her 1980 *Atlantis* article, which described the pain she experienced when dealing with status non-Aboriginal women who accused her of being disruptive in her community.[28] This type of resistance stalled legal battles until Sandra Lovelace from the Tobique Reserve in New Brunswick took her case to the United Nations, hoping to put international pressure on the Canadian government. When her marriage to a non-Native man failed, Lovelace wanted to return home, but she was prevented from doing so. In 1981, the United Nations condemned Canada for violating human rights under Article 27 of the International Covenant on Civil and Political Rights, which secures the cultural rights of minorities.[29] This embarrassing turn of events for the Canadian government laid the groundwork for changes to the Indian Act under Bill C-31. After its passage, status was then attainable for women (and their descendants) who had lost or never received status. Changes were also made to policies of enfranchisement, which took status away voluntarily and involuntarily from those who won the right to vote before 1960, owned land off reserve, or who had earned a university degree, among other things.[30] Muriel Sawyer, a self-defined "Nish Dennis the Menace," said "Miigwech!" when Bill C-31 restored her status at Nipissing First Nation. She was so thankful to Corbière-Lavell and other women who fought for these changes.[31] Similarly, Clara Corbière described it as a "great evening out of balance for Aboriginal women" who just happened to have fallen in love with and married non-Native men. She elaborated on this point later in her interview, explaining that Bill C-31 did much more than award status. It gave women "the right to own their home on a reserve, the right to own property on the reserve and things like that," allowing them to return home and gain a measure of economic security through land ownership and treaty obligations they had previously been denied.[32] When Laurie Robinson was recognized as a status Indian, she received access to the education her ancestors had exchanged for land and resources. Her older brother had not been able to exercise this right. When her parents were given status, "it changed our lives economically," explained Robinson. "If it hadn't happened I don't even know if we would've been able to go to college and university."[33] When gender discrimination is challenged and treaty obligations are fulfilled, the decisions of ancestors are given respect, cultural identities are strengthened, and economic security is made more possible for Aboriginal women.

Sawyer's and Corbiere's reactions were not universal, however. Many people argued that Bill C-31 simply repackaged gender discrimination, and the "bleeding off" of status for Native people indicative of the assimilative agendas of the Indian Act.[34] In fact, by establishing different classes of status, Bill C-31 redefined "Indianness" once again. As Lorraine Sutherland shared in her conversation with Clara Corbiere, despite important changes under the 1985 amendment the federal government still has significant power over Aboriginal identity. "The categories," explained Sutherland, "of it being 6(1) full Indian, 6(2) half breed or whatever" is the government saying "we acknowledge you as a Native woman but your offspring if they don't breed, I don't want to use that word, but that is what it is. If you don't breed your children with other status Natives that status is gone."[35] Known as the "second generation cut-off," status provisions, outlined in sections 6(1) and 6(2) of the amended Indian Act, prevent some people from securing full or even partial status for their descendants.[36] The dense language of the Indian Act makes the accessibility of the amendments difficult, but in general terms 6(1) status applies to people who have two parents who have or are entitled to status, while 6(2) status applies to people who have only one parent who has or is permitted to have status. Though rights and entitlements are equal at this level, differences emerge for the children of 6(2) parents. The offspring of people with 6(2) status may not register as status Indians. In order to maintain 6(1) status for their children, all 6(1) men and women must marry other 6(1) status Indians. In addition, it is still possible for men and women who are siblings and have the same ancestral link to have different status depending on whether they "married out" before or after 1985.[37] While the children of men who married non-status women before 1985 are considered full status, children of women in the same position would be categorized as 6(2) because one of their parents is non-status. The arbitrary nature of such distinctions, which give no consideration to cultural practice, kinship ties, or treaty obligations, is infuriating for many people. Corbiere agreed with Sutherland, pointing out that

Bill C-31 still allowed the government to keep "Aboriginal people under their thumb."[38] Certainly these status distinctions provide a powerful example of the persistence of colonial practices in Canada.

The federal government has argued that in order to protect their fiduciary responsibilities, they must retain control over who will be allowed to register as Native. There is, however, great unevenness in who has or has not been eligible to receive status after the passage of Bill C-31. Muriel Boissonneault's father should have been eligible for status, which he lost because his father was non-Native; however, he never received status because he could not locate the documents required by the government to prove his authenticity as a "true" Native man. Though Boissonneault has reconciled herself to that fact now, it is a "can of worms" she has closed; at the time she was very frustrated by the Department of Indian and Northern Affairs, who refused to recognize that her grandparents were Native. Boissonneault, of course, did not need this proof, but nonetheless managed to track down a census record of her grandmother whose nationality was listed as "Indian." To add to this, her sister paid three hundred dollars for someone to look into their heritage; that person "took her money and said goodbye." The siblings also worked with other groups, but they were never able to make any progress towards obtaining status. "You just get tired," explained Boissonneault with quiet resignation.[39] The task of applying for status can be daunting, convoluted, and filled with disappointment. And, as Boissonneault's story makes clear, the federal government has not exercised due diligence in establishing up-to-date registries. They have required Aboriginal people "to conform to multiple, almost incomprehensible, regulations for reinstatement, in an extremely time-consuming process that provides no guarantee that their status will be reinstated."[40] In the past, people were omitted regularly from registries because they were absent on the day of registration or because the Indian Agent did not make it to their region. These historical inaccuracies have made acquiring status (and thus a sense of identity and belonging) difficult.

Status has also not ensured women band membership, creating divisions within communities and contributing to greater feelings of loss and alienation. After 1985, band councils gained control over membership lists and, therefore, also the distribution of treaty rights associated with membership.[41] This was a positive development in many ways, as it allowed First Nations to establish rules based on their particular cultures. Most First Nations have welcomed members who have been excluded, making membership as wide as having Aboriginal ancestry or kinship ties to traditional lands. Others have established membership codes based on cultural ties, such as language skills.[42] In some areas, however, the issue of who does and who does not belong is very contentious, highlighting the complicated connection between identity, status, and belonging. In her interview, Muriel Boissoneault explained that she sees it as a quandary facing the Canadian government, band councils, and Aboriginal people. "I think you have to go careful on that because if you don't then some people who are not Native will get their cards and people who are Native will not. If the government doesn't have the right to tell us who is Native and who is not, would that mean the Chief of different bands in different areas have the right? It's a tricky question."[43] Controversially, some bands are applying colonial categories of "Indian" identity to determine membership, using "blood quantum" or old *Indian Act* determinations to exclude people—particularly those who have been reinstated since 1985.[44] On the south shore of Montreal, the Mohawk community of Kahnawake adopted membership rules based on blood quantum. Under Kahnawake Mohawk Law, after December 11 1984, "a biological criterion for *future* registrations requires a 'blood quantum' of 50 percent or more Native Blood."[45] The *Sawridge Band v. Canada* case, which started in 1986 and remains unresolved, is one example of outright resistance on the part of bands to changes in status rules. The Sawridge band denied reinstated women access to band resources, in keeping, they argued, with their right to determine membership; however, the Canadian government demanded that the reinstated women and one man be given band membership, arguing that such a decision was discriminatory based on gender and birth.[46] Such conflicts leave women in positions of profound alienation within their own communities.

Other bands have argued they have insufficient resources to support reinstated members. The federal government has never transferred sufficient funds to cover reinstated community members. In fact, they had no idea how significant demand would be, projecting an 80 percent overall application rate. In the first year, the Department of Indian and Northern Affairs processed only 3,200 of the 17,600 applications.[47] Band councils are, therefore, dealing with severely limited resources. For many women, however, the individual and cultural implications of inclusion are far more important than economic or housing support. This is true of Audrey Elsemere, whose grandmother refused to register for status, as "she did not want to be registered to anything." Elsemere continues to deal with being told to get off reserve. She cannot vote in her community and, most painfully for her, she cannot participate in language conferences or community workshops unless there is "extra" space. Every year there is a language conference in Sault Ste. Marie; Elsemere is willing to pay the non-status fees, but she is not allowed to ride on the bus that collects people from Nipissing First Nation. "This is a type of discrimination," said Elsemere, "because I am anxious to learn the language" to go to powwows and workshops. For her, status has closed doors in all directions.[48] A survey conducted by the Native Council of Canada in 1996 determined the actual economic impact of Bill C-31 on bands was only moderate, as the vast majority of people who regained status (70 percent) did not want to live on reserve or put pressure on resources. Instead, like Elsemere, they "wanted band membership so they could regain some of their culture."[49] Nonetheless, socially constructed categories of identity and disputes over jurisdiction continue to overshadow crucial issues of belonging, the consequences of which are lasting divisions within communities, between women and men, and among family members.

Irrespective of band council decisions, there continues to be significant antipathy within reserve communities towards both non-Aboriginal women with status and "Bill C-31 women." In her interview, Margaret O'Connor of Nipissing First Nation noted with anger that there are "so many white people on reserve because they got status." She was fed up with "people marrying out" and diluting Indian bloodlines.[50] Clara Corbiere remembered what happened to her aunt when her uncle passed away. "She was an absolutely wonderful woman. But when my uncle passed away, the community rose up and wanted her to be off the reserve. [They] made it so her life was miserable. In the end she ended up getting sick and dying." Corbiere also felt bad for her children who were still living on reserve. What message did this give them, she asked? "Did it tell them you're not really wanted because you're half white," because the government gave you status and kept it from others? Having established this, Corbiere explained she had some concerns about the distribution of status rights to some Bill C-31 people. "This is where I am racist because there are some people I wish never got status because they are sucking our education dollars dry. They are non-Native, like non-Native women, but they are going all out. They are getting PhDs on our education dollars, while there are Aboriginal students who are full [status], and they've been sitting on waiting lists for seven years to go to university. There is something wrong there." Perhaps, explained Corbiere, if there was an obligation to give something back, communities would feel differently about the distribution of resources.[51]

Corbiere is certainly not the only person who feels antipathy towards "Bill C-31 women." Many women who had their status reinstated after 1985 speak of feelings of exclusion when they return to their communities. In their report for the Aboriginal Women's Action Network and Vancouver Status of Women, Audrey Huntley and Fay Blaney found that many women felt like second-class citizens when they returned home. Some of them argued that their brothers received memberships faster, and were welcomed more readily, raising interesting questions about gender discrimination.[52] Are band councils—many of which are male-dominated—discriminating against women in particular? Bonita Lawrence's research suggests this is the case. In many communities, for instance, it has long been accepted that Native women who "marry out" "forfeit their right, and their children's, to be band members and live in the community." Meanwhile, little consideration has been given to the Aboriginal men who have "married out," or the "generations of white women who were allowed to live in Native communities passing along European culture to *their* mixed-race children."[53] The language used to describe Bill C-31 women—"strangers" or "new Indians"—is particularly indicative of this perspective.[54] This has created significant and ongoing rifts between Aboriginal women and men. The National Indian Brotherhood/Assembly of First Nations (AFN) actively opposed the Bill C-31 legislation. On top of arguing that the *Indian Act* was protectionist, they accused women such as Corbière-Laval, Bedard, and Lovelace of placing their individual needs as women ahead of the needs of their communities. As Clara Corbiere's recollections suggest, resistance is not limited to men. In an article in *Windspeaker,* Catherine Twinn of the Sawridge First Nation in Alberta argued that Bill C-31 Natives were "strangers who would bring conflict, stress, and problems" to Native communities.[55] Such divisiveness does little to move communities away from the definition of "Indian" that is a creation of colonial relationships and, more specifically, the Indian Act.

Though such resistance did not prevent the passage of Bill C-31 or the acceptance of reinstated women in most communities, the legacies of gender-based inequalities linger and continue to do damage to Aboriginal women's lives. Muriel Sawyer married a non-status Aboriginal man in 1975. Shortly thereafter, she received a letter from Nipissing First Nation. She remembered what it said with dismissive anger: "You are no longer a band member, blah, blah, blah." She never signed that letter. This act of rebellion did not, however, prevent her from feeling exiled from her reserve and angry at her own people, particularly men: "I thought, I married a Native! Why aren't people fighting for this!" In her estimation, the *Indian Act* was absurd. "Where else on the planet, when you marry someone do you take on their ethnicity…oh, now I'm Irish?!" She asked herself what Sitting Bull would have done, and then looked at the men in her community. "They had nothing to lose," surmised Sawyer. "They could marry ten women and they all had status and I was resentful of that. I am a fluent speaker and I have no status by my own people, and they're perpetuating that ignorant piece of legislation."[56] Similarly, Audrey Elsemere wondered, "where were our men? Where were our chiefs? How could they let this happen to our women?"[57] Whether Aboriginal men wanted or even conceptualized of themselves as more powerful than women, the *Indian Act* introduced gender hierarchies that were "non-Nish," as Sawyer put it. The ceremonial and political power of women was eroded, as was recognition that women and men were different but equal. Clara Corbiere's grandparents lost their treaty payments because the Indian Agent arrived on their reserve on Manitoulin Island to record names for treaty payments while her grandfather was away hunting. Her grandmother was there but the Indian Agent would not allow her to sign. As a consequence, "everyone in my family, in my bloodline, will never get a treaty payment. I don't want their two dollars anyway. Wait! Inflation! I think it's four bucks now," said Corbiere with laughter. "But that is the male thing there, because the male wasn't there to sign his name."[58]

Matrimonial property rights on reserves provide an ongoing example of this legacy. When marriages fail, Aboriginal women continue to have "no right in law" to marital assets. Unlike provincial governments, the federal government does not have any provisions to resolve these issues, leaving women and children with "no legal claim to occupy the family residence."[59] Women are typically the primary caregivers; loss of status or an inability to maintain reserve membership means they cannot access schools, post-secondary education, or other benefits for themselves and their children.[60]

Issues of status also created profound divisions within families, as daughters found themselves overlooked for or unable to take possession of reserve property because they had lost their status. This created anger and disillusionment with fathers who supported such decisions and brothers who benefited from them. When I first presented this research at the Canadian Historical Association meeting in Saskatoon (2007) an audience member reminded me that divisions are not just racial, or individual, or gender-based—status issues shook families as well. This provides an interesting counterpoint to Innes' findings among Northern Plains peoples. In fact, women's stories reveal that gender differences disrupted kinship connections in fundamental ways. They highlight, once again, the hazy linkages between status and ancestral claims to Aboriginal identity. When Katherine Sarazin's mother (who was of French and Polish background) married her Algonquian father she gained status, adopting this identity very closely. "To her, she was Native," Sarazin explained.[61] This could, however, prove difficult in family settings, said Sarazin, pausing before she explained, "in my family, my closest auntie and uncle... my dad's sister married my mom's brother." Therefore, Sarazin's aunt who was Algonquian lost status, which caused friction between the sisters-in-law. Aside from the hurt feelings that proliferated within the immediate and extended family, the situation also prevented Sarazin's aunt from passing status to her children. After the passage of Bill C-31, her aunt was not able to prove her right to status, which leaves her children who work very closely with the Algonquian Nation in Mattawa inside the community culturally, but outside it according to the law. These legacies also left some family members in more stable economic positions than others because of treaty benefits, particularly because of dental and health care. This "puts another wrench in the whole family," explained Sarazin.[62]

Family violence is the most troubling consequence of "eroded cultural identity," disenfranchisement, and European patriarchal values for Aboriginal women. Alice Desjarlais was raped by her brother, was a victim of residential schooling, and suffered years of abuse before finding ways to heal.[63] Muriel Boissonneault's father abandoned his family. "He just wasn't there. I'd have to say he just didn't want the responsibility." Boissonneault's first marriage, which lasted for thirty years, was also difficult. As she explained it, "I was a bad girl. I got pregnant." Though she was only fourteen, they got married and Boissonneault hoped things would be better but "they weren't. I was thinking and hoping they would [be], but there was nobody there to help." Her husband was very controlling; he would not let anyone in her family attend the wedding. Boissonneault's sister is still upset about this. He also strictly limited where she could work because he wanted to control her movements. Sadly, Desjarlais and Boissonneault are not alone; stories of alcoholism, abuse, and desertion are plentiful and painful.[64] Native women are three times as likely to report violence from (and eight times as likely to be killed by) their spouses. One-quarter of all Aboriginal women who were surveyed over a five-year period for a 1999 General Survey were assaulted by their spouses.[65] Such statistics are disturbing and all too unsurprising for Native women themselves. It took Audrey Elsemere some time to realize "the beauty of being a woman." It was only by embracing Native spirituality, or taking the "sweet-grass road," as she called it, that she began to understand the sources of her discontent. She "learn[ed] to walk beside men, not behind them," and in doing so embraced gender roles based on separate but equal rather than hierarchical relationships.[66] While Bill C-31 changed gender discrimination on paper, the amendment did not provide a basis for women and men to understand where "walking together" was lost; it did not provide a means for disentangling Anishinaabe, Cree, Métis, and European values, or for protecting women emotionally, economically, and physically. Genders are "made differently" in time and place and across cultures; only when we acknowledge these differences can we begin to understand the steps that need to be taken to abolish imposed and damaging power relationships.

While these realities continue to do damage to Aboriginal women's lives, many women have found ways to mend wounds and challenge the alienation and violence in their lives since the passage of Bill C-31. At the official level, the federal government, Aboriginal communities, and organizations such as the Native Women's Association, Status of Women Canada, and the Aboriginal Healing Foundation have produced reports and proposed solutions to the difficult legacies of colonialism.[67] The Report of the Royal Commission on Aboriginal People, published in 1996, uncovered several important issues necessary for healing, including "parity in medical and social services," a "focus on self-esteem," "recognition of traditional healing and traditional culture," "holistic approaches to critical symptoms," and "Aboriginal and community control of programming." As the report made clear, problems must be dealt with systematically and with a clear sense of the "culturally appropriate means and sites for change and recovery." [68] Healing has developed differently in women's individual lives. For some women it has been impossible because the wounds are too great, because understanding how social and historical forces beyond their control or the control of their parents or communities have insidiously and savagely ripped at their own lives is unfathomable. For others, struggle has given way to discernible paths and solutions for healing. For the Anishinaabe, Cree, and Métis women in this project, healing involved journeys: journeys of self and of culture.[69]

Whatever their perception of the 1985 amendment to the Indian Act, none of the women in this study felt that the "government [or] a piece of paper" determined their identity.[70] It never dawned on Muriel Boissonneault to define herself as Native or non-Native. No one ever said, "you're a Native child or of Native descent."[71] It was not until her father applied for a status card in the 1980s that she realized that these divisions existed between people. Far from feeling disconnected from her Métis identity, Boissonneault tells people about her background—she is proud of it. Laurie Robinson grew up in Hunter's Point,

Quebec. She did not have status before 1985 because her grandmother lost her status when she married. "She married Hector Lavigne [who] was French, so bang my Gran's not an Indian no more"; Robinson did not, however, feel like an "almost Indian" because of this. Status cards do not dictate Robinson's identity, they are "something that's owed. That's part of the deal man. That was part of the royalties, an agreement." The ridiculousness of the situation is sometimes a source of humour for her: "Hey, how you doing? Oh pretty good, I'm almost an Indian now...they're sending me my card."[72] In her summer 2006 interview, Audrey Elsemere exclaimed, "The government says I am not Indian. Well I look like one. I feel like one, I talk like one. Well I must be one!"[73]

Despite ongoing barriers to institutional education, including geographical isolation, funding, and resistance within families, it is one of the most important sources of healing for Aboriginal women. At Nipissing University, Aboriginal women account for close to 75 percent of the enrollment of Native students. As Erin Dokis pointed out in a special bulletin on family violence published in the Nipissing region, "education is one of the ways in which Aboriginal women can break the cycles of abuse and denigration in their own lives, those of their families and communities, and in the global community."[74] Education helped Clara Corbiere break out of the "cycle of poverty" she was facing as a single parent and prove wrong those who thought she would be on assistance for the rest of her life.[75] Muriel Sawyer's position as an educator, in the North Bay Catholic School Board and at Nbiising High School at Nipissing First Nation, has allowed her to share her strong sense of identity with others. From a young age Sawyer connected her identity to her language and not her status card. She said, "my language helped me develop my identity at a very early age and a very positive, strong identity. The language, that's my life!"[76] Many years later, she feels that the racism she faced in schools was easier to deal with because of this. "I don't remember having any feelings of inferiority. In fact, for show-and-tell time, I would sing in Ojibwe, and do some Gregorian chants. It's what I knew, right?" There was certainly discrimination, including being streamed into technical courses in high school, but facing it was much easier because of her strong identity. "Call me 'sauvagesse.' So what? I can call you other things in my language, and I can't even tell you in your language what I'm calling you!"[77] After Sawyer finished high school, she enrolled in the Native Teacher Education program at McMaster University. It was 1974, the first year the course was offered. From her perspective, this program was going to do a lot more "to further Native peoples' lives" than anything being proposed by the federal government at the time.

"There were 175 people in that course...we went to classes six days a week...and the teachers that they brought in were outstanding."

The cultural elements of this education were an integral part of the healing quality of this type of learning for Sawyer. It is the basis for what she teaches today, and is also at the heart of a language retention program with elders, which Sawyer is involved with. There is sadness in her mother-in-law, explains Sawyer. "Who do you speak with? What happens when that language dies? A way of life, a world view is lost." Margaret O'Connor participates in these meetings, where elders meet with others who are interested in learning the "Nishnabeh language." Together they teach and learn and laugh. Sawyer translates songs for them; "it's a vehicle to show them the positive aspects of that language. They have it inside. It's just a different way to release it." She received some complaints about always translating old songs, though. They wanted Buddy Holly. "Buddy Holly?" asked Sawyer quizzically. "All right, we'll do Buddy Holly!"[78] In her interview, Robinson pointed out the importance of distinguishing between institutional forms of education, which have their roots in European traditions of "philosophy and thought and discipline," and cultural education, which is equally and sometimes more important to women.[79] As Sawyer pointed out, "you can't abandon one for the other, because one is so integral to your everyday life anyway. I remember going with my grandfather on the trap lines and then skinning the animals, and we'd have to pull...and it stunk! Like hell!" Of Robinson's education as an Algonquin person, she noted, "how to live in the bush and how to know who I am and who my people are, that's way more important to me" than formal education because it strengthens cultural identities.[80]

In similar ways, cultural and community links have helped Aboriginal women like Alice Desjarlais connect to their ancestry. Though Desjarlais rejected her Native identity for most of her adult life, it was returning to the North and the teachings of elders which helped her heal. For Katherine Sarazin, Native spirituality, including "the medicines, smudging, sweat lodges," was the key to help her "through many, many things that happened in [her] life." When Sarazin started attending the North Bay Native Friendship Centre in 1985, she began to develop the cultural and personal connections that she associates with healing. In the 1980s, the Friendship Centre was "booming with youth," many of whom were from northern regions of Moose Factory or Attawapiskat but in the city for high school, college, or university. Together they started the Canadore College powwow. As Sarazin explained, "I felt like I fit in for the first time in my life. I fit in." Before this, Sarazin had little connection to her Native identity. From a very young age her father was taught "that it was wrong to be Native, and that any-thing that had to do with the culture was wrong." Though he spoke Algonkian with his grandmother and had experienced Algonquian ways of life living in the bush until he was seven, when he started attending school in Mattawa things changed. He was not allowed to speak his language at school or in public, and he learned that being Native was not positive. He transferred this feeling to his chil-dren. When she started learning about her culture, Sarazin remembers that "it was like a whole new world opened up to me, and that's what I wanted, and I fed on that." Her parents were terrified that she was in a "cult." It took her five years to begin talking to her father, to point out to him how much of his knowledge about "the bush, about medicines and animals" was part of his Native heritage. In reflecting on this time with her father Sarazin said, "it gave him a better un-derstanding… It's not going to powwows, it is how we live our life. He taught me so much about animals, and the bush, and I said 'Dad! This is who we are! And, even though you tried telling us "being Native is wrong," you taught us what we needed to know to be who we are.' So to him it was like, 'uh oh!'"[81]

Sarazin found herself developing a better connection to her past and also to her father. He finally attended a powwow with her in the summer of 2006, where he saw "the kids dance. To have him here was just overwhelming for me, because it's something I've wanted, and it's awesome."[82] Muriel Boissonneault had a Ro-man Catholic upbringing but she was not happy with the way things were done in the church. She wanted to develop a better connection to Native spiritual-ity. "It's part of my *background*. It's my *heritage*," explained Boissonneault with emphasis. "I want to know more about it. I just never had a teacher." There was "Old Annie," her grandmother's sister who lived up by the Lacave Dam near Mattawa, Ontario. Boissonneault visited her as a child, but she was too young to understand or to ask about the family's past. As for receiving guidance today, she is not sure about trust; if the person talks the talk she expects them to walk the walk as well. For women like Robinson, Sawyer, Sarazin, and Boissonneault, the path to healing the violence of lost identities has been seeking connections with their heritage, through education, language, and community.

Bill C-31 was a landmark decision that acknowledged the patriarchal legacies of the Indian Act; as individual stories point out, however, the status issues sur-rounding it have not been resolved. In fact, recent protests and court decisions have brought Bill C-31 back onto centre stage. In 2005, on the twentieth anni-versary of the passage of Bill C-31, the Native Women's Association of Canada held a protest on Parliament Hill declaring that issues of sexism and assimilation had, in fact, worsened since the 1985 amendment.[83] In a court case in British Columbia, Sharon McIvor and her son Charles Grismer challenged Bill C-31 provisions, saying that they were discriminatory based on sex and marital status. In its 2007 ruling (*McIvor v. Registrar, Indian and Northern Affairs Canada, 2007 BCSC 827*), the B.C. Supreme Court overturned the 1985 Amendments, arguing that Bill C-31 violated equality rights guaranteed under Section 15 of the Canadian Charter of Rights and Freedoms.[84] A British Columbia Court of Appeal upheld this decision in 2009. Later that same year, the Supreme Court of Canada indicated it would not hear the McIvor case, thus allowing the decisions of the British Columbia court to stand. As a consequence, on 15 December 2010, Bill C-3, the Gender Equity in Indian Registration Act, received Royal Assent. Bill C-3 makes grandchildren of women who lost their status eligible to apply for reinstatement.[85] With each legal case and amendment, Aboriginal women such as Sharon McIvor carry on traditions of protest by challenging the gender discrimination of the Indian Act.

While such steps remain essential within the present political system in Canada, individual stories provide compelling evidence that these legal initiatives and minor concessions on the part of the federal government are not a solution to the troubling damage of status categories. Irrespective of amendments to the Indian Act, Alice Desjarlais hated her status card and did not use it until the 1990s—indeed, she rejected her Aboriginal identity. For Desjarlais, as for thousands of other Aboriginal women and men, to reject her identity—to feel embarrassed and resentful of it—was toxic; it produced self-hatred, destroyed belonging, and resulted in alcoholism, suicide, drug abuse, and violence, horrible violence. In the end, Bill C-31 did not end gender discrimination or, in Muriel Sawyer's words, efforts to "destroy [Aboriginal] women." And, in an equally important sense, Indian Act amendments have done nothing to stop fracturing within communities along cultural and economic lines. Muriel Boissonneault tried without success to find the documentation necessary to prove her grandmother had Aboriginal heritage. In 2006, Boissonneault was resigned to this outcome. This does not mean she does not remain angry—angry at those who have status and, in her mind, do not deserve it. Angry that paperwork and only paperwork can prove her heritage, her right to belong. Muriel Sawyer connects her identity to her language and feels great animosity toward Native men for recognizing status definitions in the first place. Where were the men? How could they let us down? Audrey Elsemere continues to struggle with life as a non-status Aboriginal woman. She feels like she belongs, but she is not allowed to belong. Such divisions among community and family members, between women and men, make it difficult to challenge the cycles of self-hatred and the legacies of colonialism that Aboriginal women struggle with each and every day. Though none of the women in this study connect their identities directly with government-determined status categories or band memberships, as their memories make clear, the costs to them individually and to Aboriginal communities generally continue to be great.

Despite profound challenges, these women's stories make clear that solutions lie in creating and fostering a sense of belonging, through culture and language, education, and connections to the land. Alice Desjarlais learned to be a proud Anishinaabekwe when she returned to northern Ontario and, with the guidance of elders, developed a positive self-identity. She connected to her heritage, was educated in traditional ways, and came to understand that her status card was a symbol of entitlements and rights. Through language, in particular, Muriel Sawyer maintains a strong Anishinaabe identity. Among elders, in local high schools and at Nipissing University, in language workshops for beginners and fluent speakers, Sawyer shares her love of Ojibwe, challenging "ignorant legislation" designed to eliminate her language with legendary humour and a fierce commitment to her culture and her people. The school system taught Katherine Sarazin's father it was wrong to be Aboriginal, but Sarazin developed positive links with her heritage through community organizations such as the Native Friendship Centre. This helped her father heal and allowed her children to proudly perform the dances of their people. Through access to education, Clara Corbiere broke the cycle of poverty for her family. This step strengthened her sense of self-worth and belonging, a powerful achievement for her and for her children. It is through cultural education that Laurie Robinson sees great potential for healing. By recognizing different epistemological systems within our school system, Aboriginal children are offered greater opportunity to learn in culturally appropriate ways that foster belonging and pride, and make success so much more possible. Through culture and language, in community organizations and educational settings, Aboriginal women are resisting status categories with tremendous humour and strength, while also recognizing them as "part of the deal" that the Canadian government signed with their ancestors. When the Canadian government fulfills its historical obligations to Canada's First Nations—whether it is for land and resources, education, health care, or clean water—they too will foster healing that will produce far more forceful outcomes than any amendment to the *Indian Act*.

Notes

1 First and foremost, I would like to thank the women who have generously shared their stories with me, as well as Lorraine Sutherland for conducting the interviews for this project and sharing in its evolution. For their ongoing support, I thank Glenna Beaucage, Erin Dokis, Mary Lawson, John Long, and Laurie McLaren. Jennifer Evans, Johanna Kristolaitis, and Kyle Marsh provided much appreciated transcription assistance. I also acknowledge the support of the Social Science and Humanities Research Council, Nipissing University, and the Northern Canadian Centre for Research in Education and the Arts.

2 Alice Desjarlais, interview by Lorraine Sutherland, 2 June 2006, North Bay, Ontario. Unless otherwise noted, all interviews were conducted by Lorraine Sutherland in North Bay, Ontario. Sutherland, who identifies as Cree from Attawapiskat First Nation, first worked with me in 2005 as a student in my fourth-year oral history seminar. She conducted the interviews for this project as a research assistant between 2006 and 2008. Since that time we have worked together to develop trust and research relationships at Nipissing First Nation, as well as build her skills in oral history and Indigenous methodologies. She has been accepted to complete her MA in history at Nipissing University. Using Indigenous oral history and ethnographical methods, she will study the role of women in the annual goose hunt in her community. On Indigenous oral history see Winona Wheeler, "Reflections on the Social Relations of Indigenous Oral History," in *Walking a Tightrope: Aboriginal People and Their Representations,* ed. David T. McNab (Waterloo: Wilfrid Laurier University Press, 2005), 189–214.

3 On Canadian residential school experiences see Kevin Annett, *Hidden from History: the Canadian Holocaust: the untold story of the genocide of Aboriginal peoples by church and state in Canada*, 2nd ed. (Vancouver: Truth Commission into Genocide in Canada, 2005); Marlene Brant Castellano, Linda Archibald, and Mike DeGagné, "From Truth to Reconciliation: Transforming the legacy of residential schools," in *Report Prepared for the Aboriginal Healing Foundation* (Ottawa: Aboriginal Healing Foundation, 2008); Agnes Grant, *Finding My Talk: How Fourteen Native Women Reclaimed Their Lives After Residential School* (Calgary: Fifth House, 2004); *No End of Grief: Indian Residential Schools in Canada* (Winnipeg: Pemmican Press, 1996); J.R. Miller, *Shingwauk's Vision: A History of Native Residential Schools* (Toronto: University of Toronto Press, 1996); John Milloy, *"A National Crime:" The Canadian Government and the Residential School System, 1879–1986* (Winnipeg: University of Manitoba Press, 1999); Brent Stonefish, *Moving Beyond: Understanding the Impacts of Residential Schools* (Owen Sound, Ontario: Ningwakwe Learning Press, 2007).

4 Desjarlais, interview.

5 In this paper, I use naming terminologies—Aboriginal, First Nation, Indian, Métis, and Native—employed by research partners and participants. I have also used "Indigenous" when discussing issues of global importance. On naming I have taken direction from Kim Anderson's *A Recognition of Being: Reconstructed Native Womanhood* (Toronto: Second Story Press, 2000): 14, as well as *Recollecting: Lives of Aboriginal Women of the Canadian Northwest and Borderlands*, eds. Sarah Carter and Patricia McCormack (Edmonton: Athabasca University Press, 2010), 314. For the purposes of this study, northern Ontario encompasses all regions north of and including the districts of Muskoka and Parry Sound.

6 See also Martin John Cannon, "Bill C-31-An Act to Amend the Indian Act: Notes Toward a Qualitative Analysis of Legislated Injustice," *Canadian Journal of Native Studies* 25, 1(2005): 373–387.

7 The ten women who agreed to participate in this study were contacted through Nipissing University, Nipissing First Nation, the Native Friendship Centre, and word of mouth. While each woman contributed one interview lasting between two and four

hours, some participated in multiple meetings, and others became centrally involved in the development of this project, providing cultural guidance and helping to establish the relationships necessary for me to be welcomed on Nipissing First Nation territory. In this article, their names and any aspects of their stories that could be used to identify them have been changed in accordance with their wishes. Interviewees were also asked to fill out biographical information sheets, which included questions about identity, education, and employment. Six women identified as Ojibwe, two as Cree, one as Métis, and one as Algonkian-French.

8   Here I employ a definition of colonization, and its ideological impetus colonialism, similar to that of Mary-Ellen Kelm in her book, *Colonizing Bodies*. Colonization is a process of geographical, political, and economic control that results in "dispossession" and the "creation of ideological formulations around race and skin colour, which position the colonizers at a higher evolutionary level than the colonized." The process and systems of colonization were not, however, linear, foreordained, or uncontested. They play out differently in various contexts for different people. Mary-Ellen Kelm, *Colonizing Bodies: Aboriginal Health and Healing in British Columbia, 1900-1950* (Vancouver: University of British Columbia Press, 1998), xviii–xix.

9   Sylvia Van Kirk, *"Many Tender Ties": Women in Fur-Trade Society in Western Canada, 1670-1870* (Winnipeg: Watson and Dwyer, 1980); "Tracing the Fortunes of Five Founding Families of Victoria," *BC Studies* 115-116 (Autumn-Winter 1997–98): 148–179; "From 'Marrying-In' to 'Marrying-Out': Changing Patterns of Aboriginal/non-Aboriginal Marriage in Colonial Canada," *Frontiers* 23, 3(2002): 1–11; "A Transborder Family in the Pacific Northwest: Reflecting on Race and Gender in Women's History," in *One Step Over the Line: Toward a History of Women in the North American Wests*, eds. Elizabeth Jameson and Sheila McManus (Edmonton: University of Alberta Press and Athabasca University Press, 2008), 81–93.

10   See, for example, Jennifer Brown, *Strangers in Blood: Fur Trade Company Families in Indian Country* (Vancouver: University of British Columbia Press, 1980); Sarah Carter, *The Importance of Being Monogamous: Marriage and Nation Building in Western Canada to 1915* (Edmonton: University of Alberta Press, 2008); "Transnational Perspectives on the History of Great Plains Women: Gender, Race, Nations and the Forty-Ninth Parallel," *American Review of Canadian Studies* 33, 4 (2003): 565–596; *Capturing Women: The Manipulation of Cultural Imagery in Canada's Prairie West* (Montreal: McGill-Queen's University Press, 1997); "First Nations Women of Prairie Canada," in *Women of the First Nations: Power, Wisdom, and Strength*, ed. Christine Miller and Patricia Chuchryk (Winnipeg: University of Manitoba Press, 1996), 51–76; "Categories and Terrains of Exclusion: Constructing the 'Indian Woman' in the Early Settlement Era in Canada," *Great Plains Quarterly* 13, 3 (1993): 147–161; Carter and McCormack, *Recollecting*; Julie Cruikshank, *Life Lived Like a Story: Life Stories of Three Yukon Native Elders* (Vancouver: University of British Columbia Press, 1990); *The Social Life of Stories: Narrative and Knowledge in Yukon Territory* (Lincoln: University of Nebraska Press, 1998); Nancy Janovicek, *No Place to Go: Local Histories of the Battered Women's Shelter Movement* (Vancouver: University of British Columbia Press, 2007); Mary-Ellen Kelm and Lorna Townsend, eds., *In the Days of Our Grandmothers: A Reader in Aboriginal Women's History in Canada* (Toronto: University of Toronto Press, 2006); Bonita Lawrence, *"Real" Indians and Others: Mixed-Blood Urban Native Peoples and Indigenous Nationhood* (Vancouver: University of British Columbia Press, 2004); Patricia Monture Angus, *Thunder in My Soul: A Mohawk Woman Speaks* (Halifax, Nova Scotia: Fernwood Publishing, 1995); Adele Perry, *On the Edge of Empire: Gender, Race, and the Making of British Columbia, 1849-1871* (Toronto: University of Toronto Press, 2001); *Contact Zones: Aboriginal and Settler Women in Canada's Colonial Post*, eds. Katie Pickles and Myra Rutherdale (Vancouver: University of British Columbia Press, 2005); Paige Raibmon, "The Practice of Everyday Colonialism: Indigenous Women at Work in the Hop Fields and Tourist Industry of Puget Sound," *Labor: Studies*

in Working Class History of the Americas 3, 3 (Fall 2006): 23–56; Sherene H. Razack, "Gendered Racial Violence and Spacialized Justice: The Murder of Pamela George," in *Race, Space, and the Law: Unmapping a White Settler Society*, ed. Sherene H. Razack (Toronto: Between the Lines Press, 2002): 121–156; Janet Silman, *Enough is Enough: Aboriginal Women Speak Out* (Toronto: Women's Press, 1987); Mary Two-Axe Early, "'The Least Members of Our Society': The Mohawk Women of Caghnawaga," *Atlantis* 11, 2 (1980): 64–66; Sally Weaver, "First Nations Women and Government Policy, 1970–1992," in *Changing Patterns: Women in Canada*, eds. Sandra Burt, Lorraine Code, and Lorna Dorney (Toronto: McClelland and Stewart, 1993): 92–150.

11   John Lutz, *Makúk: A New History of Aboriginal-White Relations* (Vancouver: University of British Columbia Press, 2008), 43.

12   Ibid., 42–46.

13   See, for example, Carter, *The Importance of Being Monogamous*; *Capturing Women*; *In The Days of Our Grandmothers*, eds. Kelm and Townsend; Janovicek, *No Place To Go*; John Long, "Narratives of Early Encounters Between Europeans and the Cree of Western James Bay," *Ontario History* 80, 3 (September 1988): 227–245; Raibmon, "The Practice of Everyday Colonialism," in *Authentic Indians: Episodes of Encounter from the Late-Nineteenth-Century Northwest Coast* (Durham, NC: Duke University Press, 2005); Joan Sangster, *Regulating Girls and Women: Sexuality, Family, and the Law in Ontario, 1920–1960* (Toronto: Oxford University Press, 2001); "Making a Fur Coat: Women, the Labouring Body, and Working-Class History," *International Review of Social History* 52 (2007): 241–270.

14   Kathy Absolon, "Kaandosswing, This is How We Come to Know! Indigenous Graduate Research in the Academy: Worldviews and Methodologies" (PhD thesis, University of Toronto, 2008); *Research as Resistance: Critical, Indigenous, and Anti-oppressive Approaches*, eds. Leslie Brown and Susan Strega, (Toronto: Canada Scholar's Press, 2005); Julie Cruikshank, *Do Glaciers Listen?: Local Knowledge, Colonial Encounters, and Social Imagination* (Vancouver: University of British Columbia Press, 2005); *The Social Life of Stories*; *Life Lived Like a Story*; Lawrence, *"Real" Indians and Others*; Margaret Kovach, *Indigenous Methodologies: Characteristics, Conversations, and Contexts* (Toronto: University of Toronto Press, 2009); Lutz, *Makúk*; Linda Tuhiwai Smith, *Decolonizing Methodologies: Research and Indigenous Peoples* (London: Zed Books, 1999); Shawn Wilson, *Research is Ceremony: Indigenous Research Methods* (Halifax: Fernwood Publishing, 2008).

15   Tuhiwai Smith, 28–39. See also: Ken Coates, "Being Aboriginal: the cultural politics of identity, membership and belonging among First Nations in Canada," *Canadian Issues* 21 (1999): 23–41.

16   Wheeler, "Reflections on the Social Relations of Indigenous Oral History." For more on Indigenous oral history see Julie Cruikshank, *Reading Voices: Oral and Written Interpretation of the Yukon's Past* (Vancouver: Douglas and McIntyre, 1991); *Life Lived Like a Story*; *Social Life of Stories*; William Schneider, *...so they understand...Cultural Issues in Oral History* (Logan, UT: Utah State University Press, 2002). For other scholarship that employs individual stories to examine issues of status and identity for Aboriginal women, see Silman, *Enough is Enough*; Beth Brant, *I'll Sing 'til the Day I Die* (Toronto: McGilligan Books, 1995).

17   Some women reclaimed traditional leadership roles, while others initiated important political changes in their communities, allowing them to advocate for the needs of women and their families. For discussion of Indigenous women and political leadership, see Cora Voyageur, *Firekeepers of the 21ˢᵗ Century: First Nations Women Chiefs* (Montreal & Kingston: McGill-Queen's University Press, 2008), 4; Dawn Martin-Hill, "She No Speaks: Other Colonial Constructs of the 'Traditional Woman,'" in *Strong Women Stories: Native Vision and Community Survival*, eds. Kim Anderson and Bonita Lawrence (Toronto: Sumach Press, 2003), 106–120; Bonita Lawrence, "Approaching the

Fourth Mountain: Native Women and the Ageing Process," in *Strong Women Voices*, 121–134.

18   Kathleen Jamieson, "Indian Women and the Law in Canada: Citizens Minus," Canadian Advisory Council on the Status of Women and Indian Rights for Indian Women, Ottawa, 1978. See also Fay Blaney, "Aboriginal Women's Action Network," *Strong Women Voices*, 156–170. For various reports produced by NWAC and other organizations advocating for Indigenous women see Aboriginal Canada Portal: http://www.aboriginalcanada.gc.ca/acp/site.nsf/eng/ao26596.html (accessed 29 June 2011).

19   See, for example, Anderson, *A Recognition of Being*; *North American Indian, Metis and Inuit Women Speak about Culture, Education, and Work*, ed. Carolyn Kenny-Bereznak (Ottawa: Status of Women Canada, 2001); Jennifer Blythe, Peggy Brizinski, and Sarah Preston, *I Was Never Idle: Women and Work in Moosonee and Moose Factory* (Hamilton: McMaster University, Research Program for Technology Assessment in Subarctic Ontario, 1985); Brant, *I'll Sing 'til the Day I Die*; Linda Dumont and Tara DeRyk, "C-31 Women Protest," *Alberta Sweetgrass* (July 1997): 15; Regina Flannery, *Ellen Smallboy: Glimpses of a Cree Woman's Life* (Montreal & Kingston: McGill-Queen's University Press, 1995); Joan Holmes, "Bill C-31: Equality or Disparity? The Effects of the New Indian Act on Native Women," Canadian Advisory Council on the Status of Women, Ottawa, 1987; Audrey Huntley et. al., "Bill C-31: Its Impacts, Implications, and Recommendations for Change in British Columbia," *Final Report* (Vancouver: Aboriginal Women's Action Network and Vancouver Status of Women, 1999); Michelle M. Mann, "Aboriginal Women: An Issues Backgrounder," Status of Women Canada, Ottawa, 2005; Rob McKinley, "C-31 Appeal Decisions," *Windspeaker* (July 1997): 1, 4; *Windspeaker* (December 1997a): 2; Silman, *Enough is Enough*. See also: *Alberta Sweetgrass*, *First Nations Drum*, and *Writing the Circle: Native Women of Western Canada*, eds. Jeanne Perreault and Sylvia Vance (Edmonton: NeWest Publishers, 1993).

20   Muriel Sawyer, interview, 22 August 2006.

21   Edward Said's work provides a classic discussion of the process of "othering" in colonial contexts. *Orientalism* (New York: Random House, 1979). For scholarship on the creation of the "Indian" in the Canadian context see: Carter, *Capturing Women*; Lawrence, *"Real" Indians*; Perry, *On the Edge of Empire*; Bruce Trigger, "The Historians' Indian: Native Americans in Canadian Historical Writing from Charlevoix to the Present," *Canadian Historical Review* 67, 3 (September 1986): 315–42.

22   Coates, "Being Aboriginal," 24.

23   While chiefs and the heads of family lines within clans or dodems were traditionally male, according to Jean Recollet's writings for the *Jesuit Relations* women were also understood to have "liberty" that was "absolute and inviolable." For Nipissing First Nation's documentation of this history see: http://www.nfn.ca/historical/index.html (accessed 16 June 2011).

24   Status of Women Canada, "Seeking Alternatives to Bill C-31: From Cultural Trauma to Cultural Revitalization through Customary Law," 30 January 2007; James S. Frideres and René R. Gadacz, *Aboriginal Peoples in Canada*, 8th ed. (Toronto: Pearson Prentice Hall, 2008), 28–29.

25   "Seeking Alternatives to Bill C-31."

26   The crucial connection between definitions of "Indians" and the status obligations of the Canadian government have contributed to concerns about recent changes to the name of Department of Indian and Northern Affairs. See: http://www.aadnc-aandc. gc.ca/eng/1314808945787(accessed 7 November 2011); http://www.cbc.ca/news/canada/ north/story/2011/05/18/sk-indian-aboriginal-name-change-ministry-110518.html (accessed 28 June 2011). On calls by Shawn Atleo, National Chief of the Assembly of First Nations, to fundamentally alter the relationship between Aboriginal peoples and the Canadian government, see National Assembly of First Nations, http://64.26.129.156/

article.asp?id=3 (accessed 8 September 2011), and national media coverage, http://www. thestar.com/news/canada/article/838193--first-nations-head-calls-for-end-to-the-indian-act (accessed 8 September 2011).

27 Megan Furi and Jill Wherrett, "Indian Status and Band Membership Issues," Parliamentary Research Branch, Ottawa, February 2003, 3. See also Silman, *Enough is Enough*; Two-Axe Early, "The Least Members of Our Society."

28 Two-Axe Early, "The Least Members of Our Society."

29 Furi and Wherrett, "Indian Status and Band Membership Issues," 3.

30 Frideres and Gadacz, *Aboriginal Peoples in Canada*, 32.

31 Desjarlais, interview; Sawyer, interview.

32 Clara Corbiere, interview, 17 August 2006. Women have experienced significant financial loss as a consequence of status restrictions. Aside from treaty annuities, women could not access university funding, mortgage assistance, free daycare, or receive redemption from taxation. They also lost the ability to cross the border without restriction. Lawrence, *"Real" Indians*, 54–55.

33 Robinson, interview.

34 Lawrence, *"Real" Indians*, 55.

35 Corbiere, interview.

36 Holmes, "Bill C-31: Equality or Disparity?" On the twentieth anniversary of the passage of Bill C-31 in 2005, the Native Women's Association of Canada and the Quebec Native Women Inc. protested at the Human Rights Monument in Ottawa. "Loss of Indian Status: A Foremost Aboriginal Issue," *Canadian Dimension* 39, 5 (July–August 2005): 15–16.

37 For a sense of the dense language of the *Indian Act*, see http://laws.justice.gc.ca/en/I-5/. See also http://www.grantnativelaw.com/pdf/McIvorCaseComment.pdf (accessed 29 March 2009).

38 Ibid.; Mann, "Aboriginal Women."

39 Muriel Boissonneault, interview, 9 August 2006.

40 Lawrence, *"Real" Indians*, 67; J. Giokas and P. Chartrand, "Who are the Métis? A Review of the Law and Policy," in *Who are Canada's Aboriginal People?* ed. P. Chartrand (Saskatoon: Purich Publishing, 2002).

41 For more on this see Lawrence, *"Real" Indians*, 67–69; John Steckley and Bryan D. Cummins, *Full Circle: Canada's First Nations*, 2nd ed. (Toronto: Pearson Prentice Hall, 2008), 126.

42 Lawrence, *"Real"Indians*, 68. See also Patricia Monture-Angus, *Journeying Forward: Dreaming First Nation's Independence* (Halifax: Fernwood Publishing, 1999), 144.

43 Boissonneault, interview.

44 Frideres and Gadacz, *Aboriginal Peoples in Canada*, 37–38.

45 Lawrence, *"Real" Indians*, 78. *Club Native* (2006), a National Film Board documentary by Tracey Deer, follows four women in their attempt to get status, revealing the ongoing challenges of these laws for women.

46 "Seeking Alternatives." The latest appeal of the government's decision occurred in 2006: http://reports.fja.gc.ca/eng/2004/2004fca16.html (accessed 29 June 2011); http://www. nomus.ca/en/case/FCA/2006FCA228 (accessed 29 June 2011).

47 NWAC, "Implementing Bill C-31—A Summary of the Issues," Ottawa, 1988, 5. See also Stewart Clatworthy, "Re-assessing the Population Impacts of Bill C-31," Minister of Northern and Indian Affairs, Ottawa, 2001, http://dsp-psd.pwgsc.gc.ca/Collection/R2-

363-2004E.pdf (accessed 29 June 2011); "Background Notes: Bill C-31: An Act to Amend the Indian Act," F.L Barron Fonds, University of Saskatchewan Archives.

48 Audrey Elsemere, interview, 14 July 2006. For more on the issue of cultural loss, see Lawrence, *"Real" Indians*.

49 "Bill C-31: The Challenge, Classroom Edition," *Windspeaker* (March 1996): 7; Lawrence, *"Real" Indians*, 69.

50 Margaret O'Connor, interview, 18 August 2006.

51 Corbiere, interview.

52 Audrey Huntley and Fay Blaney, with the assistance of Rain Daniels, Lizabeth Hall, and Jennifer Dysart, *Bill C-31: Its Impacts, Implications, and Recommendations for Change in British Columbia – Final Report* (Vancouver: Aboriginal Women's Action Network and Vancouver Status of Women, 1999): 15.

53 Lawrence, *"Real" Indians*, 71.

54 Ibid., 70.

55 Rob McKinley, "C-31 Appeal Decision Overturned," *Windspeaker* (July 1997): I, 4. Cited in Lawrence, *"Real" Indians*, 72. See also: Joyce Audrey Green, "Exploring Identity and Citizenship: Aboriginal Women, Bill C-31, and the Sawridge Case" (PhD thesis, University of Alberta, 1997).

56 Sawyer, interview. Sawyer married a non-status Aboriginal man.

57 Elsemere, interview.

58 Corbiere, interview.

59 Status of Women Canada, "Aboriginal Women: An Issues Backgrounder," August 2005, 3. For more on the marital property law debate, see Richard Bartlett, "Indian Self-Government, the Equality of the Sexes, and Application of Provincial Matrimonial Property Laws," *Canadian Journal of Family Law* 5, 1 (1986): 188–195; Wendy Cornet, "First Nations Governance, the Indian Act and Women's Equality Rights," in *First Nations Women, Governance and the Indian Act: A Collection of Policy Research Reports* (Ottawa: Status of Women Canada, 2001). The NWAC, working with Mary Eberts, has launched a court case to challenge this ruling.

60 "Seeking Alternatives to Bill C-31," 1.

61 Katherine Sarazin, interview, 14 August 2006.

62 Sarazin, interview; Steckley and Cummins, 126–127.

63 Desjarlais, interview.

64 Emma D. LaRocque, "Violence in Aboriginal Communities," in *The Path to Healing* (Ottawa: Royal Commission on Aboriginal Peoples, 1993), 72–89.

65 Mann, "Aboriginal Women."

66 Elsemere, interview.

67 See, for example, Royal Commission on Aboriginal Peoples, *The Path to Healing: Report of the National Round Table on Aboriginal Health and Social Issues* (Ottawa: Ministry of Supply and Services Canada, 1993); Royal Commission on Aboriginal Peoples, "Gathering Strength," Ottawa, 1996; Marlene Brant Castellano, "A Healing Journey: Reclaiming Wellness," *Final Report of the Aboriginal Healing Foundation, Volume I* (Ottawa: Aboriginal Healing Foundation, 2006); Linda Archibald, "Promising Healing Practices in Aboriginal Communities," *Final Report of the Aboriginal Healing Foundation, Volume III* (Ottawa: Aboriginal Healing Foundation, 2006); Status of Women Canada, "Seeking Alternatives to Bill C-31."

68 Royal Commission on Aboriginal Peoples, *The Path to Healing*, 10–11.

69 Anderson, *A Recognition of Being*.

70 Sawyer, interview.

71 Boissonneault, interview.

72 Robinson, interview.

73 Elsemere, interview. For a discussion of Bill C-31 and its inability to disrupt women's lives, see Susanne E. Miskimmin, "'Nobody Took the Indian Blood Out of Me'": An Analysis of Algonquian and Iroquoian Discourse Concerning Bill C-31" (PhD thesis, University of Western Ontario, 1996). Miskimmin argues that academics exaggerate the divisive power of Bill C-31.

74 Erin Dokis, "Aboriginal Women find healing and hope in education," in *Taking Domestic Violence Out of the Shadows: Addressing Domestic Violence in the District of Nipissing* (*North Bay Nugget,* February 2007), 6.

75 Corbiere, interview.

76 Sawyer, interview. The connection between identity and resistance is well-developed in Beatrice Culleton Mosionier's *In Search of April Raintree* (Winnipeg: Portage and Main Press, 1999).

77 Sawyer, interview.

78 Ibid.

79 Robinson, interview. For a discussion of the use of cultural retention in programming at shelters in Thunder Bay, see Nancy Janovicek, "'Assisting Our Own:' Urban Migration, Self Governance, and Native Women's Rights," *The American Indian Quarterly* 27, 3 (2003): 548–565.

80 Royal Commission on Aboriginal Peoples, *The Path to Healing*, 10.

81 Sarazin, interview.

82 Ibid.

83 For more on this protest, see Turning Point, a web-based forum for discussion of issues important to Aboriginal peoples: http://www.turning-point.ca/?q=node/22360 (accessed 9 June 2011).

84 See http://www.grantnativelaw.com/pdf/McIvorCaseComment.pdf (accessed 29 March 2009).

85 See http://www.parl.gc.ca/About/Parliament/LegislativeSummaries/bills_ls.asp?Language=e&ls=C3&Mode=1&Parl=40&Ses=3&source=library_prb (accessed 7 November 2011).

Contributors

Jennifer S.H. Brown, FRSC, was a professor of history and Canada Research Chair at the University of Winnipeg until 2011, and directed the Centre for Rupert's Land Studies, which focuses on Aboriginal peoples and the fur trade of the Hudson Bay watershed. She is general editor of the Rupert's Land Record Society documentary series (McGill-Queen's University Press), which publishes original materials on Aboriginal and fur trade history. She has published several books and many articles on these topics and also on anthropologist A. Irving Hallowell and the Berens River Ojibwe, and now resides in Denver, Colorado.

Robin Jarvis Brownlie is an associate professor at the University of Manitoba, specializing in the history of Aboriginal people and colonization in Canada. She is working on a book-length study of racial discourses and First Nations in Upper Canada and is the author of *A Fatherly Eye: Indian Agents, Government Power, and Aboriginal Resistance in Ontario, 1918–1939* (Oxford University Press, 2003).

Victoria Freeman is the author of *Distant Relations: How My Ancestors Colonized North America* and received her PhD in history from the University of Toronto in 2010. Her dissertation was on the historical memory of the Indigenous and colonial past of Toronto. She currently co-teaches a course on the politics and process of reconciliation with Sto:lo writer and elder Lee Maracle in the Aboriginal Studies Program at the University of Toronto and has spent the last two years coordinating governance-related activities and partnerships at the university's Centre for Aboriginal Initiatives.

Franca Iacovetta is professor of history at the University of Toronto and co-editor of the History and Gender series at University of Toronto Press. The recipient of the John A. Macdonald best book prize for *Gatekeepers: Reshaping Lives in Cold War Canada* (Between the Lines, 2006), she is the first Canadian president of the Berkshire Conference of Women Historians.

Robert Alexander Innes is an assistant professor in Native Studies at the University of Saskatchewan.

Elizabeth Jameson holds the Imperial Oil–Lincoln McKay Chair in American Studies at the University of Calgary. Her research has focused on class and gender in the North American Wests, and on the U.S.-Canada borderlands. Her publications include three co-edited volumes: *The Women's West, Writing the Range: Race Class, and Culture in the Women's West*, and *One Step over the Line: Toward a History of Women in the North American Wests*.

Valerie J. Korinek is a professor in the Department of History at the University of Saskatchewan. A cultural and gender historian, she is a co-editor of *Edible Histories, Cultural Politics: Towards a Canadian Food History* (University of Toronto Press, 2012) and the author of *Roughing it in the Suburbs: Reading Chatelaine Magazine in the Fifties and Sixties* (University of Toronto Press, 2000).

Patricia A. McCormack is a professor with the Faculty of Native Studies at the University of Alberta. She has long-term research interests in Fort Chipewyan in northern Alberta but works elsewhere in the Subarctic and the northwestern Plains on the fur trade, the expansion of the state, cultural transformation and renewal, oral traditions, and material culture. She is currently completing a second book about Fort Chipewyan, developing a book about Thanadelthur, and pursuing fur trade links to Scotland.

Kathryn McPherson teaches women's and social history at York University in Toronto. Her research focuses on the history of women, work, health, and popular culture. McPherson is author is *Bedside Matters: The Transformation of Canadian Nursing 1900–1990* and co-editor of *Gendered Pasts: Historical Essays in Femininity and Masculinity in Canada* and of *Women, Health and Nation: Canada and the United States Since 1945*.

Adele Perry teaches at the University of Manitoba, where she is Canada Research Chair in Western Canadian Social History (Tier II). She is working on a book-length study of the Douglas and Connolly family.

Katrina Srigley is associate professor of history at Nipissing University. She studies the history of women and gender in twentieth-century Canada, with specific interests in Indigenous methodologies, memory, and the dynamics of race, class, and gender in our past.

Angela Wanhalla is a senior lecturer in the Department of History and Art History, University of Otago, where she teaches New Zealand, Maori, and comparative Indigenous histories. Her current project is a history of interracial marriage in New Zealand, which will be published with Auckland University Press in 2013.